A CLASS BY THEMSELVES?

The Origins of Special Education in Toronto and Beyond

In *A Class by Themselves?* Jason Ellis provides an erudite and balanced history of special needs education, an early-twentieth-century educational innovation that continues to polarize school communities across Canada, the United States, and beyond.

Ellis situates the evolution of this educational innovation in its historical context and explores the rise of intelligence testing, the decline of child labour and development of vocational guidance, the emerging trends in mental hygiene and child psychology, and the implementation of a new progressive curriculum. At the core of this study are the students. This book is the first to draw deeply on rich archival sources, including one thousand records of young people with learning difficulties who attended public school between 1918 and 1945. Ellis uses these records to retell individual stories that illuminate how disability filtered down through the school system's many nooks and crannies to mark disabled students as different from (and often inferior to) other school children. *A Class by Themselves?* sheds new light on these and other issues by bringing special education's curious past to bear on its constantly contested present.

JASON ELLIS is an assistant professor in the Department of Educational Studies at the University of British Columbia.

D1528517

A Class by Themselves?

The Origins of Special Education in Toronto and Beyond

JASON ELLIS

UNIVERSITY OF TORONTO PRESS
Toronto Buffalo London

© University of Toronto Press 2019
Toronto Buffalo London
utorontopress.com
Printed in Canada

ISBN 978-1-4426-3711-5 (cloth)   ISBN 978-1-4426-2871-7 (paper)

∞ Printed on acid-free, 100% post-consumer recycled paper with vegetable-based inks.

Library and Archives Canada Cataloguing in Publication

Ellis, Jason, 1981–, author
A class by themselves? : the origins of special education in Toronto
and beyond / Jason Ellis.

Includes bibliographical references and index.
ISBN 978-1-4426-3711-5 (cloth)   ISBN 978-1-4426-2871-7 (paper)

1. Special education – History.   2. Special education – Ontario – Toronto –
History.   I. Title.

LC3965.E45 2019   371.9   C2018-906474-9

This book has been published with the help of a grant from the Federation
for the Humanities and Social Sciences, through the Awards to Scholarly
Publications Program, using funds provided by the Social Sciences and
Humanities Research Council of Canada.

University of Toronto Press acknowledges the financial assistance to its
publishing program of the Canada Council for the Arts and the Ontario Arts
Council, an agency of the Government of Ontario.

Canada Council Conseil des Arts
for the Arts du Canada

ONTARIO ARTS COUNCIL
CONSEIL DES ARTS DE L'ONTARIO
an Ontario government agency
un organisme du gouvernement de l'Ontario

Funded by the   Financé par le
Government gouvernement
of Canada   du Canada | Canadä

MIX
Paper from
responsible sources
FSC   FSC® C016245
www.fsc.org

For Tina.

Contents

Illustrations and Figures

x   Illustrations

Tables

Acknowledgments

Many people helped with this study. I wish to thank them for contributions that improved it immeasurably.

The following individuals offered advice or read chapters, parts of chapters, or – in one or two cases – the entire manuscript: Lesley Andres, Paul Axelrod, Tarah Brookfield, Penney Clark, Katie Gemmell, Catherine Gidney, R.D. Gidney, Mona Gleason, Dale M. McCartney, W.P.J. Millar, Ian Mosby, Peter Seixas, Elizabeth Smyth, Veronica Strong-Boag, Alison Taylor, Robert Vipond, and Amy von Heyking.

Students in my EDST 504a, "History of Educational Policy," Winter 2, 2015 graduate seminar in the Department of Educational Studies at the University of British Columbia (UBC) read early versions of the introduction and chapter 3 and gave incisive commentary at a crucial moment in the manuscript's development.

Sections in chapters 2, 3, and 5 look at data compiled from pupil record cards. Korryn Broder, Jamie Michelson, and Fahd Husain designed the databases for the representative samples, and extracted and helped me interpret the findings. Funke Aladejebi and Joanna Pearce keyed information from record cards into those databases and provided other research assistance as well.

Most of the research for this book took place on site at the Toronto District School Board Archives. There the archivist and manager Greg McKinnon, archives assistant Marie Passerino, and conservator David Sowerbutts always made me welcome in their workspace, even as they juggled many priorities and projects more important than mine.

I would also like to acknowledge the Toronto District School Board Archives for granting me permission to use pupil records from the pre-1945 period in my research and the UBC Department of Educational Studies for supporting financially some of the work with those records.

At the Centre for Addiction and Mental Health Archives in Toronto, archivist John P.M. Court shared generously his tremendous knowledge of the collections and of the history of mental health.

I also did research at other archives: the Clara Thomas Archives and Special Collections (York University), City of Toronto Archives, and the Archives of Ontario, where I was assisted by excellent staff.

Librarians at York University, University of Toronto, the Education Library at Western University, and UBC, some of the institutions at which I studied or taught while completing this work, tracked down rare sources through interlibrary loans and in special collections. At the Ontario Institute for Studies in Education Library, Kathleen Imrie granted access to the Ontario Historical Education Collection. Kathy Sassonow rescued from the building's basement volumes of the *Bulletin* and the *Special Class Teacher* that were not then listed in the catalogue.

Staff at the Toronto Public Library's Reference Library and at the Urban Affairs Library, which has since closed, retrieved hard-to-find school board reports and minutes for me.

My PhD dissertation committee at York University – Paul Axelrod (supervisor), Molly Ladd-Taylor, and Jennifer Stephen – put this project on track from the beginning.

Dorothy Turnbull copy-edited the first draft of the manuscript. Her work was meticulous. Staff at University of Toronto Press were a pleasure to work with. Len Husband had confidence in the manuscript and in me from the start. Alex Wozny, the web assistant in the UBC Department of Educational Studies, helped me format computer graphics for the figures and tables. Tim Spence checked the final tables.

History of Education Quarterly and *Paedagogica Historica* granted permission to include parts of these articles in the book:

Jason Ellis, "'Inequalities of Children in Original Endowment': How Intelligence Testing Transformed Early Special Education in a North American City School System," *History of Education Quarterly* 53, no. 4 (November 2013): 401–29, doi:10.1111/hoeq.12035; and
Jason Ellis, "'All Methods – and Wedded to None': The Deaf Education Methods Debate and Progressive Educational Reform in Toronto, Canada, 1922–1945," *Paedagogica Historica: International Journal of the History of Education* 50, no. 3 (2014): 371–89, doi: 10.1080/00309230.2013.833273.

I owe my greatest debt of gratitude to my family, but especially to Christine (Tina) Paramonczyk. She has supported this project – and me – in every conceivable way. She is a loving spouse, a bread-winner and professional, and, now that Ramona has joined us, a devoted mother. She does it all without missing a beat. And when I need it, Tina reminds me to "be here now" instead of lingering in the distant past. This book is for her.

Abbreviations

ADP   Admission-discharge-promotion card
DOE   Ontario Department of Education
IQ   Intelligence quotient
OEA   Ontario Educational Association
ORC   Office record card
PER   Psychiatric examination report
PS   Public school
TBE   Toronto Board of Education
TDSB Toronto District School Board

A CLASS BY THEMSELVES?

The Origins of Special Education in Toronto and Beyond

Introduction

"Nature has put the mental defective in a class by himself, we had better take the hint."[1] A century ago, when the Canadian physician and eugenicist Helen MacMurchy wrote this advice, the idea that children and youth with disabilities or learning difficulties belonged in separate, special classes in public schools was a relatively new one. This book is a history of those classes – what readers today will recognize as special education. The term "special education" is in fact newer than the first special classes in public schools and came into widespread use only in the 1930s.[2] Prior to that time, people would have said "auxiliary" instead, as in "auxiliary class" and "auxiliary education." I use both these terms in this book. Since they mean slightly different things, I will clarify them before I begin, along with a few related concepts. "Auxiliary class" was what people called separate classrooms for children with learning difficulties or intellectual disabilities – for so-called mental defectives, as one example. There were also oral classes for the deaf, orthopaedic classes, sight-saving classes, speech correction classes, classes for hard-of-hearing students, classes for foreign students, open-air classes, and forest schools. As early as the mid-1920s, Toronto's public school system had all of these programs. It also had special schools for adolescent auxiliary students, called "junior vocational schools." Put together, all of these programs were referred to as auxiliary education. To complicate matters, in 1935 the Toronto Board of Education (TBE) changed the name of "junior vocational schools" to "handicraft schools," and in 1937 the Ontario Department of Education (DOE) changed the name of "auxiliary classes" to "opportunity classes." When I write "handicraft school" or "opportunity class," I refer to the later period.

Language matters in more ways than one in this book. Many of the terms once used for pupils in auxiliary education are bound to jar modern readers. "Feebleminded," "mental defective," and "cripple" are three such terms. They appear in this book because they were at one time common expressions, and sometimes official linguistic forms as well. Even the epithet "moron" was coined as a specialist word by a clinician. It later became a derisive term, while its technical origin faded from memory.[3] Sanitizing my text of the historic language of disability would risk, as the Canadian historian of eugenics Erika Dyck also argues, forfeiting opportunities to explore the meaning of being labelled in these ways at different points in time. Some authors place such terms in scare quotes every time they appear in their texts. Like Dyck, I believe that it is better to explain language once at the beginning of a book, rather than to subject the reader to tiresome extra punctuation.[4]

This book is primarily intended to contribute to educational history, though I hope that it will also engage other audiences. It is the first book to look at auxiliary education and disabled children and youth in a Canadian city public school system – the TBE.[5] It begins with auxiliary education's origins as a headline-grabbing reform when TBE officials founded the first four classes for mentally defective children in 1910. It ends in 1945, when the city's public schools had many special programs and auxiliary education sat on the edge of the postwar expansion of public schooling. By that time, auxiliary education was poised to develop into modern special education, a major part of schooling today. The book should interest readers who wish to learn more about the history of children, youth, and families and about disability history during this period. It will appeal as well to educational researchers, policy-makers, and other parties curious about how the past contributes to current debates on inclusion, educational equity, and special education policy.

The story this book tells does not concern Canadian schools alone. In 1919, Edith L. Groves, a Toronto school trustee and leading proponent of auxiliary education, visited special classes in several American cities. "I feel that the United States is far in advance of us in this particular," she would tell her trustee colleagues upon her return.[6] But Groves was wrong about that. From 1910 to 1945 the TBE's growing slate of auxiliary services rivalled those of comparable US city public schools. The historian of education David Tyack describes the urban school reformers of this era as an "interlocking directorate" for their tendency to share their reform plans through nascent professional networks that spanned the United States.[7] It turns out that those connections did not terminate at the international border.[8] Groves's foray, and professional excursions by other Toronto educators to the United States before and after it, reveal a pattern of educational exchange that sent Canadians south in search of solutions to use in auxiliary education – and occasionally brought Americans north for the same reason. Since Toronto's public schools kept pace with urban systems on both sides of the border, and provided practically identical services, my study of Toronto contributes to the history of education literature in the United States.[9] It draws upon and complements, and in a few instances may even correct, studies of special education history in that country by Robert L. Osgood, Barry M. Franklin, Scot Danforth, and others.[10] Canadians exchanged ideas with British authorities, too, though almost exclusively in the early period when eugenics had its most formative influence on special classes in both countries.[11]

"The history of special education is beset with contradictions," Marvin Lazerson once wrote.[12] These contradictions call for an approach that argues – as this book does – that different stakeholders tried to accomplish dissimilar things through auxiliary education.[13] A rosy aura surrounds some existing historical accounts of the topic. These works celebrate the field's pioneers.[14] Or they present the history of special classes as one of inexorable progress from a dark nineteenth century to an enlightened present where the full inclusion of people with disabilities draws ever nearer.[15] A social control thesis hangs over other accounts like a forbidding cloud, with its theory of elite manipulation and lack of positive change over time.[16] Auxiliary education's roots in eugenics – the discredited science of improving the human race through selective breeding – knock it out of the running as a munificent reform. Yet social control makes a poor description of the dedicated work of many passionate auxiliary education teachers, the large majority of them women, who went to great lengths to teach and care for students whom other teachers sometimes did not even want in their classes and who probably, had it not been for auxiliary education, would have been ignored, ostracized, or institutionalized. Instead of stumping for a single explanation to account for the way that auxiliary education developed historically, this book looks at the overlapping chain reactions that were actually involved.

Any examination of auxiliary education's historical development is incomplete if it does not also include the stories of auxiliary pupils and their parents. Like scholars Mona Gleason, Cynthia Comacchio, Tamara Myers, and Veronica Strong-Boag, I believe that young people's lives matter to history.[17] So do the lives of people with disabilities. Not that long ago, historians did not take disabled people or disability very seriously. If they considered them at all, it was from a limited medical standpoint. Like other scholars taking a "new" approach to disability history, I do my best to portray young people in ways that allow them to be more than diagnoses and labels, and to appear as historical actors in their own right.[18] This book synthesizes the widest possible range of their experiences, from the positive to the negative. It happens that disability was a remarkably common and diverse part of people's lives historically, as scholarship by Geoffrey Reaume, Nic Clarke, Dustin Galer, and others attests. However, these scholars remind us that not just age and disability count.[19] The young people in my book were also girls or boys. Some were immigrants or ethnic minorities, while others were Anglo-Canadians. They came from working-, middle-, or upper-class families. Analysis of auxiliary pupil data that I present in chapters 2, 3, and 5 also takes into account these factors in the demographic make-up of auxiliary programs.

But beyond that, this book brings more young people's and their parents' experiences to bear on auxiliary education than any other history to date. Adding these perspectives alongside those of school officials, medical experts, and teachers cultivates an even greater appreciation of the complexity that rules the history of auxiliary education. For this study, I draw on the pupil records of more than 1,300 auxiliary students who attended three Toronto public schools: Coleman Public School (PS), Duke of York PS, and Hester How PS.[20] (I describe these schools and explain this source and my methodology in appendix A.) Pupil records, or any case files for that matter, pass through the hands of interested parties and institutions before the historian gets them.[21] Like other historians who read case files "against the grain," I am reasonably sceptical about the assumptions and judgments of teachers, principals, psychologists, and other adults who had a hand in putting information into the records.[22] A school nurse's notes about a physical examination, or a psychologist's record of a child's intelligence quotient (IQ), might indicate a physical deformity or a learning problem. But the story seldom ends there. Pupil records contain many more subtle clues about why a child landed in an auxiliary program. Sometimes the record reveals a girl or boy new to Canada. Or it shows an academic past checkered with absences, failing grades, or visits to the principal's office. It may even expose a home life disrupted by frequent changes of address that sometimes signify parental unemployment and poverty.

Chapter by chapter, this book's arguments are as follows. Chapter 1 explains why by about 1910 many urban school systems had adopted a policy of placing exceptional children in separate classes. The popularity of eugenics, the search by school reformers for bureaucratic efficiency, and the earnest desire of child savers to improve conditions for underprivileged youngsters played a part. In Toronto, these developments together prompted the establishment of auxiliary classes for mental defectives in 1910 and then, in 1912, classes for children labelled "merely backward" but not defective.[23] Forest schools began to operate in 1910, and open-air classes in 1916, for "pre-tuberculous,"[24] sickly, and malnourished children, and foreign classes began in 1913 for immigrant youngsters handicapped because they did not know English and were unfamiliar with Canadian ways.

Somewhat uncertain reform origins gave way to auxiliary education becoming entrenched in urban schooling, a process that culminated in the 1920s. Chapter 2 looks at the rise of IQ testing and its influence on the expansion of auxiliary education during that time. Historians who have studied IQ testing in schools, such as Paul Chapman, focus on its effects on sorting pupils by ability into different classrooms, programs, or sometimes even schools.[25] In Canada this is known as "streaming," which is how I will refer to it in this book. In the United States "tracking" is the more common term for the same practice.[26] While I do not dispute its significance for streaming, I argue in chapter 2 that IQ testing had much broader effects on auxiliary education than streaming alone. The science of IQ fundamentally altered prevailing notions about the nature and treatment of learning problems by suggesting that most were caused by low innate intelligence that was forever fixed and totally impervious to even the best teaching. Thus, when IQ testers such as Stanford University's Lewis Terman began to peddle their tests on the North American educational services market, they were also selling a new set of ideas about dealing with exceptional youngsters. Local officials who adopted IQ testing, including Toronto school inspectors and trustees, invested in these ideas and used them in turn as the basis for transforming policies and practices that city school systems had only just begun to put into place for auxiliary education.

Theories derived from IQ studies on the possibilities and limitations of adolescents' educational abilities and occupational prospects were a vital ingredient in 1920s vocational guidance, as were evolving beliefs about class, gender and sexuality, and adolescent development. This brew of ideas, plus a volatile post-First World War juvenile employment market and a subsequent provincially legislated increase in the school leaving age from fourteen to sixteen in 1920, closely shaped the aims and objectives school officials had for Toronto's gender-segregated junior vocational and handicraft schools. Chapter 3 focuses on that program. Rationally planned and IQ-based auxiliary education mirrored the progressive approach that defined curriculum-making by the 1920s, a new curriculum science that Amy von Heyking and Theodore Christou study in Canada and that Herbert Kliebard analyses in the United States.[27] Despite the careful planning and deep educational science that went into Toronto's junior vocational program, the actual schools were unpopular with many – though not all – pupils and families, for reasons that chapter 3 also explores.

Meanwhile, developments in rehabilitation science and deaf education suggested that the Victorian concept of disability, with its overtones of pathos, was being replaced by the idea that education could help some disabled people to eventually get past their handicaps. By the mid-1920s, the TBE had created the programs that chapter 4 examines: sight-saving classes, oralist day school classes that taught lip-reading to the totally deaf, classes for the hard-of-hearing, speech correction classes, and orthopaedic classes for children with physical disabilities. Disabled and deaf children who attended these new programs, which went to surprising lengths to accommodate them, nevertheless faced an uneasy paradox. They could now be integrated into mainstream schools – as long as they learned to move, act, and communicate like their able-bodied or hearing peers. Some of them could adapt. Others could not and were labelled failures. Still others who were capable, particularly some deaf students, did not want to adapt because they did not want to give up part of who they were.

Its years of expansion and consolidation behind it, auxiliary education in Toronto weathered the 1930s and the Great Depression remarkably well. It also underwent significant changes during that time and in the first half of the 1940s. Chapter 5 is about the discovery of special-subject disability by an international assortment of brain injury experts, remedial education experts, and psychologists, and the effect of that discovery on auxiliary education after 1930. The IQ testers had claimed that almost all children who failed to learn did so because they lacked mental capacity. The theory of special-subject disability would eventually throw that idea into doubt. Finally, chapter 6 examines another important influence on auxiliary programs after 1930: mental hygiene ideas about personality adjustment. Mental hygienists, like special-subject disability advocates, believed that mental states were built in environments and that treatment could improve, and sometimes even remove, a disabled child's condition. The rise of special-subject disability and adjustment theory marked a steep decline in eugenics' direct influence over auxiliary education by about 1945.[28]

In the chapters that follow, I explain the rise of auxiliary programs as a reform and describe how special classes became commonplace. The history I recount here raises and answers questions about which factors, forces, and individuals produced change in auxiliary education over time. It addresses how pupils and parents lived with that change and occasionally contributed to it. Certain themes loom large: urban school systems, as bureaucracies, accommodating pupil difference through greater and greater program differentiation; poverty, foreignness, and ill health as disadvantages that educators characterized as handicaps; changing ideas about the nature, cause, and treatment of disabilities and learning difficulties that were translated into policies, classroom practices, and curricula; schools incorporating modern instructional techniques, novel educational and psychological tests, and medical discoveries and cures into their approach to disabilities and learning difficulties; and questions about whether auxiliary education enhances or restricts pupil opportunity – or whether it has the capacity to do both, depending on the situation.

Familiar discussions in education today raise questions that resonate with these historical themes. Should schools approach varying pupil abilities, capacities, and interests by differentiating the setting – ability-grouping in elementary schools and streaming in secondary schools – or should they adopt inclusive settings or a common curriculum, and leave it to teachers to differentiate instruction in mixed classrooms? How much input should pupils and parents have in the way exceptional young people are educated? Are disabilities deficits to treat, or differences to acknowledge or even celebrate? How can we make policies that will actually improve how schools teach and generally handle disabled, disadvantaged, and different students? History is present in each and every one of these questions, but it is seldom mentioned in the debates they engender.

More than that, the way people entered the special education debate in the past is similar to how they engage it today. Readers who look to history for fresh insights about the present should pay extra close attention to the discussions in this book about the varied motives of different contestants in the special education debate and the changing coalitions they formed; to the constantly evolving theories about the cause, nature, and treatment of learning difficulties; to the politics that shaped educational research; and to the school system bureaucracy that framed it all. These are the very same factors that create the contours of debates in contemporary special education. By bringing auxiliary education's often-curious past to bear on special education's constantly contested present, this book contributes to and enriches the living conversation.

One last note about terminology before I go on: until the late 1930s, Ontario public schools used the lingo of "forms" instead of today's "grades." In the elementary schools, there were four (and in some cases five) forms after kindergarten, and each had a "junior" and a "senior" division. Junior first form was effectively equivalent to grade 1, senior first to grade 2, junior second to grade 3, senior second to grade 4 – all the way up to junior fourth, i.e., grade 7, and senior fourth, i.e., grade 8.[29] A few elementary schools even had junior and senior fifth, representing grades 9 and 10, although Toronto students completing work at this level mostly attended high schools.[30] In this study, when I write junior first, senior first, and so on, I am referring to forms and to the period prior to approximately 1937, after which the terminology changed. Where I use grade 1, grade 2, and the like, I am referring to the time after that change.

Chapter One

Eugenics Goes to School and Other Strange Legacies: Auxiliary Education's Origins

Auxiliary education for children with disabilities, learning difficulties, and disadvantages was an innovation of the 1910s, and one drop in an early-twentieth-century outpouring of reform. Trickles of reform sentiment had been collecting and pooling for more than a decade in North American cities, including Toronto, before the buildup finally overflowed.[1] The wave that followed would last only a moment, but nevertheless enveloped many social, moral, educational, and municipal matters. In Toronto, mayor Horatio Hocken rallied progressives with his appeal for a "New Spirit of Municipal Government," which called for greater state intervention in public services.[2] Toronto's civic government formed public electricity and transit companies in 1910 and 1911. City officials created a municipal social services commission to coordinate city-wide charitable giving in 1912. City government made a first foray into public housing in 1913.[3] The Toronto Board of Education (TBE) initiated its school medical inspection service in 1910 to improve the health of the city's young people. Within a few years, the service had become, as Neil Sutherland writes, "one of the most comprehensive and widely reported school medical systems in the world," serving tens of thousands of pupils.[4]

Auxiliary education was, at its outset, an urban educational reform. It arose at a time when cities like Toronto were straining under unprecedented growth and change. At the turn of the twentieth century, Toronto was rapidly becoming one of eastern North America's leading industrial and commercial centres. As with other metropolises of the age, people poured in from the surrounding towns, villages, and farms – as well as from overseas. Toronto's population reached 200,000 people in 1901, swelled to over 520,000 by 1921. It would reach nearly 700,000 by 1946.[5] Migration to Toronto was remarkably Anglo-Saxon. The city was no New York, Chicago, or Winnipeg, but it still had enclaves of Jews, Italians, Chinese, and agglomerations of other ethnicities.[6] At 7 per cent of the Toronto population, Jews were the largest visibly non-Anglo-Saxon group.[7] New arrivals – foreign and domestic – were drawn to the city's "intensive industrial expansion," especially between approximately 1900 and 1920.[8] The city's largest industry was clothing. Significantly feminized, with over 50 per cent female employees by 1911, it was characterized in part by a Jewish employment ghetto and was profoundly transformed by the encroaching factory system.[9] The fruits of Toronto's economic growth were massively unequally distributed, and wage earners saw a stagnating standard of living in the decades of expanding industrial capacity while freewheeling markets perilously exposed them to cycles of boom and bust, work and joblessness.[10]

Toronto's reformers watched industrialization, immigration, and urbanization with trepidation. They believed that poverty, labour unrest, vice, and ignorance accompanied these changes and were sullying the city's reputation as "Toronto the Good."[11] These reformers were not radicals, although a small number, such as politician Jimmy Simpson, were socialists. Instead of reforging society, progressive reforms were intended to blunt the sharper edges of the social hierarchy while also serving middle-class and business interests.[12] The progressives of the 1910s rarely lobbied on behalf of just one cause.[13] The same people trying to extend the reach of the social safety net by getting government into public housing might also be fighting against the profiteering private streetcar and electric lighting "rings"[14] or trying to wipe out corruption at city hall. Or, as a number of the city's busiest reformers were in the 1910s, they might be combating feeblemindedness.

Auxiliary education was not peripheral to reform efforts, mainly because it was closely connected to the campaign against feeblemindedness that loomed large in the 1910s and often rode shotgun to other reforms. Auxiliary education was advanced by individuals such as city controller J.O. (Jesse) McCarthy, one of the elected members of the Board of Control that functioned as a form of municipal cabinet government for Toronto. The historian John C. Weaver describes McCarthy, whose place as a controller made him one of the city's most powerful politicians, as "a dynamic and versatile reformer, who bridged the social gospel and business efficiency elements of progressive reform." McCarthy, a Liberal, was known for his support of temperance, revered as a backer of public health modernization, and respected for his attempt to have the city enter the public housing sphere.[15] He was the main voice on city council speaking out in favour of "special classes" and "custodial care" for feebleminded girls and boys, and he stated in 1914, for example, that "in the field of Social Welfare Work in Toronto there is no more pressing problem than that of caring for feeble-minded children."[16]

Progressive causes were supported by high-profile voluntary organizations as well as by individuals. The Toronto Local Council of Women (LCW) was one of the most vocal and powerful lobbies arguing for greater attention to the problem of feeblemindedness and for auxiliary classes in the city's public school system. The local council was a branch of the National Council of Women of Canada, an organization that after 1893 had federated women's groups that flourished across the country. The local and national councils were maternalist feminist, mainly Anglo-Saxon, middle- or upper-class reform outfits. The Toronto LCW had an impressive range in its activities, and touched on moral, social, and municipal reform concerns.[17]

Less obviously, auxiliary education also fit into the plans of mostly male progressives who wished to make major changes to how municipal government conducted business. The Bureau of Municipal Research was formed in 1913 as a "voluntary association of citizens," consisting mainly of business interests organized under the patronage of members of the city's elite.[18] The bureau set its sights on cleaning up city politics with "scientific methods of accounting and reporting the details of public business."[19] It wished to apply these bureaucratic measures to Toronto's public school system through a campaign to attack "educational waste" and "unscientific methods of school administration" that drove up property taxes. In the 1910s, the bureau repeatedly called for auxiliary classes as a way to curtail educational inefficiencies and save ratepayers, it boldly promised, hundreds of thousands of dollars.[20] Canadians sometimes tend to think of special classes as an isolated, and perhaps unremarkable, educational issue. But at their outset, demands for auxiliary education were deeply nested within a broad reform movement that exceeded the bounds of education alone.

Popular with system outsiders, auxiliary education certainly punched its weight with people directly involved in public schooling as well. It represented one extension of bureaucratic school reforms that had been underway in urban systems since the nineteenth century. As cities and their school systems grew rapidly, authorities had trouble keeping up – especially, many of them believed, because school systems were haphazardly organized and inefficient, lacked clear administrative hierarchies, and did not have sufficiently standardized routines and procedures. Educational reformers historians have called "administrative progressives" pursued a strategy to transform these disorderly city school systems into sleek bureaucracies. Generally this involved three measures: centralization of educational decision-making authority; standardization of educational practices, curricula, and administrative routines; and – especially from approximately 1890 onwards – implementation of differentiated instructional settings to more efficiently meet the diverse needs of increasingly large and heterogeneous urban school populations.[21] Toronto public schools initially adopted many bureaucratic features under James L. Hughes's long reign (1874–1913) as inspector. He introduced age-grading, regularized promotion practices from grade to grade, standardized curricula by setting an approved textbook list, and opened the City Model School to train teachers and prepare them to a uniform standard.[22]

Other reforms to the system during Hughes's tenure also contributed to bureaucratization and gave the TBE the governance and administrative structure it would enjoy throughout the period of this study. A municipal plebiscite, followed by provincial legislation, led eventually in 1904 to school board amalgamation. The TBE replaced three formerly distinct boards that had represented public schools, collegiate institutes (high schools), and technical schools. Dozens of trustees governed the three predecessor boards. The new TBE consisted of fourteen trustees elected by public school taxpayers and two appointed trustees who represented Catholic ratepayers on high school matters only. At the head of the administrative bureaucracy, which was not elected, was Hughes, who took the title of chief inspector. When he retired and R.H. Cowley replaced him in 1913, Cowley assumed responsibility for a central office with five inspectors who worked under him and oversaw groups of elementary schools; a senior principal to whom the other high school principals reported; and six elementary school supervisors of specialized curriculum areas such as kindergarten, drill, drawing, and domestic science.[23]

It was mostly after the start of Cowley's term as chief inspector that TBE enrolment exploded. In 1910, enrolment was 43,000 pupils. By 1920, it had more than doubled to 90,000.[24] By about this time the board had nearly one hundred elementary schools and ten high schools (with several more soon to come), and employed about 1,900 teachers.[25] The TBE was Canada's largest school board by a long shot.[26] In fact, in about 1920, there were as many pupils enrolled in TBE schools as there were in the public schools of the American metropolises of Los Angeles, Baltimore, or St Louis.[27] Like school officials in those and other cities, Toronto's officials struggled with rapid school building to accommodate population growth. There was enormous overcrowding in the younger grades, caused in part by repeaters who could not keep up with the regular program, and intense enrolment pressures on high schools burdened with outdated facilities. School officials faced mounting questions about how to meet the varied needs of a student population that had become not just much larger, but also much more diverse in terms of ethnicity and race, class, and ability. They answered with a bureaucratic solution and differentiated school programs along many distinctive lines, including for children with disabilities and learning difficulties.[28]

In this context of drastic urban and educational change and reform, auxiliary classes owed their origins to eugenics entering education, to the discovery of widespread grade repetition and the efforts of school officials to curb it through program differentiation, and to the child-saving spirit that infected some school officials and spurred them to improve conditions for the growing city's most vulnerable young people. On the one hand, auxiliary education benefitted from the wide support of a calico collection of elite school system insiders, rank-and-file teachers, and layperson and expert outsiders of vastly different political stripes and with manifestly different social leanings. Auxiliary education was like other educational reforms of the progressive period that William J. Reese argues drew together people "who had diametrically opposed political and ideological perspectives" but who nevertheless often "endorsed the same innovation." On the other hand, as Reese also points out, "even the acceptance of the need for the same reform produced noticeable conflict."[29] Educators, school administrators, social reformers, child-savers, eugenicists, and others – including even a few parents of disabled schoolchildren – who joined the consensus supporting auxiliary education lacked a common vision for the system they were creating. Friction was unavoidable and contestation shaped early auxiliary programs.

The Fight against Feeblemindedness and the Desire for Eugenics

No one worked harder on behalf of the early lobby for auxiliary classes in Toronto public schools than Helen MacMurchy. To make sense of auxiliary education as a reform, especially the disputed intentions behind it, MacMurchy must be situated in the fight against feeblemindedness. Historians have debated her as a historical figure because of her conflicted legacy as a pioneering female physician, accomplished civil servant, and respected maternalist feminist – but also ardent eugenicist.[30] Groundbreaking professional women of this period, unlike their male contemporaries, have been held to a higher standard and a double standard. They have been called upon to atone for their prejudices, which were widely shared with men, before they can be celebrated for their accomplishments. Yet as the feminist historian Veronica Strong-Boag advises, adopting a situated approach that locates women such as MacMurchy in their times helps to avoid the false dichotomy of either castigating them as villains or celebrating them as heroes.[31] MacMurchy's personal background, her career in teaching, her aspiration to be and later success as a medical doctor, and her efforts to influence public health reform at a time when women struggled to have their views respected in these fields shaped her thinking. So did the events of the 1910s and her personal connections in that decade to like-minded reform women. All of these influences on MacMurchy in turn marked the direction that auxiliary education took in Toronto.

Steadfastness was one of the most important traits in MacMurchy's personality and in her professional career, which she began not as a physician but as an educator. In 1880, at age eighteen, MacMurchy joined the staff at the Toronto Collegiate Institute on Jarvis Street, where her father, Archibald MacMurchy, was headmaster. Until 1898, MacMurchy would live under her father's roof and teach at his school. At thirty-six, she left teaching to embark on a completely new career as a doctor. In 1901, she graduated from the University of Toronto with first class honours in medicine and surgery and started in private practice.[32] MacMurchy was a "proud and brilliant woman," and her politics and character were staid. Her opinion of those living in poverty, most immigrants, and people with disabilities was unforgiving.[33] Much like her father – who the school board's official history describes as "Highland by birth and temperament" and "a strict Presbyterian and a severe disciplinarian" – MacMurchy, although not humourless, was often unrelenting in how she dealt with people.[34] In 1910 and 1911, she became embroiled with the head of the school system, Chief Inspector Hughes (himself known to be "ill-mannered and assertive"), in an acrimonious public fight over medical inspection at the TBE. MacMurchy had sought an appointment as head medical inspector. The board refused because it did not want a woman in charge of its medical inspection service and offered MacMurchy only a joint position with a male counterpart, which she turned down on principle.[35] MacMurchy was angered and hurt but not defeated by the experience. Indeed, as Diane Dodd explains, "early professional women like MacMurchy had to battle for the privilege of filling even a small niche."[36]

MacMurchy eventually found that niche in the care and control of the feebleminded. In establishing herself in that area, she had help from the women who formed the Toronto LCW – especially the group's leader, Florence Huestis, who had been unable to pursue the medical career to which she, like MacMurchy, aspired.[37] The LCW's interest in the care and social control of feebleminded women – an interest that other women and women's organizations shared – was piqued as early as 1897.[38] In 1906, a Toronto LCW delegation convinced Ontario Premier James Whitney, head of the Conservative provincial government, to appoint MacMurchy to investigate feeblemindedness in the province.[39] Whitney made MacMurchy Ontario's official provincial inspector of the feebleminded. In that role, she would go on to submit more than a dozen detailed and startling yearly reports on what she defined as the feeblemindedness problem, finding solutions to it in eugenics and auxiliary education.

By about 1900, the science of eugenics was already significantly shaping an emerging debate about feeblemindedness. Francis Galton invented the term "eugenics" in 1883, and used it to refer to measures to encourage the reproduction of the fit, who would pass their laudable traits, such as intelligence and morality, on to their progeny. Eugenics referred as well to measures to prevent the unfit from passing on their less desirable traits, such as alcoholism, criminal tendencies, or feeblemindedness.[40] Specious claims perhaps, but eugenics was no junk science in its heyday. Historians who have studied it without imposing presentist judgments have convincingly demonstrated that eugenics was in the forefront of reputable scientific endeavour.[41] Carolyn Strange and Jennifer A. Stephen write: "Over the first half of the twentieth century, eugenics in Canada was modern, scientific, and respectable."[42] Moreover, although many people rightly associate eugenics with sexual sterilization surgeries, coercion, and racism, the movement – as Erika Dyck shows – encompassed much more and should be understood in broadened historical terms. In Canada and many other countries, eugenics also reached into public health, social welfare, and the birth control movement. It attracted support from the political left and right.[43] Eugenics was influential in early efforts to introduce auxiliary education.

People like MacMurchy who were drawn to eugenics as a way to address feebelmindedness believed that it was hereditary, transmitted from generation to generation by "germ plasm."[44] MacMurchy once wrote: "There is no escape from the taint of Feeble-Mindedness. If it is there it descends."[45] By the 1900s, the feebleminded individual had been reclassified by mental deficiency experts, such as the American H.H. Goddard, as the "moron" (a clinical term he also coined) or "highest grade" of intellectual deficiency. This group was distinct from more severely deficient individuals, such as "idiots" and "imbeciles" (also clinical terms a century ago).[46] Goddard and others claimed that feeblemindedness could be found in about 2 per cent of the population.[47] In Britain and Canada, the term "feebleminded" was used much more often than the term "moron" to refer to so-called higher-grade defectives.[48] For Canadians, both expressions, but especially the former, were also interchangeable with "mental defective," which was the term that Canadian educationists tended to use most.

As a higher grade of mental deficient, the feebleminded fit more seamlessly into mainstream society, eugenicists argued. "Capable of some development or of some degeneration," as MacMurchy put it, they often looked physically typical.[49] To eugenicists, this made them dangerous. They were especially concerned about the threat posed by feebleminded women as potential childbearers. They sometimes referred to these women (and to feebleminded men as well, but less often) as "moral imbeciles." This notion drew upon Goddard's theory that morons suffered from arrested development. That theory in turn relied on the ideas of G. Stanley Hall, the pioneering expert on adolescence who was Goddard's mentor and graduate school professor. In his recapitulation theory, Hall proposed that as children developed into adults they passed through the different stages of humanity's journey from savagery to civilization. (Hall said as well that different racial groups moved along the same developmental road, but that only whites reached its civilized terminus.) Morons, who had a mental age of between eight and twelve, were arrested at the adolescent mental stage. Incapable of progressing beyond it, they grew physically and sexually into normal adults, but never attained a fully mature moral sense. Eugenicists consequently either maligned them as immoral and sexually irresponsible or pitied them for being morally weak and susceptible to seduction. Either way, they believed feebleminded women were inherently sexually available. This explained why they also claimed that feebleminded women bore more children proportionally than women of the respectable classes, who increasingly chose to limit their fertility.[50] MacMurchy was persuaded that under these conditions, within a few generations, the feebleminded would outnumber the fit, leading to the decline of "the race."[51]

Racial decline was not the only threat that feeblemindedness posed. Eugenicists added that it was plain to see that the developmentally arrested and morally compromised feebleminded who did not know right from wrong were responsible for much more than their fair share of the most pressing social problems of the immediate age – crime, prostitution, delinquency, poverty, unemployment, industrial unrest, and "inefficiency in educational institutions."[52] MacMurchy's reports as inspector frequently ran to a single theme for a solution that would address the long-term threat and short-term consequences of unchecked feeblemindedness: segregation. Like many superintendents of asylums; medical experts on mental deficiency; and reformers in the United States, Canada, and England by the 1900s, MacMurchy believed that if an entire generation of feebleminds was permanently segregated, "there would be such a drop in their numbers that soon we should be practically rid of this terrible problem."[53] (Later, eugenicists would turn to sexual sterilization legislation to attempt to accomplish this aim.)[54]

Eugenics Goes to School

MacMurchy's desire to exert segregation and control over the feebleminded – which outweighed her impulse to educate and care for them – brought her to auxiliary classes as a eugenic solution to the feeblemindedness problem. Her dedication to solving this problem and her interest in eugenics made her into Canada's first devoted auxiliary education advocate, although she would quickly share this terrain with others. In her 1908 report as inspector, and in several subsequent reports, MacMurchy wrote that the auxiliary class could serve as a "clearing house" for assigning mental defectives to a custodial institution when they reached an appropriate age, placing them under the "continuous authority" of an institution that would monitor, care for, and segregate them for the rest of their lives.[55]

Such a plan was not without precedent. Similar measures involving special classes as clearing houses and a custodial institution were planned, or already in place, in the United States and England.[56] In the 1900s, auxiliary classes for feebleminded children were instituted in several North American public school systems. MacMurchy visited three – in New York City, Boston, and Cleveland – in 1908 and watched the classes in action.[57] With a design for the reform she wanted firmly in mind, MacMurchy began to try to convince Toronto public school authorities to adopt auxiliary classes as clearing houses for a custodial institution, to be built as soon as possible.

The Toronto LCW once again stepped in to help MacMurchy advance her cause, although on this occasion the involvement was more inadvertent than deliberate. The Toronto local council hosted the International Council of Women meetings in June 1909. The gathering attracted female reformers from around the globe. Mary Dendy, the leading British expert on the control and care of the feebleminded, attended the council meetings and lectured on mental defectiveness and education in England.[58] MacMurchy surely would have admired, if not envied, Dendy's accomplishments. She had achieved in England much of what MacMurchy set out to do in Toronto. Elected to the school board in Manchester in 1896, she prepared the report that led to the board establishing special classes and day schools for feebleminded children in 1898. That year, Dendy also founded the Lancashire and Cheshire Society for the Permanent Care of the Feeble-Minded. By 1902, the society was welcoming the first girls and boys to the Sandlebridge Boarding Schools, a custodial institution for the life-long segregation of the feebleminded that it operated at Alderley Edge, south of Manchester. English school boards were permitted to send mentally defective pupils to Sandlebridge, provided that the board or the Poor Law Union covered fees. The school boards of Manchester, Salford, and Bolton sent pupils to Dendy's school.[59]

Shortly before the International Council of Women meetings opened, MacMurchy invited Dendy to accompany her for a day as she inspected Toronto public schools to look for mentally defective pupils. Dendy was also formally invited to address a TBE meeting at City Hall. Speaking that evening on the subject of "weak minded children attending public schools," she described how she and MacMurchy had uncovered eleven worrisome cases of children who were "defective minded." "The worst case was that of a lad of fifteen years," Dendy told school trustees, "who, though having had the best instruction, had gained no knowledge." She "expressed the hope that a separate school would be set apart in the Toronto schools for the benefit of those so afflicted" and also praised the city's public schools on having a feebleminded population "under the European average."[60]

With Dendy's address, MacMurchy's efforts to establish auxiliary classes took a big step forward. Before the school board adjourned that evening, trustee Jimmy Simpson announced that he would introduce a motion at a later meeting to ask the board's Management Committee to counsel trustees on the "advisability of classifying the weak minded and otherwise physically incapacitated children in our public schools, with a view to giving special instruction that such children require."[61] The fact that Simpson was the board's sole socialist trustee[62] and cooperated with MacMurchy, a Conservative, is just one indication of how support for eugenics and auxiliary education cut across many lines in Canada.[63]

The board would wait approximately a year before it finally established special classes. But first, in February 1910, trustees hired Mac-Murchy to conduct a survey of the exact number of feebleminded children in the schools.[64] By the spring, she had confirmed more than one hundred cases.[65] To identify them, MacMurchy conferred with principals and teachers and personally visited fifty TBE schools to observe pupils. When a child was identified as possibly feebleminded, the school board wrote to the child's parents, inviting them to bring the child to a formal clinic at City Hall. There, MacMurchy performed a fifteen- to thirty-minute examination of each child and delivered a clinical diagnosis.[66] She does not appear to have used an intelligence test. At this time, standardized intelligence tests were still not widely available in North America; only by the mid- to late-1910s would they become the standard for diagnosing learning problems (see chapter 2). After MacMurchy had concluded her investigation, in the summer of 1910, Toronto trustees authorized the city's first auxiliary classes for mentally defective children, to open in the 1910–11 school year as some of the first auxiliary classes in Canada.[67] In March 1911, Ontario passed An Act Respecting Special Classes, giving Toronto's program provincial sanction.[68]

After several years of relentlessly publicizing her cause through her reports as inspector of the feebleminded, and with the help of highly placed allies in the LCW and associates such as Dendy and Simpson, MacMurchy achieved her initial goal of establishing special classes for mental defectives in Toronto public schools. Her work, however, had only just begun. Her next endeavour, lobbying for a custodial institution where pupils from these new clearing house classes could be sent for permanent control after their schooling, would call on even more of her legendary determination.

Going to School with Eugenics

The TBE selected four schools for its first auxiliary classes for mental defectives. Grace Street Public School (PS) and Essex Avenue PS were in the city's west end, while Elizabeth Street PS and George Street PS were more centrally located. Inner-city Elizabeth Street stood at the centre of the Ward, Toronto's most notorious neighbourhood. (Elizabeth Street would become Hester How PS in 1912, one of three schools whose pupil records feature prominently in this study.) Reformers knew the Ward for its poverty and significant immigrant population.[69] The auxiliary classes for mental defectives at the four schools were offered, in half-day sessions only, to between sixty and seventy pupils in total.[70] Two teachers were selected to conduct them. Lillian Carruthers was in charge at Essex Avenue and Grace Street, switching schools at midday. She was a veteran who had received her teacher preparation at the City Model School, graduating in 1892 and starting her first teaching position in Toronto public schools a year later.[71] Florence Sims handled classes at Elizabeth Street and George Street through the same half-day arrangement.[72] She had more than twenty years' experience as well and had worked with children at the challenging Elizabeth Street school for some time.[73]

In fact, Sims's early experience at Elizabeth Street was in the sort of class that prefigured the auxiliary classes for mental defectives that she would teach beginning in 1910. Starting around 1890, she taught an ungraded class for formerly truant boys at the school. Ungraded classes became more common in urban schools from the mid- to late-nineteenth century, and arose when enrolments mushroomed and compulsory attendance laws tightened, confronting urban schools with a small but significant number of children who previously might not have come to school at all. At mid-century reformers had often derisively labelled them "street Arabs," a bigotry-laden reference to the nomadism or vagrancy of street children – the orphans, waifs, and child beggars who cropped up in cities and alarmed reformers who suspected them of criminality.[74] By the later nineteenth century, children who appeared in the streets during school hours were more likely to be recognized as truants or child labourers than as homeless or mendicants. Predominantly boys, they worked full time during the school day (and into the evenings), selling newspapers or blacking boots and shining shoes. One Toronto police report from 1887 claimed that nearly 700 young people worked in street trades that also included performing; vending small items such as pencils, fruit, or shoelaces; and teenage prostitution. Many of these youngsters lived at home. A few newsboys, however, emancipated themselves from their parents and rented rooms in cheap boarding houses or lived in the Newsboys' Lodging and Industrial Home or in St Nicholas Home for Catholic children.[75]

These types of formerly non-attending children, when reformers and child-savers forced them to go to school, did not fit well into a system of age-graded classes.[76] Officials sometimes resorted to placing children with gaps in their schooling who were not accustomed to regular attendance, or who were unable to attend during normal hours because of work obligations, in special classes for newsboys that had flexible scheduling, or in ungraded classes for children of varying ages whose lack of school experience meant that they could not fit into the grade their age dictated they were supposed to be in. As early as 1881, a TBE teacher named Hester How was instructing truant boys, part of a former "unruly gang" that had been inhabiting a coal shed, in a special class in downtown premises the school board rented. In 1885 her class moved from temporary quarters to Elizabeth Street.[77] Hughes selected How for the class because he thought she was the only Toronto teacher with the right combination of pluck and compassion to handle unschooled street boys. The TBE would go onto rename How's long-time school, Elizabeth Street, in her honour in 1912. "Your voice and your smile," Hughes would later claim to have said to How when he hired her, "are the best positive reformatory agencies I have yet discovered, and I believe you can do this great work better and with less friction than any other woman or man I know."[78] Sims joined How in this work when the TBE opened a second class for former truants at Elizabeth Street around 1890.[79] The board established classes with flexible schedules specifically for newsboys around the same time, also at Elizabeth Street, under Jennie Warburton.[80] These classes would persist until about 1918 before disappearing for good.[81]

A few historians, such as Robert Osgood, have argued that ungraded classes were the antecedents to the auxiliary classes that came several decades later.[82] Some of the earliest ungraded classrooms anywhere in North America opened in Boston in 1879. Osgood writes that these classes, which he calls "undifferentiated," were for "a highly diverse collection of students" who did not fit into the grades for many different reasons.[83] He charts the decline of ungraded classes against the rise of special classes specifically for feebleminded children, which he calls "differentiated," and which first opened in Boston in 1898.[84] Auxiliary classes were ultimately far more sophisticated than the ungraded programs they replaced. Osgood helpfully distinguishes between these two settings. The former undifferentiated classes were more generic. More common before 1900, when they could be found in Boston, New York City, Cleveland, and New Haven, these classes were for children who did not fit into the grades for a variety of reasons. They might include habitual truants, or newsboys such as in the Toronto case, but often also encompassed older and immigrant children, children whose behaviour teachers could not control, and probably some disabled children. The latter differentiated classes, for feebleminded or mentally defective children who were disabled, had a more specific demographic. School systems largely implemented these auxiliary classes after 1900, supported by a rapidly emerging science of learning difficulties that eugenicists developed and that intelligence quotient (IQ) testers would soon elaborate. Ungraded classes, by contrast, were not backed by a cohesive theory of learning problems. Increasingly after about 1900, auxiliary class teachers received special training in learning problems and in teaching children who had them. Ungraded class teachers lacked formal training of this sort.[85]

The science of eugenics supported the newer and differentiated auxiliary classes for mental defectives in Toronto and other cities that eventually crowded out ungraded classes. Without eugenicists to put meat on the bones of the category of mental defectiveness, differentiation might not have occurred. Eugenics underwrote distinctive training for auxiliary class teachers that prepared them to work with mentally defective children. Toronto's auxiliary class teachers had access to that training from virtually the inception of the city's special classes for mental defectives. Carruthers travelled by train to New Jersey in the summer of 1911 to take courses in the characteristics of mentally defective learners and in auxiliary education methods at the Vineland Training School, a custodial institution in New Jersey.[86] The instruction that she and other teachers from the United States and Canada received at Vineland, regarded at the time as the preeminent training centre for special class teachers, introduced them to eugenics-supported theories about the learning ability and other characteristics of mental defectives.[87] Like any experienced educator placed in a novel teaching situation, Carruthers and other early auxiliary class teachers relied on their professional intuition to develop auxiliary class approaches, and often adapted kindergarten methods, manual training, and physical exercise such as dance for use with feebleminded children.[88] But at a time when there were few other sources of information about mental deficiency – or even about what caused learning problems of any sort – teachers had to call on a few experts for information not just about the characteristics of mental defectives but also about what and how much they could learn and the best ways to teach them. Custodial asylum superintendents, who were the first to offer specialized training to auxiliary class teachers, were intent on actively disseminating their expertise on these matters. The Canadian-born superintendent of Vineland, E.R. Johnstone, believed that "with all these [children] as laboratory material we ought to announce ourselves (every institution in the country ought to announce itself) as a laboratory for the public schools of America."[89] In this way, superintendents, who were often eugenicists but might actually have had very little sustained contact with exceptional children in classrooms, enjoyed virtually unchallenged authority to clinically construct differences in pupils' abilities. They also had wide latitude to develop knowledge about how pupils with disabilities and learning difficulties learned and therefore how they should be taught. Through the training they received at institutions such as Vineland, early auxiliary class teachers helped to carry down to the school level the outlines of categories that in the 1910s would shape instruction and policies in auxiliary education. This did not mean, however, that teachers never questioned expert knowledge, as we shall see.

The courses for auxiliary class teachers at Vineland were led by the foremost authorities of the day. Goddard and Johnstone taught some classes.[90] Both men subscribed to the view that mental defectiveness was inherited, intractable against efforts to educate it away, and made children a social menace to control.[91] Johnstone instructed teachers to prepare mentally defective children for institutional life. These children had no use for academic knowledge, he told their teachers, asking rhetorically: "What in the world is the use of any feebleminded child in any institution knowing how to multiply two hundred and fifty-six by twenty-seven?"[92] Starting in 1915, "Auxiliary Teachers' Summer Classes" were offered in Ontario as well. MacMurchy delivered lectures. Peter Sandiford, an educational psychologist at the University of Toronto and a eugenicist, joined her and taught "Psychology of Mental Defectives," among other topics.[93] MacMurchy prepared a nearly 200-page instructional manual for educators, *Organization and Management of Auxiliary Classes,* which the Ontario Department of Education (DOE) published in 1915. In the manual, she wrote about mental defectiveness: "The school must take its place as the greatest preventive agency against this great menace to society."[94] She also wrote: "The best place to train teachers for Auxiliary Classes" was in institutions like Vineland and Sandlebridge.[95]

Laggards in Toronto's Schools

Mentally defective children were not the only group of academically struggling youngsters to attract educational reformers' attention in the 1900s and 1910s. Experts in mental deficiency, as well as educationists during these decades, in fact distinguished between two types of schoolchildren who had trouble learning: mentally defective children and backward children. Although experts and educationists were concerned with both groups, eugenicists such as MacMurchy tended to be preoccupied with mental defectiveness, while school inspectors and other administrators tended to be preoccupied with backwardness. This second group comprised many of the administrative progressive reformers who sought to enhance the efficiency of schooling through bureaucratic reforms, including greater program differentiation in the form of auxiliary programs. Their separate interest in auxiliary education overlapped partially with the interest of eugenicists, strengthening the movement for auxiliary education as a reform.

Mentally defective children struggled to learn because, experts in the 1910s said, they inherently lacked the mental ability to succeed. Backward children also struggled to learn in the schools. But unlike mentally defective children, experts and educators contended, backward children had the necessary capacity for academic success. They had been prevented from succeeding, it was thought, by one or more factors usually not related to intellectual disability.[96] When describing the causes of backwardness in his district in 1913, the Toronto school inspector W.H. Elliott blamed the "carelessness of parents," overcrowding in the primary grades, the "in-elasticity of our school programme of study," the promotion system from grade to grade, and the proliferation of small schools.[97] From his more clinical standpoint, the chief medical inspector of Toronto public schools, Dr W.E. Struthers, asserted: "Many pupils are backward, purely and simply because of defective vision, defective hearing, adenoids, which may also cause deafness, enlarged tonsils, enlarged glands, or general malnutrition and physical weakness."[98]

The foremost expert on backward pupils at the time, however, was the American Leonard P. Ayres. He listed contributing factors such as "the constant influx of non-English speaking children, the enrolling of children in the first grade at a comparatively advanced age, slow progress of children on account of physical defects or weaknesses, inefficient teaching, unsuitable courses of study, and the shifting of children from school to school by reason of the frequent changes of residence of their families."[99] Despite so many causes of backwardness, educators, school administrators, and medical personnel were still confident that it could be overcome by removing the external causes one by one. Mental defectiveness, by comparison, had a cause that was "irremovable": "little or no mind to educate."[100] Struthers summed up the difference perfectly in 1911: "The mentally backward child can be educated, trained, and developed into a useful, self-supporting, responsible citizen; the mentally defective child never."[101] This distinction was crucial to the emergence of different auxiliary education programs for each group in the 1910s. Yet, as we shall see in the next chapter, at the end of this decade and the beginning of the next one, this distinction would also be challenged and undone – in somewhat dramatic fashion and with significant implications for exceptional pupils.

Backwardness bore a close relationship to "retardation," a major challenge in urban education at the time. In 1909, in his book *Laggards in Our Schools*, Ayres coined the term "retardation" to refer to large numbers of American schoolchildren who were "older than they should be for the grades they are in."[102] These backward girls and boys were the bigger and older children (even some teenagers) who were grade repeaters or had started school late. In most urban schools, legions of them crowded into the early grades with smaller and younger beginners. When Chief Inspector Cowley finally surveyed retardation in the TBE in June 1917, he found that there were twice as many children enrolled in junior first form (the first grade after kindergarten) as there were enrolled in senior third form (the system's sixth grade).[103] Of the nearly 11,000 children enrolled in junior first, there were approximately 9,000 seven- and eight-year-olds. But there were also 1,500 nine- and ten-year-olds, one hundred eleven- and twelve-year-olds, and handfuls of teenagers.[104]

Although mentally defective children could also, by Ayres's definition, be retarded (they too could be over-age for their grade), retardation, Ayres wrote, was "not at all a problem concerning a few underdeveloped or feeble minded children. It is one affecting most intimately perhaps 6,000,000 children in the United States."[105] The dollar sum associated with reteaching grade repeaters was thus massive, pegged by Ayres at about $27 million a year nationwide.[106] He also drew attention to how repeating grades led to discouragement and eventually to "elimination" (dropping out), an equally important "evil" that educational progressives sought to conquer.[107] To forward-thinking administrative progressives, including many Toronto school inspectors, retardation was very nearly a calamity.[108] Not only did it create enormous inefficiency, it had, according to Ayres, an "evidently close bearing on the question of the adaptation of the school to the needs of the child," yet another core progressive concern.[109]

Why did worry about retardation become so dire and so widespread? David Tyack writes that "the classification of pupils was not divinely inspired or embedded in the order of nature."[110] That is to say, there is not now, nor was there in the 1910s, a natural age when a child should begin schooling, nor any ordained reason a child should progress at a rate of one grade every twelve months. However, the bureaucratically and efficiency-minded administrative progressives in charge of city school systems in the 1910s were, to a fault, intent on changing precisely the sort of haphazardness that retardation represented by standardizing educational practices and by differentiating the functions of schooling to better adapt the academic program to varied individual needs.[111]

By 1913 concern had spread deeply into Canada, and nearly all of the Toronto school inspectors, and more than a few school systems outsiders as well, were talking about retardation.[112] Inspector J.W. Rogers had discovered close to 3,900 over-age pupils in his inspectorate. With alarm, he reported that numbers ran as high as 60 per cent at one school.[113] His counterpart, Elliott, declared that close to one-third of pupils in his district were over-age for their grade. "This is a most serious situation," he warned, "and measures should be taken at once, towards its amelioration."[114] Even more concerned about the seriousness of the issue than the inspectors, perhaps, was the Bureau of Municipal Research. Turning its earnest attention to the city's retardation problem, the bureau applied considerable pressure to the TBE, and published no fewer than fifteen pamphlets on the issue of "educational waste" between 1915 and 1920.[115] In the fourth pamphlet, "Are All Children Alike?," the bureau estimated that Toronto's retardation problem cost the city (and ratepayers) "from $250,000 to $500,000 a year in impaired productiveness or actual expenditure, or both."[116]

To school officials searching for a solution to the retardation problem, auxiliary classes for backward children beckoned for several reasons, and Toronto opened its first at Queen Alexandra PS in 1912 followed by another half-dozen or more at different schools by 1920.[117] Unlike auxiliary classes for mentally defective children, auxiliary classes for backward children were expected to help their pupils return to regular graded classrooms by giving them remedial instruction that would enable them to do so. Describing the ideal auxiliary class for backward children in 1913, Inspector Elliott wrote that it "should be relatively small, and its pupils should remain only so long as is necessary for them to develop sufficient power to proceed with the work of the grades from which they were taken."[118] Also in 1913, John Seath, the province's superintendent of education, observed backward pupils in auxiliary classes in the United States. "They have the future of pupils of normal intelligence," he reported, and "it is expected that they will take their place in one of the regular grades."[119] Indeed, the average stay for a child in a "backward class" in Toronto in 1914 ranged from three or three-and-a-half months in some schools to eight months in others.[120] Educators believed that backward children were not universally delayed like mentally defective children, but instead "backward in only one," or perhaps two, subjects.[121] With individual remedial instruction in those weak subjects and hard work, backward children, it was thought, could catch up to their peers. In her class for backward children at Queen Alexandra, teacher Bessie Bowling practiced "individual teaching" and encouraged her pupils to "acquire habits of industry."[122] While students caught up in the backward classes, they were also removed from regular classrooms where it was thought they absorbed too much of the teacher's attention, sometimes causing still more pupils to fall behind.[123]

In the grander scheme, the impact of a few auxiliary classes for backward children on the retardation problem was minimal at best. Retardation, it was believed, afflicted students by the thousands in Toronto. It was changes to grading and promotion practices, arriving at the end of the 1910s, that helped urban school systems like Toronto's to reduce retardation significantly.[124] Nevertheless, the need that school officials felt to respond to retardation, like the pressures they felt to address feeble-mindedness, helped to propel auxiliary education forward as a reform.

Defining Disadvantage as Disability

Auxiliary education as a reform in Toronto schools did not end with the classes the school board initiated for mentally defective children under

Carruthers and Sims in 1910, nor with the classes for backward children it first opened in 1912 under Bowling. Social and moral reformers, child savers, and educators also turned to special classes as a way to improve the lives of other Toronto children who had not necessarily been identified as backward or mentally defective but who lived in poverty, were unhealthy, or spoke little English. Between 1912 and 1916, to serve some of these pupils, the TBE opened two forest schools and one open-air classroom for children at risk of tuberculosis or in otherwise poor general health. In 1913, the first auxiliary education rooms specifically for immigrant children also opened. By 1917, DOE regulations officially recognized all forest school, open-air, and what the TBE called "foreign" classes for immigrants as falling under the province's auxiliary education legislation.[125] By locating classes and services designed to address poverty, ill health, or lack of English language ability within the emerging auxiliary education system, reformers and educationists in the 1910s both constructed (or conflated, as Mona Gleason argues) and formalized poverty, ill health, and foreign language as disabilities.[126]

Forest Schools and Open-Air Classrooms

In June 1912, the TBE established its first forest school with outdoor classrooms in Victoria Park in Toronto's east end. It added a second school in High Park in the west end two years later.[127] In 1918, the two schools enrolled 203 students and employed six teachers.[128] The forest schools were part of "the Open Air School Movement," as one of its supporters, the Toronto school inspector N.S. MacDonald, called it. Open-air schooling, which found adherents in North America and Europe in the 1900s and 1910s, was influenced by the awakening interest in the effects of good and bad air on well-being that moral reformers, child savers in the playground movement, and especially public health doctors shared.[129] The movement had from the beginning, MacDonald observed, been "intimately connected with the work of the anti-tuberculosis organizations."[130] Doctors saw bad air as a major contributor to the spread of tuberculosis, the dreaded and deadly infectious "white plague."[131] Struthers, another Toronto supporter of open-air schooling, wrote that "vitiated" air could contribute to "anaemia, malnutrition, poor physical development, sluggish mentality, and all the conditions that so frequently end in pulmonary tuberculosis."[132]

Forest schools and open-air classes merged educational work with public health work, a combination that by the 1910s was becoming much more common in city school systems in Canada and the United States.[133] The TBE's forest schools and open-air classes, at least at first, were primarily for children at risk of contracting tuberculosis. However, these programs also admitted children with other illnesses and children who were "ill-nourished with poor home surroundings."[134] The journalist W.A. Craick, who wrote a popular set of profiles of city schools for the *Toronto Star Weekly* in the 1910s and early 1920s, called the forest school "one of the most unique institutions of learning in the city." Describing the physical setting for his readers in 1917, Craick wrote: "Not far from the north-east corner of High Park in an open space among the trees two large tents are to be seen standing close together. Nearby on low wooden platforms rows of benches and desks face portable blackboards propped against the tree trunks. A little further an odd-looking group of objects, which on closer scrutiny resolve themselves into tarpaulin-covered cots, are ranged in even ranks under the sheltering branches."[135] Unlike regular schools, where academics had priority, "health first, then education" was the forest school motto, stated proudly by Fred Dent, the principal of Victoria Park Forest School for part of the 1910s.[136] Pupils studied academic subjects for just two hours and fifteen minutes in a seven-hour-and-forty-minute school day.[137] Under the health-first approach, most of their time was devoted to hygiene lessons, play, nature walks, meals, and a nap period. One of the forest schools' greatest achievements, according to Struthers, was pioneering step-by-step toothbrushing and nose-blowing drills.[138]

Toronto's forest schools welcomed a crop of new and returning pupils each May, kept them over the summer (class was in session from Monday to Saturday), and returned them to their regular schools in November.[139] The seasonal interruption in open-air schooling was a challenge that the board took strides to overcome in 1916 when it opened its second type of open-air educational facility at the newly constructed Orde Street PS.[140] The school was "built and arranged in every detail for open-air work," with the top storey consisting of two wall-less classrooms, cooking and eating facilities, washrooms, and a playground. (Today, the open-air classroom, now closed, on the school's roof is still visible from the street.) Unlike the forest schools, the Orde Street open-air classrooms followed the regular school calendar.[141] To shield the children from the winter cold, the school board outfitted each of them with an "Eskimo suit," a "combined toque and coat of flannel, and big felt boots over ordinary ones."[142]

1.1 "High Park Forest School class at work, girl writing," 1926. City of Toronto Archives, *Globe and Mail* fonds, fonds 1266, item 7744.

Over the course of the 1910s, forest schools and open-air classes evolved from a program for children at risk of tuberculosis to a program principally for children authorities believed were handicapped by ill health. The schools could not admit children with open, contagious cases of tuberculosis; consequently, they turned their efforts towards children who medical personnel judged to be at risk of the disease because of their poor general health. In 1913, the TBE hired a tuberculosis officer, Dr F.S. Minns, to help identify students for the forest schools.[143] Children were also identified through the routine checkups that came with the start of a school medical inspection service in 1910.[144] MacDonald, who had acknowledged the open-air school's origin in anti-tuberculosis work, said that it was "not merely 'a school in the open air,' nor is it a sanatorium or convalescent

1.2 "Forest School – Board of Education," 1913. Children and teacher in an impromptu nature study lesson at Victoria Park or High Park Forest School. City of Toronto Archives, Former City of Toronto Fonds, Department of Public Works photographs, Board of Education photographs, item 76.

home. It comprises a way of life and a system both of education and medical treatment."[145]

Forest schools were enlisted in the city's effort to cut down retardation as well, with the idea that they could treat some of its root causes. Dr A.C. MacKay, who replaced Struthers as chief medical inspector in 1915, commended them for these efforts: "In a large percentage of the [forest school] pupils, the mentality increased in a few months at least a grade, much of the backwardness seemed to be due not so much to an inherent mental deficiency but rather to the fact that they had not enough vigor and strength for both physical and mental growth. Teachers have told me of pupils who were 'repeaters' in their

1.3 "Orde Street Open Air School," 1919. Wearing "Eskimo" suits, late autumn. City of Toronto Archives, Former City of Toronto Fonds, Department of Public Works photographs, Health Department photographs, item 613.

grade, after a season at a Forest School were able to advance normally in their studies."[146]

Open-air schooling also helped such children overcome what reformers saw as the handicap of ill health, caused, they further believed, by the poverty and ignorance of families, especially recent immigrant ones. In the 1910s, Toronto's forest schools enrolled mostly poor and "foreign born" students; the latter composed 61 per cent of the High Park Forest School population in 1915, while students "of Jewish parentage" composed 44 per cent.[147] This meant that the forest schools actually served some of Toronto's newest and most impoverished residents. Many Jewish families arrived in Canada from Eastern Europe in the 1900s and 1910s practically penniless, and lived in shocking poverty in the Ward's cramped and dilapidated cottages – approximately

1.4 "Forest School – Board of Education – High Park," 1913. Children and staff sit for a meal. City of Toronto Archives, Former City of Toronto Fonds, Department of Public Works photographs, Board of Education photographs, item 59.

one in ten dwellings had no running water, for instance.[148] Like other middle-class urban social reformers, educators and school health inspectors such as MacKay, Dent, and Struthers believed that their own class-bound health norms (which they could achieve because of their relative financial comfort) were naturally superior to those of the children and families they served.[149] The education of the "whole child" at the forest schools was not just for the children themselves, MacDonald wrote, but also for their parents and even their eventual offspring: "The State profits indirectly from the lessons in sanitation and hygiene which are carried into the child's home, and are applied as a matter of course in the home of the future citizen."[150]

By the late nineteenth century or early twentieth century, various educators, reformers, and others were beginning to recognize that hunger, like poor general health, had a deleterious effect on learning.[151] In addition to hygiene lessons, forest schools went to considerable lengths to attempt to correct what school authorities perceived as immigrants' deficient practices around food and nutrition. This was a common theme of domestic science instruction generally.[152] Immigrants' nutrition practices, authorities believed, contributed to the malnourished, underweight, unhealthy children who showed up at schools across Toronto. The forest schools measured their success in part by feeding their students what school officials believed were the correct foods, and then meticulously tracking any weight they gained.[153] Principal J.C. Copp of Victoria Park Forest School talked about his pupils' initial preferences "for pastry, cakes, pickles and heavy foods." He taught them to adjust their palates by the time they left: "Evidently they had never had proper food at home, and of the greatest accomplishments of the school was to train the children to like and eat proper food."[154] E.W. Linklater, the principal of High Park Forest School with its large Jewish population, affirmed that at the school "the boys and girls were trained to like good, plain, wholesome food, well cooked, served cleanly and at regular hours. Many of the Hebrews are used to dining at very irregular hours and eating anything but the proper food."[155] Struthers, for his part, told delegates to the Ontario Educational Association (OEA) meetings in 1914 that "the Science of Nutrition has a close and practical relation to the Science of Eugenics, and both to Education, for it boots little to have a child well born if it is not well fed, trained, and disciplined."[156] Struthers had earlier written that "our children are suffering, degenerating, dying, not from want of food but because of improper and unwholesome food ... I do not know whether it is from parental lack of knowledge or indifference or both."[157]

Hunger was a fact of life for many poor children in cities in this period, and Toronto was no exception.[158] Such children welcomed food that eased their hunger pangs. In her study *Small Matters*, Gleason interviewed adults who had grown up poor in Canada from the 1900s to the 1940s and spoke about being hungry.[159] In this sense, Linklater did not exaggerate greatly (although he did point, at least indirectly, to Anglo-Canadian or Protestant ways he believed superior) when he wrote that "meal time" at the forest school "was soon much anticipated by the boys and girls. It was a source of pleasure to hear them lustily sing the tune of the doxology:

We thank the Lord for this our food,
For life and health are very good;
Let manna to our souls be given
The Bread of Life sent down from heaven.[160]

However, the adults who told Gleason about their hungry child-hoods also spoke about their mothers' valiant struggles to stretch good food as far as they could to fill many hungry stomachs on sparse bud-gets.[161] A sense of cultural superiority and the notion that the wrong food, not a lack of food or other structural factors related to poverty and class in cities, was the cause of malnourishment in schoolchildren clearly drove forest school officials' views. They shared those views with many, though not necessarily all, moral reformers in the United States and England during this period.[162] These adults were misguided, but this did not mean that hungry children did not benefit from the forest school bounty.

Foreign Classes

Along with ill-health caused by malnutrition and other factors, another mounting concern for educationists was foreignness, which they be-lieved contributed to retardation and backwardness. They defined for-eignness as a deficit in some children's abilities in English if it was not their first language. To an only slightly lesser extent, they understood foreignness as a cultural or racial deficit in the ability of children from some immigrant groups to adapt to Canadian life. To address foreign-ness as an educational challenge, the TBE created special classes spe-cifically for immigrant children, which had much the same purpose as those for backward children: to bring new immigrants who were just learning English up to the pace of their same-age, Canadian-born, English-speaking peers, so that they might join them in the regular grades. In 1913 and 1914, the TBE opened several "ungraded class[es] for foreign children."[163]

This timing was no coincidence. 1913 was a banner year for Canadian immigration, with 402,000 foreign-born persons entering Canada as the nation's economic opportunities beckoned and war clouds gathered in Europe.[164] This influx – a single-year record high for immigration that has yet to be surpassed – included many non-British immigrants. The schools that the TBE selected for new foreign classes in 1913 and 1914, including Victoria Street PS, Ryerson PS, and Hester How PS, had sizeable immigrant populations, mainly Eastern European Jews. At Victoria Street in 1913, according to a survey conducted by TBE inspector G.H. Armstrong, 190 students had Russia, Austria, or Romania as what he called their "nativity or land of birth."[165] In comparison, 160 pupils had been born in Canada, 129 in England, forty in the United States, and seventeen in Scotland. Smaller numbers of children at the school were born in Italy and China. At Hester How, Russian-, Austrian-, or Romanian-born pupils made up slightly more than two-thirds of the school's entire population.[166] Inspector W.F. Chapman, who made a similar survey in his district, reported that approximately 46 per cent of pupils at Ryerson were "foreign."[167]

Foreign classes in largely immigrant schools had two goals. One was to teach immigrant children English so that they could enter a mainstream class. Educators viewed a lack of English language skills as a disability to be overcome as quickly as possible. In Inspector Chapman's district, foreign classes at McCaul PS and Ryerson were modelled after the "Steamer Classes" that Cleveland public schools pioneered and that Boston and New York City had as well.[168] These classes, according to Ayres, who surveyed the Cleveland school system in 1917, were for the "rapid acquirement of the English language" by immigrant children who spoke little or no English, "before they are placed in a class with 30 or 40 other children who are not similarly handicapped."[169]

The other goal of foreign classes – a goal public education shared more generally – was to assimilate foreign children into Canadian ways. Public school administrators, including those in the Toronto system, made no effort to conceal that assimilation was the objective.[170] With the number of public school pupils in Toronto who had been born outside of Canada or other English-speaking countries far exceeding the spaces available in just a handful of foreign classes, however, most immigrant children were in mainstream classes from the beginning. There, they were promptly inundated by the Lord's Prayer, the Union Jack, Empire Day celebrations, and the prose and poetry of Rudyard Kipling and Sir Walter Scott.[171]

Educators in the 1910s generally believed that most foreign pupils, those from Europe at least, were capable of learning English quickly and assimilating into mainstream Canada – that is, overcoming their foreignness.[172] In 1913, John Seath investigated the length of time children spent in Toronto's foreign classes before being promoted. At Lansdowne PS, thirty-five children attended, nine were promoted, and one transferred schools. On average, children spent three-and-half months in these classes. Pupils in foreign classes at Hester How, McCaul, Ryerson, and Victoria Street spent on average between six-and-a-half and eight months there, with slightly more than one-third promoted within the year to regular grades.[173] Inspector Chapman observed pupils in foreign classes in his district, including at McCaul and Ryerson, reporting: "The progress these pupils make is marvellous. The teachers do not know the language of these foreigners and the results obtained prove that it is not necessary that they should to teach these people. The children are industrious, intelligent, respectful and obedient; they are exceedingly appreciative; they have that greatest incentive to effort, viz. feeling the need of what you are after, and their progress delights the teacher as it so visible and rapid."[174] This perspective on immigrant students stands in contrast to the views held by Canadian eugenicists. MacMurchy and prominent psychiatrist C.K. Clarke believed that most immigrants at Canada's doors were of poor heredity, were largely unassimilable for this reason, and that the entry of yet more newcomers should therefore be restricted.[175]

Although more accepting than eugenicists of immigrants in general, teachers in Toronto (like other North American educators) nevertheless held distinct opinions on the relative educability and assimilability of different ethnic and racial groups.[176] Teachers and inspectors especially lauded newly immigrated Jewish students for rapid headway in their studies, a result they attributed to Jewish cultural and supposedly racial traits. Mr Lavis, a senior third teacher at Victoria Street, told Craick, who interviewed him in 1918, that "Jewish children are always quick and clever," going on to discuss the reasons that Jewish children succeeded as a group.[177] Referring to various supposedly racial characteristics affecting schooling, Miss Cooper, who taught a foreign class at Victoria Street also, remarked that "in the case of foreigners of some nationalities ... especially for example the Chinese, their methods of thought seem so different from our own that it is difficult to get into touch with them."[178]

In short, educators and school officials in the 1910s, the decade when auxiliary education began in Toronto, believed that such instruction could help children who were backward, foreign, or unhealthy to return to the mainstream classroom. They did not assume that all exceptional children were educationally unreachable, only one group of them. Mentally defective children, the most seriously handicapped because – as eugenicists went out of their way to point out – their defect was hereditary, were deemed out of reach for most types of instruction and for any improvement. The Bureau of Municipal Research summarized the issue in 1915: "The foreigner can be assimilated. The feeble-minded child can never be assimilated, but must always remain a stranger in his home land, whose genius, institutions and national life he cannot by any tour de force be made to understand."[179]

Reform Plans and Oppositions, 1912–1920

Neither the form that auxiliary education took in the 1910s nor its success as a reform was predetermined. Both were manufactured amid debate on overlapping and opposing visions of special classes, articulated by eugenicists, teachers, school trustees and inspectors, politicians, reformers, parents, and others. For the most part, the forest schools and open-air classes seem to have gone relatively unquestioned, except perhaps near the end of the 1910s when conservatives in municipal government asked for spending reductions at the TBE. The foreign classes faded in importance after the onset of the First World War made immigration difficult. However, the auxiliary classes for mental defectives and backward children engendered competing viewpoints throughout the 1910s. Much of the controversy surrounded a planned custodial institution to accompany the classes for mental defectives.

After successfully convincing the school board to set up auxiliary classes for mentally defective children, MacMurchy turned next to convincing school authorities, the city's Board of Control, and the provincial government to execute the next step in her plan to manage feeblemindedness in Toronto. She wanted a "Farm Colony" that would accept mentally defective graduates of the auxiliary classes as well as other mental defectives. The proposed institution "should be as far as possible self-contained – should grow its own food – do its own work – assist materially in building the necessary houses, even make its own pavements and weave the cloth for the inmates' clothes, and raise produce and make things for sale. ... This is done now at practically every progressive and modern Institution for the Feeble-Minded. ... It is the right way."[180] In fact, the farm colony that MacMurchy described bore many similarities to the Sandlebridge institution that Dendy had established outside of Manchester.[181] A separate facility for the feebleminded was needed, MacMurchy said, because too many feebleminded patients had been dumped at the provincial Asylum for Idiots at Orillia, which was for the most severely disabled cases only, individuals MacMurchy would have classified with the technical terms idiots and imbeciles.[182]

The farm colony plan gathered momentum in 1912. On 26 March, "the first-ever convention in Toronto to consider the whole problem of the mentally deficient child" was held. Mayor G.R. Geary presided, and a subcommittee, chaired by McCarthy and including MacMurchy, school board chairman and local dentist Dr Fred Conboy, Reverend J.B. Starr of juvenile court, and others, formed to publicize the issues.[183] The subcommittee's subsequent report called on the city to create a register of its feebleminded population – estimated at 625 children under age fourteen and 500 individuals who were older than that. It also called on the school board to institute more auxiliary classes for mental defectives and on the province to construct a "training school of the residential colony type."[184] Another meeting took place in November 1912, during which a formal group called the Provincial Association for the Care of the Feebleminded (PACFM) was founded to pursue these goals. MacMurchy was an organizing force in the founding of the PACFM (its name is reminiscent of Dendy's Lancashire and Cheshire Society for the Permanent Care of the Feeble-Minded), as were McCarthy and members of the National Council of Women of Canada.[185]

Parents of children with disabilities also took an interest in efforts to establish auxiliary programs. Later, in the 1950s, formal parent associations would come together to advocate for their children,[186] but private pursuit of services was the norm in the earlier period. In December 1915, Toronto school trustees heard directly from a local woman, Mrs L. Fares, who requested that "her son be allowed to attend the class for defective children."[187] Another parent, a father of "a mental deficient," took his appeal to the newspapers. In a letter to the *Toronto Globe*, he pleaded with the city's medical officer of health, Charles Hastings, to take action: "Will Dr Hastings try to get a school? Do you, sir, or does Dr Hastings know the heartless and hopeless problem [of] an only son is who is a mental deficient? ... For ten years my home has been wrecked and our hearts broken ... To send a boy to Orillia [Asylum for Idiots] who is merely a deficient ... is in effect equal to all the pangs and sorrows of a sentence to prison for both child and parents."[188] Like the parents who did send a child to custodial institutions such as Orillia, parents who requested special classes acted in complex circumstances and with complicated feelings about their own children – love, shame, fear, and hope. The historian Nic Clarke notes that even at the height of fears about the feebleminded in the early decades of the twentieth century, people both "daemonized" mentally defective children as dangerous or as a drain on resources and also "sacralised" them as deserving of the same special care and consideration increasingly extended to other children. Parents in particular wrestled with these difficult emotions.[189]

Not surprisingly, while some parents sought auxiliary education services, others shunned them. When MacMurchy conducted her clinic at City Hall in 1910, summoning children whom schools had identified as possibly feebleminded and their parents, many families did not show up at all. One father sent what MacMurchy regarded as a haughty letter, informing her "that it would not be convenient for him to bring his daughter at the time and place appointed, or at any other time and place."[190] C.K. Clarke, who had considerable experience in his own clinic at the Toronto General Hospital diagnosing feeblemindedness and speaking with parents about it, recommended to his colleagues that they avoid issuing an insulting label, such as feebleminded, that parents might take as "a serious reflection upon their own creative powers."[191] In the 1910s, the popularization of eugenics through family studies, such as Goddard's 1912 *The Kallikak Family: A Study in the Heredity of Feeblemindedness*, cast doubts on the genetic and therefore moral past of any family with a child or other member with a disability.[192]

Newspaper coverage of feeblemindedness and of the lobby for auxiliary classes, which was regular and frequently sensational, placed both issues squarely in the public eye. Journalists were present at the high-profile March 1912 convention on feeblemindedness in Toronto. At least two newspapers, the *Toronto Daily Star* and the *Globe*, reported on a remark, seemingly innocuously enough, that Conboy made at the conference. According to the *Globe*, Conboy said that "fifty percent of the [mental] defectives" attending Toronto auxiliary classes "cannot be educated."[193]

The reporting of Conboy's remarks in the press, which likely were not all that different from statements others uttered at the convention, would contribute to a commotion about the city's auxiliary classes for mental defectives. Carruthers, who taught the classes to which Conboy was referring and who read what he had said about them, was angered by his flippancy. In a letter to the *Star*, Carruthers responded to Conboy's "gratuitous statement," writing that "from my experience of almost two years with these children, I have no hesitation in stating that they are all unmistakably educable." There were only two exceptions, she said. The first was a child who might have been educable but had been in her class for too short a time for her to tell for certain; the second was a child for whom "insanity had supervened upon mental defect."[194]

The views on mental deficiency on the part of officials such as Conboy or experts such as MacMurchy usually received more ink than the views of teachers such as Carruthers. Some historians have commented negatively on professional women who in this period used their relatively new status in fields like children's health or disability to promulgate racist or ableist ideas.[195] These historians have less readily acknowledged that the views of professional and elite women varied greatly. Professional hierarchies gave disproportionate attention to the ideas of a few expert women and men, over-representing these opinions. The much larger numbers of women working on the frontlines, as teachers or nurses, for example, had far fewer opportunities to make their views known.[196] Teachers, for that matter, formed their own opinions on the nature of mental deficiency, suitable education for exceptional pupils, and the most appropriate goals for auxiliary classes. At different times, these views could be similar to or dissimilar from reformer or expert views. The historian Kate Rousmaniere's persuading analysis in her book on New York City teachers in this period is that many urban educators encountered administrative progressive and other reforms "as confusing and contradictory intrusions into their already stressful workday and that they responded to their chaotic workplace by alternately accommodating, adapting, and resisting certain aspect of their working conditions."[197]

Some Toronto teachers shared eugenicists' way of thinking about exceptional children and fully welcomed auxiliary education as a reform. Others did not, or at best did so only partially. Writing about auxiliary classes in *Public Health Journal* in 1914, the Toronto teacher Mary Blackwell used the same phrasing that MacMurchy invoked frequently in the 1910s: "Nature has put the mental defective in a class by himself, we had better take the hint."[198] Carruthers, in contrast to Blackwell, had views on the education of mental defectives that differed from those of the experts. In addition to believing that, by and large, mentally defective children were educable (which experts did not believe), Carruthers treated these children, whom she knew personally, with great compassion. She defended them as vulnerable and valuable, children "whose gentle manners and loving hearts are worth tons of intellect."[199] Yet she did not differ categorically from other commentators in her views. Like MacMurchy and TBE chairman Conboy, she also supported the farm colony (claiming "sincerest sympathy" with the cause), and her understanding of mental deficiency, acquired initially in her studies at Vineland, stressed a firm line between backwardness and mental defectiveness.[200]

Relations between Carruthers and school officials grew even tenser about a month after Conboy made his remarks and Carruthers sent her first letter to the *Star*. Carruthers had been asking for medical inspection of several of her pupils for some time. Ignored by the medical inspection office, she was forced to wave down a school nurse who happened to pass by her school. She also protested deplorable conditions in her classrooms. Essex PS had become overcrowded, so the school board moved the auxiliary class to a rented room nearby. (It was common at this time to rent premises even for regular classes to relieve overcrowding.)[201] The new classroom, located in the basement of a Baptist church, flooded regularly, and the walls were perpetually "sopping wet." Conditions were little better at Grace Street PS, where Carruthers and her other half-day class were crammed into two inadequate enjoined rooms, also in a rented house.[202]

Carruthers conveyed some of this information in another letter, this time addressed to the school board.[203] The *Star*, which obtained an advance copy (probably from Carruthers) and printed it, called the letter "a direct charge of neglect" against Struthers. Sensing a good opportunity for muckraking, the *Star* quickly dispatched a reporter to talk to Struthers about Carruthers's allegations. "These are not normal children, and they should be cared for in government institutions," he told the reporter. "I shouldn't have to bother with them." The reporter pressed further, and asked him, "So long as the classes are in the charge and care of the Board of Education should they not receive as much or more attention than ordinary classes?" Struthers grudgingly admitted that they should. "But," he added, "those children in her classes are abnormal, some of them even approach imbecility, and, what are we expected to do with them? Can we put brains in them? Are we to perform operations on them? If a child is not normal you cannot make it so. There are some very absurd notions prevalent as to this matter."[204]

When the school board met the next day, Conboy demanded to know who had leaked Carruthers's letter to the press. An unnamed trustee referred resentfully to her "brass band method" of protest, while the board's management committee made plans to call her before trustees to explain herself. Yet the trustees, like Struthers, were forced to admit that the board had a duty to medically inspect the classes, as Carruthers had requested.[205] No one in Toronto in 1912 – not Conboy or Struthers, not even MacMurchy – could claim as much day-to-day experience with mentally defective children as Carruthers had. Yet it would be the expert view, especially the view that mental defectives were not educable, that would dominate auxiliary education to the end of the decade.

Around the same time, another Toronto educationist was questioning the value of auxiliary classes. His target, however, was the other type of auxiliary classes in Toronto: the ones for backward children. Inspector Armstrong agreed with the other inspectors that "retardation of pupils in the grades," which auxiliary classes for backward children were supposed to resolve, "is a very present problem." He also agreed that "irregular attendance, overcrowding of the classroom, under-feeding, improper feeding, and the passive attention of city children to formal studies, owing to the many passing, dissipating interests of artificial life" contributed to retardation and should be addressed. But, attempting to set himself apart from the other inspectors, Armstrong blamed retardation on "a common cause often overlooked, the tendancy [sic] of most teachers to concentrate attention upon the bright children of the class, adapting the lessons to contribute to the progress of those who readily reflect credit, and ignoring largely the slow and unkindled children." Armstrong's solution thus was different from that of the other inspectors. "This procedure should be reversed, the teacher should concentrate on the fringe of the class, those who are behind, and who see not the way, ignoring to a large extent the clever and the normal who will find the way almost alone. Herein lies a better solution to this problem than is to be found in ungraded classes." Teachers, Armstrong continued, should use some of the lunch period and all of the period from 3:30 to 4 p.m. "for individual work with backward children ... the bright ones being sent off home or to the playgrounds."[206]

Armstrong was not alone among North American school officials in proposing alternatives to auxiliary classes for backward children. Between the late 1890s and the early 1910s, before separate special classes became the dominant model for educating backward children, a surprisingly wide variety of alternatives were employed. Historians have yet to fully explore them. However, in 1908, principals and "heads of department" in Manhattan and Brooklyn public schools investigated grading and promotion practices and educational provisions for exceptional children nationally in the United States (with a few inquiries in Canada and some US territories as well) through an extensive school survey. They received a total of 965 clear responses from superintendents, principals, and teachers – the groups that were by far the most common respondents – as well as some teacher educators. Their replies indicated experience with thirteen different models for educating academically struggling schoolchildren.

One hundred and thirty-five promotion survey respondents, for example, had experimented with the "Batavia Plan."[207] Now largely forgotten, the plan was developed in 1898 by John Kennedy, superintendent of the schools of Batavia, New York.[208] The plan called for two regular classes to be combined in one classroom and two teachers assigned. While "the class-teacher went on as usual conducting classes all day long," Kennedy wrote, the second teacher "did her work at a table, calling the child to her as she became ready for him, and detaining him as long as she deemed it expedient." Kennedy recalled telling the inaugural teacher appointed for this work "to go into that room, find the most backward children, and make them the most forward." Continuing, he wrote, "she did that, of course. And for the first time in the history of education there was a large room leveled up, a large room in which there was no child dragging and no child retarded."[209]

The 1909 Manhattan-Brooklyn survey asked respondents whether they favoured or did not favour each of thirteen identified models. "Special Classes for over-age or foreign-born children" and "ungraded classes" were the approaches that educators were most likely to report they "favored": 92 per cent of respondents liked the former and 93 per cent the latter. Just 37 per cent favoured the Batavia Plan.[210] Alternatives were clearly giving way to a model of separate settings. Armstrong persisted nonetheless in his 1916 report against separate classes for backward children in Toronto, and instead proposed cutting class sizes in regular classrooms to give teachers more opportunities to work with these children. He also argued that Toronto public schools were winning the battle against retardation by addressing "wooden or unscientific teaching, irregular attendance, underfeeding of children, physical defects capable of removal." Once school officials had fully mastered these "other causes" of retardation, he wrote, "the backward child will seldom be found. Herein is the remedy; not special or ungraded classes."[211] This would be Armstrong's last recorded stand on the issue.

Meanwhile, by the mid-1910s, auxiliary classes for mentally defective children in Toronto were not faring nearly as well as those for backward children. In early 1914, about a year and a half after the brouhaha involving Carruthers and school trustees, Inspector Elliott visited her class at Grace Street. He noted that "three of the pupils were incapable of receiving any benefit from the class and four others were unfit to be with other pupils." In a report to Chief Inspector Cowley, he recommended closing the class. Cowley and the Toronto inspectors agreed to shutter Carruthers's class, the last remaining of the original four of their type taught by her and Sims. (It is not clear when the other classes closed.) Only one trustee protested: Miles Vokes accused the board of shirking its responsibilities and called for provincial legislation, to little avail.[212]

Vokes may have been the only one willing to champion the cause at the school board, but MacMurchy – true to form – was certainly not giving up on auxiliary education for mental defectives. In fact, she was already hard at work on the provincial legislative front when the inspectors closed Carruthers's class. In 1914, MacMurchy collaborated closely with R.A. Pyne, the Conservative government's Minister of Education and a member of provincial parliament (MPP) for Toronto, and his staff to redraft the 1911 auxiliary class legislation An Act Respecting Special Classes.[213] Her objectives were to strengthen the act's provisions on mental defectives and to lay the legislative groundwork for a custodial farm colony. Although ultimately it would mainly be used to administer auxiliary classes, the 1914 rewritten and expanded Auxiliary Classes Act said nearly as much about farm colonies as it did about auxiliary education in public schools. The act authorized public and separate school boards to operate "a suitable residence and home" for any mentally defective children in their jurisdiction and empowered school board trustees to acquire property for that purpose. Any child admitted to one of these custodial institutions became a ward of the school board until her or his twenty-first birthday. The act stipulated that school boards could establish auxiliary classes for mentally defective children but not children "whose mental capacity is incapable of development beyond that of a child of normal mentality at eight years of age." This excluded idiots or imbeciles, who would continue to be sent to the Asylum for Idiots at Orillia.[214]

As specific as it may have been about custodial accommodations, the act left key aspects of auxiliary education in non-custodial classes in public school systems for the government to define through regulations. When these appeared, around 1917 (if not earlier), they specified the types of programs that would count as auxiliary. They stipulated that auxiliary teachers needed an Auxiliary Class Teacher's Certificate,[215] which likely few had and which the inspector does not seem to have rigidly enforced. (The training course for the certificate was offered in Ontario in 1915 and then not again until 1919.)[216] The regulations capped auxiliary class sizes.[217] The regulations also defined the terms of the government grant to school boards for auxiliary education: a very modest $100 for each class. Up to $50 additional funding was available to pay for a teacher if her salary was above the "usual" school board pay, and up to $100 more could be requested for "*approved* special equipment" if the inspector deemed it acceptable. Lest auxiliary education become too lavish, the regulations also confirmed that the minister could reduce, pro rata, the grant if the total expenditures under it exceeded the amount the legislature had voted for auxiliary education that year.[218]

The new act also created the position of provincial inspector of auxiliary classes.[219] The government appointed MacMurchy to this role; she retained her title as inspector of the feebleminded as well. In 1915, W.J. Hanna, the provincial secretary and government-side Conservative Party MPP, appointed an advisory committee on feeblemindedness that included MacMurchy and other PACFM members. The committee promptly recommended a farm colony, as well as other measures eugenicists had proposed in the past.[220] Thus, even as Toronto public schools shuttered classes for mental defectives, MacMurchy could still claim, for a while at least, that the farm colony plan was gaining support.

Attempting to deepen that support, in 1916 MacMurchy prepared and distributed a petition at the Canadian Conference of Charities and Correction meeting in Toronto. The petition asked the federal and provincial governments to fund "farm colonies ... for the care and control of the mentally defective," whom it described as a "great menace ... to the moral and social life of our communities, and our public institutions, including the public schools." The 2,046 signatures MacMurchy's petition garnered represented a wide swathe of influential people. Signing were famous reformers and feminists Adelaide Plumptre, Florence Huestis of the LCW, and Augusta Stowe-Gullen. *Star* editor J.E. Atkinson signed. A near-full roster of spiritual leaders did as well. This included H.P. Plumptre, Adelaide Plumptre's husband and Rector of St James Cathedral; Rabbi Jacobs of Holy Blossom Synagogue; the Methodist preacher Reverend Peter Bryce; and Lancelot Minehan, parish priest of St Vincent de Paul Church. Psychologists, psychiatrists, and physicians with connections to eugenics were represented in force. Peter Sandiford and Clarence Hincks signed. Clarke and Dr O.C.J. Withrow did as well.[221] Incumbent TBE trustees William Houston, W.W.

Hodgson, and Dr Caroline Brown signed. They were joined by school inspector D.D. Moshier, the supervisor of school nurses E.M. Paul, and the "Teachers of Balmy Beach School Toronto" and their principal, N.J. Yeo, who signed them en masse this way.[222]

However, a farm colony for Ontario was not to come. Harvey Simmons suggests that its cost – more specifically, the issue of who would assume that cost – was ultimately what led to the plan's undoing by about 1920.[223] Despite MacMurchy's many efforts, the unravelling was underway by late 1916. In December, the TBE received a massive delegation of farm colony supporters from the PACFM. Trustees unanimously passed a motion supporting the construction of two farm colonies for mental defectives.[224] Conservative Premier William H. Hearst publicly authorized the city in 1917 to issue debentures to construct farm colonies. In private, Hearst fretted over the expense. Finally, as the city treasurer tried to calculate the municipality's cost, difficulties arose.[225]

Municipal and provincial officials ran up against two problems while trying to prepare a cost estimate for the farm colonies. The first was the confusing and haphazard estimates of the number of mental defectives who would be housed in the colonies, which the PACFM was notorious for issuing and which made it impossible to pin down just how many spaces would be needed. The PACFM's Hincks would admit that "figures gathered ... were not convincing and so when we went to the Parliament Buildings and the Board of Control the apple cart was often spilled when direct questions were asked. We simply had to guess and if I might use the vernacular of the street we not only guessed, but we gassed, and our efforts invariably ended in the latter."[226] The second problem the farm colony faced was the closing window for reform. Incumbent progressive mayor Hocken did not run in the 1915 mayoral election, and the standard for the reformers was picked instead up by the Liberal Party's McCarthy. The "Grit" McCarthy stood against, and was defeated by, Tommy L. Church and his Conservative "Tory machine."[227] With McCarthy out of municipal politics, MacMurchy, the PACFM, and the other allies of the farm colony plan were deprived of their strongest voice on the Board of Control. As mayor from 1915 to 1921, Church would largely repudiate the "new spirit of municipal government." Eventually, by 1920, he would campaign aggressively against "fads and frills" in the public school board budget, and demand that the board hold the line on tax increases and cut spending. The school trustees, the Bureau of Municipal Research, and the LCW (among other groups) retorted with a pageant staged by students titled "Fads and Frills," which defended the expansion of school board services over the previous decade.[228] But the spirit of reform was under pressure at the board as well.

A new provincial government elected in 1919, and formed for the first time by the United Farmers of Ontario and Independent Labor Party MPPs, was not favourable to the reformers either.[229] The PACFM had managed to squeeze a Royal Commission on the Care and Control of the Mentally Defective and Feebleminded in Ontario out of the outgoing Hearst government in 1917. The sole commissioner, Justice Frank Egerton Hodgins, delivered his report in 1919, just before the United Farmers took office. In the report, on the matter of auxiliary education, Hodgins wrote that "the future solution of the major part of this great problem [feeblemindedness] lies in the schools" and endorsed, once again, clearing house auxiliary classes and a farm colony.[230] Although the United Farmers government supported some reform causes, the party was wary of urban Ontario and its issues. That would have made it reluctant to act on the Hodgins report, as one historian suggests.[231] Adding to that reluctance, in all likelihood, was that many of the Hodgins recommendations, like the farm colony, were expensive. As C. Elizabeth Koester argues, the cost and the continuing uncertainty about which level of government would bear it frightened politicians and diminished the likelihood that many of Hodgins's proposals would ever become policies.[232]

MacMurchy also left the Toronto reform scene in 1920 to take up a prestigious position in Ottawa as the first head of the federal government's Division of Child Welfare, a post she would hold until her retirement in 1934. With her departure, the eugenics movement in Toronto lost a powerful and persistent voice. It is not completely clear why MacMurchy chose to leave. She may have believed that the new post in the federal government offered a better opportunity for her to pursue her calling. She may have felt that she could make little headway against the new provincial government. Or, as Dodd argues, she may have been disappointed that the government passed her over yet again for a key position when Hearst appointed a man, Hodgins, to head the royal commission. With MacMurchy's departure, the post of provincial inspector of the feebleminded was abolished, and the PACFM, without MacMurchy's tenacity to breathe life into it, dissolved.[233] The farm colonies were never built.

Conclusion

Reformers, eugenicists, their school board allies, and others who attempted to put auxiliary classes in place on an established basis in Toronto schools in the 1910s encountered opposition that curtailed some of their efforts. Despite the failure of the farm colony plan in particular, the auxiliary classes succeeded as a reform. By decade's end, separate special classes were engrained as the preferred mode for educating many exceptional children. Toronto was not unique in adopting this approach. At approximately the same time, in processes that seem to have been as idiosyncratic as Toronto's, other urban school systems in places such as Atlanta, Vancouver, New York City, Chicago, Cleveland, Boston, and St Louis also implemented auxiliary classes.[234] As these reforms from different cities gradually began to resemble each other, auxiliary education services would expand dramatically along the lines laid out by early teachers, mental deficiency experts, eugenicists, and others during the decade of reform and debate that was the 1910s.

These myriad individuals did not merely establish the segregated approach to educating exceptional children – they also defined types of exceptionalities and methodologies for how educators and schools should deal with each type, classifying feeblemindedness or mental defectiveness as an intractable condition. In the view of these powerful constituencies, schooling for mentally defective children would consist of preparation not for social integration and independence but for exclusion and dependency. Teachers such as Carruthers may not have completely agreed with this prognosis, but segregation and dependency defined the eugenic approach to mentally defective children's education all the same. Meanwhile, backward and foreign children and children with health problems were defined as handicapped as well. The duty of educators to these children was different – to remediate them by removing the impediments to their normal development, whether learning challenges, health problems, or lack of English skills. The reverberation of all of these categories, constructed mainly in the 1910s, and the echoes of assumptions about the best education for each type of labelled child may still be felt in public schooling more than a century later.

Chapter Two

"Inequalities of Children in Original Endowment": IQ Testing Transforms Auxiliary Education, 1919–1930

"There are few if any more significant events in modern educational history than the developments which have recently taken place in methods of mental measurement," wrote Lewis Terman, a Stanford University psychologist who did more than any other individual to promote intelligence quotient (IQ) testing in schools, in 1923.[1] Historians have explored in great detail how school authorities used IQ tests to sort and stream students of all ages and abilities.[2] But I argue in this chapter that IQ testing's historical significance was greater than just its influence on pupil sorting. The rapid rise of IQ testing in the 1920s completely remade auxiliary education, which itself was still emerging, in decisive ways and with long-lasting effects. In Toronto, IQ testing contributed to the proliferation and complete reorganization of auxiliary classes. More than that, the science of IQ radically altered the leading theories among psychologists and educators about the causes, nature, and treatment of most young people's learning difficulties. The experts of the 1910s, Leonard Ayres among them, had presented a theory of learning problems and retardation that accounted for multiple potential causes – from illness, to school absences, to students' lack of English, to poor teaching, to improperly organized schools. The IQ testers, especially Terman, repudiated Ayres's theory. They argued instead that low IQ was virtually the only cause of children's learning problems and that it was innate and intractable, totally resistant to educators' efforts to raise it. They fashioned entirely new categories of disability and learning difficulty, such as "subnormality," that were based directly, and for the first time, on IQ scores. The use of IQ tests on a widening scale in schools created discernible changes in how children were diagnosed and admitted to auxiliary classes, and generated new types of interactions between schoolchildren and the adult psychologists that public schools now employed. Intelligence testers also successfully advanced a new philosophy for curriculum in auxiliary education that was based on their theories. This led to a complete revamp of the program of study in auxiliary classes in the 1920s that saw the remedial instruction of the 1910s dropped entirely by about 1925.

This chapter looks at auxiliary classes for a group of children who, in the 1920s, IQ testers labelled "subnormal." Chapters 3 and 4 will focus on auxiliary education's expansion in Toronto, also in the 1920s, into dedicated auxiliary vocational schools for adolescents and into new specialized programs for children with physical disabilities and impairments.

The Origins and Rise of Intelligence Testing and IQ

Without special education, the concept of IQ as we know it likely would not exist. This is because IQ's very origins lie in the tests of "mental age" that were first developed for use in special classes.[3] It is ironic, then, that the IQ tests employed in auxiliary education by the 1920s significantly distorted the original meaning of the concept of mental age. In 1904, the French government tasked the psychologist Alfred Binet with identifying children for the new special schools it was planning.[4] Seeking a means of measuring a wide range of mental faculties, Binet and his student Théodore Simon devised an ingenious work of synthesis. They developed a set of small and widely varied tests in the form of problems and puzzles, which they used in concert to estimate the mental ability of the children they examined. By 1908, Binet had also developed a scale that ranked his small tests by order of difficulty.[5] He claimed that his scale could approximate "mental age." Any child who could pass the same easy tests that most three-year-olds whom Binet had tested could pass was said to have a mental age of three, any child who performed to the level of most five-year-olds was said to have a mental age of five, and so on. Binet compared a child's tested mental age to the child's chronological age. This comparison was crucial: a child whose mental age was significantly below her or his chronological age became a candidate for the special class.[6]

At about the same time that Binet was developing the concept of mental age in France, on the other side of the Atlantic, in New Jersey, H.H. Goddard, the research director of the Vineland Training School, was looking for a reliable and efficient way to diagnose different grades of feeblemindedness. In 1908, Goddard toured several European psychological laboratories. Eventually, he happened upon Binet's mental age scale. Although at first he was sceptical about Binet's method, he brought Binet's tests back to the United States and had them translated into English. When he began giving the tests at Vineland, he discovered to his great excitement that they were as effective at identifying the different grades of feeblemindedness as was a more time- and resource-consuming clinical diagnosis.[7] The Vineland inmates whom institution staff had classified clinically as idiots tended to test at a mental age of one or two on the Binet scale. Imbeciles tested between mental ages three and seven. Morons tested between eight and twelve.[8]

In importing Binet's concept of mental age, Goddard took liberties that changed its original meaning – the first of several to significantly remake Binet's vision. Binet had stated that "intelligence" possessed "an artificial character."[9] What he meant was that although there are variations in the relative mental capacities of different people, intelligence does not exist as a unitary, tangible thing that can be observed and measured in the same way something such as body temperature or bone density can be observed and measured.[10] "The scale, properly speaking," Binet wrote about mental age, "does not permit the measure of intelligence, because intellectual qualities are not superposable, and therefore cannot be measured as linear surfaces are measured."[11] Goddard ignored Binet's cautions about the abstract meaning of the term intelligence. Instead, he was seduced by what Stephen Jay Gould calls the "reification fallacy": he took an abstract concept, i.e., intelligence, and treated it as though it were concrete and measurable.[12]

In 1911, Binet died.[13] Within about a year, yet another psychologist, the German William Stern, brought a further significant change to his method. Binet had always subtracted mental age from chronological age to determine how far a child was behind. Stern proposed division instead of subtraction. He then multiplied the quotient that resulted by one hundred to eliminate the decimal. Thus a child with a mental age of six and chronological age of seven was said to have an IQ of 86. (Six divided by seven, times one hundred, equals eighty-six.) This is where the modern concept IQ was born.[14]

Terman executed the final significant reinterpretation of Binet's original work. Like Goddard (and unlike Binet), Terman treated intelligence as though it were a concrete thing, and he treated IQ as a true measurement of that thing.[15] He embraced Binet's use of small and varied tests of ever-increasing difficulty to measure mental age, devising his own set of tests. He gave these tests to a sample of one thousand school-children in order to establish norms, then used the results to calibrate his own, psychologically derived classification of mental ability, which he published in 1916 in a book called *The Measurement of Intelligence*. Terman based his classification not on mental age but rather on IQ, the first scale of its kind to use IQ ranges. The scale contained seven ranges that comprised, Terman confidently claimed, the entire spectrum of human intelligence: "'near' genius or genius" (IQ above 140); "very superior intelligence" (IQ 120 to 140); "superior intelligence" (IQ 110 to 120); "normal, or average, intelligence" (IQ 90 to 110); "dullness, rarely classifiable as feeble-mindedness" (IQ 80 to 90); "border-line deficiency, sometimes classifiable as dullness, often as feeble-mindedness" (IQ 70 to 80); and "definite feeble-mindedness" (IQ below 70). Terman, covering the same ground Goddard had earlier traversed, qualified the final grouping further, stating "of the feeble-minded, those between 50 and 70 IQ include most of the morons (high, middle, and low), those between 20 or 25 and 50 are ordinarily to be classed as imbeciles, and those below 20 or 25 as idiots."[16]

Binet had designed his tests to identify children for special classes by approximating their scholastic aptitude, at which tests could only guess or estimate. Mental age, Binet said, was an artificial gauge. But by the time Terman put the final touches on his reinterpretation of Binet's work in 1916, more than a decade after Binet had begun, mental age had a totally new meaning. It had become IQ, and IQ, Terman now claimed, was an accurate representation and measurement of a person's actual mental ability. An IQ test, properly administered, could reliably discover that mental ability.

Intelligence testers, such as Terman or Goddard, made a further set of claims about intelligence and IQ testing that had significant ramifications for schooling, especially for auxiliary education. They insisted that intelligence was innate. That is, they argued that intelligence was inborn, that it was passed down from forebears, and that a person's native intelligence remained more or less fixed.[17] They also argued that meaningful intergroup differences in intelligence existed. In 1916 – at a time when no one had yet to conduct a large-scale study of group intelligence norms – Terman was nevertheless already claiming that immigrants, African Americans, and workers were innately intellectually inferior. He speculated liberally about the existence of "enormously significant racial differences in intelligence, differences which cannot be wiped out by any scheme of mental culture."[18]

In 1917, when the United States entered the First World War, Terman joined a team of psychologists studying the intelligence of US Army recruits. With Goddard, as well as Harvard University professor Robert Yerkes, he oversaw the administering of IQ tests to 1.75 million army enlistees. The three men used data from the massive survey to claim that whites were more intelligent than blacks and that immigrants from Northern Europe were more intelligent than those from the south and east.[19] Other researchers disseminated similar claims. Carl Brigham, who also worked on the army testing program, published *A Study of American Intelligence* in 1923. In this popular book, he argued that IQ data from the army tests confirmed that so-called Alpine and Mediterranean races were "intellectually inferior" to what he called the Nordic race.[20]

All such claims were highly dubious. The test questions were culturally loaded, even though intelligence testers insisted otherwise. The army recruit data was of very suspicious quality. Faulty test procedures that saw illiterate recruits taking tests designed for the literate, and the testers' underacknowledgment of environmental influences, such as prior education, all badly skewed the test results. Nevertheless, most early claims about group differences were based upon the original army data.[21]

Peter Sandiford was Canada's preeminent IQ tester and held views about intelligence, measurement, and racial differences that were similar to those of Terman, Goddard, and Brigham. Born in Derbyshire, England, in 1882, Sandiford completed graduate work and lectured at the University of Manchester in the early 1900s. He then went to New York in 1909, teaching and finishing his doctorate at Columbia University. In 1913, he was appointed an associate professor of educational psychology at the University of Toronto. He would hold professor of educational psychology posts at that university and at the nearby Ontario College of Education until his death in 1941. Sandiford laid much of the groundwork for the wide use of IQ tests by academics, educators, and administrators in Canadian schools during the interwar period.[22]

The army tests and the slew of IQ studies by people like Brigham and Sandiford that followed them popularized for ordinary Americans and Canadians the idea that everyone's intelligence was innate and inherited. Eugenicists in the 1910s had tended to assert that only feeblemindedness was passed down. Post-First World War IQ studies, looking at the whole range of human intelligence, appeared to confirm what was already popularly supposed: like begets like at all points on the intelligence spectrum.[23]

Finally, the intelligence testers – Terman especially – insisted that IQ tests should form the basis for school organization. Terman proposed "a mental test for every child" as a new slogan for school reform.[24] Tests could be used to "create class groups of homogenous ability" as the basis for differentiated streams in the elementary grades.[25] Sandiford promoted intelligence tests as early as 1919 as a tool that could be used for school reorganization, for "dealing with delinquents and with retarded school children," and for university admissions decisions.[26] Schools in Toronto were early adopters of tests for streaming. By 1921, Principal A.W. Ross Doan at Queen Victoria Public School (PS); C.C. Goldring, then an assistant master at Bolton Avenue PS and later the Toronto Board of Education (TBE) superintendent; and Principal John Wallis at Queen Alexandra PS had experimented widely with IQ tests in their schools. Wallis tested the entire student body of 1,300 pupils at Queen Alexandra in 1920–1 and used the results to stream students into "classes of slow, average and bright children," as Terman had recommended.[27]

Terman deliberately made intelligence testing simple in order to popularize his tests for use in school reorganization. His first book, *The Measurement of Intelligence*, explained IQ testing without resort to complicated scientific lingo. "The aim," Terman wrote in the preface, "has been to present the explanations and instructions so clearly and in such an untechnical form as to make the book of use, not only to the psychologist, but also to the rank and file of teachers, physicians, and social workers."[28] The book contained a complete and standardized IQ test that Terman had composed and named the Stanford-Binet. The book also contained IQ norms, which the person giving the test could easily use to determine whether the test subject's IQ was higher or lower than average and by how much. The Stanford-Binet was simple to give and score, with the test questions, the answers, and the scoring guide included in the book.[29] (The Stanford-Binet is a one-on-one verbal test, not a mass pencil-and-paper test, as later tests were.) Anyone using the book could measure another person's IQ virtually on the spot, in as little as twenty-five minutes when testing very young children and in certainly no more than ninety minutes when testing adolescents.[30]

Ease of use largely explains why the tests were adopted so quickly and so widely in schools, even amid early opposition from some who questioned their scientific validity and social value. The most outspoken critic was the journalist Walter Lippmann, who hounded Terman in the pages of the liberal American periodical the *New Republic*.[31] But by the time Lippman debunked Terman in 1922 and 1923, it was too late. Terman and Yerkes had already turned the army tests into the first pencil-and-paper IQ test for schoolchildren. They published it as the National Intelligence Test in 1920. Unlike the Stanford-Binet, a single adult could administer the National Intelligence Test to more than one child at once. It swamped the school market immediately: its publisher, World Book, printed 400,000 tests in the very first print run.[32]

IQ Testing and the Transformation of Learning Difficulties

Terman was not content with just changing the course of the history of education by shaking up the definition of intelligence, altering forever the way people measured it, or introducing IQ tests as the basis for streaming. He also took on auxiliary education. He successfully used his Stanford-Binet test and the new concept of IQ to aggressively promote an entirely new outlook on the nature and causes of retardation and learning difficulties.[33] These efforts pitted Terman against a long-time rival, Ayres.[34] As chapter 1 discussed, in the early 1910s Ayres had tallied an extensive list of factors responsible for backwardness and retardation – children's health problems; infrequent attendance; non-acquisition of the instructional language, English; improper school organization; and so on. Ayres included feeblemindedness, or innate lack of intelligence, as only one relatively minor cause of retardation.

Terman's refutation was based mainly on his views on the nature of intelligence – that it was inherited and largely immutable – and how they affected his understanding of learning difficulties.[35] In his 1919 book, *The Intelligence of Schoolchildren*, Terman took aim at Ayres directly. He wrote: "Notwithstanding the persistent campaign which has been waged against the evils of retardation over the last dozen years, the number of retardates remains to-day much the same as it was when the campaign began." Using "data from intelligence tests," Terman promised to demonstrate – against Ayres – that "innate differences in intelligence are chiefly responsible for the school laggard; that the so-called 'retarded' children on whom we have expended so much sympathy are in reality nearly always *above* the grade where they belong by mental development." (By this, Terman meant their mental ages were lower than their chronological ages.) "In other words," he concluded, "it will be shown that the retardation problem is exactly the reverse of what it is popularly supposed to be."[36]

Terman not surprisingly, given his criticisms of Ayres, rejected as ineffective conventional remediation measures that school systems had up to that point used to combat retardation, measures adapted from Ayres's ideas about retardation's primary causes. School inspectors in Toronto in the 1910s had encouraged the development of auxiliary classes for backward children as one way to reduce retardation. The classes were introduced to provide these children with remedial instruction that would help them catch up academically with their peers. Open-air classes, foreign classes, and forest schools were initiated, at least in part, because school officials also believed these programs curbed retardation by addressing some of its causes like unfamiliarity with English or poor health. Terman regarded all of these sorts of measures as basically futile because he rejected the theory of variable causes of retardation that they were intended to address. "The chief cause of retardation is not irregular attendance, the use of a foreign language in the home, bad teeth, adenoids, malnutrition, etc., but inferior mental endowment," he wrote. "Educational reform may as well abandon, once and for all, the effort to bring all children up to grade."[37] However, despite Terman's ultimately successful insistence on minimizing the myriad factors that Ayres had said caused most learning difficulties, these factors did not go away. They still frequently continued to cause young people to fall behind. IQ testers simply paid less attention to them. After about 1919, auxiliary educators did as well.

IQ Testing and Auxiliary Education in Toronto, 1919–1930

The Reorganization of Auxiliary Classes

Terman's ideas about the nature, cause, and treatment of learning difficulties quickly came to exert considerable sway over auxiliary education in Toronto public schools. In 1919, the TBE instituted a mental testing program. Trustees hired the city's first-ever school "pychitrist [sic]," Dr Eric Kent Clarke. (In fact, Clarke would work mainly as a psychologist.) The board also hired Clarke's sister, Emma de V. Clarke, a nurse, as his assistant.[38] Eric Clarke, the school trustees, and many of the inspectors enthusiastically accepted all of the intelligence testers' major premises about IQ and education. Beginning that year, they embarked upon a major reorganization of Toronto's auxiliary classes based on the science of IQ. Clarke was the main architect of the reorganization.

Clarke was a eugenicist, with a predilection for frank talk about the "spread of mental defect and its associated evils."[39] Trained as a medical doctor, not a psychologist, he was just twenty-five years old when the TBE hired him in 1919.[40] What he may have lacked in experience, he compensated for with connections. His father, C.K. Clarke, was Canada's most famous psychiatrist. The elder Clarke, who was a medical director of the Toronto General Hospital and the founder of the hospital's psychiatric clinic, was a contemporary of Helen MacMurchy. Like MacMurchy, C.K. Clarke enthusiastically evangelized eugenics, a vocation with which Eric was eager to help him.[41] Around the same time that MacMurchy's Provincial Association for the Care of the Feebleminded entered its decline, C.K. Clarke and Dr Clarence M. Hincks started a new organization with similar goals. The Canadian National Committee for Mental Hygiene (CNCMH) would mature in the 1920s into the main national lobby for eugenics.[42] Eric Clarke served for a time as the group's associate medical director.[43]

Clarke's first act as school psychologist was to coordinate a major intelligence survey of Toronto public schools. He assembled a survey team that consisted of himself, his father C.K., his sister Emma, Hincks, and Dr E.J. Pratt. Pratt was surely the most unusual member of the group, soon to become an erstwhile psychologist. In 1920, Pratt traded in his psychology lecturer position at the University of Toronto for a post in the Department of English. There he found more time to write the verse that would help him become the "Grand Old Man of Canadian poetry," the most celebrated Canadian poet of his time.[44] In 1919, Pratt the psychologist worked as one of Clarke's team of five – all CNCMH members – that visited seventy TBE schools over a two-year period to give IQ tests. The team administered tests to students for whom teachers and principals had requested examinations. Many of these children had been identified as academically struggling or disabled.[45] Clarke's main objective for the survey, like that of similar surveys MacMurchy had carried out approximately a decade earlier without the benefit of the Stanford-Binet tests Clarke used, was to determine how many mentally defective or subnormal children there were in the schools. Clarke used these two terms interchangeably, although the latter would soon mostly replace the former in Canadian educational settings.

SPECIAL CLASSES FOR MENTAL DEFECTIVES

Special classes for feeble-minded children are of value in training mental defectives to become useful citizens. At present there are 100 such classes attached to the public schools of Canada but 1,000 are needed.

The Canadian National Committee for Mental Hygiene gives a stimulus to the establishment of special classes.

2.1 "Special Classes for Mental Defectives," 1924. One in a series of posters created as a national tour in department store windows by the CNCMH. The thirty-one posters in all publicized the social problems the CNCMH said were caused by unchecked feeblemindedness and the policy solutions, including special classes, it proposed for dealing with those problems. Centre for Addiction and Mental Health Archives. Canadian Mental Health Association fonds, studio photograph CNCMH-14.

2.2 "Mental Hygiene in Primary Schools," 1924. From a series of posters created as a national tour in department-store windows by the CNCMH. Centre for Addiction and Mental Health Archives, Canadian Mental Health Association fonds, CNCMH-19.

2.3 Eric Kent Clarke, undated, ca. 1910. Watercolour and ink drawing by the caricaturist Will Frost. C.K. Clarke commissioned Frost to do private caricatures of his friends and family, of which this is an example. (The author thanks John P.M. Court for details about the artist Frost's life.) Centre for Addiction and Mental Health Archives. Clarke Family fonds, original artwork, 10–06.

Crucially, Clarke also used IQ ranges to set the limits for subnormality, which was a first for Toronto schools. Clarke classified as subnormal any child with an IQ lower than 75.[46] This range was derived from Terman's work, although Clarke adapted it slightly in that Terman had set an IQ of 70 as the cut-off for subnormality or "definite feeblemindedness."[47] Through his team's surveys, Clarke eventually found a total of 1,422 subnormal children in Toronto public schools.[48]

Clarke embraced Terman's argument, against Ayres, that low native intelligence was the root of most learning difficulties and asserted that "the real cause" of "mental defect" was "heredity."[49] His survey covered the city's "three classes for 'backward' children" who were receiving remedial instruction so that they could return to their grades, which he referred to as "primarily promotion classes." Clarke claimed to have discovered in these classes not simply backward pupils, but rather "mental defectives, of a low order" who were not supposed to be there. In most of these children's cases, he said, their learning problems should be attributed not to any of backwardness's varied causes but to low native intelligence, which remedial instruction could not help. In his view, Toronto's existing auxiliary classes for backward children "rather defeated their purpose, as the children were in no way suitable for promotion."[50]

Consequently, Clarke recommended a reorganization of auxiliary classes, a plan that was implemented after quickly garnering support from school trustees and most school inspectors. Clarke proposed that "industrial classes be substituted" in the place of "promotion" classes.[51] In November and December 1919, the trustees approved plans for two existing auxiliary classes, one at Lansdowne PS and one at Queen Alexandra, to "be reorganized, as advised by Dr Clarke" (and as further recommended by the TBE's inspectors) into special classes for subnormal pupils.[52] The trustees would keep one special class open as an "'Ungraded Class for Backward Children' ... to be used for 'catch-up' work."[53]

One inspector who supported the reorganization was N.S. MacDonald, who also advocated for open-air education in the 1910s (see chapter 1). In his 1919 inspector's annual report, MacDonald quoted Terman directly (and without attribution), advising that "instead of wasting energy on the vain attempt to hold mentally slow and defective children up to a level of progress which is normal to the average child, or superior child, it would be wiser to take account of the inequalities of children in original endowment and to differentiate the course of study in such a way that each child will be allowed to progress at the rate which is normal to him, whether that rate be normal or slow."[54] The only opposition to reorganization came from Chief Inspector R.H. Cowley, although his reservations were not severe enough to slow the plan's adoption. Cowley wrote in his 1919 report: "The reports of the psychiatrist should be a valuable guide to the educator, not in multiplying special classes but in arranging the individual assistance required to fit as many backward pupils as possible to remain in the regular grades of the school, and thereby share as possible in its normal social life."[55] Despite the chief inspector's reluctance, Clarke upped the ante by recommending that in addition to reorganizing existing auxiliary classes, the TBE should open twenty-two completely new "industrial classes" that would house "many, if not all" the "unfortunate subnormal pupils" in the city. The new classes, Clarke confirmed, would not be promotion classes. They would constitute a special stream for subnormal youngsters, with a course of study "that will interest them, and advance their education along lines not heretofore attempted in Toronto."[56] Auxiliary education for the new group – subnormal children whose learning problems were attributable to low IQ (75 or below) and were therefore innate and fixed – was rapidly replacing education for backward children who educators thought could benefit from remedial instruction, improve, and eventually return to the grades.

By September 1920, reorganized "industrial" (auxiliary) classes were in place in at least six Toronto public schools.[57] By 1924, the TBE reported 658 children enrolled in "Training Classes for Sub-Normal Pupils," with no mention of "promotion" auxiliary classes for backward children at all.[58] The Ontario Department of Education (DOE)'s "Regulations for Auxiliary Classes," a circular that it reissued every couple of years, included, in the 1917 and 1922 versions, provisions for "promotion classes," an option "for children who are backward on account of some remediable cause, but are not mentally defective." The 1925 version dropped that phrasing. The term "promotion classes" was still present, but now referred to an entirely different type of class: "For children who are eligible for a training class, thirteen years of age and over, in school areas where there is no special industrial class."[59] The idea of an auxiliary class as a place where backward children could go to receive instruction and opportunities to catch up to their peers (see chapter 1) all but disappeared as IQ became the primary consideration in auxiliary education in the 1920s.

IQ Testing, Diagnosis, and Auxiliary Class Placement

Following Clarke's appointment as psychologist, IQ tests became the most common way to select schoolchildren for auxiliary classes for subnormals in Toronto.[60] Under this system, which continued throughout the 1920s, the main benchmark for placement in the classes became an IQ score in the 50 to 75 range and the diagnosis of subnormality that usually followed. Other tested youngsters, whose IQ scores fell a few points above or below 75, could be diagnosed as "borderline" and could sometimes be admitted to auxiliary classes on the basis of that diagnosis as well. The changeover to IQ in admissions did not necessarily mean, however, that all of Toronto's auxiliary class pupils in the 1920s had been diagnosed as subnormal. Earlier in the decade in particular, before the IQ testing service was fully established, some children were still admitted to auxiliary classes without IQ examinations. Moreover, despite a swift shift to a theory of low IQ as the principal cause of learning difficulties, the same variety of factors that had contributed to young people's learning problems in the 1910s continued to do so in the 1920s. Intelligence testers simply minimized their importance or did not acknowledge them at all.

The use of IQ testing for diagnosis and auxiliary class admissions was made possible by the steady expansion of Toronto's IQ testing service. What began as a single survey conducted by Clarke and others became, by the close of the 1920s, an established and sophisticated mental testing service to rival those of major American and Canadian city school boards.[61] In 1925, the Toronto Department of Public Health absorbed Clarke's position into its Division of Mental Hygiene. Clarke left a year later, to be replaced by E.P. Lewis. As the director of the division, Lewis was also the school board psychologist. The transfer of Toronto's testing service from the school board to the municipality did not change the service's predominant work of attending to the schools.[62] Young people were referred to the Mental Hygiene Division by teachers, principals, social agencies, and even parents, though most referrals came from the schools. Any principal could request a complete mental "survey" of her or his school to identify potential candidates for auxiliary classes. Two afternoons a week, a clinic was held at Hester How PS, "which is centrally located, for those cases which come up from time to time in the various schools throughout the City." Between 1926 and 1930, the division surveyed between forty and sixty public and Catholic separate schools per year, and tested and individually assessed approximately 1,500 to 2,000 pupils per year.[63] Clarke and Lewis could have used Terman's mass pencil-and-paper test – the National Intelligence Test – as their main diagnostic instrument, as a number of American school systems did, and at times they employed it.[64] However, both men preferred the Stanford-Binet test and the face-to-face testing that came with using it. They used it more often than not, sometimes supplementing it with other "performance and educational tests."[65] While other staff administered many of the tests, Clarke and Lewis as mental hygiene division directors and head psychologists were responsible for examining individual children and for making diagnoses and placement recommendations that they based largely on IQ test results.[66]

Pupil records reveal a great deal about how auxiliary education functioned at a school level as IQ testing became the primary, but still not exclusive, criterion for auxiliary class admissions. The next several paragraphs examine the pupil records of students who attended Hester How between approximately 1920 and 1930. The process of admitting students from that school to auxiliary classes for subnormals went as follows: A teacher, or the school principal, initially referred a child for IQ testing by Mental Hygiene Division staff. (Pupil records do not say why particular children were selected, although we can infer some reasons.) If the child scored below 75 to 80 on the IQ test, Clarke – and later Lewis – usually diagnosed her or him as "borderline" or "subnormal" and recommended the child for placement in an auxiliary class for subnormals. The placement recommendation was entered on the child's Admission-discharge-promotion card (ADP).[67] The child was then transferred to an auxiliary class, usually at the start of the new term in September, February, or May.

David P., a Hester How pupil, was ten years old when Lewis tested him in June 1927. At the time of the examination, David was already older than most of the seven- or eight-year-olds in his junior first form class. It could be speculated that he was sent for an IQ test because he was over-age for his grade. David's score on the IQ test was 75. On this basis, Lewis diagnosed him with borderline intelligence and recommended him for the auxiliary class. When school opened the next fall, David was in that class. He attended it for two years, before his family left Toronto in 1929.[68]

Like David P., Emily L. was placed in an auxiliary class as the result of an IQ examination. Emily started kindergarten elsewhere at age five and transferred to Hester How shortly afterward. In September 1922,

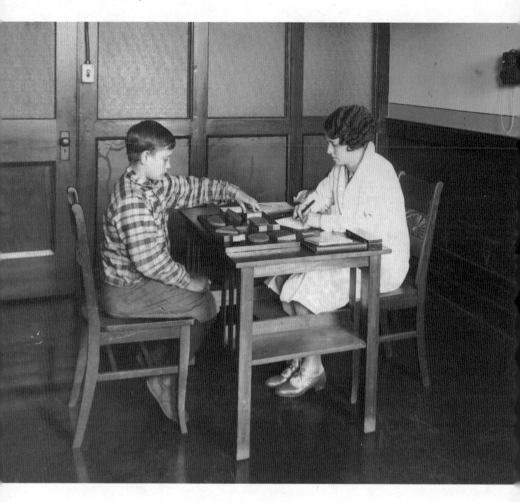

2.4 "Auxiliary class mental test," ca. 1930. A woman, possibly a teacher or more likely a Division of Mental Hygiene staff member, administers what appears to be the Stanford-Binet test to a schoolchild. The writing instrument and paper before her are probably for recording the child's answers to later calculate IQ. The child appears to be doing a construction puzzle, possibly the Healy-Fernald. The Stanford-Binet test consisted mainly of oral questions but some manipulable materials were optionally used for years IX and X test items. City of Toronto Archives, William James family fonds, item 3038.

she entered junior first. That May, Clarke diagnosed her as subnormal on the basis of an IQ test score of 71 and recommended her for auxiliary class training. In September, Emily started out in junior first again. However, her school transferred her to the auxiliary class in February.[69]

An IQ test was the official and primary means by which a young person entered the auxiliary class, but a number of pupils continued to be admitted to the classes in the 1920s without the test and without a psychologist's examination. The only evidence of this lies in pupil records. Twenty-four pupils who attended Hester How in the 1920s left behind pupil records with enough detail to reveal auxiliary class admissions in greater depth.[70] Of this group of twenty-four, slightly less than one third (n = 7) were placed in the auxiliary class without an IQ test for that purpose. The other two thirds (n = 17) were tested before placement. Most of the students who joined the auxiliary classes without a test entered between the 1919–20 and 1922–3 school years,[71] when Clarke was still establishing the IQ testing service.

The students who did not have their IQs tested were placed in the auxiliary classes for what appears to be a variety of reasons. George W. was born in China. He had recently moved to Toronto at the time he was moved to the auxiliary class at Hester How in September 1922. Although most pupil record cards for children admitted without an IQ test give no reason for admission, George's card stated that he was admitted (likely by the principal of the school) "for special help with language." George remained in the auxiliary class for one school year. In September 1923, he returned to junior first. Six years later, George left school, having obtained no more than a senior second form education.[72] Other more mundane reasons also contributed to auxiliary class admissions in the 1920s for children who did not sit an IQ test. Aaron N. was placed in the class after a school nurse examined him and judged him "dull + backward," apparently without an IQ test and without a diagnosis and placement recommendation from the psychologist.[73]

When school psychologists actually used IQ testing to make decisions, the tests rendered diagnosis and placement more efficient and consistent. These are the advantages of a rigid instrument. But the use of IQ testing for diagnosis and placement had disadvantages as well. Just as the IQ testers theorized, the application of IQ testing in auxiliary education reduced a myriad of learning problems, with numerous potential causes, into a singular problem and cause: low IQ.

Psychologists who employed IQ tests overlooked children's specific learning difficulties and also specific strengths, even if the IQ test had revealed them. In 1926, Lewis tested Bessie L. and entered his findings on her Psychiatric examination report (PER) attached to her pupil record. According to that report, Bessie lacked what Lewis referred to as an "idea of form." ("Form" on the Stanford-Binet test referred to a sense of how shapes relate to each other – for example, how a rectangle is more like a square than a circle.[74]) Bessie, her PER says, was also more awkward than other children her age at manipulating the few physical test materials, such as cubes, triangles, and other shapes, that could be used with the Stanford-Binet. Yet her assessment reveals that if she lacked manual and reasoning skills, she nonetheless possessed "fair" general knowledge.[75] Lewis distilled these diverse and ranging intellectual traits down to just her IQ. It was 65, and he assigned Bessie the same diagnosis of subnormality that all other children in the same IQ range usually received. That different children displayed very different strengths and weaknesses to arrive at a similar IQ score was never factored into placement recommendations. Based on Bessie's subnormal IQ, Lewis recommended her for placement at junior vocational school, which took subnormal adolescent girls (see chapter 3). This recommendation flew in the face of what the intelligence test itself seemed to suggest about the appropriate type of education for Bessie. Thus Bessie, whose "manual dexterity" he rated "poor," Lewis still recommended for a junior vocational school, where the program was decidedly manual.[76]

Their over-reliance on IQ scores at times even caused psychologists to change placement recommendations just because they had computed IQ incorrectly. In November 1928, Lewis tested David P. for a second time. Lewis wrote in David's PER that he had "a very contagious smile," was "quite talkative during the test," and was "ever ready to make a joke out of anything." He determined that David's IQ was 79, diagnosed his intelligence as borderline, and recommended David this time not for an auxiliary class but for placement in an "ordinary grade," which might "give him an impetus to get down to work." However, Lewis discovered after the examination that David was eleven years old, not ten. A recalculation of his IQ would have to occur. Lewis subsequently revised the IQ downward – from 79 to 72 – and without further comment altered his placement recommendation from "ordinary class" to "auxiliary class."[77]

The IQ Testing Moment

The use of IQ testing to place students in auxiliary classes created a new and often arduous school experience: "the testing moment."[78] This was another major change, in addition to the new ideas about learning difficulties and the subsequent reorganization of auxiliary classes, that the science of IQ brought to auxiliary education in Toronto in the 1920s. An IQ test and the follow-up meeting with the school psychologist could determine the course of a child's education. Most often the testing moment helped to confirm what people already suspected: that a child was a candidate for an auxiliary class. More fleetingly, it helped some children to shape, and occasionally even improve, their school circumstances. Young people's reactions to IQ testing ran from compliance to confusion, to indifference, and, much more rarely, to defiance. These reactions, which ordinarily are overlooked in the historical record, sometimes appear in pupils' PERs.[79] Kathleen Jones, in her study of American child guidance clinics in the first half of the twentieth century, argues that historians should take seriously the small actions of children who engaged with adult clinicians, such as forgetting, lying, fibbing, and avoiding examinations.[80] If young people sometimes demonstrated in these ways that they were historical actors, as Jones observes, they were also always vulnerable to the adults, psychologists, and educators who still largely decided what would happen to them. The testing moment was crucial because it often helped determine whether or not a child would be placed in an auxiliary class. Once that decision was made and a submornal label applied, the direction of a child's schooling could change drastically and often permanently. In this sense, each child's fate lay partly in the balance when the test began.

Probably only a tiny number of Toronto youngsters in the 1920s consciously attempted to resist IQ testing. In the fall of 1927, Lewis examined Emma C., a ten-year-old student. Emma was referred to the Mental Hygiene Division because frequent school transfers, including to one of the forest schools, had interrupted her schooling seven times over the previous four years. Lewis remarked that Emma "was not co-operating to the fullest extent of her ability" in his mental examination. When he reached the "Year X" (mental age ten) tests in the Stanford-Binet, Emma refused to do the "Healy A" test, a "construction puzzle" that asks the subject to fit five different rectangles into a wooden frame. (Only one configuration works, and the subject must complete the puzzle three times within five minutes to pass.)[81] Emma informed Lewis: "'I'm not going to do that.' 'I am not so crazy.'" She refused the "ball and field test" and "weighted cubes" at other year levels as well. Her insubordination forced Lewis to change his approach. He reported taking "great care ... to make everything seem as natural as possible" so that he could obtain an accurate IQ for Emma. Ultimately, Lewis failed. Unable to give credit for parts of the test that Emma refused to complete, he had no choice but to calculate that her IQ was 83. Guessing that had Emma cooperated she would have scored higher, Lewis wrote that "the above mental age and I.Q. are probably too low." He recommended her for a regular grade, not an auxiliary class.[82] Emma's small-scale defiance complicated the testing moment for the adults involved.

Other students undid the test's effectiveness as well but without being overtly or consciously disobedient. To take a Stanford-Binet IQ test properly, a child must pay careful attention to the adult administering the test, who gives all the questions orally. It can be difficult for an adult to secure the trust and attention of a child, especially a young child, for long enough to complete the test. Terman learned this prior to publishing *The Measurement of Intelligence*, which consequently contains a whole section of tips for creating "rapport" with a child in order to carry out the test. A brief "stroll" with the child out of doors before the examination formally began would have many children "chattering away as though to an old friend" in no time. "Exclamations like 'fine!' 'splendid' etc. should be used lavishly" because tactful praise was the sure-fire way to achieve rapport, Terman surmised. The inability to establish rapport was an obstacle that contributed to "misleading" test results.[83]

By several accounts from PERs, Clarke was not especially good at establishing rapport. He wrote about Katie L. on her PER in 1925: "It is hard to keep [Katie's] mind on anything, as she is easily distracted and wants to talk at random of things that have no bearing on the case."[84] Katie L.'s brother, Jack L., a "shockheaded youngster to whom life is one big joke," caused Clarke equal consternation: "Everything he does," he complained, "is careless, haphazard and inaccurate – ten to one it won't be finished unless he is forced to keep at it."[85] Jack and Katie had an equally easy-going sister, Ida L. Her PER notes that she took great pleasure in depositing small gifts of apples, peanuts, and chocolates on her teacher's desk. In spite of Ida's good nature, Clarke could not establish rapport with her, either. "She seemed very pleased with herself that she was brought up for examination. Pays absolutely no attention to what is said to her, but giggles behind her hand instead." Clarke complained that Ida "cannot concentrate at all scarcely[.] Cannot remember what is said to her, but must have all instructions repeated several times."[86] He had great difficulty obtaining complete scores from all three siblings. There are no indications that such problems caused Clarke to seriously question Terman's claims or methods. In his actions, he appeared to remain confident that IQ tests could measure what Terman said they could, when rapport was successful and the tests could be properly administered.

With a few exceptions, the rigidity of IQ testing, when it was used in auxiliary class admissions, was restricting for children. But the testing moment also conferred on a few others modest opportunities to challenge what their teachers thought about them and even to improve their school circumstances. In September 1930, Fred V. began to attend senior first at Duke of York PS. Fred's PER indicates that one of his teachers reported that he could not do arithmetic, could barely read or write, and was poor in "handwork." Lewis was brought in to examine him. He remarked in his report that Fred's "appearance is very much against him. If one judged solely from appearances, one would put him much below par both physically and mentally." Lewis described Fred as small, pale, and soft-spoken. His parents had fibbed about his age to get him admitted to school a year earlier than when he should have begun. When quiet Fred sat down with Lewis and was coaxed into conversation, Lewis reported he "shows signes [sic] of intelligence." But an IQ test was still necessary confirmation. Fred managed an IQ score of 99, which was good enough to persuade Lewis to label him "quite up to normal." On this basis, Lewis rebuked Fred's teacher's rather dim assessment of his abilities. Fred V. may well have changed the course of his school career with his solid performance in the testing moment. He was never placed in an auxiliary class. He made steady progress academically at Duke of York and, by 1937, had passed the difficult entrance examination for high school.[87]

Strong performance on an IQ test could also help to surmount a language barrier that made a child appear academically slow. In 1926, Lewis examined Will C. He wrote that Will was "very slow and his English is very poor, although he was born and brought up in Canada. It takes him a long time to take things in and his answers were expressed in the poorest way." (Will's other language was likely Yiddish.) Will, however, was not moved to the auxiliary class because his IQ score, 105, was deemed too high to justify that placement.[88]

Demographics: Who Attended Auxiliary Classes for Subnormals?

As we have seen, IQ testers liked to claim that workers and many immigrants, especially immigrants not from Western or Northern Europe,
had lower than average IQs. Toronto's school psychologists fully expected this to be reflected in the composition of auxiliary classes for
subnormals. Clarke stated in 1923, on suspicious evidence, that his
TBE IQ surveys showed that 70 per cent of the city's subnormals were
immigrants or children of immigrants. He further asserted that most
subnormals came from families with "unskilled labour, low wage earners" as family heads.[89] In 1930, Lewis claimed, also on the basis of IQ
test results, that Toronto schools in areas with what he called "poor"
social conditions had between seven to eleven times as many mental
defectives than schools in areas where social conditions were "good."[90]
Clarke and Lewis attributed these findings to innate mental defects in
immigrant and working-class groups. With their scientific veneer, big-
oted views about group differences slipped into auxiliary education
via IQ testing in the 1920s, just as similar views had slipped in through
eugenics in the 1910s. The demographics of actual auxiliary classes,
however, did not always bear out Clarke or Lewis's claims.

There were significant numbers of working-class, immigrant, and
non-Anglo-Canadian youngsters in Hester How auxiliary classes in
the 1920s. But enrolments from these groups were not necessarily disproportionate to the groups' shares of the total Hester How school
population. Hester How is the only school from which I have enough
pupil record card data from the 1920s to make a reliable examination
of auxiliary class demographics in that decade. Of all Hester How students in the 1920s, 63 per cent came from working-class households
(see table 2.1). The school's auxiliary classes for subnormals were
little different: 60 per cent working-class pupils. Within the broader
working-class category, however, there are some differences between
auxiliary classes and the school generally: children from households
headed by members of the skilled and semi-skilled category were over-
represented in auxiliary classes, while children of unskilled labourers
were under-represented.

There are other variations between the two populations represented
in table 2.1 that also bear on class and are significant. There are clear-cut
differences between the column on the left and the one on the right for
the category "none/not available." (See appendix A for an explanation
of this category.) Close to 11 per cent of auxiliary class students fell into

2.1 Occupational group and class of Hester How PS pupils, 1920–1 to 1929–30 school years

	% of Aux. Class for Subn. Pop.	% of School Pop. as a Whole[a]
Owners and managers	2.2 (n = 2)	5.4
Agents on commission	0 (n = 0)	.6
Self-employed	23.7 (n = 22)	30.1
Middle class	1.1 (n = 1)	.6
Working class (subtotal of three categories below)	60.2 (n = 56)	63.2
Skilled and semi-skilled	38.7 (n = 36)	28.9
Unskilled	21.5 (n = 20)	32.5
White collar	0 (n = 0)	1.8
None/not available	10.8 (n = 10)	0
Miscellaneous (cannot be classified)	2.2 (n = 2)	0

[a] Based on a representative sample of pupil records from the school, discussed in appendix A.

this category. In the total population of the school, however, the category was negligible (nil).[91] Moreover, 3.3 per cent of auxiliary class pupils came from families headed by owners and managers or by middle-class employees. For the school population as a whole, the percentage of these families was nearly twice as much: 6 per cent. It can be said that students from the wealthiest backgrounds were under-represented in auxiliary classes for subnormals. The under-representation in auxiliary classes of pupils from the "self-employed" category may be saying this as well. But that category must be read especially carefully. Applied to families of Hester How pupils in the 1920s, self-employed is a particularly diverse grouping that is difficult to read in class terms. It included better-off families, like those headed by shop proprietors, but also very poor families, like those headed by pedlars.

The general picture that emerges from all of the variations that appear in table 2.1 is as follows: Auxiliary classes at Hester How in the 1920s were more likely to enrol pupils from the least well-off backgrounds (occupational category "none/not available"). They enrolled about the same percentage of working-class pupils that could be found in the general Hester How school population. However, there were important variations within that category between skilled and semi-skilled working-class household heads (over-represented in auxiliary classes) and unskilled working-class household heads (under-represented). Finally, the classes were slightly less likely to enrol better-off students, even if we look only at the owner and manager and middle-class groups and set aside the more difficult to interpret self-employed group.

Twenty-seven per cent of Hester How pupils were born abroad, which is not surprising for a school at the heart of an immigrant neighbourhood. The percentage for auxiliary class pupils was only slightly higher: 30 per cent (see table 2.2). If, however, pupils for whom birthplace information is not available are removed from the tally, the percentages are 32.9 per cent immigrants in auxiliary classes for subnormals, against their 27.7 per cent share in the total school population – a marginally wider spread. This can probably be explained by many first-generation pupils who were unfamiliar with English when they began to attend school in Canada and by first-generation pupils' greater likelihood of being over-age for their grade at some point in their school lives.[92]

In this same period, 89 per cent of Hester How students hailed from non-Anglo-Canadian ethnic origins. (See appendix A for the way I constructed this variable.) Most of them were Jewish, Italian, or Chinese. Almost the same percentage of auxiliary pupils – 91 per cent – were ethnically non-Anglo-Canadian (see table 2.3).

It is a bigger challenge to explain fine-grained group differences in table 2.3. I cannot definitively say why Jewish pupils were 32 per cent of the total Hester How population while they were 47 per cent of the population of auxiliary classes.[93] Nor can I account for why Italians seem under-represented in auxiliary classes. Neither finding seems to be explained by students' place of birth (Canada or abroad), by IQ test results recorded on ADP cards, or by varying class backgrounds.

Interestingly, the over-representation of Jewish pupils in auxiliary classes at Hester How defies common beliefs in the 1920s about race, intelligence, and the scholastic aptitude of the Jews as a group. At that time North American educators and psychologists widely believed that Jews were exceptional, and that their children excelled at school because they were naturally cleverer than other groups (see chapter 1).[94] One Toronto school inspector, P.F. Munro, completed his DPaed thesis on this subject. He published it as a book in 1926 under the peculiar but memorable title *An Experimental Investigation of the Mentality of the Jew in Ryerson Public School Toronto*. Comparing Jews and gentiles on different intellectual and academic measures, Munro's conclusion

2.2 Hester How PS students by birthplace, 1920–1 to 1929–30 school years

	% of Aux. Class for Subn. Pop.	% of School Pop. as a Whole[a]
Born in Canada	61.3 (n = 57)	71.1
Not born in Canada	30.1 (n = 28)	27.2
Information n/a	8.6 (n = 8)	1.7

[a] Based on a representative sample of pupil records from the school, discussed in appendix A.

2.3 Hester How PS students by top four ethnic origins, auxiliary classes and school as a whole, 1920–1 to 1929–30 school years

	% of Aux. Class for Subn. Pop.	% of School Pop. as a Whole[a]
Jewish	47.3 (n = 44)	31.9
Italian	15.1 (n = 14)	19.6
Chinese	10.8 (n = 10)	9.5
Anglo-Canadian	9.7 (n = 9)	10.6
All others	17.2 (n = 16) (9 other groups)	28.5 (12 other groups)

[a] Based on a representative sample of pupil records from the school, discussed in appendix A.

was that "taken as racial groups ... the Jews are slightly superior."[95] He claimed confirmation for his hypothesis elsewhere in the book by referring to similar conclusions he said had been reached by "Dr Terman and Dr Root in California, and investigators in New York City."[96]

The discussion so far has been about just one school: Hester How. Statistics on the class, birthplace, and ethnic origins of auxiliary pupils city-wide might divulge a different story. That sort of data would not become obtainable until many decades later.[97] But there is one demographic area where Toronto-wide auxiliary pupil data was available for part of the 1920s: gender. Boys were over-represented in auxiliary classes for subnormals, not just at Hester How but in all Toronto public schools. DOE statistics, which are available for Toronto classes for subnormals in 1928–9 and 1929–30, show that boys were 60 per cent of enrolments.[98] Pupil record card data from Hester How reveals that between the 1920–1 and the 1929–30 school years, 63.4 per cent of enrolments in classes for subnormals were boys and 33.3 per cent were girls. (Note that 3 per cent of record cards contained no information that would make it possible to identify the pupil's gender.)[99]

Educators and psychologists were aware in the 1920s – in fact even earlier – that boys experienced higher rates of elimination (dropping out) and retardation (over-age for grade) than girls.[100] Ayres, for example, attributed these problems to schools "better fitted to the needs and natures of the girl than of the boy pupils." But he rejected as conjecture any argument about the "alleged bad effects of too exclusively feminine instruction on the moral fiber and character of the boys."[101] E.D. MacPhee, a psychologist at the University of Toronto, in contrast to Ayres, claimed in a 1927 speech to the Ontario Educational Association (OEA) that "the Auxiliary Class has been used in some schools as a disciplinary class to which bad boys – usually boys – are sent."[102]

Historians have also attempted to explain why there were more boys than girls in auxiliary classes. Much like MacPhee contended in the 1920s, two modern historians, Joseph L. Tropea and Julia Grant, argue that special classes and curricula evolved chiefly as a cover that educators and school officials adopted as a convenient way to deal with difficult boys.[103] Tropea claims that teachers and principals ignored the stated purpose of the auxiliary classes – to educate children identified as disabled – and instead implemented a set of "backstage rules" that used the classes as a secret dumping ground for pupils with behavioural problems, disabled or not.[104]

We should not discount the likelihood that teachers or principals nudged a few boys (and girls, too) toward auxiliary classes because of difficult behaviour. However, I could find no evidence in the Hester How pupil record cards I examined that anyone systematically dispatched troublemaking boys to the classes. My analysis of pupil record cards does, however, show that Hester How boys in this period were two-and-a-half times more likely than girls to have had their IQs tested at least once.[105] Regardless of whether or not the test led to an auxiliary class placement every time, with testing the main gateway to admission, simply being tested raised boys' chances of placement in the classes. Teachers and principals probably more frequently selected boys for IQ testing because boys were more likely to be behind in school or over-age for their grades. Laggardly students in the 1920s were still good candidates for auxiliary classes even if educators now explained their delays with a low IQ theory instead of with the other factors they had cited in the 1910s.[106] But there is no evidence to support a strong-hand social control thesis of schools consistently or deliberately streaming misbehaving boys into special education.

A New Course of Studies for Auxiliary Education

There was one final area where IQ testing helped to transform auxiliary classes in Toronto in the 1920s: the course of studies. In the 1910s, the auxiliary classes for mentally defective children prepared them for life in an institution. The auxiliary classes for backward children gave them remedial instruction and special attention in their areas of academic weakness. Educators believed that this instruction, combined with pupil diligence, would lead to improvements. In the 1920s, auxiliary education moved away from the remedial approach for backward children and developed a more coherent and differentiated course of studies specifically tailored to a merged group now defined not as mentally defective or backward, but as, in the new IQ terms, subnormal.

This shift in the basic curriculum philosophy in auxiliary education occurred at a time when, curriculum historians argue, rationalized approaches to curriculum-making were on the rise.[107] Auxiliary educators advocated for a rationally planned course of studies rooted in IQ testers' theories that would displace the earlier remedial approach of auxiliary classes for backward children. In a speech to the OEA in 1925 on "Classification and Time-Table in Auxiliary Classes," Dr E.T. Seaton, a Hamilton educator, described curriculum change:

> At first the aim of Auxiliary Class workers was very ambitious, being nothing less than to make all, or nearly all, normal, and so be able to return to the regular grade classes. If the children were merely slow or even dull this might be attained, but we now know how different the case has proved to be.
>
> *Now*, i.e., to-day ... the aim is to try to make the children healthier and happier, both during school life and after school life. To obtain this result we strive to teach – the useful – the pleasurable – the healthful – the most fundamental adjustments.[108]

The program in auxiliary education was reconceptualized in the 1920s by psychologists and by auxiliary educators such as Seaton. Many of the details of the new program are laid out in a pamphlet that the DOE published in 1925, *Suggestions for Teachers of Subnormal Children*. The unnamed author grounded the new program in what the science of IQ appeared to reveal about subnormal schoolchildren's supposedly specific and limited mental capacities, about the particular manner in which these children learned, about their special vocational needs, and about the proper place of the subnormal adult in a stratified social order.[109]

One rationale for the new program included the argument that subnormal schoolchildren were not only less intelligent than normal schoolchildren, but also possessed a different form of intelligence. Sandiford distinguished between the "concrete" intelligence of subnormals and the "abstract" intelligence, or the "the highest form of intelligence," that only youngsters with higher IQs possessed.[110] Abstract intelligence he further associated with the "rarer," and therefore more "valuable," professional skills and careers. "In terms of intelligence," he stated, "we say that a person needs a higher I.Q. for the successful learning of sciences, languages and mathematics than he needs for the successful learning of carpentry, plumbing, bricklaying, dressmaking and cookery."[111] Harry Amoss, a psychologist and instructor at the Hamilton Normal School (and eventually the provincial inspector of auxiliary classes, 1929–39), stated along similar lines that a subnormal child "can be taught concepts of concrete things, mountain, lake, quart, mile, etc., but will never gain concepts of abstract things that is, doubly abstract concepts, such as honesty, justice, predicate adjective, or repeating decimal."[112]

Psychologists, IQ testers, and auxiliary educators transferred these sorts of ideas about intelligence into the new curriculum. Thus, Amoss wrote that "the subnormal pupil will require a slower, more detailed, more concrete and more intensive course of study."[113] Seaton described a program for auxiliary education that included "much concrete object teaching" (i.e., accompanying a lesson with an object or image representative of that lesson), alongside "reading, writing and numbers – slowly and rarely beyond senior second [form]," and "manual training."[114]

The program of studies introduced rudimentary pre-vocational subjects as well, based on the notion that, as Inspector N.S. MacDonald put it in 1921, auxiliary classes should give pupils "something to do with their hands which will enable them to become useful members of society as far as they are capable."[115] Seaton recommended "woodwork, cardboard construction, raffia, braiding, weaving, stencilling [sic], card sewing, paper folding, etc."[116] By 1928, schoolchildren in Toronto's auxiliary classes for subnormals reportedly followed a curriculum that was 50 per cent academic and 50 per cent pre-vocational manual training.[117]

In addition to program changes, auxiliary class teaching also became more formalized and specialized in the 1920s as it was reoriented

2.5 "Boy caning chair, auxiliary class," ca. 1920. The curriculum in auxiliary classes changed over time. In the 1920s, perhaps as much as 50 per cent of class time was dedicated to the sort of manual training or pre-vocational work that this photograph depicts. Academic studies were present at all times in at least some quantity. City of Toronto Archives, William James family fonds, item 3039.

around IQ. Teaching specialization established auxiliary instruction and curricula as distinct from general education. In the 1910s, a small number of auxiliary class teachers, such as Lillian Carruthers, studied at American custodial institutions or, after 1915, at the summer school that the DOE offered from time to time.[118] By about 1917, provincial regulations stipulated that all auxiliary class teachers had to have three years of teaching experience (at any grade level) and had to hold an "Auxiliary Class Teacher's Certificate."[119] At this point, auxiliary class teachers became more like kindergarten "directors" and "assistants," manual training teachers, household science teachers, and other certified specialists that occupied an expanding number of niches within bureaucratizing city school systems.[120] By 1929, a "trained" auxiliary class teacher in Ontario was supposed to have taken "a five-weeks summer course" that included instruction on the unique methods and program in "training, promotion and special industrial" classes.[121]

Conclusion

In the 1910s, auxiliary education was experimental and contested. In that decade, the TBE had but a few auxiliary classes, some for backward children and others for mentally defective children. The board even closed the latter type of class by about 1914. After 1919, however, auxiliary classes were reorganized and the new classes for subnormals proliferated to become an established part of the city's school system. By the 1929–30 school year, 760 Toronto students were enrolled in auxiliary classes for children labelled this way.[122] The rise of intelligence testing and IQ were significantly responsible for the direction these classes took in the 1920s. In part, this was because IQ testers, such as Terman, had helped to alter drastically theories of intelligence and of learning difficulties. He and others successfully appropriated Binet's concept of mental age and successfully challenged Ayres's theory on the causes of retardation. The IQ testers argued that low native intelligence, measurable with new IQ testing tools, was responsible for most young people's learning difficulties. The IQ testers' theory about learning difficulties ascended in the 1920s. But, as we shall see in chapter 5, after approximately 1930 this theory's grasp on auxiliary education began to slip. Remedial educators and others proposed different ideas about the nature and cause of some children's learning problems that challenged it.

The other effects of IQ testing on auxiliary education in the 1920s that the present chapter has examined were also profound. The rise of IQ introduced the testing moment, which became a significant experience in the school lives of many young people. School psychologists in Toronto's Division of Mental Hygiene increasingly relied on IQ tests in the auxiliary class selection process, with a child's low score on a test usually leading to placement in an auxiliary class. Not very many young people were as fortunate as Fred V., whose high IQ score may have changed his educational fate. Children who upset the testing process – through defiance or simple inattention – also exerted some control, however little and fleeting it might have been.

Intelligence testers claimed group variations in IQ test results not only demonstrated that there were real differences in the intelligence of various racial, ethnic, and class groups, but also that such differences were inherited and innate. Psychologists heralded studies based on IQ test results that allegedly showed that neighbourhoods with significant poverty and significant numbers of immigrants contributed disproportionately to the subnormal population. Enrolment patterns in auxiliary classes for subnormals in one Toronto school in the 1920s, Hester How, both affirmed and challenged such claims. Auxiliary classes at Hester How enrolled predominantly working-class students and large numbers of immigrant students as well. But this is not surprising, given that the school's population was overwhelmingly working-class and included many immigrants. The proportions of working-class and immigrant youngsters in Hester How auxiliary classes were practically the same as the proportions of these groups in the school as a whole. And while IQ testers suggested that supposedly naturally low IQs were the main justification for auxiliary education placements, other factors, such as language barriers or a late start to school causing a child to become over-age for grade, continued to play real and underacknowledged roles in why some children struggled and eventually fell under auxiliary education's purview.

The course of studies that educators proposed by the 1920s for auxiliary education was based on the theory, which IQ testers promoted, that subnormal learning was unique and that a concrete, manual, and vocationally oriented program was the one best suited for auxiliary class pupils. Abandoning the notion that auxiliary instruction could add to the scholastic abilities of pupils formerly labelled backward, curriculum planners after 1920 began to educate subnormal children based on the belief that their learning abilities were more restricted than other children's. This belief in turn justified the argument that subnormal students, by virtue of their unique and limited learning ability, required a pre-vocational or industrial education that would prepare them for their appropriate place in a workforce supposedly defined by a hierarchy of intelligence. As we shall see in the next chapter, assumptions like these figured prominently in the design of new junior vocational auxiliary programs for adolescent subnormals that the TBE also initiated in the 1920s as yet another branch of its expanding auxiliary education programs and services.

Chapter Three

Avoiding "Blunders and Stupid Mistakes": Auxiliary Education for Adolescents, 1923–1935

In September 1927, Mr Gillespie, a young teacher at Central Technical School, was summoned to the school's basement. Years later, Gillespie would become principal of Central Tech, but his task this time was more prosaic than captaining the city's flagship technical high school. A coal heap needed moving so that another class could be squeezed into the bowels of the bursting building. Gillespie took up a shovel and pitched in.[1] Overcrowding in Toronto's secondary schools by the late 1920s had become dire. Even Central Tech – a mass of neo-gothic architecture, and the most costly high school ever built in Ontario when it opened in 1915[2] – was overflowing with students. All of the city's secondary schools were swamped throughout the 1920s. Enrolments seemed to climb even faster than teams of workers could erect new high school buildings.[3] In 1919–20, the Toronto Board of Education (TBE)'s academic high schools (called collegiate institutes) enrolled 4,300 students. In addition, approximately 4,000 vocational students were enrolled in technical or commercial secondary schools.[4] Within just ten short years, by 1929–30, there were 11,846 vocational students in Toronto. They now outnumbered the 9,646 scholars who attended collegiate institutes.[5] This unprecedented enrolment growth brought new heterogeneity to the high school population. The Ontario high school student body in the 1920s was more female, more working class, and more immigrant than ever before.[6] In Toronto, working-class enrolments grew from 19 per cent of the total secondary school roll in 1901, to 33 per cent in 1914, and to 45 per cent by 1929, according to one historian.[7]

The causes of unprecedented and rapidly increasing high school enrolments in the 1920s – a fact of pedagogical life in Canadian and

American schooling – were economic, social, and educational. The consequences of the increase were very important for the future shape secondary school programming would take, including in auxiliary education. Educationists in the 1920s coped with the help of expanded vocational programs, greater use of vocational guidance, and initial yet serious use of intelligence quotient (IQ) testing to differentiate secondary programs of study and to stream pupils. At practically the very same time that this response to increasing enrolments was occurring, ideas about the expected social roles of people with intellectual disabilities were changing. In the 1910s, a significant sector of auxiliary education was still concerned with preparing mentally defective youngsters to transition to institutions, such as the proposed farm colonies, for permanent custodial care (see chapter 1). But by the 1920s, a new consensus among mental deficiency experts was that with proper training and guidance, subnormal youth (as they were now more likely to be called) could become functioning community members.[8] Amid these various changes, adolescent auxiliary class pupils were thrust to the centre of policy.

To begin, this chapter examines the ways that educational and other changes, specifically new laws that raised the school leaving age in Ontario, generated anxiety among school inspectors and trustees about the fate of adolescents. This prompted school leaders to develop a new type of senior auxiliary program. The "junior vocational schools," for thirteen- to sixteen-year-olds, focused on the transition from adolescence to adulthood, predominantly (but not exclusively) for teenagers with low IQs. They pioneered new forms of vocational guidance that tried to compensate for intellectually disabled youngsters' many supposed inherent occupational deficiencies and that encouraged junior vocational pupils of all abilities to be satisfied with menial jobs when they left school. The schools' wholesome extracurricular activities were promoted as an effective way to keep adolescent pupils on the straight and narrow path.

At first, educational officials in Toronto planned junior vocational schools only for students they labelled subnormal, but they would soon realize that they could use the very same programs and curricula to instruct youngsters labelled dull-normal and some unlabelled young people as well. Junior vocational schools streamed pupils primarily by ability. They were also populated by students who were largely working class. However, these schools were not responsible for streaming all, or even very many, of the city's working-class secondary school pupils into basic vocational programs. The vast majority of Toronto's working-class high school students attended academic collegiate institutes and technical and commercial schools. Despite this reality, IQ theories about dull-normality, ideas about vocational education for working-class adolescents, and, from the founding of the new junior vocational schools, the strong presence of the offspring of unskilled and unemployed workers in this program helped to create powerful associations that still exist today between special education for secondary school students and some forms of vocational training and preparation.

This chapter's final section examines how young people and their parents interacted with junior vocational schools. Young people – once they reached age fourteen – and their families had options that included different forms of schooling, waged work, or unpaid domestic labour at home. The nature of the industrial economy, relations between workers and employers, and a changing juvenile employment market squeezed working-class youth and families, and created tense conditions that hung over the very serious decisions they made about work and schooling, including whether or not to attend junior vocational schools.

Educational and Industrial Change in Toronto, 1900–1930

In 1918, Premier William H. Hearst, of the Conservatives, appointed the Toronto Anglican clergyman Canon H.J. Cody as Ontario's new minister of education. Cody had a reputation as a "brilliant scholar and outstanding Christian leader," the historian Robert Stamp writes, who had served the nation as a staunch patriot during the First World War, the Conservative Party as a stalwart, and the provincial university (Toronto) as a reliable member of its board of governors. Not about to disappoint Hearst's high expectations, Cody promptly brought forward an ambitious education policy proposal to extend compulsory attendance in the province's schools. Only more schooling, Cody urged with a clergyman's conviction, could prepare youth for a dawning postwar world where, he believed, they would need more training to join the workforce, more guidance about living a righteous life, and more education to intelligently execute the duties of citizenship.[9] Cody successfully oversaw the passage of the School Attendance Act, which obliged school boards to hire attendance officers and strengthened

enforcement against truancy, and the Adolescent School Attendance
Act, which raised the normal leaving age from fourteen to sixteen.
But with the defeat of the Conservatives at the hands of the United
Farmers of Ontario in 1919, Cody would have to watch from the opposition benches as his bills took effect. With some changes introduced
by the new government, the legislation was implemented in stages in
1920 and 1921.[10]

The Adolescent School Attendance Act set a youngster's sixteenth
birthday as the legal school-leaving age. But it also contained clauses
that made fourteen- or fifteen-year-olds who met specific conditions
eligible for exemptions from compulsory attendance to age sixteen.
Fourteen- or fifteen-year-olds who lived in urban areas could be exempt
if their parents or guardians could prove they needed their labour "in
or about the home" and applied for a "home permit" from the school
attendance officer. Fourteen- or fifteen-year-olds engaged "in some
permitted gainful occupation for the necessary maintenance of such
adolescent or some person dependent on him" were also potentially
exempt. Eligible youth in urban areas who found themselves in this
situation could obtain an "employment certificate" that permitted them
to work for wages. There were slightly different rules for farm youth.[11]

Stricter attendance laws alone did not result in enrolment increases.
Industrial changes –to the workplace and workforce – helped to expand enrolment as well. In a masterfully detailed study of the family
wage economy and juvenile labour and school attendance in Hamilton,
Ontario, Craig Heron shows how even before new attendance laws the
industrial capitalist economy was changing in a way that undercut
the need for young workers. From about 1914 onward, apprentice-
ships for youth slumped; light manufacturing that had given them
work was replaced by heavy industry using adult male labour; and
work processes were transformed through mechanization in a way
that eliminated young people's traditional jobs, such as fetching
and carrying materials. Adult male immigrants now competed for
work at young people's wages as well.[12] Employment opportunities
for working-class teenagers withered throughout the 1920s as these
changes pushed them out of industries, warehouses, and shops. As
a result, enrolments of working-class youth in Hamilton's secondary schools substantially increased.[13] In a case study of Edmonton,
Rebecca Coulter observes very similar changes in that city within the
same time frame, and shows how such declines in youth employment

opportunities confronted working-class youth with the new "harsh realities" of a difficult entry into the industrial capitalist economy.[14]

Working-class youth, when they had the choice, did not turn all at once to more schooling, or to vocational education, to fill the hole left by declining work opportunities. Their reasons for not doing so were conditioned by class, culture, parental expectations, the types of jobs available, and what sort of secondary education (if any) was necessary to obtain those jobs.[15] Yet over the course of the first half of the twentieth century, secondary school attendance increasingly became a necessity for youth from all classes, one that might even yield some worthwhile payoff, so young people and parents began to feel high school's pull.[16]

The schools were also adjusting to change, with work preparation becoming one main objective by about the turn of the twentieth century. To be sure, before this time, preparation for work was a function of schooling, although in high schools it mostly involved grooming for the respectable upper crust and lucky middle-class few – mostly boys, although less overwhelmingly so than before – who had professional, commercial, or genteel futures before them.[17] But after 1900, "vocationalism" increasingly defined all schooling. Vocationalism was the notion that schools, like proverbial tool and die makers, should mould, cut, and polish the pupil masses – not just the elite – to slip as frictionless cogs from the schoolroom into the precision human machinery of the factory or another workplace.[18]

Vocationalism in Ontario was bolstered through the passage in 1911 of the province's Industrial Education Act. The government used the act to contribute capital to vocational school construction. In testament to the breadth of support for vocationalism, two old foes, the Canadian Manufacturers' Association and the Trades and Labour Congress, both supported the legislation.[19] The federal government's new Vocational and Technical Education Act in 1919 provided even more construction capital.[20] Canada's legislation resembled the American Smith-Hughes Act passed in 1917.[21]

Of no less importance, vocationalism bonded with the functional differentiation that the administrative progressives had introduced as they further bureaucratized public schooling after about 1890. In elementary schools, curriculum differentiation sometimes took the form of auxiliary classes and programs (see chapter 1). More commonly, differentiation was represented in ability grouping within regular classrooms in the lower elementary grades. It was on occasion present in more formal streaming of students into classes by ability in the higher grades of some large urban elementary schools. It could intermittently be found in those elementary schools where boys and girls from the same classes separately received manual training or domestic science instruction for a few hours a week.[22] At the secondary level, vocationalism held one of the keys to curriculum differentiation as well. A variety of vocational courses promised to adapt schooling to what educators perceived to be the varying needs of young people facing employment in workplaces that were vastly different than in years before.[23] Chief Inspector R.H. Cowley stated the significance of vocationalism for Toronto public schools in 1922: "How best to bridge the way, for thousands of young people, between the public schools and occupational life is a problem of the first importance, worthy any prominence it may achieve in order of attention."[24]

How, on the transition to work, to bridge terrain that was uneven, even rocky and dangerous, was a concern that educationists shared with employers in the first three decades of the twentieth century, a time of industrial upheaval and strikes as employers stepped up efforts to tighten controls over work and workers.[25] Alongside vocational education, vocational guidance in the schools promised a science for smoothing and efficiently managing industrial relations.[26] Vocational guidance was intended in no small part to mitigate the problem of "occupational wanderers" – the description, according to the historian Jennifer Stephen, that a 1916 Ontario unemployment commission used for young female workers who experienced high turnover, but that could easily apply to young workers of any gender at this time.[27] Low pay, poor conditions, and lack of opportunity for advancement motivated youthful workers to switch jobs often. Industrial efficiency experts, such as the University of Toronto psychologist E.A. Bott, bemoaned the capricious attitude of juvenile workers or blamed the inadequacies of the home and school for the turnover.[28] Only very reluctantly did experts recognize structural economic problems as factors. Vocational guidance was designed to coordinate the home, the school, and the workplace in a manner that would train the young worker to find the right job from the beginning and to keep at it.[29]

In Toronto, the combined result of the new attendance laws that raised the school leaving age, the changes to juvenile employment in a transforming industrial economy, and the rise of vocationalism was the high-school overcrowding that Central Tech's Gillespie battled in 1927 with a shovel.

Creating the Junior Vocational School:
The Problem of Adolescent Subnormals in the Schools

In Toronto – amid these roiling changes to schooling, to the industrial workforce, and to class relations – school officials also worried about an increasing number of subnormal adolescents turning up at school. As we saw in chapter 2, by the 1920s educationists equated a diagnosis of subnormality to an IQ in the 50 to 75 range. Virtually from the moment that provincial attendance laws were changed, Toronto school inspectors and trustees seem to have become gravely worried about what to do with older auxiliary-class pupils and other youth who fell in this IQ range. Inspector G.K. Powell, for instance, observed in 1920 that whereas up to that point, many "mentally defective" children left school when they reached age fourteen – "and it is a blessing that they do" – the new attendance law meant these youngsters would now remain until their sixteenth birthdays. The "impossible task" of educating them, Powell wrote, promised to overwhelm teachers and normal youth alike. "If under the operation of the Adolescent Act, such young people as I have described are compelled to remain at school the work for them must be very different from that of the ordinary class," Powell also stated. "We must introduce still more 'fads and frills' so that the school may be of use to them and not be merely a prison."[30] Powell's colleague, Inspector N.S. MacDonald, asked in 1922, "What value is there in keeping a subnormal adolescent in regular class-work until he is sixteen?" He added: "It is true that we have auxiliary classes but these are for junior pupils only."[31] A year later, Eric Clarke, the TBE's psychologist, wrote that complying with the attendance act was "a really serious problem" because it would "compel the subnormal to two extra years [sic] work." He recommended new forms of schooling "along manual training lines" for subnormal youth.[32]

In response to concerns such as these, in February 1923 trustees on the Advisory Industrial Committee of the TBE – one of the board's standing committees – approved a motion to open "a boys' and girls' school, respectively, for sub-normal adolescents." Temporary sites adjacent to existing TBE schools on Wellesley Street and Huron Street were chosen.[33] Equipment was secured and teachers and principals appointed.[34] Both facilities opened their doors to pupils in April 1923.[35]

Around the same time, S.B. Sinclair, the provincial inspector of auxiliary classes, had been working the back corridors of Queen's Park to garner the provincial government's support for junior vocational schools. In 1924, he got an amendment to the Vocational Education Act authorizing vocational education for adolescent pupils "who have been in attendance in auxiliary training, or who are eligible for admission to such classes." Sinclair, with evident pride, called the amendment the "most progressive and far-reaching legislation" of its type.[36] In 1925, the TBE relocated the girls' junior vocational school and renamed it Edith L. Groves School for Girls, after the pioneering school trustee and auxiliary education advocate at whose reforms chapter 4 will look more closely. The boys' school was named Jarvis Junior Vocational School around the same time. (It should not be confused with Jarvis Collegiate Institute, one of the academic high schools.)[37] In 1927 the TBE opened a second girls' junior vocational school in the east end, Bolton School for Girls, bringing the total number of junior vocational schools to three.[38]

At first, junior vocational schools were for former auxiliary class pupils only. Very quickly this would change, but the original intent to educate youth who had grown too old for elementary school auxiliary classes is apparent in the reference to subnormal adolescents in the Advisory Industrial Committee's initial motion described above. It is also evident in a subsequent motion that authorizes the TBE's director of technical education, A.C. MacKay, to "obtain from the Chief Inspector a list of pupils of thirteen or over who have passed through the Auxiliary Classes of the Public Schools, and from same make a selection of pupils for the Auxiliary Schools on Huron and Wellesley Streets."[39] Junior vocational schools were further set apart from the TBE's other vocational institutes – the technical and commercial schools – by their dramatically lower academic standards. Standards at technical and commercial schools were high. It was difficult to gain admission – nearly as difficult as it was to win a place in traditional collegiate institutes, which required a student to pass the high school entrance examination after senior fourth. Commercial and technical high schools awarded diplomas for programs ranging in duration from two to four years for courses that packaged substantial academic classes with technical or commercial studies.[40] Ontario's four-year commercial course, for example, offered literature, history, geography, business law, economics, and French alongside commercial subjects.[41] Technical and commercial schools even had a matriculation stream, accessed by perhaps 5 to 10 per cent of students, that provided the necessary academic courses for a matriculant to be admitted to university.[42] Compared to these rigours, junior vocational schools were anything but academic. They were basically ungraded, a terminal program that students completed more or less when they turned sixteen, rather than when they finished any particular set of studies.[43]

IQ and the Expanding Junior Vocational School Clientele

Inspector G.W. McGill wrote in his annual report in 1928: "We have made provision for the auxiliary type of pupil by establishing a large number of auxiliary classes for the junior pupils and the two Vocational Schools for the seniors." But like some of his inspector colleagues, a handful of trustees, and E.P. Lewis, who was by then the city's school psychologist, McGill had grown concerned about yet "another equally important group" of young people, "those pupils having IQs between 75 and 90, for who [sic] little is being done."[44] Between approximately 1926 and 1930, the TBE would extend junior vocational education to adolescents with IQs in that range, "dull-normals." Unlike subnormals, these young people were not defined as disabled; however, they were seen as having educational needs in common with subnormals, especially for particular forms of vocational education and guidance.

Lewis Terman, who influenced auxiliary education so profoundly in Toronto in the 1920s, also developed the category of dull-normals. He described it in 1916 in *The Measurement of Intelligence*, the book that set off the testing craze in schools. On Terman's scale, dull-normal (IQ 80 to 90) sat in approximately the adjacent IQ range to feeblemindedness (IQ 50 to 75).[45] (The latter category, by the 1920s, had become subnormality.) Terman characterized dull-normals as the particular victims of what he believed was the poor heredity of the working-class and of some racial groups. Among dull-normals, Terman wrote,

> are included those children who would not, according to any of the commonly accepted social standards, be considered feeble-minded, but who are nevertheless far enough below the actual average among races of western European descent that they cannot make ordinary school progress or master other intellectual difficulties which children are equal to. A few of this class test as low as 75 to 80 IQ, but the majority are not far from 85. The unmistakably normal children who go much below this (in California at least) are usually Mexicans, Indians, or negroes.[46]

In addition to displaying his racial prejudices as a white Californian (albeit a transplant from Indiana), Terman was making a subtle but still important point about dull-normals: race and class, he believed, contributed to their low intelligence.[47] Terman expanded on this point in his discussion of what he called "border-line" cases: "The border-line cases are those which fall near the boundary between that grade of mental deficiency which will be generally recognized as such and the higher group usually classed as normal but dull." Border-line cases were not intellectually disabled, but poor heredity, class, and race factored in the diagnosis.[48] "Among laboring men and servant girls there are thousands like them. They are the world's 'hewers of wood and drawers of water,'" Terman contended. Moreover, the typical border-line cases he introduced in *The Measurement of Intelligence* "represent the level of intelligence which is very, very common among Spanish-Indian and Mexican families of the Southwest and also among negroes. Their dullness seems to be racial, or at least inherent in the family stocks from which they come."[49]

Consequently, intelligence testers characterized dull-normals not primarily by intellectual disability, but in part by their belonging to the working class or to what Terman and other white psychologists saw as less desirable racial or ethnic groups. Lewis did his own survey of dull-normality in Toronto in 1930. Observing that schools in communities whose "economic conditions" he classified as "poor" had dull-normal student populations far above the expected norm, he concluded that "it would seem that there is a definite relationship between unsatisfactory social and economic conditions and this condition of being non-academic." (Lewis had recently updated the terminology he used for dull-normals, i.e., pupils "whose intelligence quotient fell between 75 and 90," settling on the emerging term "the non-academic child."[50] The constant updating of language, often for propriety's sake, never seemed to alter the descriptions or IQ ranges associated with the terms.) Lewis probably did not quite think that all working-class youngsters were dull-normal, but when he pictured the archetype of a dull-normal youth, he likely had a working-class girl or boy in mind.

A group of Toronto school trustees, led by Adelaide Plumptre, began to study the dull-normal adolescent problem.[51] An auxiliary class booster in the 1910s, Plumptre won election to the school board in 1926.[52] A year later, she joined a Toronto delegation travelling to Pittsburgh to "study work in connection with dull normal pupils" in that city. This junket would lead to the expansion of the aims of Toronto's junior vocational schools to include educating dull-normals. Plumptre, along with T.I. Davis, the principal of Park PS in working-class Cabbagetown, made up two-thirds of the visitors from Toronto. The board's new chief inspector, D.D. Moshier, rounded out the group.[53]

In Pittsburgh, Moshier, Plumptre, and Davis discovered a system of "trade schools" that they found greatly appealing.[54] The person behind these unique schools was Frank Leavitt, the city's associate superintendent of education and a former professor of industrial training at the University of Chicago, who was known for pioneering work in vocational education that dated back nearly two decades.[55] The trade schools were distinct from Pittsburgh's composite high schools, which had "academic, technical and commercial departments." Instead, they admitted students regardless of academic ability. "These trade schools," the three Torontonians wrote in their report, "offer an opportunity for the 'dull-normal' pupils, who have reached the junior fourth grade, to acquire some skill which is useful in earning a living." However, the trade schools, because they also admitted a wider range of students including subnormal, dull-normal, and normal, had a more extensive program of studies than "the type of work carried out in the Junior Vocational School and Edith L. Groves School," they remarked. Moshier, Plumptre, and Davis regarded this "extended" program of studies as a great virtue. While they were cagier about the seemingly "far less distinct line of demarcation between the 'normal' and the 'subnormal' child than obtains in the Toronto schools," they were clearly inspired by Pittsburgh's model of vocational schools that integrated in the same program subnormal, dull-normal, and "bright" working-class students "who cannot afford to take a High School course."[56] Pittsburgh was not the only city to operate this model of vocational education successfully. A US Office of Education bulletin from 1931 showed Boston, New York, Minneapolis, Cleveland, Portland, Milwaukee, and a host of others running similar trade schools.[57]

By 1928, Plumptre had become head of the Special Committee of the Board on Dull Normal and Retarded Pupils in the Public Schools.[58] The special committee finally identified the nub of the problem when it came to adolescent dull-normal pupils in Toronto: "These pupils have an 'intelligence quotient' above that of the pupils for whom auxiliary education is provided; and they are therefore not eligible for admission to the Junior Vocational School or the Edith L. Groves School into which auxiliary pupils can pass on reaching the age of fourteen. On the other hand, their intelligence quotient is too low to allow them to qualify satisfactorily for admission to the Technical, Commercial and Academic High Schools."[59] "It seems hard," the special committee concluded, "that there should be a large group of our public school pupils who are at once too bright and too dull to be educated! Why would we have to label boys and girls as 'subnormal' in order to procure for them the type of education they most need?"[60] It recommended the Pittsburgh trade school model for Toronto as a solution to this conundrum.[61]

Toronto's junior vocational school enrolment grew partly through the admission of new types of pupils, just as the special committee had hoped. Mental Hygiene Division psychologists made hundreds of new admissions recommendations for junior vocational schools yearly, for example: 298 in 1929,[62] and 325 in 1935.[63] In the 1925–6 school year, the first year for which Ontario Department of Education (DOE) enrolment statistics are available for junior vocational schools, there were 493 junior vocational school students in Toronto, compared to 754 younger auxiliary class students in the city's public elementary schools. By 1929–30, Toronto's three junior vocational schools enrolled a total of 1,012 pupils (see appendix B). This far exceeded the 760 pupils found in auxiliary classes for subnormals in elementary schools. And these younger students were spread across a wider age range. The auxiliary classes for subnormals simply did not churn out enough adolescent pupils to fill up the junior vocational schools, even if every thirteen- to sixteen-year-old former auxiliary class pupil had attended. Other pupils, including those labelled dull-normal and those not labelled at all, filled the remaining junior vocational seats.

Pupil Selection for Junior Vocational Schools

In the 1920s and early 1930s, many of the children at Hester How Public School (PS) and Duke of York PS, two schools whose pupil record collections I examined in depth, who attended an auxiliary class moved directly from that class to a junior vocational school upon reaching their early teens. This included the likes of Andrew H., who spent three years in the auxiliary class for subnormals at Duke of York in the 1930s. In June 1935, he was discharged from that class to Jarvis Junior Vocational.[64] Maxine F. was also a former auxiliary class attendee who moved on to a junior vocational school. After repeating several grades at Hester How, Maxine was placed in the auxiliary class in September 1932. At the end of the school year, by which time she had turned thirteen, she was transferred to Edith L. Groves School.[65]

3.1 "Edith [L.] Groves school, group of 5," 1929. City of Toronto Archives, *Globe and Mail* fonds, fonds 1266, item 18778.

However, there were also adolescent students who – unlike Andrew or Maxine – had not attended an auxiliary class immediately prior to transfer to junior vocational school. Herman I., a Hester How student, was sent to Jarvis Junior Vocational in 1933, even though he had not been in the auxiliary class for subnormals. When Hester How staff finally successfully moved Herman to Jarvis Junior Vocational, he was nearly sixteen and still in junior fourth.[66] Sarah B. entered junior first in September 1925. Nearly four years later, she was still in that form. In September 1929, she began senior first at Duke of York. After repeating that form once and registering in the second form (a combined junior and senior second class), she was transferred to the Bolton School for Girls in the fall of 1931. By that time Sarah, who had started school

3.2 "Junior vocational school, pyramid by gym class," 1930. City of Toronto Archives, *Globe and Mail* fonds, fonds 1266, item 19904.

at age six, was thirteen, yet had completed just the first two grades of primary school.[67] Donald R. is still another example of a student moving from elementary school to junior vocational school without passing first through an auxiliary class for subnormals. He attended public schools in suburban York County before his family relocated to Toronto in 1930 in time for the new school year. Lewis examined him in February 1931, recorded an IQ of 74 and diagnosed Donald as borderline. However, he made no placement recommendation. A month later, Donald – who was nearly fourteen – was transferred from Duke of York to Jarvis Junior Vocational.[68]

In fact, more junior vocational school students than not were like Herman I., Sarah B., and Donald R. and had not been attending an auxiliary class when they transferred to junior vocational schools. Close

3.1 Former auxiliary education status, pupils admitted to junior vocational schools (JRV) from Hester How PS, 1923 to 1934–5 school years, and Duke of York PS, 1929–30 to 1934–5 school years

	Boys (n)	Girls (n)	Total (n)	%
Hester How PS				
Transf. from the aux. class for subn. to JRV	20	9	29	41
Transf. from another class to JRV	24	18	42	59
Duke of York PS[a]				
Transf. from the aux. class for subn. to JRV	6	15	21	42
Transf. from another class to JRV	20	9	29	58

[a] Duke of York PS opened in the 1929–30 school year.

to 60 per cent of the students who transferred to those schools from Hester How between 1923 and 1935 and from Duke of York between 1929 and 1935[69] came from regular classes (see table 3.1). In a survey she conducted in 1932, Grace Mackenzie, the principal of Bolton School for Girls, reported a similar finding. Only 31 per cent of the students at her school had come from an auxiliary class in an elementary school; the remainder came directly from the grades.[70]

At Coleman PS, the third school whose record card collection I looked at, there was no auxiliary class for subnormals. At that school, a pattern of sending students who were over-age for their grades to junior vocational schools developed as early as the mid-1920s. Coleman was a small school (only four rooms) and did not have classes higher than junior third.[71] Upon completing junior third, many Coleman pupils went on to finish higher grades at the nearby and more spacious elementary school Gledhill PS. For other pupils, schooling simply stopped at junior third if they were old enough to go to work or to obtain a work or home permit. A third, small group continued on, but not to Gledhill. This group transferred to junior vocational school, even though they had not attended an auxiliary class for subnormals.

Fiona N. entered junior first at Coleman in September 1918, a few days shy of her ninth birthday. She repeated junior second in 1921 and spent the first half of the next school year in the second form as well. By September 1923, Fiona was nearly fourteen and still in junior third. An entry for the grade she attended in 1924–5 is missing from her Office record card, though she was probably in junior third again that year because there was no higher grade at Coleman for her to attend. In September 1925, Fiona – now nearly fifteen – was discharged to Edith L. Groves School.[72] Her brother, Vernon N., experienced a similar pattern of slow progress through the grades and eventually was discharged to Jarvis Junior Vocational when he became old enough to attend.[73] Like Fiona and Vernon, eleven other Coleman students who were transferred to junior vocational schools between approximately 1925 and the 1934–5 school year had made relatively poor school progress before they reached junior third and were subsequently moved to Jarvis, Bolton, or Groves.[74]

Junior vocational schools did not primarily enrol former auxiliary class pupils, though this was their original intent, but instead youngsters the likes of Herman I., Sarah B., Donald R., and Vernon and Fiona N. Some of them, such as Donald, school psychologists had labelled dull-normal or borderline. Others, like Fiona and Vernon, had become considerably over-age for their grades, and had not been tested for admission to an auxiliary class but were becoming too big to remain in elementary school classrooms with younger children.

Junior Vocational Schools, 1923–1935: Laying the Groundwork for Future Streaming

There is a sizeable sociological and historical literature on special education, vocational schooling, and streaming. That literature shows that youth in Canada and the United States who are working-class, black, male, or immigrants are frequently over-represented in special education programs for older pupils that often offer only a very basic, vocational curriculum. Most studies look at the post-1950 period, with earlier demographic data usually unavailable.[75] This section presents pre-1950 demographic data from pupil record cards and, where available, data from the DOE annual reports.

The analysis of pupil data in this section is used to assess the earliest origins of special education as a form of streaming for secondary school students. With only limited and imprecise data for the pre-1950 period, it is difficult to fully evaluate the extent, causes, and consequences of this early streaming. I can say that junior vocational schools in Toronto in the 1920s and early 1930s may have established the theoretical basis for forms of streaming that would later channel some working-class youngsters into the "dead end division" of the system, as critics called it by the 1970s.[76] But in this earlier period, junior vocational schools did not stream all, or even a very large percentage, of working-class Toronto youth. There are several reasons for this. First, unlike today, prior to about 1950 most school-age Canadian adolescents, even when they were the right age for it, did not attend high schools. Quite unlike the situation in United States, which achieved something resembling mass secondary school enrolment much earlier, Canadian youth continued for many more years to be carried by economic currents right out the school door before high schools could stream them anywhere.[77] Second, it is true that of the pupils who remained, a considerable number were working class. But most of these pupils attended not junior vocational schools but rather academic, technical, and commercial secondary schools, and made up very large percentages (and sometimes large pluralities) of the populations of all three in the interwar years.[78] Nor do Toronto's junior vocational schools in the 1923–35 period seem to have streamed large numbers of immigrant youth. Social sorting on a grand scale in secondary schools had not arrived.[79]

Occupation and Class

The ideas that school officials, educators, and psychologists advanced about the aims of vocational and auxiliary education and about class, race, and IQ explored above certainly would have made it possible, even seemingly natural (to them) to have overlapping groups of subnormal, dull-normal, and working-class students streamed into the same secondary school programs. Most of the class patterns in discharges to junior vocational schools from Hester How and Duke of York (tables 3.2 and 3.3) are generally quite similar to more or less cognate patterns that characterized auxiliary classes at Hester How in an overlapping period (1920–30) (see chapter 2).[80] Working-class students are well-represented in discharges to junior vocational schools. To be sure, Hester How and Duke of York were both working-class schools, so this is not surprising. Students from households where the head had no occupation, or no known occupation ("none/not available") are present in high numbers as well, especially at Duke of York.

The DOE gathered its own statistics on the occupations of heads of junior vocational school pupils' families, which also supply some perspective on questions of occupation, class, and streaming. Table 3.4 draws on DOE statistics from 1931 to 1933. (There are gaps in the earlier data, and the DOE stopped collecting it altogether after 1933.) It should be noted that the DOE's categories, which table 3.4 uses, and its

3.2 Occupation group and class of pupils discharged to junior vocational schools (JRV) from Hester How PS, 1923 to 1934–5 school years

	% discharge to JRV
Owners and managers	1.2 (n = 1)
Agents on commission	0 (n = 0)
Self-employed	9.9 (n = 8)
Middle class	0 (n = 0)
Working class (subtotal of three categories below)	74.1 (n = 60)
Skilled and semi-skilled	25.9 (n = 21)
Unskilled	48.1 (n = 39)
White collar	0 (n = 0)
None/not available	7.4 (n = 6)
Miscellaneous (cannot be classified)	7.4 (n = 6)

3.3 Occupation group and class of pupils discharged to junior vocational schools (JRV) from Duke of York PS, 1929–30[a] to 1934–5 school years

	% discharge to JRV
Owners and managers	0 (n = 0)
Agents on commission	6 (n = 3)
Self-employed	10 (n = 5)
Middle class	0 (n = 0)
Working class (subtotal of three categories below)	60 (n = 30)
Skilled and semi-skilled	20 (n = 10)
Unskilled	40 (n = 20)
White collar	0 (n = 0)
None/not available	22 (n = 11)
Miscellaneous (cannot be classified)	2 (n = 1)

[a] Duke of York PS opened in the 1929–30 school year.

3.4 Secondary school enrolment by family head (father's) occupational group, selected schools/programs, TBE, 1931–3

	1931		1932		1933	
	n	%	n	%	n	%
Jarvis Junior Vocational (boys)						
Commerce	65	11.7	55	9.7	44	7.2
Agriculture	7	1.3	10	1.8	6	1.0
Law, Medicine, Dentistry, Church	5	0.9	3	0.5	2	0.3
Teaching	0	0	0	0	0	0
The Trades and Industries	168	30.2	172	30.2	181	29.8
Labouring Occupations	73	13.1	83	14.6	89	14.7
Other Occupations	164	29.4	173	30.4	230	37.9
Without Occupation	75	13.5	73	12.8	55	9.1
Total	557	–	569	–	607	–
Edith L. Groves and Bolton (girls)						
Commerce	6	1.2	12	3.3	12	2.0
Agriculture	1	0.2	0	0	0	0
Law, Medicine, Dentistry, Church	0	0	1	0	1	0.2
Teaching	0	0	0	0	1	0.2
The Trades and Industries	124	24.2	62	17.0	88	14.9
Labouring Occupations	162	31.6	79	21.6	194	32.9
Other Occupations	30	5.8	9	2.5	0	0
Without Occupation	190	37.0	202	55.3	294	49.8
Total	513	–	365	–	590	–
Central Commerce High School						
Commerce	603	34.7	507	31.5	496	30.5
Agriculture	0	0	0	0	0	0
Law, Medicine, Dentistry, Church	27	1.6	24	1.5	28	1.7
Teaching	11	0.6	16	1.0	12	0.7
The Trades and Industries	697	40.1	491	30.5	622	38.3
Labouring Occupations	131	7.5	282	17.5	150	9.2
Other Occupations	148	8.5	89	5.5	154	9.5
Without Occupation	120	6.9	201	12.5	163	10.0
Total	1737	–	1610	–	1625	–

3.4 Secondary school enrolment by family head (father's) occupational group, selected schools/programs, TBE, 1931–3 (*cont.*)

	1931		1932		1933	
	n	%	n	%	n	%
Central Technical School						
Commerce	670	24.2	421	12.1	527	20.3
Agriculture	9	0.3	5	0.1	11	0.4
Law, Medicine, Dentistry, Church	44	1.6	84	2.4	65	2.5
Teaching	15	0.5	12	0.3	18	0.7
The Trades and Industries	724	26.1	747	21.4	595	22.9
Labouring Occupations	318	11.5	325	9.3	432	16.6
Other Occupations	698	25.2	1539	44.2	545	21.0
Without Occupation	293	10.6	352	10.1	402	15.5
Total	2771	–	3485	–	2595	–
Harbord Collegiate Institute						
Commerce	416	34.3	463	33.7	506	36.9
Agriculture	0	0	4	0.3	8	0.6
Law, Medicine, Dentistry, Church	72	5.9	62	4.5	63	4.6
Teaching	60	4.9	25	1.8	25	1.8
The Trades and Industries	552	45.5	575	41.8	544	39.7
Labouring Occupations	42	3.5	156	11.3	96	7.0
Other Occupations	54	4.4	60	4.4	77	5.6
Without Occupation	18	1.5	30	2.2	51	3.7
Total	1214	–	1375	–	1370	–

Source: Ontario, Legislative Assembly, *Report of the Minister of Education Province of Ontario*, Part II, Statistics of Elementary and Secondary Schools, Detailed Statistics (Toronto: various publishers, various years).

method of collecting information were rudimentary. It classified large numbers of students as belonging to the "other occupations" category, which distorted statistics for some schools. This makes interpreting table 3.4 especially tricky when it comes to Jarvis Junior Vocational and Central Tech, where this problem is particularly manifested.[81] As well, the Depression wreaked havoc on employment in the years table 3.4 covers, affecting what local school officials reported to the DOE about occupations and what ended up in published statistics.[82]

With their imperfections, the DOE statistics on table 3.4 still essentially show – like the pupil record card data in tables 3.2 and 3.3 – that junior vocational pupils came predominantly from households in which the head held a roughly working-class occupation, i.e., "labouring occupations" or "the trades and industries" (see table 3.4). This, however, did not distinguish junior vocational schools significantly from other Toronto high schools – for example, Central Tech and Central Commerce or even Harbord Collegiate Institute, as table 3.4 equally shows. All of these schools had sizeable working-class populations, and often pluralities of working-class students. Junior vocational schools, however, can be distinguished from these other programs by the former's relatively very large numbers of students from households in which the head in the DOE statistics is "without occupation," and by their relatively very small numbers of students from the owner-manager or professional categories: "commerce," "law, medicine, dentistry, church," and "teaching."

Ethnic Origin and Gender

It is possible, using pupil record card data, to tentatively explore ethnic origin and streaming in junior vocational schools. At Hester How, the five ethnic groups that contributed the largest proportions of pupils discharged to junior vocational schools between 1923 and 1935 were Jewish (37 per cent of discharges), Italian (17 per cent), Anglo-Canadian (13 per cent), English (9 per cent), and Polish or Russian (6 per cent each)[83] (see table 3.5). I have chosen to look here only at Hester How. The school's large and diverse non-Anglo-Canadian population supplies numbers significant enough from which to draw conclusions.

One thing that stands out in table 3.5 is that Jewish youth were the only ethnic group at Hester How from which more girls than boys were discharged to junior vocational schools. In the other ethnic groups, usually considerably more boys than girls transferred to junior vocational schools. There are different possible explanations: boys in those ethnic groups were more likely than girls to be streamed into this program; or, families from those ethnic groups preferred it as an option for boys rather than for girls. The other options for boys and girls who were not transferred to junior vocational schools at the end of public school were leaving school for work on a permit; leaving school after their sixteenth birthdays; or attending a different type of secondary school, such as an academic collegiate institute or technical or commercial school. What

3.5 Ethnic origins of girls and boys discharged to junior vocational schools (JRV) from Hester How PS, 1923 to 1934–5 school years

	N girls dischrgd to JRV	N boys dischrgd to JRV	N total pupils dischrgd to JRV	% of total dischrgd to JRV
Jewish	14	12	26	36.6
Italian	3	9	12	16.9
Anglo-Can.	2	7	9	12.7
English	2	4	6	8.5
Polish	2	2	4	5.6
Russian	1	3	4	5.6
...				
Chinese	0	1	1	1.4
All other	3	6	9	12.7

then might account for Jewish youth not fitting into the same pattern as most other ethnic groups in table 3.5? Jewish boys may have been more likely to be discharged to work, or to other secondary programs. Clues as to why may lie in historians' analysis of immigrant beliefs about education and schooling, which varied from group to group and formed patterns that can help us to explore the actions of individuals and families. The historian Lynne Marks, in a case study of Harbord Collegiate Institute in the 1920s, examined education and "patterns of cultural continuity and adaptation" among Toronto's first- and second-generation Jewish immigrants.[84] She argues that by the 1920s Jewish families had "modified" – although not completely "transformed" – their "traditional perceptions of proper female roles."[85] What she calls modifications may say something about why Jewish girls were disproportionately discharged to junior vocational schools. Traditional gender perceptions in the Jewish immigrant community, Marks argues, tended to significantly favour male education. In the sending society, the *shtetls* (Jewish towns) of Eastern Europe, boys had a longer period of formal education than girls. Families gained status from extending a son's religious studies for as long as they could afford. Daughters received very little formal schooling. "They spent most of their girlhood at home," Marks writes, "learning domestic skills, until they became *kale meydelach*, girls of marriageable age."[86] Around the time that many Canadian Jews emigrated, this sharp gender distinction in Jewish education was breaking down in Eastern Europe. It was modified even further after immigrants landed in Canada, to the point where families by the 1920s had long since dropped any opposition to public schooling for girls.[87] Yet, Marks also writes, "some continuity with Old World patterns of male privilege" in education still remained after immigration. Academic education in Toronto's collegiate institutes was a preserve for Jewish young men. In 1923, Marks demonstrates, 71 per cent of Jewish pupils entering Harbord for the first time were boys. Two years later the gap, though smaller, was still wide at 59 per cent boys.[88]

Sending a girl to a junior vocational school could both challenge and reinforce the existing gendered attitudes of Toronto's Jewish immigrants towards schooling. The junior vocational school represented a sort of happy medium for girls' secondary education; it was the kind of modification that Marks and other historians describe as reconciling traditional and emerging values.[89] On the one hand, junior vocational schools offered schooling past the elementary grades. On the other hand, they emphasized domestic skills. For Jewish families who conceded that their daughters would be educated beyond elementary school but did not wish to sacrifice their traditional view of girls' education, junior vocational schools were a potentially attractive option: gender segregated, they were also more domestically oriented than academic, technical, or commercial high schools and could be seen as preparation for marriage. The schools apparently did not carry an overpowering stigma from any association with subnormal pupils. These characteristics could explain why girls, and not boys as with the other ethnic groups in table 3.5, made up the larger proportion of Jewish discharges to junior vocational schools. However, with the relatively small numbers involved (twenty-six Jewish girls or boys discharged over a dozen years), this theory, even though the secondary literature would support it, is largely speculative.

A Final Word on Streaming in Junior Vocational Schools Prior to 1935

What do we learn about the critical question of streaming from the foregoing discussion focused on demographic analysis? One thing is that from the very beginning, Toronto's junior vocational schools enrolled proportionally larger percentages of students from some groups than from others. None of the discussion, however, should leave the impression that junior vocational schools streamed the entirety of Toronto's working-class or immigrant student populations prior to 1935. They did not. For one thing, relatively few pupils actually attended junior vocational schools; at their height in the mid-1930s, they represented only about 6 per cent of total enrolments in Toronto public secondary schools (see appendix B). There is also no evidence to support the notion that working-class pupils were forced en masse into dead-end vocational classes prior to 1935 or, for that matter, that Toronto students from modest and manual backgrounds in this period did not find their way into academic high school programs. In fact, large numbers of working-class pupils attended collegiates and technical and commercial high schools.

But this is not quite the same as saying that junior vocational schools had no relationship to streaming prior to 1935. The schools laid the theoretical basis for streaming two groups of high school students – working-class and intellectually disabled – into a single program. The existence of the junior vocational program – in particular its development as an option for a relatively broad clientele not limited to subnormal students – reinforced the emerging view that the same vocational programs that supported youth labelled this way, or labelled dull-normal, could also support a general vocational school population that in every practical sense would have been mostly working-class.

Practical Training and Successful Citizens: Programs of Study and Guidance at Junior Vocational Schools, 1923–1935

Jane Little and Grace Mackenzie, the principals of Toronto's two junior vocational schools for girls, writing jointly in their 1932 annual report, stated, "the purpose of these schools is to train the pupils to the utmost of their limited capacities that they may become good citizens."[90] Curricula at Jarvis Junior Vocational, Edith L. Groves School, and Bolton School for Girls were designed to prepare youth for citizenship in distinct ways. Part of that preparation was vocational training, including general training for occupations and industries for boys and domestic science education for girls. Junior vocational schools also tried to inculcate students with habits and attitudes that would make them compliant workers and moral citizens. As they constructed the programs of studies for junior vocational schools, auxiliary educators, school board officials, and school psychologists always kept front of mind their assumptions about what Little and Mackenzie called the "limited capacities" of their pupils, a description that referred mainly to intellectual ability but sometimes incorporated gender and class assumptions as well.

The Curriculum: Industrial and Domestic Subjects

In practice, junior vocational schools never offered much specific occupational preparation. In the 1920s and early 1930s, most of the subjects at Jarvis Junior Vocational were general. Every boy took English,
arithmetic, history, and drawing. Technical subjects were deliberately
basic. The school's shops contained only "the most inexpensive hand
tools," the school's principal W.J. Tamblyn claimed in 1930, because
"it is recognized that the vast majority of our boys can never become
skilled artisans in the highly technical trades. The majority can only
help to be mechanic's helpers. The greatest field of opportunity lies in
the factories where semi-skilled machine operators are employed."[91]
When the school made specialized options available – this was seldom – usually only a very small number of boys actually took the
courses. In the 1925–6 school year, only sixteen boys took plumbing.
In 1929–30, out of a total population of 746 pupils, 426 boys took au-
tomotive mechanics and 418 took machine shop – the two specialized
subjects with the largest enrolments. But the third most common specialized subject, carpentry, enrolled just thirty-two.[92] Other special-
izations that appeared sporadically on the course of study included
barbering, typewriting, shoe repair, pressing and cleaning, tailoring,
and caretaking.[93]

The courses at Groves and Bolton featured the same core of English,
arithmetic, and history. Vocational subjects were even less specialized.[94]
Courses at Groves and Bolton related to domestic science and were
oriented towards a quick transition from adolescence to adulthood.
The schools usually offered cooking, housekeeping, home economics,
laundry (which had a "two-fold aim"[95]), and sewing and dressmaking. Specialized options, never offered all at once, included typing,
embroidery and lacework, and millinery.[96] Stenography and banking
were offered only in intermittent years and attracted less than half the
student body. A machine-operating course (likely with electric sewing
machines) existed briefly and enrolled only a dozen girls, who had to
trek to Central Tech to use the equipment.[97] The list of subjects closely followed the mainstay workforce opportunities available to young
women at the time.[98]

Domestic science curricula at the girls' junior vocational schools reflected what the historians David Tyack and Elisabeth Hansot argue
was a "deeply ambivalent" set of feelings about young women, vocational education, and work. Educators generally did not want female

3.3 Junior vocational school, auto shop, 1930. H. James photographer. Pupils at Jarvis Junior Vocational School in the auto shop appear to pose for a newspaper photographer. In 1929–30, half the school took auto mechanics. Most vocational studies at the school were not nearly as specialized. Toronto Star Photograph Archive, courtesy of Toronto Public Library.

graduates to become permanent members of the waged workforce, an outcome that would disturb the gendered social order.[99] In the Toronto junior vocational schools, girls followed domestic science lessons they could apply in domestic service in someone else's home or as a home-maker in their own. The lessons in "plain cookery" at Bolton School for Girls are a good example of this. They were necessary, MacKenzie wrote, "as most girls are likely to do a considerable amount of cooking after they leave school, either in their own homes or as domestics in the homes of others."[100]

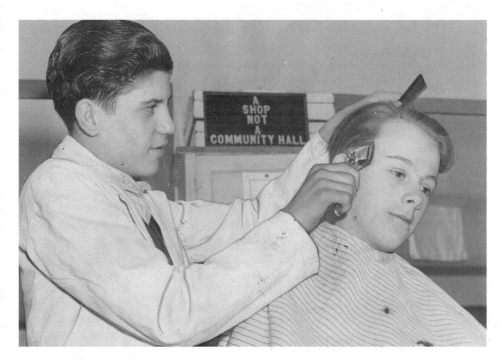

3.4 "All the trimmings," 1939. One pupil in the barbering class at Jarvis Junior Vocational School cuts the hair of another. Barbering classes like other specialized classes were offered in sporadic years. Toronto Star Photograph Archive, courtesy of Toronto Public Library.

In addition to general domestic science subjects, there was a program at Groves and Bolton that prepared and placed some girls as household servants. The Home Service and Apprenticeship course sent girls from the two schools out during school hours to act as substitute domestics in the homes of Toronto's lace-curtain elite. Little and MacKenzie described it this way in 1929: "By interesting Women's organizations in the school, we carry on an extensive employment bureau. During illness or when extra help is required for entertainment, these ladies employ our girls. The school provides a uniform, made on the power-machines in the Sewing Class, and the girl is counted as 'present' at school, if satisfactorily employed in these desirable homes. Our girls thus enjoy higher standards of living, and are made more ambitious to better their home condition at present and in the future." Wages for the pupil apprentices are not mentioned, and there probably was not pay.[101]

Domestic service was the least desirable form of female work of this era. It badly needed recruits because it was plagued by turnover. Backbreaking work, the penetrating eye of the senior servants and the mistress of the house, and the unwanted attentions of male servants and employers competed poorly against the possibility of a waged job. Waged jobs for women were toilsome and low-paying. But at least young female factory workers, office staff, store clerks, and waitresses living in the city had the small measure of freedom that came from a wage. Nor did they have to live in their employer's house.[102]

The Extracurriculum: Regulating Girls' Leisure and Sexuality

The Home Service and Apprenticeship course served a purpose beyond preparing and placing junior vocational school girls in domestic service positions. It also placed them in situations where their school could carefully monitor their personal conduct. The suspected sexual habits of subnormal girls bothered auxiliary educators in the 1920s much as they had preoccupied eugenicists a decade earlier. Jane Little wrote openly about her school's prophylactic effect on female subnormal and working-class adolescents: "This type of girl, often attractive in appearance and agreeable in manner, becomes a menace to boys of higher mentality and social position. If these girls can be taught to be self-supporting and respecting, they do not turn to an illegitimate way of earning a livelihood (always open to girls in a poor environment) in a city of this size."[103] In her book *Toronto's Girl Problem: The Perils and Pleasures of the City, 1880–1930*, the historian Carolyn Strange argues that reformers defined young, urban, wage-earning "girls" (school-age teenagers right up to wage-earning women in their twenties or even early thirties) as a social problem. Male heads of government agencies, gender-mixed groups of reformers, and women's clubs characterized the girl problem as "the vulnerability and moral irresponsibility of young working women in the city." This definition encompassed specific fears that too many young women, freed from the oversight of kin, would be victimized and seduced into casual prostitution (the "illegitimate" way of earning to which Little referred), as well as broader fears that wage-earning, footloose women threatened the labour market with their irresponsibility and inefficiency and the patriarchal social order because they would abdicate wifely and motherly responsibilities.[104]

Junior vocational schools for girls participated actively in efforts to help resolve the girl problem by attempting to regulate their students' behaviour, especially their leisure and, by extension, their sexuality. The historian Cynthia Comacchio argues that in the 1920s, Canadian schools, drawing on the ideas of experts in the emerging field of adolescence, such as the psychologist G. Stanley Hall, began to seriously consider the extracurriculum as a device for regulating young people.[105] In 1927, the TBE hired Helen Robinson, a recent graduate of the University of Toronto's social work program, as a permanent social worker at Groves and Bolton. The schools became the only two in the city to have this sort of professional on staff. The Big Sisters paid Robinson's salary.[106] Her main duty was to plan the leisure time of girls who were "potential social problems."[107] It was precisely this sort of leisure reform, Strange and Stephen argue, that was on the front lines of the battle moral reformers waged against moving pictures, theatres, amusement parks, vaudeville shows, dance halls, and other supposedly unhealthy pleasures.[108] Robinson and the Big Sisters schemed to keep junior vocational girls away from cheap urban thrills. They cooperated with other organizations, such as the Neighbourhood Workers Association, to provide supposedly more wholesome alternatives through the extracurriculum: a swimming club (at the Central Tech pool), a weekly gym class, and three-week summer holidays for some of the girls at the Bolton Fresh Air Camp. In 1930, the city's Department of Mental Hygiene took over the social work role from the Big Sisters, and Robinson moved on.[109]

For a very small number of selected junior vocational school girls, regulation extended beyond the school day, and even beyond the extracurriculum. In 1932, the TBE partnered with the Haven, a small, private charitable organization funded by the Federation for Community Service and the Ontario government, to open Ross Cottage. This "boarding home for students" was located a few blocks from Edith L. Groves School. It housed about fifteen girls, aged thirteen to sixteen, who attended Groves during the day. These were girls, Little claimed, "whose environment and home conditions were such that they could never become successful citizens" if they remained with their families. In Ross Cottage, the girls lived with "a Home Mother, under twenty-four hour supervision."[110] The Haven also managed a parallel institution, Lorimer Lodge, which was a "half-way house" for girls released from the Ontario Hospitals at Orillia and Cobourg where they had been institutionalized.[111] It was located a block from Ross Cottage.

(Remarkably, it continued to operate until 1987 and at this same location.) Some of the Lorimer Lodge girls attended girls' junior vocational schools as well.[112] There were no similar services for the boys of Jarvis Junior Vocational.

Blunders and Stupid Mistakes: Vocational Guidance and Junior Vocational Schools

In the 1920s, there was a new orientation towards preparing youngsters with intellectual disabilities to join the community instead of permanently institutionalizing them in farm colonies as people had advocated in the 1910s. Despite this change, vocational guidance experts remained troubled by their belief that subnormal, and even dull-normal, youth were unable to adapt to the community without significant assistance.

Vocational guidance at Jarvis, Groves, and Bolton was intended to help the subnormal, or for that matter dull-normal or unlabelled, student find the correct occupational niche and take her or his place in the workforce and society. Guidance specialists at the time believed that any young person who was not directed immediately upon entering the workforce to the correct employment for their gender, social station, and aptitude would become an inefficient, maladjusted, and perhaps even malcontented worker.[113] In the junior business course at Groves and Bolton in the late 1920s, for example, training in basic office skills ranked fourth after the course's three main objectives: "to help the pupil get a position; keep a position, and to make her an economical asset to the community."[114] Put another way, as historian David Hogan does, the "effort to study and reconcile the individual to the available job structure became the principal feature of the vocational guidance movement," ahead even of specific job training.[115]

Guidance for subnormal and dull-normal youth focused on selecting appropriate employment for them in the industrial economy based on their supposedly limited abilities.[116] Often, IQ score was the basis for assessing a young person's level of ability and for selecting the proper job. "Suppose there are four types of work to be performed," Sinclair wrote in his 1931 book *Backward and Brilliant Children*, before listing a factory worker who fastens nuts onto bolts, a letter carrier, a bank manager, and a university professor. "Suppose, further, that there are four children, A, B, C, and D, to be trained to fill these four positions." A, Sinclair informed his reader, was "dull and backward," B and C were more or less average, and D was "superior." Predictably, Sinclair stated that A should be trained for the factory job, B for the postal position, C to manage the bank, and D to teach undergraduates: "It would be a serious mistake to make a different allotment."[117] In fact, Sinclair went so far as to argue that "dull and backward" workers might prefer factory work over other options because they were less intelligent: "Putting nuts on bolts all day would drive D to distraction, but A finds the work quite congenial. He discovers his self-realization in doing this work well (can even do it better than C or D could do it), and may be as worthy a citizen as any."[118] All of Sinclair's thinking about guidance, he wrote, was derived from "a fundamental and far-reaching educational principle ... Namely, that a knowledge of an *exceptional* child's I.Q. at any stage of his life furnishes the master-key to unlock in large measure the hidden secrets of his adult life, the kind of work he will be able to do, the course of study he should have."[119]

Teaching students to be satisfied with low-skill occupations, or even with periods of unemployment in an economy that counted on plenty of cyclical joblessness to create a reserve labour force that drove down wages, was built into the guidance program's goal of preparing good, compliant workers. Tamblyn, in the first year of the Great Depression, credited his school with preparing students who knew enough not to "join in with unemployed gangs." Instead, he wrote reassuringly, unemployed "graduates of the Junior Vocational Schools" were "pooling" money and starting businesses, staying off "the bread line." "Throughout our whole school curriculum," Tamblyn wrote, "an effort is made to teach our pupils to render a service rather than to expect that society owes them a living."[120]

Vocational guidance for subnormal and dull-normal youth was also intended to be compensatory. Powell remarked in 1922 that "the average employer is not in business as a charity. He would not put up with the blunders and stupid mistakes these mental defectives would make when he could as easily employ young people of normal mentality who would give him less trouble." He urged special manual training for adolescent mental defectives to supposedly give them a better chance to compete with normal young people.[121] Vocational guidance for girls with disabilities emphasized the importance of attitude and appearance to make up for other shortcomings. Mona Gleason argues about this period that "conventional understandings of 'beauty' precluded bodies that were considered in any way 'abnormal.'"[122] Hence, Little and MacKenzie had ominous warnings for the pupils in their schools: "If these girls are going to keep a job, it is essential that their physical condition be the best possible to compensate for their deficiencies."[123] They continued: "If we can train these girls to support their emotions, to become obedient, courteous, and willing to co-operate, there are many positions in Toronto for the mentally limited." They further wrote: "The processes involved in these positions are very simple, usually monotonous, but, if the girl is stabilized, punctual, and willing, she is more successful than her more highly endowed sister, who has not learned to restrain her emotions. It is not the girl with the highest mental age, who is making the most successful citizen."[124]

Youth and Families Encounter Junior Vocational Schools, 1923–1935

Did junior vocational schools actually help their graduates get jobs? Were these jobs worth getting? More to the point: just how attractive was this form of schooling to youth and their families? Junior vocational school pupils possessed one advantage that younger auxiliary class pupils did not: they were adolescents. They were close to reaching – or in some cases had reached – the age when compulsory education laws no longer touched them. The parent or guardian of any pupil who reached the age of fourteen could apply for an employment certificate or home permit for that pupil. Any student, as of her or his sixteenth birthday, could exit the school system for good. Toronto junior vocational schools struggled to retain adolescents who could choose to leave. They appealed to young people through dispensing vocational guidance, providing an extracurriculum, and especially by offering programs of study that school authorities claimed would lead to stable employment. Exploring the degree to which junior vocational school pupils were swayed by the purported advantages the schools offered against the economic realities they faced offers one way to examine and evaluate the effectiveness of auxiliary education policies. It takes the assessment beyond school authorities' claims that junior vocational schools helped to prepare teenagers for work and life to examine what young people and their families actually gained from them.

With the exception of a few special cases, such as the daughters of Jewish immigrants, junior vocational schools' efforts to recruit and retain pupils failed. Given the opportunity to leave for work, students fled the schools in large numbers. They remained only when there were no jobs, such as during the Great Depression's nadir. The decision to leave junior vocational school was conditioned not only by economics

– in the cases of families who needed their youngsters' wages – but by other interests and needs that in many cases the schools did not meet.

Psychologists, school staff, and other school authorities went to great lengths to persuade and compel adolescents to attend junior vocational schools. One way they did this was through testing in the Division of Mental Hygiene. The division's psychologists had the power to diagnose and label and to recommend young people for junior vocational schools. The use of IQ tests helped to manage the admissions process as well as, much more insidiously, young people's expectations. Marvin K. discovered this as a twelve-year-old at Hester How in 1926. In June, and then again the following fall, Marvin met Lewis for a psychological examination. Marvin's Psychiatric examination report (PER) contains the details of these encounters. He had been struggling academically and trailed his same-age peers by three grades when Lewis encountered him. Marvin disliked academic work because he believed he was poor at it. Lewis commented on his "inferiority complex in regard to spelling," an indication, he surmised, that Marvin was quick to "give up." Marvin's dislike for school, however, was not total. "He pitches for the school baseball team," Lewis wrote, "and is very proud of this accomplishment, although shy in speaking of it." Marvin's work ethic was expressed not where Lewis looked for it, in his studies, but in the way that he helped his family by selling the evening newspaper on street corners every day. After his work ended at 8 or 9 p.m., Marvin stayed out until 11 p.m. every night and twice a week used the few pennies his mother left him from his pay packet to go to the movies. As to Marvin's family circumstances, Lewis noted on Marvin's PER that his father was a plumber and Jewish immigrant from Galicia.

Marvin had his own aspirations. He told Lewis that he wanted "to be a doctor or a lawyer." Lewis commented that Marvin was, however, "a bit lazy about the method of being one." He pushed a trade for him instead, putting forward furrier as a recommendation. Lewis's diagnosis, based on consecutive IQ scores of 76 and 75, was that the boy was borderline (neither subnormal nor dull-normal). He recommended a junior vocational school for Marvin when he turned thirteen. In fact, Marvin remained at Hester How and managed to make it to senior third before he left for work as a fifteen-year-old in September 1929.[125]

With young people Marvin's age, families could exercise some decision-making about further schooling. The most basic choice they faced was more schooling and the possibility that this might increase wage-earning power, or immediate access to the young person's wages or unpaid household labour. The choice had significant consequences. For working-class families – that is, for the majority of Toronto families – children's wages, however small, were at times all that stood between the family and poverty, starvation, or homelessness. The historian Michael Piva found that a working-class Toronto family of five could never hope to reach the minimum threshold for food and shelter on the wages of a single adult breadwinner. The wages of a second adult earner (spouse), and even a third earner (usually an older child), were often essential.[126] It was precisely with this predicament in mind that the new attendance laws contained the clauses granting work permits not to adolescents who were dependents but to adolescents who had dependents – their younger siblings, parents, and other kin.[127]

Junior vocational school officials acknowledged the choice families had to make. They tried to promote their programs by arguing that a short-term sacrifice was worth it for families because attending their schools increased long-term earning power. One promotional forum was the annual published school board report. In 1932, Little and Mac-Kenzie listed in it the occupations of successfully employed former students and their wages while optimistically claiming that "the training in these schools has given our graduates an advantage over those seeking employment through the employment bureau."[128] Another forum was direct interaction with parents. The very active Home and School Association of Jarvis Junior Vocational, with a board composed of involved parents and sympathetic teachers, undertook efforts to convince parents that junior vocational schools were a worthwhile time investment.[129] Open houses and parents' afternoons invited mothers and fathers to observe their boys hard at work in the school's shops.[130] At the first Home and School Association meeting of the 1929–30 school year, Tamblyn presented information to parents that he claimed showed that his school leavers earned $176 per month on average, an amount higher than other boys of the same age who had not attended the school. By further comparison, Tamblyn added, two-thirds of youth who had made the wrong choice and left the school before their training was complete had become trapped in "blind alley jobs" that paid less. Tamblyn's message: it was worth enrolling, and worth staying enrolled.[131]

The Home and School Association's boosterish approach reflected a belief, or perhaps a hope, that Jarvis Junior Vocational was effective at preparing boys for work. Perhaps sometimes it was. But boosterism betrays as well the concern on the part of the Home and School

Association's executive that other parents in the city were not sold on the program's merits. In 1934, the association made educating parents citywide about the school's mission its "main project of the year."[132] There had been "considerable discussion" at an executive meeting that year about "the name and opinion of our school as expressed around different public schools in the city, and how difficult this makes it for a parent, who has not seen the school at work, to decide to allow their boy to come." Three mothers planned to visit the school board superintendent to find out "what steps could be taken to counteract this tendency and make the work of our school better known."[133]

Despite the occupational and other benefits that junior vocational schools claimed to offer and despite the Home and School Association's lobbying, there are other indications that these schools were unpopular with pupils and parents.[134] In September 1933, her pupil record shows, Ruthie S. was supposed to attend junior third at Hester How for the fourth school year in a row. Ruthie was thirteen and apparently fed up with being in a form with mostly younger children. Lewis had examined Ruthie and had measured her IQ at 74, and the principal at Hester How had recommended her transfer to Edith L. Groves School. "To this the mother, and therefore the child, is strongly opposed," Chief Inspector Moshier wrote after he became involved in Ruthie's case at the principal's request. In an effort to sway Ruthie and her mother, Moshier drafted a letter to a Toronto physician as a third party who could meet with mother and daughter to convince them of the junior vocational school's merits. The doctor was also unable to influence Ruthie or her mother. Meanwhile, Mrs S. had asked the principal at Hester How for a transfer for Ruthie to another school. As the situation approached stalemate, the principal gave in, informing Moshier that she believed that "it would injure [Ruthie's] health to force her to attend [Groves]." Reluctantly, Moshier agreed to a transfer for Ruthie to the other school that her mother had requested.[135]

It is impossible to know how many youngsters like Ruthie there were. Her record was a rare one to which correspondence was appended, and it is in that correspondence that Ruthie's case is explained. Other types of sources that are not anecdotal, however, can provide a sense of a program's popularity, if read inferentially. A strong indication that junior vocational schools were not popular comes from average daily attendance (ADA) statistics. The DOE calculated ADA statistics for the province's schools and published them in its annual reports. The statistics were supposed to show what percentage of the school's attendance roll was present on average on any given day of the school year. R.D. Gidney and W.P.J. Millar sound a note of caution to historians using these statistics. The way that the DOE calculated ADA significantly embellished absenteeism. "To arrive at ADA," they write, "one divided the total number of days attended by all pupils during the year by the number of legal days in the school year." This crude method took too little account of students who were neither sick nor playing hooky but had in fact dropped out entirely. Students who left the school permanently – by moving to a new city, for example – were retained on the roll until the new school year and thus for the purposes of ADA were counted absent for every day remaining in the existing year. Nevertheless, ADA statistics are still helpful for making relative comparisons of absenteeism in different schools, if not exact comparisons.[136] And ADA statistics are also a good measure of the turnover rate at a school, although the DOE never intended them for this purpose.

Junior vocational schools in Toronto attained very poor ADA numbers in the period 1925 to 1935. (See figure 3.5. Data prior to 1925 are not available for junior vocational schools.) ADA at Jarvis Junior Vocational was about 70 per cent in 1925. It slipped as low as the mid-forties in subsequent years, only increasing – and then dramatically so – in the first year of the Depression. Edith L. Groves School fared about the same as Jarvis, while Bolton fared somewhat better. However, all three junior vocational schools had much worse ADAs than Harbord and Central Commerce and somewhat worse ADAs than Central Technical School.

Junior vocational schools not only achieved relatively poor ADA numbers but also leaned hard on pupils and parents to keep the former in school. Little and MacKenzie reported ominously that at their schools "the Juvenile Court and the Attendance Department of the Board of Education give valuable assistance where parents refuse to give these girls an opportunity for education."[137] Meanwhile, the Juvenile Court of Toronto offered its detention home to lock up any truant from Jarvis Junior Vocational long enough to give him "an opportunity to think seriously of his situation."[138]

If these were the sticks necessary to compel attendance, the carrots were financial aid that the Ontario government's Mothers' Allowance Commission and the Children's Aid Society doled out to encourage it. One of the main goals of mothers' allowances for single women was to remove the need for adolescent children to go to work by replacing that youngster's wage with a supplement from the state.[139] Little and Mackenzie credited the allowance with helping some women to send

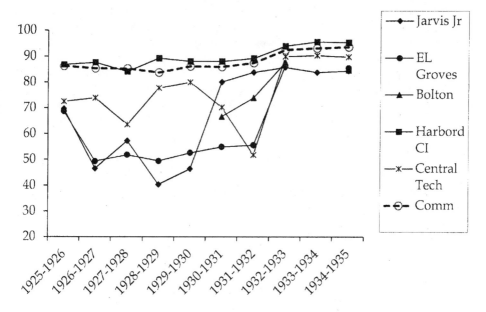

3.5 Average daily attendance (ADA). As a percentage of school's total attendance roll (*y*–axis), by year (*x*–axis), selected Toronto secondary schools, 1925–35. Source: Ontario Legislative Assembly, *Report of the Minister of Education Province of Ontario* (various publishers, various years).

their daughters to junior vocational schools "where otherwise, the girls would have to enter industry to support the home."[140] The cash must have been welcome. But there were stringent conditions to receive benefits. The Children's Aid Society had a mandate to investigate all families on its caseload and a legal option to seize any children its agents thought were being neglected.[141] The Mothers' Allowance Commission imposed strict requirements on women and had the power to cut off benefits.[142]

Even though the ADA statistics exaggerate absenteeism because of the way the DOE calculated them, they can also tell us something about drop-outs. Low ADA rates can indicate a revolving door of admissions and departures at a school. Permanent leavers, steadily streaming out of the school, depress the ADA when they are retained on the roll for the remainder of the year. A much lower ADA than other schools suggests a constant stream of drop-outs or truants – either way, a silent but not-so-subtle commentary by youth and parents on a school program that could not compete effectively for youngsters' attentions on either daily basis or a more permanent one.

Drop-outs from junior vocational schools were only reliably pre-vented by times when there was nothing to drop out for. The num-ber of adolescent students who remained in junior vocational schools increased during periods of economic collapse.[143] When jobs could be had, families pulled their children out of junior vocational schools; when jobs were scarce, families left them in. (To an extent, this was true of enrolments in all types of school program, which tended to increase during hard times when young people could find less work or no work at all.)[144] The Great Depression beginning in late 1929, for instance, pushed up ADA in junior vocational schools, especially Jarvis. The ef-fect of the Depression downturn on ADA at other secondary schools in Toronto seems less dramatic (see figure 3.5). Pupils who we could speculate were in junior vocational schools attended them because they could not find anything else to do with their time.

The Depression also spiked total enrolments in junior vocational schools (see figure 3.6). Between 1929–30 and 1932–3, junior vocational school enrolments increased by approximately 20 per cent. The highest enrolment year was 1934–5, when more than 1,400 pupils were on the registers. As was the case with increased ADA, higher enrolments coin-cided with the worsening Depression and the decline of other options.

Conclusion

Junior vocational schools started out in the early 1920s as a response to the prospect of adolescent subnormals being compelled for the first time by new provincial attendance laws to remain in school until age sixteen. The mandate of these schools was soon enough enlarged to include dull-normal pupils and others who had not previously attended aux-iliary classes. In fact, the majority of students discharged from Hester How, Duke of York, and Coleman to junior vocational schools did not transfer from an auxiliary class but rather directly from the grades.

The curriculum goal of this new form of vocational schooling was to prepare boys for low-wage jobs in the industrial economy, and girls for servant positions or homemaker roles. All junior vocational stu-dents, it was thought, required special guidance to become functioning and compliant workers. Subnormal youth especially, it was believed,

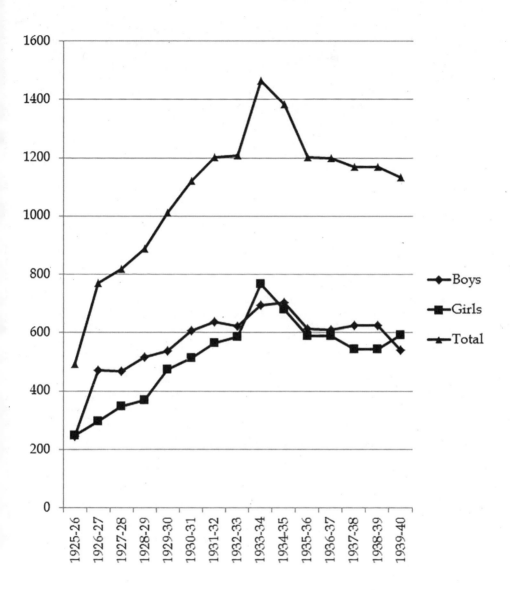

3.6 Junior vocational school enrolments, 1926–40. Number of pupils enrolled (*y*–axis), by year (*x*–axis), girls, boys, and total. Source: Ontario, Legislative Assembly, *Report of the Minister of Education Province of Ontario* (various publishers, various years).

needed guidance that could compensate for their supposedly manifest intellectual and moral shortcomings.

Junior vocational schools comprised large numbers of students from working-class backgrounds. The least well-off, such as students from households in which the head was unemployed or an unskilled worker, usually contributed large numbers of pupils to junior vocational schools. Studies of streaming, special education for adolescents, and vocational schooling conducted after 1950 would show that working-class and immigrant children were often streamed into the lowest levels of the system, including special classes. However, prior to this time, Toronto's junior vocational schools could not be said to be participating in streaming of working-class or immigrant populations, because the number of students who attended these programs was more of a trickle than a torrent. Even in 1935, when the board changed "junior vocational schools" to "handicraft schools," there were just 614 boys and 588 girls in the program out of total high school enrolment exceeding 23,000.[145] Most working-class students who attended high schools in Toronto after 1920 – and they were an increasingly large group – went to collegiate institutes or technical and commercial high schools, not junior vocational schools.

True, some segments of the city's working class seemingly readily accepted junior vocational schools for what they could do for their children. It could be speculated that some Jewish immigrant families saw advantages in junior vocational schools because these schools enabled them to enrol girls for further education as well as traditionally sought-after domestic instruction and preparation for marriage. For the most part, however, despite the boosterism of school authorities and the Home and School Association at Jarvis Junior Vocational, the families that interacted with junior vocational schools found little to suit their interests. Low ADA and low enrolments in better economic times speak for the many silent choices of junior vocational students to leave for work when it existed. Anecdotally, there was also vocal opposition to the schools, such as the sort Ruthie S. and her mother expressed.

Junior vocational schools nevertheless played a crucial role in shaping ideas about auxiliary education for adolescents, vocational guidance for young people with disabilities, and streaming. These effects reverberated through time and were still felt as late as the 1970s, when critics would eventually accuse the TBE's "special vocational" program, the direct successor program to junior vocational schools, of discriminatory streaming.[146]

Chapter Four

"A Mental Equality Where Physical Equality Has Been Denied": Sight-Saving, Speech and Hearing, and Orthopaedic Classes, 1920–1945

In 1920, R.H. Cowley called Toronto's small number of auxiliary classes "but the beginning of special provisions that must become much more extensive if wisdom and humanity are to regulate educational opportunity for all receptive children." There were still youngsters, the chief inspector continued, "for whom as yet the public schools have done little or nothing." This included "cripples, stammerers, epileptics, mutes, the blind, etc."[1] Within just a few short years, the Toronto Board of Education (TBE) would begin to do something for almost all of the children that Cowley had identified. Trustees inaugurated sight-saving classes for partially sighted youngsters, hired a specialist teacher of the deaf, opened day school classes for youngsters who were totally deaf and another type of class for youngsters who were hard of hearing (partially deaf), started a speech correction clinic, and finalized arrangements for "orthopaedic" classes for students with physical disabilities.

These new auxiliary programs were some of the most specialized, technical, and treatment-oriented yet. Their appearance by about 1920 followed significant changes to thinking about disabilities that had taken place over the previous two to three decades. Orthopaedics' late arrival as a respected medical discipline in the 1890s, the early stirrings around the same time of rehabilitation and occupational therapy, and later the heightened visibility of thousands upon thousands of disabled First World War veterans pushed popular ideas about disability partly away from a Victorian "affliction narrative." In the Victorian way of thinking, disability was incurable and dependency inevitable. Disability was God's will, and there was nothing people could, or should, do to change it. Secular ideas about disability never fully displaced religious ones in the first half of the twentieth century.[2] But modern surgical and therapeutic advances now suggested that many adults and children with disabilities could, with proper treatment and through their own perseverance, eventually conquer disability, escape dependency, and attain a level of normalcy that the Victorians would not have believed possible.[3]

Writing about polio in a similar time frame, the historian Daniel Wilson argues that restoring the children it affected to the most able state possible was considered the pinnacle of successful treatment: "Prevailing cultural values held that the only acceptable response to the disabilities caused by polio was to try as hard as possible to overcome any disability; to walk if at all possible; and to return to home, school, and work looking, behaving, and moving as normally as possible."[4] Auxiliary educators by the 1920s reassured mostly grateful parents and a receptive public that the young who successfully conquered disability on these sorts of terms could achieve the status of near-equality with non-disabled people. H.J. Prueter, the principal of Wellesley Public School (PS), which held Toronto's first orthopaedic classes, wrote that young people in those classes were capable of "a mental equality" with their normal schoolmates "where physical equality has been denied."[5] Or as Jean Hampson, a teacher and occupational therapist at the same school, described her work: "It is simply trying to make handicapped children as normal as possible."[6] With this belief about achievable normalcy in mind, all of the auxiliary classes described in this chapter used the regular academic program, and modified it as little as possible. This made them much different from classes for subnormals and junior vocational schools, which used a revamped academic program.[7] Pupils in the programs this chapter describe completed more grades and attained higher levels of schooling than any other auxiliary pupils. But if these programs offered some disabled children an education more equal to that which non-disabled children received, disabled children were still expected to pay a high price. The schools expected them to adapt their bodies and senses in order to achieve normalcy. While some were able and willing to adapt, others were not capable or were reluctant. Educators at this time simply did not yet possess the modern sensibility that disability is not a deficit – the perspective that would have been necessary for them to acknowledge that integration could come without normalcy, if the schools adapted to their pupils instead of expecting their pupils to adapt to them.

Education as Prevention, Therapy, and Correction:
Attempts to Foster Normalcy

Sight-Saving Classes

The TBE inaugurated sight-saving classes at Orde Street PS in 1921.[8] The classes modified instruction in ways intended to preserve the remaining eyesight of partially sighted students whose vision was less than one-third of normal. Youngsters whose vision was less than one-tenth of normal ordinarily were transferred to the provincial boarding school, the Ontario School for the Blind at Brantford.[9] An eye specialist visited the sight-saving classes weekly to check for signs of eyestrain, which this program went to great lengths to try to prevent. Teachers vigilantly forbade excessive reading and drawing.[10] Classrooms were modified to reduce glare. A special TBE committee on sight-saving recommended purchasing "doubles [sic] shades in unglazed dull buff fabric" and "a clock with unglazed surface," and also requested approval from the administration department for a budget to paint classroom walls with a special dull finish.[11] Students in the classes were issued sight-saving editions of Ontario school texts. Authorized in 1931, these were identical to standard textbooks but had been "multigraphed in large type." Before they became available, one devoted teacher, Miss Rush, had retyped textbooks herself, a significant investment of her time and energy in her pupils.[12] For children who had difficulty seeing even large type, the board purchased two pairs of "Easy Read" glasses, a mechanical device that could be opened up over a book page to further magnify it.[13]

Educators believed that children whose eyesight was already compromised were at high risk of further damage, disability, and eventual dependency.[14] But with the correct intervention in the sight-saving class, and by teaching the regular curriculum, these challenges could be prevented or partly overcome. "Through the years the idea of 'an equal chance for all children' has been exemplified by the sight saving classes," TBE chief inspector D.D. Moshier, Cowley's successor in this post, wrote in 1930. "The recognition that their aims and objectives include those of the regular classes has changed the outlook of the pupils from one of inferiority and dependence because of physical difference to one of preparedness and independence in facing a limitation with which they have learned, in a measure, to cope."[15]

Speech and Hearing Classes

In 1922, a year after it opened sight-saving classes, the TBE hired expert teacher Imogen Palen to develop special hearing and speech classes. Palen had previously taught at the Ontario School for the Deaf (OSD), a provincial boarding institution at Belleville. She had also received teacher training at the School for the Deaf at Columbia University in New York City and at the Central Institute of the Deaf in St Louis. Her first position in Toronto involved going school to school to instruct individual children with hearing and speech difficulties. In 1924, trustees approved permanent classes for "very-hard-of-hearing" children (who had some residual hearing) at Rose Avenue PS, classes for "totally deaf" children at Clinton PS, and speech correction pull-out classes at several other schools. The trustees made Palen "senior teacher" for these programs. They also appointed her director of the speech correction clinic that treated such "defects" as "stuttering, stammering, lisping, defective phonation and foreign accent and articulation."[16] It was important to correct speech problems such as stammering, Palen once wrote, because "stammerers cannot take and hold positions in the community which their original mental endowment and their educational opportunities should fit them to occupy, they are an economic loss to the state."[17]

Palen was an ardent advocate of "pure oralism." She successfully implemented this pedagogical method as the only one used in Toronto's auxiliary programs for deaf and hard-of-hearing pupils, although her efforts were not without controversy.[18] Palen and other oralists taught deaf and hard-of-hearing children to read lips and speak. They did not teach sign language. In fact, their pure oralist method totally forbade teachers from using and teaching manual signs.[19] Bolstering pure oralism were eugenicists, nativists, progressives, and many medical professionals. They feared the expansion of a deaf community that used only sign language and intentionally separated itself from hearing people, disdained signing deaf people as backward, or viewed deafness as a pathological condition that needed modern medical treatment. Pure oralism, used in day school classes in public schools, was presented as a powerful corrective to these problems.[20] Palen wrote that speech and lip-reading instruction represented "the making of the deaf child *a part of* the community, instead of *apart from* the community."[21] The TBE's still relatively new superintendent, C.C. Goldring, who had replaced Moshier at the head of the bureaucracy in 1932, agreed.[22] He stated in a 1935 radio address (an ironic medium given the subject matter) that oralist teaching, used alongside the regular public school curriculum, would make deaf children "as nearly like hearing children as possible."[23]

Oralist day school classes like the ones at the TBE immersed deaf children in a public school environment where signing was not common. This made day schools not only unlike the provincially or state-operated boarding schools for the deaf, such as the OSD (although it also was oralist by this time), but also very controversial because deaf people saw them as endangering sign language. Though by the early twentieth century signing was under serious threat from oralists even at the boarding schools where it had originated, deaf people still managed to keep it alive. It was a struggle to preserve their identity. The historian Douglas Baynton explains that deaf people cannot do without signs, "for they are both members of a species that by nature seeks optimal communication, and inhabitants of a sensory universe in which that end cannot be achieved by oral means alone." For that reason, he continues, "it is also no accident that deaf people continued to use sign language throughout the long years of its proscription in the schools, and that the living language today called American Sign Language has been handed down, generation to generation, for nearly two hundred years without interruption."[24] Toronto was only one of a relatively small number of cities to establish oralist day school classes that attempted to interfere with the sign language tradition, joining Boston, Erie, and others.[25] The TBE's decision to open day school classes for deaf children at Clinton – a regular public school – was immensely provocative, with the deaf-led Ontario Association of the Deaf strongly opposed on the grounds that the classes were an attempt by hearing educators to suppress sign language.[26]

The other type of class – the hard-of-hearing classes, for partially deaf students – were also oralist and taught lip-reading. By the late 1930s, pupils in them at TBE schools were using brand new group hearing aid technology that was closely aligned with oralist goals. Mechanical hearing aids augmented residual hearing, enabling teachers to more quickly teach pupils to read lips, which in turn cleared timetable space for the regular curriculum.[27] (Hearing aids could not be used with totally deaf children at Clinton, who had no residual hearing to enhance.) A 1946 school board booklet for parents referred to hearing loss as "a serious handicap to a child since it prevents him, in a measure, from entering the world of ideas about him," but also reassured parents that the board "provided expert teachers and modern mechanical aids to assist children to overcome this handicap."[28]

Orthopaedic Classes

School trustees cut the ribbon on Toronto's first orthopaedic class at Wellesley PS in April 1926.[29] Prior to opening the orthopaedic classes, the TBE had employed visiting – or "extramural" – teachers who went to the homes of children who were disabled or had serious illnesses and could not come to school. Miss Hannah Milne became the TBE's first visiting teacher in 1921 and later taught orthopaedic classes at Wellesley as well. Opening the orthopaedic classes never completely curtailed extramural program enrolments, which in 1930 comprised 105 pupils taught by seven visiting teachers.[30] Orthopaedic classes in the schools resembled sight-saving classes and hearing and speech classes in that they were supposed to help young people surmount disabilities and achieve greater normalcy, leading eventually to adult independence.

Orthopaedic classes enrolled children that the schools classified "crippled," such as "spastics" (children with what is now called cerebral palsy); others with different forms of paralysis; and youngsters with disabilities caused by muscular dystrophy, tuberculosis of the bone, or another illness. The largest group enrolled, however, were young people who had become disabled from the effects of polio, also known then as infantile paralysis. This group included scores of casualties who contracted the disease in a particularly serious national epidemic that in autumn 1937 closed Toronto schools for more than a month.[31] Nearly all of the children who attended the orthopaedic classes wore braces or splints or used crutches or wheelchairs.[32] Principal Prueter, expressing a common view in this period, wrote that "the crippled child in a wheel-chair daily watched the procession of normal children pass on their way to school and was compelled to realize that for him life held no promise of future independence or self-sufficiency. His lot was cast, – a burden to himself, to his parents and to society at large."[33]

Educators believed that to foster educational equality for crippled children it was necessary to bring them to the schools. This required transportation services. The board was reluctant at first to transport crippled pupils because of the cost and danger involved. Milne and trustee Edith L. Groves were instrumental in convincing school officials that it could be done cheaply enough and safely.[34] Achieving transportation services for crippled children was just one way that Groves contributed to auxiliary education in Toronto. Her wide involvement with auxiliary programs over more than a decade is a prime example of the sometimes-complicated motivations that drove people to work on behalf of auxiliary education in this period. A former teacher, Groves's eclectic accomplishments included minor literary fame as a published children's poet and playwright. She also served on the executive of the Toronto Committee on Mental Hygiene and was the secretary of the Ladies' Canadian Rifle Club. (The rumour was that she was a "crack shot."[35]) After her step-son's death in the First World War, and the death of her husband, the respected school principal W.E. Groves, in Toronto shortly afterwards, Groves turned to elected politics to further her interests in education and reform. In 1919, she campaigned successfully for school trustee in Ward 7. Its electors would return her a further twelve times until her death in 1931. Her fellow trustees chose her in 1929 as the board's first woman chair. Drawn from the outset of her trustee tenure to eugenics – she was a personal friend of Helen MacMurchy's and may have even been her pupil at Jarvis Collegiate in the 1880s – Groves was also sympathetic to the plight of physically disabled children who were cut off from schools. The TBE would name a girls' junior vocational school after Groves in recognition of her deep commitment to auxiliary education.[36]

It was in 1926 that, partially thanks to Groves, "grey buses" belonging to the Toronto Transportation Committee began to bring crippled children to Wellesley. The cost to the board was twenty-seven dollars per day for just thirty students, though the Ontario Department of Education partly subsidized the expense. The buses delivered the children by 10 a.m. and returned them home no later than 3 p.m., making for an abbreviated school day. Two school custodians greeted the children upon arrival and helped to carry them off the buses. Busing was celebrated by progressives, including the National Council of Women, and by auxiliary education promoters, such as Groves, as a historic achievement.[37]

Busing crippled children to school was one thing; getting them into classrooms was another. The early twentieth century's urban "egg-crate" schools, as one historian calls them, with their stacked-up storeys and steep staircases, were far from barrier-free.[38] To Milne, inaccessible public school buildings represented the "absolute neglect" of crippled children's education. "The last time you passed our City Public Schools," she wrote in 1926, "Did you notice the entrance? Did it look as if it were built with a view to encouraging a lame child to come in? Did you see any way by which a mother could wheel an invalid chair into a class-room? Did the inevitable flight of concrete steps have a friendly hand-rail by the help of which the chap with the dragging foot or heavy brace could help himself up? NO!"[39] The school board authorized a series of building renovations at Wellesley that were remarkably similar to modifications that are made to schools today to accommodate disabled young people. A photograph of the school from 1926 shows a newly erected wooden ramp running up the outside of the building that bypassed stairs to give wheelchair access. Handrails were installed in a few bathrooms to create "special lavatory accommodation."[40] Modifications improved the building in noticeable ways, but they did not make Wellesley, a school constructed in the nineteenth century, fully accessible. The school had a completely wood interior, from walls to staircases. The teaching staff was particularly concerned about fire, especially since the building had nearly burned to the ground in 1923. They eventually decided that if another fire were to occur, "sturdy" senior boys would rush to the orthopaedic classes and carry their schoolmates to safety. The children practiced this emergency plan successfully in drills.[41]

Innovative in accommodations, Toronto's orthopaedic classes also boasted some of the most modern and radical forms of treatment and correction available in any of the new auxiliary programs of the 1920s. In 1927, the TBE hired Hampson to the Wellesley staff.[42] She was a First World War veteran and "pioneer in the application of remedial therapy for children."[43] Judith Friedland explains that women such as Hampson trained initially during the war as "ward aides," a type of work that later in the 1920s evolved into occupational therapy. Hampson took the ward aides course that the University of Toronto began to offer in 1918.[44] Her training would have prepared her to teach "bedside occupations," such as basketmaking and painting, to recovering hospitalized soldiers who had suffered injuries like the loss of a limb. Bedside occupations were intended to keep the soldiers busy and to motivate their recovery until they were well enough to be vocationally retrained for the workforce.[45] Hampson would later leave Wellesley during the Second World War to work at the Astley-Ainslie Institute, a rehabilitation hospital in Edinburgh.[46]

At Wellesley in the 1930s, Hampson taught academic subjects and carried out occupational therapy and "remedial" regimens with crippled students. She described starting out with "handwork" and "manual arts," leading children in activities such as "making book covers" and

4.1 "Vocational school opening, Mrs Groves and Premier Ferguson, key," 1929. City of Toronto Archives, *Globe and Mail* fonds, fonds 1266, item 16937.

other craft work. But she moved quickly from this to what she called "remedial work." This involved children in activities that made them practice movements their disabilities made difficult. Hampson offered as examples: "One girl has a very weak arm and while playing badminton is required to pick up the bird with it." Another boy developed his ability to move his shoulders by throwing beanbags and balls. Only a few children could not engage in remedial work and stuck with crafts.[47] The craft and remedial work that Hampson described are consistent with occupational therapy's shift by the 1930s towards medicine and away from the ward aide work Hampson did in the late 1910s – "from restoring people to productivity to fixing their broken parts," Friedland writes.[48] Chief Inspector Moshier recounted approvingly in 1930 that of fourteen Wellesley spastics who worked with Hampson, two had been

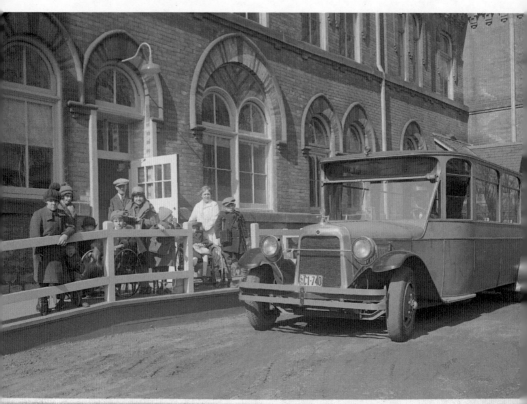

4235 Transportation Crippled Scholars (Executive) Apr.15/

4.2 "Transportation, crippled scholars," 1926. Alfred Pearson photographer. A Toronto Transportation Commission bus waiting at Wellesley PS. Note the special wooden ramp that was constructed to enable children to exit the bus and enter the school building. City of Toronto Archives, Toronto Transit Commission fonds, Central photograph series of the Toronto Transit Commission, item 4235.

"taught to balance on their feet," three had learned to walk, and nearly all now wrote. "The majority of spastics have improved in speech, finger movements, and in walking," he added.[49] Therapists and special educators believed that children who learned to walk, write, and execute other movements would be more normal, which they also defined in part as being less reliant on others. Hampson contributed to the section on "orthopedic work" in the 1933 manual for Ontario auxiliary class teachers – Harry Amoss and L. Helen DeLaporte's *Training Handicapped Children* – which contains lines such as, "No single phase in the education of an orthopedic child is so important as the development of a spirit of confidence and independence."[50]

In addition to occupational therapy, more dramatic treatment was available to some orthopaedic class pupils. By the 1930s, Prueter and Moshier promoted surgery for crippled children.[51] Surgery represented a radical attempt – not always successful – to correct physical disabilities by restoring normal function or appearance.[52] Moshier reported enthusiastically on visits to Wellesley by the paediatric surgeon Dr R.M. Wansbrough, and by Dr Goldwin W. Howland, who founded Canada's first occupational therapy department at Toronto General Hospital.[53] In 1930, these visits resulted in several Wellesley pupils going for operations. One who had successful surgery to address the effects of polio, Moshier wrote, "now walks without crutches for the first time in fifteen years." He added that "three others, seeing the result, have had successful operations. More are to follow."[54] Moshier, like many auxiliary educators and physicians, eschewed adaptations that did not correct disability – for instance, crutches or wheelchair uses – even if wheeling and other adaptations were functionally as good as or even superior to walking. Only in the 1940s would Canadian rehabilitation professionals begin to perceive, and then eventually accept, that the wheelchair offered a mobility benefit that helped disabled people rather than hindering them.[55]

Vocationalism: Minimizing Handicaps, Becoming Self-Reliant

Vocational training and guidance took on special importance when educators attempted to turn disabled children, whom they perceived to be at great risk of becoming social dependents, into productive members of society. A primary objective of vocational guidance for this group was to get them to see themselves as future workers and citizens. "The school may do much to prepare the handicapped for future employment by developing in them the proper point of view," Goldring wrote in a report he authored on this subject titled *Occupations Available for the Physically Handicapped*. "They must be made to feel that they are just like other people ... The school can train the handicapped to be self-reliant and self-respectful."[56]

Once self-respect and self-reliance were instiled, vocational preparation for young people with physical disabilities was supposed to get them ready for employment that was deemed appropriate in light of their perceived or actual physical limitations and of their gender.[57] Goldring wrote that the schools should help young people with disabilities "to choose an occupation which will minimize their physical handicaps." He added that "training for them should be essentially vocational and boiled down so they can go to work as soon as possible."[58] His report on employment opportunities for the physically disabled contained a lengthy list of occupations, with detailed classifications of the suitability of each one for women or men with a range of incapacities. The statement "in general, people with leg deformities can perform any of those tasks requiring hands and brains, where continuous standing or walking are not required" is typical of the observations made in the report. Based on his appraisal of "a recent survey in New York City," Goldring listed two dozen positions he considered suitable for men with leg disabilities, occupations such as "bookkeeper, draughtsman, pharmacist, printer, optical mechanic, [and] assemblers of automobile parts, radios, electrical appliances, and fountain pens." For women with the same form of disability, Goldring endorsed a more limited list of careers, including "all kinds of hand and machine sewing" and some secretarial work. For other groups of physically disabled people, Goldring had entirely different lists that were equally detailed and divided by gender. He recommended that deaf young people, even though they "can be taught to become good lip readers," steer away from "occupations where fluent speech is necessary, such as selling, telephone operating, and certain professions." He also recommended that young people with visual impairments avoid most professions because they were "sometimes handicapped by their inability to do the necessary amount of reading."[59]

Adolescents who attended Toronto's orthopaedic, sight-saving, and speech and hearing classes, however, could actually prepare for a relatively wide range of occupations because these programs offered high school-level classes that were only slightly modified. This made them quite unlike the programs in junior vocational schools, which did not offer secondary-level work leading to a diploma or to a transfer to an academic, technical, or commercial high school. In 1928, the board implemented "a modified course in High School work" for students in the Orde sight-saving classes who had passed the high school entrance examination.[60] Students in 1932 were doing all of the work that fully sighted young people did in the lower high school forms. In June, a handful wrote the departmental examinations that at that time were required to move from one high school grade to the next.[61] For a time, Moshier and Inspector N.S. MacDonald thought that strictly academic work, with its heavy reading load, would damage the eyesight of sight-saving class students. Although Moshier allowed academic education for them to continue, he preferred that they take less reading-intensive studies in the technical, vocational, and commercial branches of the secondary schools. The other reason to pursue these courses, he wrote, was that sight-saving students had a "crying need ... for vocational training under conditions suited to their handicap."[62]

The orthopaedic classes offered upper-level elementary school-work. By 1932, sixteen pupils had achieved high school entrance standing or had completed senior fifth. Of these, five continued on to high school.[63] It is not clear how the high schools, just as physically inaccessible as the lower schools, accommodated former Wellesley pupils. In 1934, the TBE opened high school classes for adolescents who were deaf but could read lips at Central Technical School (for girls) and at Jarvis Junior Vocational School (for boys).[64] A small number of students who attended these classes graduated high school. A few went on to university.[65]

Goldring was aware that employers discriminated against disabled people in hiring. The schools, he believed, had a duty to prepare disabled pupils to face hard prejudice and to help them to surmount it. In his report on occupations for physically disabled people, he observed that: "in addition to the limitations in choices of available occupations, because physical defects prevent the performance of certain tasks, the physically handicapped individual must face certain other disadvantages due to the attitude of many employers. There are some employers who do not like to see disabled persons around their building, or claim that other employees object, or that their customers may object. This anti-social attitude is sometimes fairly strong and it is difficult to overcome."[66] He continued that "probably the real solution of this difficulty rests chiefly with the handicapped people themselves, and in that, the school has a function." Schools, Goldring seemed certain, could improve attitudes – if they promoted normalcy for disabled people: "The school should train the handicapped to think of themselves as normal people and the handicapped and non-handicapped should mingle freely in work and play. If the handicapped are thus trained from childhood to associate on terms of equality with normal people, and if normal children in turn are accustomed to associate freely with the handicapped, the differences present in some industries will be minimized."[67] Although he placed the onus on people with disabilities to conquer discrimination, Goldring still acknowledged its existence as a problem.

Parents of Disabled Children Encounter Auxiliary Education

Parents often responded enthusiastically to prevention, treatments, academic instruction, and vocational guidance that promised greater normalcy for their physically disabled, deaf, hard-of-hearing, or partially sighted children. Some were prepared to go to significant lengths to gain auxiliary education and services for their offspring. Robert Hedley and his parents lived in suburban York County, beyond the TBE boundary. Hedley's parents petitioned the school board in 1926 to allow him to enrol in the orthopaedic class. The trustees approved the request on the condition that the Hedleys would daily convey Robert from their suburban home to a point inside city limits where he could meet the bus that would take him the rest of the way to Wellesley.[68] Palen reported in 1928 that "several families moved to Toronto from outside points" for their children to attend the Clinton oralist day school. Other parents relocated to gain access to classes at Rose Avenue and Dovercourt PS for children who were hard of hearing.[69]

The TBE usually charged non-resident tuition fees to out-of-district pupils who attended its schools. Sometimes a child's local school board paid part, or all, of those fees. The Forest Hill School Board (serving an affluent inner suburb of Toronto) paid Catherine W.'s fees, more than $300, to attend a sight-saving class at Hester How PS in 1941.[70] That same year, a Toronto resident who was a Catholic separate school supporter – one Mr Ferrari – asked the public school board to admit his child to one of its sight-saving classes. Ferrari pledged to redirect his school taxes from the separate school board to the TBE. The trustees, however, only agreed to admit Ferrari's child if the separate board paid the TBE more than $200 to make up the difference between Ferrari's tax assessment and the estimated $275 the public school trustees determined it would cost to school his child. (It is not known whether the separate school board agreed to the request.)[71] Better-off families could afford fees without assistance or even private instruction. In 1934, Donnie B.'s father, who was a manufacturer, withdrew Donnie from the sight-saving class at Hester How and sent him to a private tutor.[72] Private lip-reading lessons also existed in Toronto for children whose parents could afford them.[73] Even if fees and other costs were nearly out of reach, it was relatively common for less well-off families in this period to care enough about treatments for disabled children that they made significant financial sacrifices to pay for them.[74]

There are fewer accounts of parents trying to prevent their children from having to attend one of the auxiliary programs this chapter describes. Pat F.'s parents refused to send him to a sight-saving class when he was eight years old because they worried he could be injured taking the streetcar to the school on his own. Only when he reached age twelve did Pat begin to make that trip from his east-end home to a sight-saving class at Hester How. Other parents who refused sight-saving classes offered different reasons.[75] Toronto school inspector D.D. MacDonald – whose DPaed thesis was on this auxiliary program – cited the example of the parents of one boy who reportedly declined to send him to a sight-saving class because they feared that putting him in "with other children of defective eyesight"[76] would disadvantage him.

Progressive ideas about child development and child-rearing that influenced reformers swayed parents of disabled children as well. The psychologist G. Stanley Hall found considerable support from both groups for his view that for proper development to occur, children should be placed under their mother's direct care wherever possible and not in institutions. This marked a significant departure from the "scientific charity" of the late nineteenth century, which often promoted institutionalization as preferable to a child continuing to reside in an unsuitable home.[77] By the 1920s, the desire to keep mothers and children together motivated parents, as well as educators, to seek options for deaf and partially sighted children that bypassed the provincial boarding schools that had loomed so large in the education of these children in the nineteenth century.[78] Groves lamented cases in which parents sent a deaf child to board at the OSD "at a tender age."[79] "By establishing day classes for these children," Palen wrote in 1929, "we are preserving for them their birthright of a childhood in their own homes and providing an education as well."[80] Nellie MacDonald, another Toronto lip-reading teacher, went so far as to claim that the board opened its oral day school classes "for the sake of the mothers of Toronto deaf children," who despaired at their child's early departure from the home.[81]

One mother whose child attended Clinton, in a bid to improve her child's speech and lip-reading abilities, took the unusual measure of enrolling herself in correspondence courses for Mothers of Little Deaf Children given by the Wright Oral School in New York City. She later moved to New York with her daughter to continue their studies.[82]

A few Toronto parents willingly lobbied for programs such as day school classes or devices such as hearing aids that were known to support oralist instruction. Oralism's appeal was especially powerful when it beckoned to hearing parents who longed for their child to be normal or to experience a normal childhood. Hearing parents felt strong, frequently negative emotions about their child's lack of hearing. The principal at Clinton wrote in a letter to Goldring in 1945 that at learning unexpectedly that a child was deaf, "most parents are utterly bewildered and heart-broken."[83] In 1925, Toronto parent Owen Elliott, whose son attended the OSD, wrote a letter to the *Toronto Daily Star* seeking out other parents of deaf children who would help him request more day school classes in city schools. The emotional weight of sending his child off to Belleville for nine-month stretches with no break for Christmas, Elliott wrote, was "difficult to bear" for the whole family. He wanted his son and others like him to "attend day classes and spend their time at home the same as normal children."[84] Florence Gilchrist, whose daughter attended a class for hard-of-hearing children at Kimberley PS, petitioned the TBE in 1943 for hearing aids for her daughter and her classmates. As a result of her efforts, it eventually agreed to purchase the devices for all of its hard-of-hearing classes at a cost of more than $5,000. A shortage of materials caused by the Second World War prevented the company that made the hearing aids from delivering for over two years.[85]

Compared to support for pure oralism, parents' objections to it as an ineffective method in deaf education were rare, although not unknown. Don Moore's parents initially enrolled him at the OSD. But Don had difficulty with lip-reading and speech and floundered academically as a result. His father at first "scolded" him for laziness. But, as Don's father would tell the Ontario Association of the Deaf as its invited guest at its 1944 biennial meeting, Don's problem was in fact pure oralism. Realizing this, Mr Moore withdrew Don from the OSD and registered him instead at the MacKay School in Montreal, a provincial boarding school for Protestant Quebecers that at that time allowed signs. Telling his story to the association membership as a convert to sign-language instruction, Moore stated that signing had "given the boy his chance."[86]

Pure oralism was especially contentious as a method in deaf education precisely because many deaf adults, including Moore's association audience, rejected it as ineffective and impractical – or worse, as an affront to a separate deaf culture.[87] Deaf adults argued that deaf children should not be made to "imitate hearing people," as David Peikoff, the Ontario Association of the Deaf's activist president, stated in 1945.[88] The separate deaf culture was based on "the sign language," which is what deaf people called their rich manual language, consisting of its own unique grammar, syntax, and expressions.[89] In education, deaf people usually preferred the combined method over pure oralism.[90] Unlike pure oralism, it permitted teachers of the deaf to use and to teach sign language combined with lip-reading and speech instruction. But the combined method was seldom found in day schools and never found in avowedly oralist ones such as Toronto's.[91] The city's day school erupted in controversy in deaf circles when Peikoff publicly challenged oralism there in 1945.[92] He accused Goldring of being over-committed to an ineffective method that did not meet the progressive test of child-centredness. He wrote in a letter to the *Star* that "beneath all the glitter and glamour of prepared public demonstrations, the Clinton Street day school has not been able to equip the greatest number of their graduates with a truly liberal education." Ninety per cent of Clinton's deaf graduates, Peikoff alleged, abandoned lip-reading upon leaving school. The imposition of "strict oralism" was "wishful thinking" that was damaging when most pupils failed to learn to read lips.[93] "The humanitarian rule is that the method should be fitted to the child, rather than the child to the method," Peikoff stated, repeating a slogan that by the 1940s deaf organizations in different parts of Canada and the United States had adopted.[94]

Parents of deaf children were thus in a double bind. They were criticized by oralist educators and by deaf adults. Even though oralists preferred the home as the ideal setting for children's development, this did not stop them from judging how some parents raised children who were deaf, were hard-of-hearing, or had speech problems.[95] Palen scolded parents who did not consent to lip-reading instruction for their hard-of-hearing child, telling them that they were risking the child's mental health.[96] Deaf adults, however, who sought to defend sign language and deaf culture against the perceived oralist foe, upbraided hearing parents for collaborating with oralist teachers. "A Friend of the Deaf" wrote to the *Star* in 1925 in response to some alleged oralist "boosting" in that paper.[97] The letter-writer attempted to shame hearing parents into revealing their true reasons for opposing sign language, and suggested they felt signing was indecorous with its "vulgar" hand motions and drew attention to their child's difference in public.[98] It was largely mothers who carried the burden of blame laid on parents of all manner of children with disabilities, including deaf, partially sighted, and physically disabled youngsters. Canadian mothers in this period, as Kari Dehli and Mona Gleason show, were routinely expected to assume responsibility for their child's education, even for their offspring's "successes and failures."[99] By the 1930s, as we will see in chapter 6, with the rise of child guidance and adjustment theories, psychologists even more regularly blamed mothers for disabled children's problems.

Young People Encounter Auxiliary Education: Acceptance, Avoidance, and Ambivalence

Young people were less likely than their parents to wholeheartedly embrace the new auxiliary programs, their methods, and educators' promises of normalcy and greater integration into schools with majority non-disabled populations. But they did not steadfastly reject these things, either. Instead, they experienced, and often also expressed, a range of acceptance, avoidance, and ambivalence.

The schooling experience of a deaf Toronto boy named Julius Wiggins is a good example of ambivalence towards auxiliary programs, methods, and normalcy. His remarkable memoir, *No Sound* – a book he signed to a translator who transcribed it into written English – describes these experiences, including his schooling in oralist classes at Clinton. In the sign language debates that adults waged around him, he was not strongly committed to one side or the other. He had little regard for lip-reading and speech instruction and found oralism tedious. "The entire speech and lip reading business was an awful bore," he signed, "because there never were any explanations. We did as we were told, no more and, if possible, less."[100] Wiggins resented the time-consuming process of learning to read lips and to speak because, he stated, it held him and other deaf children back academically. At the OSD, he did not learn to read and write English until grade 3. Many students at the school, because they had to learn to read lips first, began academic subjects such as arithmetic, history, and nature study much later than public school pupils of the same age.[101]

One reason that many children disliked lip-reading was that learning to read lips and learning to speak – the two interdependent components of the pure oralist method – were very difficult, especially for children who were born deaf and infants who were deafened before they first spoke. Typical instructions written by oralist teachers for their colleagues described a complicated method with many challenges. First, deaf children learned through touch how to speak. In this initial phase of instruction, the teacher placed the child's finger on the teacher's face. This way, the child could feel the vibration in the teacher's voice when she spoke. The child then practiced reproducing an identical vibration with her or his own voice. These exercises were repeated over and over until the child began to comprehend. There were no other direct aids, although sometimes children heightened their sense of touch by feeling vibrations made by chords their teacher played on a piano. Mastering even a little speech took a great deal of energy and practice. Lip-reading was the method's second instructional phase, and was every bit as difficult as learning speech. The pupil had to very carefully observe the movements on other people's faces when they spoke. Then she or he had to learn, with patience and practice, to associate each movement, or set of movements, with a particular sound or word.[102] Nellie MacDonald, an experienced Toronto lip-reading teacher, warned her colleagues that it typically took up to four years of intensive lip-reading work before a child learned enough vocabulary to attempt other school subjects.[103] Even Palen – the city's greatest proponent of pure oralism – confessed that "not even the expert lip-reader, after years of practice, can follow all the rapid and intricate movements of the lips in speech."[104] Palen also knew that children who were born deaf or were deafened at a young age experienced the least amount of success under pure oralism.[105] She would have known as well that oralists often denigrated pupils who struggled to learn lip-reading and speech, questioning the intelligence of a group called "oral failures."[106]

Even if acquired painstakingly, lip-reading and speech were nevertheless not nearly as useful for deaf young people as oralist educators claimed. Wiggins discovered this attending Central Tech in Toronto in the 1940s, where he and a few other deaf pupils took regular classes with hearing teenagers: "We were taught the usual subjects, but found that trying to understand our teachers was fruitless. None of them made much effort on our behalf. Instead of using the blackboard they spoke from their desks and, as none of them tried to enunciate or speak visibly, we could not lip-read. In addition, we could not find anyone to inform us about our assignment or from whom I could copy notes. I felt entirely at sea and complained bitterly to Father."[107] Wiggins could read lips under favourable conditions, but doing so did not necessarily bring him into closer communication with hearing people, even his own family. "Hearing people pick up information by listening," he explained, including in the case of children, snippets of adult conversations of which they are not directly a part. "Deaf people must have things explained, and are so often foreigners in our own homes."[108] Wiggins, who was Jewish, "knew very little concerning our religion" as a young man – only what his father managed to explain to him and what he saw watching "my family celebrate Passover and other holidays." He had no Bar Mitzvah because he was unable to read aloud Torah verses or repeat prayers in Hebrew. "Years later I was to learn our history and the meaning of ritual from the deaf Jews in New York," he signed for his memoir.[109] Yet Wiggins did not feel totally attached to the deaf culture that existed at the OSD either. With the chance to return to that boarding school after he had been attending the Clinton day classes and living at home, Wiggins told his parents he wanted to go back. His mother would not give permission, and he resented this at first. However, one of his Clinton friends, who had gone back to the OSD, did not last long there, and told him that the boarding school environment was stifling for a teenager. Wiggins "realized that I had been saved from making a mistake."[110]

Deaf pupils such as Wiggins, and hard-of-hearing pupils as well, were most often segregated in separate classrooms. However, when they occasionally joined regular classes, they experienced varying levels of academic success and integration. After his negative experience at Central Tech, Wiggins quit school altogether in frustration.[111] Other deaf young people persevered in regular schools, and graduated with high school diplomas and even university degrees – still a relatively rare accomplishment for any young person at that time.[112] Some hard-of-hearing students persevered just as successfully. Unlike deaf pupils, these children had residual hearing and, later, access to hearing aids, which made it much easier to learn lip-reading. Children who did not lose the ability to hear until after they had learned to speak were in a preferential position as well. Palen received a letter from a hard-of-hearing boy thanking her for the opportunity to learn how to read lips. In the letter, the boy described how a bout of meningitis had partially taken away his hearing and kept him out of school for four years. "We came to Toronto and I was put in an auxiliary class for backward children as I could not hear the teacher in the regular class," he wrote Palen:

The teacher set me the easiest subjects to do and I was doing the same work for two years. When the new class for hard-of-hearing pupils was opened at Rose Avenue School, I was transferred there. The teacher gave us vowel exercises and lip-reading every day in our ordinary work. With the help of the teacher and the [sic] lip-reading I was able to pass my Entrance Examination ... I think that without a knowledge of lip-reading and [sic] hard-of-hearing children have a very hard task to converse with hearing people.[113]

Like this hard-of-hearing boy, a few young people who attended the orthopaedic classes at Wellesley and received rehabilitative therapy there were eventually able to return to mainstream classrooms.[114]

Of all auxiliary students, young people in sight-saving classes enjoyed probably the greatest integration with children in regular classes. The historian Robert Osgood notes how American auxiliary educators promoted "careful articulation of sight-saving classes with regular classes and combined instruction as much as possible."[115] In Toronto, older sight-saving students joined students in the regular grades for oral recitation. According to D.D. MacDonald, "The [sight-saving] pupils themselves are delighted to be able to measure up with the pupils of the regular classes." MacDonald and others thought that mixing and competition with non-disabled peers benefited sight-saving students.[116] Some of these students went on to attend regular academic, technical, and commercial secondary schools. Donald N. attended a Hester How sight-saving class for most of the 1930s. He completed junior fifth there and went on to Harbord Collegiate.[117] Florence R. went from the Hester How sight-saving class to a collegiate institute.[118]

Of course, sight-saving students were not immune to the factors that prevented Toronto youth in this period from attending high school. These impediments included a working-class family's need for its adolescent members to have a job, perceptions about the proper limits to place on girls' education, prejudices against working-class students continuing in school, and lack of academic inclination or proficiency. Franklin C., a sight-saving student at Hester How whose mother supported the family with her factory job, left school to take a job "on the boats" (likely meaning as a fisher or shipyard worker).[119] After attending sight-saving classes at Hester How throughout the 1940s, Raymond C. turned sixteen in 1951 and left school for a job as a helper at Wonder Bakeries.[120] In the middle of the Second World War, Shirley T. quit the grade 9 sight-saving class at Hester How about a month before final examinations, and took a messenger bindery position in the print and mailing branch of a downtown department store. The roughly $15 per week that the job promised would have gone a long way for Shirley and her single mother.[121]

For sight-saving, deaf or hard-of-hearing, and physically disabled students, mixing with regular program students occurred beyond the classroom. The results of extracurricular mixing varied. According to Prueter, when one crippled boy at Wellesley could not participate in baseball games as a player, he transformed himself into an umpire and – in a rare victory for umpires everywhere – "invariably won the commendation of both teams by his knowledge of the game and by the keen impartiality of his decisions."[122] Verna M. Morrison, a hearing student who attended regular classes at Clinton, recalled schoolyard integration with deaf pupils in the 1920s: "The hard-of-hearing [sic] classes got on well with us. We learned to read lips and signs too."[123] Yet Wiggins remembered separation on the same schoolyard two decades later: "At recess, although we all played the same games, the deaf and the hearing students never mixed. The deaf were interested in their own conversations, usually in sign-language, and the hearing were interested in speech."[124] Several students that Robert Vipond interviewed for his history of Clinton confirm Wiggins's recollection. Vipond adds that "most students on either side of the divide had very little contact with each other for one very practical reason: the classrooms for deaf students were located in the original (now dilapidated) school, and the students entered and exited from a completely different set of doors – out of sight and out of mind."[125]

One barrier to greater integration was the teasing that disabled children endured from classmates.[126] This was one thing these pupils shared with children labelled subnormal, who suffered taunts such as "dummy, dunce, [and] nut," and probably with any other child who seemed very different from peers.[127] Gleason argues that embodied identities and bodily differences were particularly important in the childhood hierarchies found on schoolyards and in other places where children ruled.[128] The Canadian children's author Jean Little, who went to sight-saving classes in Toronto at Duke of Connaught PS and Jesse Ketchum PS around 1940, put up with taunts of "cross-eyed" from other children for years.[129] Teachers sometimes put down disabled students as well. Ernest S.'s mother complained to the principal at Duke of York PS in 1937 that his teacher had called Ernest, who was an auxiliary pupil, a "dumbbell."[130]

4.3 Children on ramp, Wellesley Public School, ca. 1926–30. The bigger girl on the left appears to be supporting the smaller boy in front of her. The girl in the middle is wearing a brace on her left leg. Toronto District School Board Museum and Archives Department, Historic Photograph Collection.

While ridicule was real and often raw, over-pitying children with certain disabilities was common as well. Pity's presence belied the degree to which attitudes towards disabled children had actually fully shifted, even by the 1920s. Charitable works with crippled children, in particular, continued to draw heavily on the Victorian idea of affliction. The film historian Martin F. Norden writes that the "Sweet Innocent," a sort of Dickensian Tiny Tim, was one of several popular archetypes of disabled people. In early-twentieth-century films, the Sweet Innocent "was an embodiment of the deeply ingrained mainstream belief that disabled people must depend on others for their every need."[131] Orthopaedic class pupils in Toronto were recurrently made the pitiable objects of charity. In 1928 alone, for example, the Wellesley orthopaedic class attracted the patronage, and often accompanying financial support, of no less than Rotary, Kiwanis, the Shriners, the Imperial Order Daughters of the Empire, the Local Council of Women, several Masonic Lodges, several local Trades and Labour Congress groups, and a few other organizations besides.[132] There is no record of Wellesley pupils

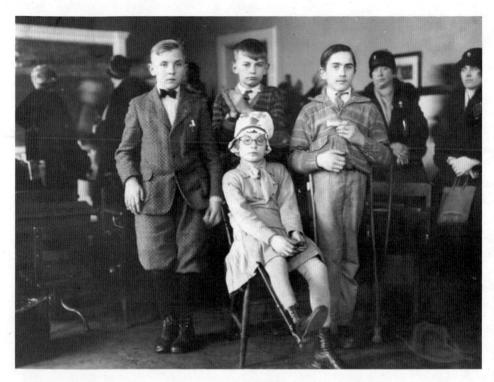

4.4 Children at Christmas event, Wellesley Public School 1927. Four children pose for a photograph at a Christmas event put on at Wellesley PS. Toronto District School Board Museum & Archives Department, Historic Photograph Collection.

directly expressing how all this attention made them feel, or whether they liked or disliked it.

Orthopaedic class pupils also became a source of object lessons for their peers to learn about charity and fair play, or became a focus of a peer's pity. Prueter argued that integrating crippled children into schools had important benefits for normal children: "The normal pupils readily develop a spirit of individual responsibility for the welfare of the cripples which is as commendable as it is fraught with desirable character-training possibilities."[133] Principal W.J.Tamblyn encouraged teaching staff at Jarvis Junior Vocational School to build character in troublemaking older boys by getting them to "encourag[e] the weaker fellow" instead of bullying him. Although there might be reason to doubt how successful this approach would have been, Tamblyn was undaunted. He wrote optimistically that it was an important part of teaching quarrelsome teenaged boys to become good citizens "with the proper attitude toward life."[134] Ruth Dewsbury, a non-disabled pupil who attended Wellesley in the 1930s, recalled the more harmless satisfaction she felt in assisting disabled schoolmates: "Our special pleasure was being allowed to help serve lunch to the pupils" in orthopaedic classes, she wrote decades later in a recollection.[135]

Disability historians such as Paul Longmore and David Goldberger as well as Richard Altenbaugh argue that settings such as special education classrooms and hospital wards created unique opportunities for young people to form peer groups around their common identities as disabled children and youth.[136] This permitted them to avoid ridicule and cloying sympathy. Edna Barg recalled decades later how good it was to attend separate sight-saving classes in Toronto in the 1930s. Regular classes made her feel slightly "left out." This feeling lasted until she switched to a sight-saving class in grade 3. In that setting, "all my fellow classmates had the same problem that I had. I could compete and succeed." She believed that the small, mixed-grade class encompassing children of all ages had helped her build stronger and more lasting friendships.[137] She was certain that the separate sight-saving class helped her to get into high school: "As it was, by the time I had reached grade ten I had learned to cope. I studied from the text and stayed after school to copy notes. This class was a godsend to all of us. We were able to excel, to compete equally, instead of always being at the bottom of the class. Then we would have felt stupid."[138] Little's memories of the sight-saving classes she went to in Toronto were much more positive than those of regular graded classes in Guelph, Ontario, when her family later relocated there. At Duke of Connaught, Little "loved Miss Burton's [sight-saving] class. ... Outside its walls, we might feel different, but once we walked through our classroom door, we knew we belonged."[139] Moshier observed in 1930 that in the Wellesley orthopaedic classes, "children aid each other by constantly reminding them [sic] what is best to do. They live in company with their equals and no inferiority is felt."[140]

A few pupils challenged school or medical officials' perspectives on their disabilities and what type of education they should receive as a result of them. They bargained rules and expectations with adults as

well as young people can or sometimes flouted them. Dick H. contracted polio in the 1937 epidemic and became disabled as a result.
He was an extramural instruction pupil in 1938 and 1939. In 1940, he
asked to return to regular classes at Duke of York. He had difficulty
walking, and for this reason the school principal worried that he would
not manage. However, Dick and his mother – who also tried to get him
admitted to an orthopaedic class – were persistent. After two months
and "much fussing" to convince school officials to allow him to return,
Dick took his place in a regular class.[141] Pauline N. first enrolled in a
sight-saving class in 1930. Five years later, her doctor forced her to
leave school, telling her that she needed to save what remained of her
dwindling eyesight. Shortly afterwards, Pauline defied physician advice by returning to the junior fifth sight-saving class at Hester How
in the fall of 1936. She missed barely any school at all that year and
received "recommendations" (advanced standing that exempted a student from writing the final examination) in four subjects. Pauline later
completed most of senior fifth. In April 1938, her doctor again advised
her to leave school. This time Pauline left permanently. She had, however, achieved almost two years of extra education through her own
perseverance and against her doctor's advice.[142]

Children with disabilities often did not think they were as delicate
as adults believed them to be. At Coleman PS, seven-year-old Gene M.,
who wore glasses, enthusiastically roughhoused with other boys and
broke his spectacles on "at least" six occasions.[143] In another example,
when medical officials recommended treating Clara T.'s eyes, she refused. She was insistent that she could see "quite well" because she sat
close to the blackboard.[144] Pupils in wheelchairs circulated among other
students at Wellesley during lunch time, even though they were told to
stay in their own special schoolyard where they supposedly would be
safer.[145] Children with physical disabilities, who were frequently the objects of charity, turned the tables by canvassing for school charity cam-
paigns. The Star Brights, a group of youngsters in an orthopaedic class,
raised enough money for the Junior Red Cross to help pay for the hos-
pitalization costs of three patients at the Hospital for Sick Children.[146]
Other children in the orthopaedic classes – who themselves were former Hospital for Sick Children patients and had joined a harmonica
band there – performed for disabled adult veterans in the Dominion
Orthopaedic Hospital.[147]

Finally, some disabled youngsters – and occasionally some non-disabled ones – cleverly used their knowledge of adults' preconceived notions about disability and delicateness or dependence to their advantage to avoid school punishments and skirt schoolwork. The principal at Duke of York desperately "wish[ed]" to strap Carl F. for misbehaviour, he wrote on Carl's pupil record card. But Carl could act up without fearing a strapping because he had a heart condition, which meant that the principal would not use corporal punishment on him.[148] In 1927, psychologist E.D. MacPhee reported a claim that Albert E., a Toronto sight-saving class pupil whom he had examined, was "using visional [sic] defect for getting out of all types of work."[149] Children who knew they were entitled to medical services to treat disabilities sometimes used that knowledge to demand treatment. In 1938, Peter O., with his mother's backing, threatened the Duke of York principal that he would change schools unless he received treatment for his eyes. The principal punished him for being "saucy," but the school arranged for the treatment nonetheless.[150] Non-disabled children occasionally tried to obtain improved treatment at school by claiming to be disabled. Frankie C., nine years old and a Duke of York pupil, did not show up for punishment when the principal summoned him. The principal eventually caught up to Frankie, who told "a long story about Doctor's orders of no whipping." Another boy had suggested to him that lying about having a condition was a good way to get out of corporal punishment. His lie exposed, Frankie was sentenced to a strapping: six whacks.[151]

Conclusion

Between just 1921 and 1926, public school trustees in Toronto established sight-saving, deaf and hard-of-hearing, speech correction, and orthopaedic classes. These classes employed new and often technical ways to treat and educate the pupils who attended them. This included measures such as rehabilitative therapy, speech correction, or lip-reading instruction. Adults in the schools required disabled youngsters who received this type of education to readapt "to society as society is presently constituted," as one historian describes the prevalent able-bodied attitude towards disabled people in this era.[152] This was challenging for students who could not adapt, and for some others, deaf students in particular, who did not wish to because they saw no benefit in it or even saw it as harming their community. Still, we cannot expect educators to have known that they were largely subscribing to what some scholars and activists would much later describe as a "medicalized" view of disability, which wrongly perceives disabled people as perpetually broken and in need of constant fixing.[153] In trying to help their pupils overcome limitations and achieve elusive normalcy, auxiliary educators in Toronto were doing their best as they understood it to help the pupils they worked with every day to obtain at least some of the same benefits from schooling – preparation for citizenship or employment – that pupils in the regular classes did. It should be acknowledged as well that in modestly transforming the physical plant of the school by adding ramps and railings, by developing special large-type texts for partially sighted students, and even by promoting hearing-aid use for some pupils, auxiliary educators and public school officials sometimes also adapted schools to disabled youngsters. In doing so, they brought many young people into schools who might not have been included in previous decades.

Parents of disabled schoolchildren generally supported normalcy initiatives. There is more evidence of parents attempting to gain access for their children to sight-saving, orthopaedic, and oral day school classes and other programs than there is evidence of them trying to keep their children out of these classes, although such evidence does also exist.

Young people seemed to display more ambivalence about normalcy than adults did. Wiggins did not enjoy learning to read lips. Acquiring this skill did not help him when he entered Central Tech, and it did not help him fit in with his hearing family. Yet he considered living round the clock in a dormitory at the OSD too restricting for a teenaged boy, even though it meant being with other deaf young people. While some youngsters resisted the programs, or could not adapt to meet educators' expectations of normalcy, others benefitted a great deal from the new auxiliary programs examined in this chapter. Learning to read lips, speech correction, and sight-saving enabled some youth to enter regular elementary and high schools, allowing them to co-mingle and compete with non-disabled youngsters. The legacies these programs have left behind are as diverse as the pupils who attended them.

Chapter Five

The "Remarkable Case of Mabel Helen": Special-Subject Disabilities and Auxiliary Education, 1930–1945

Intelligence quotient (IQ) testing dominated wide swathes of auxiliary education in the 1920s, but the decade and a half after approximately 1929 weakened its hold. The IQ testers had argued that low intelligence lay behind nearly all learning problems. But now others successfully made the case that there were children who possessed normal intelligence but had a disability in one or more individual subject areas, such as reading or arithmetic. This concept would become known as a "special-subject disability" or by such terms as "reading disability," although some children in this period were more simply recommended for "special help" in an area of academic difficulty.

Unlike a low IQ, a special-subject disability could be corrected. Educators and experts in the 1930s and early 1940s developed elaborate tests, special materials, and remedial teaching techniques for diagnosing and treating special-subject disabilities. In 1937, the Ontario Department of Education (DOE) even changed the name of "auxiliary classes" to "opportunity classes" to reflect a shifting expectation that at least some pupils enrolled in such classes could correct their learning problems and then return to regular graded classes. But access to a diagnosis of a special-subject disability, other new diagnoses, and recommendations for special remedial help were not available to all. Low intelligence was no longer seen as the cause of every child's learning problem – but that did not necessarily rule it out as the cause of any particular child's problem. Moreover, school psychologists continued to employ IQ tests to diagnose pupils and develop recommendations for auxiliary classes. In 1933 in Ontario, the term "direct learner" replaced "subnormal"; in the 1940s "dull-normal" was changed to "slow learner" or "non-academic." Although the official names changed, the category definitions and even the IQ ranges – 50 to 75 for direct learn-ers, 75 to 90 for slow learners and non-academic children – remained stable.[1] Youngsters who recorded the lowest IQ scores were seldom given access to new diagnoses or to remedial instruction. What is more, youngsters from some class and ethnic backgrounds continued to be over-represented in auxiliary programs, just as had been the case in the 1920s.

Only a few historians have looked at special-subject disabilities, re-medial education, or diagnostic tests for learning difficulties.[2] This con-trasts with the much larger number who have studied IQ, intelligence testing, and mental deficiency. Barry Franklin, in *From "Backwardness" to "At-Risk": Childhood Learning Difficulties and the Contradictions of School Reform*, convincingly shows how discoveries in the cognitive sci-ences beginning in the nineteenth century eventually led to psycholo-gist Samuel Kirk giving the name "learning disabilities" in 1963 to an amorphous set of learning problems, syndromes, and conditions that were not caused by mental retardation.[3] In *The Incomplete Child: An Intellectual History of Learning Disabilities*, Scot Danforth also traces the prehistory of learning disability to much earlier clinical forays in cogni-tive science. Remedial reading research, he also shows, contributed just as meaningfully to learning disability's origins.[4] The present chapter builds on Franklin and Danforth's ground-breaking work, but also re-considers a few of their conclusions.

Challenging IQ Dominance in the Theory of Learning Problems

In 1936, Emmett A. Betts, an American professor of education, pub-lished *The Prevention and Correction of Reading Difficulties*. "Scientific discovery is gradually re-defining our problems," he wrote. "No longer can the teacher and school administrator account for all learning dis-abilities on the basis of low intelligence."[5] However, new educational theories do not appear out of thin air. The idea of a child with a normal level of intelligence but a marked disability in one academic area was not totally new in the 1930s: it had been around in some form at least since the nineteenth century. But the rise of eugenics in the 1910s, and then of the IQ testers' theories in the 1920s, had grossly overshadowed it. After 1930, what Betts called learning disabilities, and other people called special- or subject- or special-subject disabilities, enjoyed a resur-gence in educational thought and practice. Two currents in particular contributed to this development.

Aphasia and Brain Injury

The sciences of aphasia and brain injury fed one current. Aphasia researchers understood the brain as consisting of regions responsible for different mental functions. If a region of a patient's brain was defective or became damaged, the patient exhibited characteristic difficulties. German physician Carl Wernicke discovered in 1874 that an injury to a region in the left temporal lobe – he dubbed it "Wernicke's Area" – cost patients the ability to make coherent speech. Something sounding like words still flowed, but what came out was gibberish, meaningless neologisms seemingly haphazardly forced together from muddled sounds.[6]

Other medical researchers around the same time noted peculiar and seemingly inexplicable reading problems in some of their patients. Within two decades of Wernicke, British doctors James Hinshelwood and W. Pringle Morgan brought to light unusual cases of what they referred to as "word-blindness" (sometimes also called "alexia"). A patient, previously perfectly able to read, out of the blue lost the ability completely. Hinshelwood in 1895 described an educated patient who awoke one morning to find that he could no longer read a word. Another form of word-blindness afflicted seemingly normal, even very bright young people. Printed words had no meaning for them. No amount of instruction given these youngsters, and no amount of effort on their part to learn letters, made any difference to that fact.[7]

By the 1920s, Samuel Orton, a neurologist at the Iowa State Psychopathic Hospital, was attempting to improve upon earlier aphasia findings. He conducted systematic research on brain defects or injuries that he believed caused language problems, and his special interest was hemispheric studies of the brain. Orton showed that right-handed adult patients with damage to the left side of their brain, and left-handed patients with damage to the right side, exhibited identical reading problems, reversing letters and word order. They might, for example, read the letter "n" when "m" was on the page, or read the word "men" as "nem." Orton also studied children who had not achieved cerebral dominance and who made the same reversals. Cerebral dominance normally appears in early childhood and causes dominant handedness. The similarities in the reading problems of his adult and child research populations suggested to Orton a common cause for language and learning problems. He suspected injury to or defect of a specific area of the brain.[8]

Auxiliary educators were aware of aphasia research and conditions such as word-blindness from the inception of special classes in the 1910s. Helen MacMurchy's 1915 manual *Organization and Management of Auxiliary Classes* covered both. She attributed word-blindness to damage to the "visual speech-centre" in the brain of a child with "normal mental powers." But it occurred only very rarely, she wrote – in just one of every 2,000 children.[9] By the 1930s, however, some psychologists were asserting that this type of condition was much more common than people had previously believed.

Two of these psychologists were Alfred A. Strauss and Heinz Werner. Both men had fled the Nazis in 1933 for America. In 1937, the director of the Wayne County Training School invited Strauss and Werner to join that Michigan custodial institution's active research department.[10] They formed a dynamic team with Laura Lehtinen, a young teacher at the school. Strauss had the expertise in aphasia and brain injury. He had studied at the University of Heidelberg under Wernicke's star pupil, Kurt Goldstein, who worked extensively with brain-injured First World War combat veterans. Werner's expertise was in the psychology of learning. He had worked at one time under William Stern in Germany, the man who invented the IQ to replace Alfred Binet's concept of mental age (see chapter 2).[11] By the 1930s, Werner had serious reservations about IQ. He did not believe that learning and intelligence could be as easily conflated as IQ theories tended to suggest they were. In the IQ testers' theory of learning difficulties, people failed to learn when they lacked the capacity to learn – they did not possess enough intelligence. Werner believed that there was more to learning than mental capacity. Learning was also mental processing and, he thought, a processing breakdown could lead to learning failure as well.[12]

Strauss, the brain injury expert, and Werner, the learning expert, became convinced that not all children who experienced learning problems were mentally deficient in the conventional sense. They postulated that a localized brain injury interfering with mental processing was the cause of some children's learning problems. Over several years, they physically examined Wayne County Training School pupils, put them through an extensive battery of tests of all kinds, and took detailed familial histories. The results of their intensive research led them to hypothesize that there were in fact not one but two types of mentally deficient children. There was the "endogenous" type, a child with an inherent lack of intelligence and therefore a low IQ and global learning delay. But there was also the "exogenous type," an intellectually normal child who had sustained an injury to one part of the brain. This injury was responsible for the child's learning problem in reading or in comprehending numbers and figuring, or for another specific learning delay.[13]

Reading Difficulties and Remedial Education

It was not just clinicians such as Werner and Strauss, or before them Orton, who sought more complex explanations for learning problems. Research by reading experts such as Marion Monroe, Betts, Donald D. Durrell, Kirk, and the Canadian David Harris Russell – and by remedial educators such as Grace Fernald and Leo J. Brueckner – was the second current that contributed to the emergence of special-subject disabilities. Several of them took graduate training with brain injury experts or were assistants in their laboratories. Monroe and Durrell both worked under Orton at the State Psychopathic Hospital in Iowa City.[14] Kirk paid his way through doctoral studies at the University of Michigan by teaching reading at the Wayne County Training School.[15]

Reading experts and remedial educators, especially in the 1930s, challenged the idea that low IQ was responsible for nearly all learning problems. A decade and a half earlier, a handful of psychologists had also expressed their reservations about that idea. But in IQ's heyday, their findings were awash in a sea of flashier and more popular IQ studies.[16] In *The Psychology of Special Abilities and Disabilities*, for instance, Augusta Bronner described word-blindness and other forms of aphasia. She criticized Terman's IQ test and other tests of general intelligence for their failure to account for specific abilities and disabilities:

> I shall not here enter into any criticism regarding these tests, for their inadequacies have already been so widely discussed. ... None includes tests for a wide range of different functions; indeed, many mental functions are not tested at all, and thus we are given very few clues to particular abilities or disabilities. While it is of great value to gauge a person's general intelligence – if there is such a thing – and to place him on a scale as compared to other individuals, yet this throws but little light upon the problems we are here discussing.[17]

Bronner, however, published this particular study in 1917, just as IQ testing burst onto the scene, and as a result her work had very little impact on auxiliary education. Fernald, a professor at the Calfornia State

Normal School at Los Angeles (which eventually became the University of California at Los Angeles), later recalled that when she published her first remedial reading education research in the 1920s, "the supposition that there could be children of normal intelligence who had been unable to learn to read was considered absurd by many educators." At an education conference in 1926, one Midwestern school superintendent even remarked to her: "Perhaps you do have children like that on the Pacific coast but we don't have any east of the Rockies."[18]

In the 1930s, special-subject disabilities knocked louder at the doors of educational psychology and auxiliary education. A brilliant psychometrician and diagnostician, Marion Monroe was pivotal in confirming scientifically that reading difficulty was separable from intellectual disability. Monroe had worked in Orton's Iowa laboratory, and butted heads with him because she disagreed strongly with his purely neurological theory about the origins of reading problems. She suspected that other factors besides brain injury were involved. A more positive influence on her was the University of Chicago's William S. Gray. Danforth writes that Gray, a reading expert like Monroe, believed the potential origins of reading problems were "almost innumerable."[19] The two collaborated often in the years that followed, most famously as co-authors of the *Dick and Jane* readers.[20]

In her 1932 psychology monograph, *Children Who Cannot Read*, Monroe presented a straightforward and ingenious formula that isolated the variable of reading disability from general intelligence. She first collected a child's chronological age, IQ-tested mental age, and score on a basic test measuring aptitude in arithmetic, and used the three variables to compute the child's "Expected Reading performance," expressed as a number. She then turned to four popular standardized reading tests that she also gave the child to compute a second number, the child's "Actual Reading level." Dividing the child's actual by her or his expected score, she called the result a "reading index." An index of approximately 1.02 was normal. Any child with a reading index of 2.75 standard deviations less than that, Monroe concluded, could properly be identified as having normal intelligence and a reading disability. "By teasing apart reading defect and intelligence level," Danforth writes, "Monroe created the possibility of a child of average or even high ability having a reading disability."[21]

None of what has been described so far in this section is meant to suggest that remedial educators or reading experts rejected the science of IQ outright. Monroe, we have just seen, used IQ tests to help diagnose reading problems. Bronner as well found some use in the tests, even if she was mostly a sceptic. And Fernald had fellow Californian Terman write the foreword to her 1943 book *Remedial Techniques in Basic School Subjects*.[22] Remedial educators and reading experts conceded that low innate intelligence existed and that in at least some children it was the cause of their learning difficulties. What they objected to was overreliance on the tests and on IQ theories about learning problems, which meant that too many children who were intelligent but had special-subject disabilities were diagnosed as mentally deficient. Betts, who believed that IQ testing mislabelled many youngsters, dedicated *The Prevention and Correction of Reading Difficulties* to "misunderstood children."[23] Misdiagnosis by IQ test was a strong bone of contention for Durrell as well. After leaving Orton and Iowa behind, Durrell took a PhD at Harvard University with Walter Dearborn, an authority on word-blindness.[24] Durrell wrote scathingly about pencil-and-paper intelligence tests with too many reading items. Test makers had "apparently assumed that in a system of compulsory education all children have had equal opportunity to learn to read and that achievement in reading is in proportion to the native intellectual ability of the child."[25] Durrell's conclusion, however, was that "the presence of this large factor of reading in intelligence tests will allow many children to be classed as dull who are really normal or bright but who have poor reading ability." Never rejecting that IQ could be measured, he nonetheless recommended not using the pencil-and-paper IQ test: "It appears to be a reading test incorrectly labeled."[26] Durrell was a former small-town high school mathematics and science teacher from the Midwest who lived up well to a regional stereotype of folksy plain-spokenness. His biographer tells the story of Durrell's reaction to Orton attempting to coin his own medical term for reading difficulties, "strephosymbolia."[27] Durrell scoffed at the pomposity. "Damn bad teaching," he said, was a likelier cause and a better description, too.[28]

Franklin argues, in *From "Backwardness" to "At-Risk,"* that Orton, Werner, and Strauss had begun to "medicalize the condition of childhood learning difficulties."[29] Elsewhere in the book, he asserts that over the ensuing decades, "this medicalized discourse" enabled "school managers to enhance their capacities for dealing with low-achieving children," and to control and contain in separate classrooms different and troublesome pupils.[30] Franklin's book is indispensable to understanding how brain injury research fits into the story of auxiliary education, and he deserves considerable credit as the first historian to make the connection. His arguments about medicalization and social control, however, are not convincing. One would expect Orton, Strauss, Werner, and others like them to be interested in defining some learning problems as medical in origin. They were clinicians and this was their work, after all. But medicalization does not describe what remedial educators and reading experts wanted to accomplish. Durrell and Monroe departed early from Orton and his research into the murky origins of learning problems deep within the brain. Betts, for his part, downplayed medical language and explanations: "Such terms have been bandied about and seized upon all too quickly to account for reading difficulties. The very fact that many so-called word-blind children have been taught to read discounts the emphasis placed upon this condition by early investigators."[31] As a youth, Kirk showed the illiterate farmhands who worked his parents' property straddling the Manitoba-North Dakota border how to read. Later, he taught reading at the Wayne County Training School. A large part of his career, according to Danforth, "was devoted to replacing medical explanations of learning difficulties with educational concepts that he believed were more useful."[32]

Educators at heart, these reading and remedial experts poured enormous energy into developing diagnostic instruments and remedial methods. They were sincere in wanting to help, rather than control, schoolchildren with learning problems. Fernald's *Remedial Techniques in Basic School Subjects* defined the field for years. Among other pedagogical innovations, she invented the "kinesthetic method" for teaching non-readers.[33] Hypothesizing that visual or auditory processing deficiencies impeded learning to read for some children, Fernald taught children to rely on their other senses to help them. The kinesthetic method added a tactile element, with teachers training non-readers to trace words with their fingers as they attempted to say them aloud. In a child with a visual processing difficulty, Fernald wrote, "the tracing and writing of the word give him kinesthetic-sensory experiences that supplement the defective visual cues."[34] Monroe reported using, with struggling readers at her clinic, "all possible secondary or vicarious steps in word-recognition which are not usually presented in ordinary instruction."[35] This included the "sounding-tracing method" from her earliest kinesthetic work, the "'sound dictation' method" whereby children wrote words that the teacher dictated letter by letter, and reading specially prepared "phonetic stories" that repetitiously drilled in one type of vowel sound.[36]

Educator-led diagnosis was integral to the new remedial instruction of the 1930s. Teachers up to date on the latest methods were supposed to be capable of analysing reading problems scientifically, a form of educator expertise that the reading specialist David Harris Russell, among others, promoted. Ottawa-born, Russell spent most of his career at University of California, Berkeley.[37] In a 1940 article, he wrote: "The skilful teacher today no longer gives such descriptions as 'John can't seem to read at all' or 'Florence is such a poor reader for a girl in the fourth grade.' These are blanket statements which mean little or nothing. Rather, the skilful teacher looks for specific causes of reading difficulties; that is, she diagnoses."[38] Calgary Normal School's George K. Sheane advised aspirant teachers that "a knowledge of the causes of the failure to learn and of the specific skills that make up a [learning] process, and the ability to diagnose and apply remedial teaching, are the factors that distinguish a good teacher from a poor one."[39] Sheane also wrote a series of mathematics texts for elementary pupils with American remedial arithmetic expert Leo J. Brueckner. The latter's 1930 book, *Diagnostic and Remedial Teaching in Arithmetic*, presented "the techniques for diagnosing pupil difficulties in all phases of arithmetic, and the types of remedial exercises which have been found by experiment to eliminate the difficulties that are located."[40]

Remedial and reading experts composed their own diagnostic tests for teacher use. Betts, for instance, published his reading-readiness test in 1934. There was also the eponymous *Monroe Aptitude Tests* (1935), Gates's *Diagnostic Reading Tests* (1935), and Durrell's *Procedures for the Analysis of Reading Difficulties* (1936).[41] Diagnostic tests had a very different purpose than IQ tests. Terman and others designed their tests with classification in mind, using them nearly compulsively to rank the intelligence of human beings by race, ethnicity, class, and other measures. The authors of diagnostic tests were not interested in rankings, or in classifications, or in fact in group differences at all. Like Binet several decades earlier, before others appropriated his work and made it into IQ testing, the authors of diagnostic tests were making tools for identifying children's learning problems with a view to correcting them.

The Remarkable Case of Mabel Helen B.: Auxiliary Classes Become Opportunity Classes

Theories about special-subject disabilities, new ways to diagnose these problems, and new forms of remedial instruction to treat them became

significant parts of auxiliary education in Toronto schools surprisingly quickly after about 1930. A good place to begin examining this is
Inspector P.F. Munro's description of "The Remarkable Case of Mabel
Helen B___," which appeared in 1935 in *The School*. This monthly magazine for educators was published in Toronto and attained wide national
circulation.[42] Munro's discovery of Mabel's reading disability, his observations about the remedial instruction that helped her to overcome
it, and the questions about IQ testing that he subsequently raised based
on her case capture the tone of changes in auxiliary education in the
city's public school system.[43]

Mabel, Munro recounted, had repeated junior first twice. She seemed
bright enough, and the scores she registered on many parts of an IQ test
that E.P. Lewis administered were up to par. But she reportedly "fell
down on language work" and could not read "even very simple sen-
tences."[44] "Six weeks of systematic teaching" were later devoted to her
case, Munro wrote, "to remedy the reading condition that manifestly
caused her to score an I.Q. of 86 when it should have been higher."[45]
When the time was up, Mabel had overcome her reading disability.
Lewis, who re-examined her, was impressed; he reported to Munro that
"her teacher has succeeded in getting Mabel to read intelligently. The
child knows what she is reading, expresses herself well, and can re-
call the content. Very important, too, has been the replacement of tears
by smiles." Mabel's score on the IQ test, which Lewis readministered,
jumped to 92.[46]

"Surely this case proves that ability to read, or the lack of it," Munro
would later stress in his article in *The School*, "has a very important
bearing on the matter of determining intelligence quotients."[47] Munro –
who had made substantial use of intelligence tests in his DPaed thesis
just a few years before[48] – now seemed uncertain about IQ, and pro-
claimed that it was high time to review the theory of its immutability.
As he observed about Mabel's case:

> In six weeks this child's I.Q. rose from 86 to 92. How many other chil-
> dren have been tested and not given the opportunity accorded Mabel? If
> Mabel's I.Q. in the first test had been 70 and nothing done about it, she
> would have been recommended for the Auxiliary Class. How many, there-
> fore, are actually relegated to Auxiliary Classes solely because of inability
> to read well enough to make six extra points in the mental test? Does this
> case not indicate that the theory *that the I.Q. is constant* should be revised,
> especially in reference to children between the ages of 7 and 10 years?[49]

Much like Munro, other Toronto educators in the 1930s also reconsidered their views on IQ and learning problems, and especially about their causes and treatment. They began to talk about remedial instruction again. Diagnostic testing and special-subject disabilities entered their professional vocabulary as well. As noted in chapter 2, Inspector N.S. MacDonald had professed deep faith in intelligence testers' claims that learning capacity was inborn and that remedial attempts to improve children's abilities would forever be in vain. That was in 1919. By 1932, his perspective had changed; he now devoted a section of his inspector's report to "Remedial Teaching."[50] "In almost every class there are pupils retarded in one or more subjects," he wrote. He added: "For all such pupils remedial teaching is necessary. The nature of the deficiency can be readily discovered if the pupil's attainment be carefully diagnosed and studied. A teacher may know in a general way that a pupil is handicapped in this or that subject. This is not enough; a careful diagnosis should be made and specific methods for remedial teaching used."[51] In 1939, C.E. Stothers became Ontario's inspector of auxiliary classes. Two years later, he commissioned surveys that asked special class teachers across the province to summarize their pupils' abilities in reading, arithmetic, and handicrafts.[52] The responses showed that upwards of 90 per cent of auxiliary class pupils had a reading disability and more than 70 per cent had an arithmetic disability, according to their teachers. Stothers concluded that "educational handicaps tend to be multiple instead of single, and that the failure in school of retarded, slow-learning, average, and even superior students will likely be due to more than one single, mental, academic, physical, emotional or environmental handicap."[53] At Jarvis Junior Vocational School, Walter Koerber, one of the school's two reading teachers, rejected IQ as the main cause of learning problems and embraced evolving complex views of learning and intelligence. "Participation for more than a decade in the teaching of reading to these non-academic adolescents," he wrote in 1947, "led to the conviction that the pattern of achievement was being developed by a combination of contributory factors of which intelligence, or the lack of it, was not necessarily the most influential."[54]

What front-line teachers like Koerber and others thought about special-subject disabilities is important. Larry Cuban argues that a theory of learning that teachers do not accept will not pass easily – if at all – through the classroom doorway. Conversely, one that teachers find acceptable and applicable will more often make it over the threshold to become practice. "If content knowledge counts, so do the teacher's professional and personal beliefs about how children learn," he writes.[55] In the 1930s, C.C. Goldring polled teachers at a Toronto elementary school about "handicaps to progress." Staff at McMurrich Public School (PS) were aware of special-subject disability, and ranked it sixth of fifteen causes of learning delays they identified in their school – nearly as important as "lack of intelligence" but trailing the leading causes "lack of persistence" (on the student's part) and "previous training" (or students poorly prepared by their former teachers).[56]

Evolving educator attitudes, as Cuban writes, are necessary if change is to occur. But so are new policies. The schools and the DOE phased out remedial instruction as one of the purposes of the auxiliary classes as they moved the classes in the early and mid-1920s towards a new program of studies specifically for youngsters with IQs in the subnormal 50 to 75 range (see chapter 2). It was argued that this group had no need for remedial instruction because their inherent low intelligence both caused their learning difficulties and limited what teachers could do about them.

Remedial instruction probably had never entirely disappeared in Toronto, although its place in auxiliary education diminished remarkably.[57] By the 1930s, however, evolving provincial education policies somewhat revived remedial instruction within auxiliary classes so that at least some pupils would not have to remain there for as long as they stayed in school. For almost all of the decade, Harry Amoss, a psychologist formerly on the academic staff of Hamilton Normal School, was the provincial inspector of auxiliary classes and promoted significant reforms. One of them was "mixed auxiliary training classes," which had three purposes: "(i) to readjust the more capable in their backward studies and return them to regular grade work, (ii) to provide the less capable with such minimum accomplishments in reading and arithmetic as will enable them to carry on with the ordinary activities of life, and (iii) to restore shattered confidence and build up a good citizenship attitude in all."[58] Three purposes, that is, to replace just one that had dominated auxiliary education in the 1920s, providing a basic program to limited pupils. In 1933, Amoss, with the assistant auxiliary class inspector L. Helen Delaporte, also published a much-updated provincially authorized text for auxiliary class teachers, *Training Handicapped Children*. Amoss and DeLaporte banished terms they considered "offensively discriminative, not to say snobbish" and vowed to see the day when "the use of such terms as subnormal, mental defective, etc., is taboo throughout the schools of the province."[59] They substituted "children of the direct-learning type" for "subnormals," although the new and the old groups' characteristics were for all intents and purposes identical.[60]

In 1937, Amoss changed the name of the province's auxiliary classes to "opportunity classes." The aim was to reflect the inclusion of remedial instruction – "an indication that the door of the room should, in the future, swing both ways."[61] By 1939, Stothers, Amoss's replacement as provincial auxiliary education inspector, reported that the province's opportunity classes were devoting more attention than ever to remedial instruction: "It is becoming quite common to find on inspection that from two to six pupils have been re-adjusted in reading and arithmetic, and have been returned to regular grade work at the end of the school term."[62]

Local changes in the 1930s and early 1940s slowly but surely built up remedial instruction in the auxiliary and opportunity classes of the Toronto Board of Education (TBE) and in the regular grades as well. In 1935, TBE inspectors approved in principle "a catch-up class to which a child may be sent at any time for any length of time, then returned to a regular class." (It is not clear from this source precisely when this policy was implemented.)[63] The provincial policy on opportunity classes, with a door that revolved instead of only opening in, applied to Toronto from 1937. The city's public schools bolstered their remedial programs further in the 1940s. Concerned about the lack of a "widespread programme" or coordinated approach to remedial instruction in reading, Inspector A.G. Leitch proposed in 1945 hiring extra teachers to work in this area.[64] Less than one month later, the TBE Management Committee agreed to engage them "for the purpose of assisting regular teachers with slow pupils, with problem cases, and with pupils who are having special difficulty with a particular part of the school work."[65] The inspectors wanted these teachers to help primary students with reading difficulties, either in separate small classes or in small withdrawal groups of four to six students.[66] "These teachers," Goldring wrote, "would be expected to give particular attention to children who find difficulty in reading with normal speed and efficiency. They would diagnose the mistakes being made by such children, and would apply remedial measures."[67] Goldring appointed seven early-career women teachers to this work in September 1945, and assigned them to large elementary schools such as Dewson, Ryerson, and Regal Road. The Management Committee set aside funds for them to study methods in the summer at suitable American universities.[68] That same year, the inspectors, in a concerted effort to boost remedial instruction, also directed principals to assign teachers of senior elementary grades who had "free time" during the school day to spend half of it with struggling students.[69]

The Limited Application of Special-Subject Disabilities: Diagnosing, Recommending, and Placing Students after 1930

Although special-subject disabilities and remedial methods became more accepted in the 1930s and early 1940s, the Toronto Department of Public Health's Mental Hygiene Division, still responsible for officially diagnosing schoolchildren's learning problems, continued to depend on IQ tests. Such reliance restricted the extent to which new ideas about learning difficulties and remedial instruction actually applied to individual auxiliary class pupils in the city's schools. "With regard to the general attitude towards intelligence tests," as C.G. Stogdill, the Mental Hygiene Division's director and the school board psychologist, said in an address to auxiliary class teachers in 1932, "it appears that the pendulum is swinging towards the other extreme from the attitude of a few years ago, which was that I.Q. was going to answer all of our questions about mentality. To-day, in some quarters, there is a tendency towards disregarding intelligence tests. As usual the truth is to be found somewhere between the extremes."[70] Indeed, school principals still depended on IQ tests, and relied on the division to identify and diagnose pupils for auxiliary programs. They could request a complete IQ survey of up to all the children in their school. The division did many of these surveys throughout the 1930 to 1945 period – for instance, it surveyed eighty-four TBE schools and examined 4,500 TBE students in 1935, and ninety-one public schools and 5,400 students in 1936.[71]

The Mental Hygiene Division kept basic statistics tracking the diagnoses and placement recommendations of its psychologists. Special-subject disability was not an included category in the diagnosis statistics and cannot be tracked this way (it was likely subsumed into the category "apparently normal" that covered all children with normal IQs).[72] When the placement statistics are analysed over time, however, they show a slight – though perceptible – swing of the pendulum Stogdill described in the direction of recommending pupils for remedial instruction, though the bob had yet to actually enter that zone of its arc. The category for auxiliary education remedial instruction – that is, pupils recommended for "special academic help" in an opportunity class

("SH, Opp") – first appeared in division statistical reports in 1939 (see figure 5.1). (There is evidence in individual pupil records that division psychologists used this recommendation earlier than that, discussed below.) From 1939 to 1941, this recommendation hovered at around a mere 2.5 per cent of all of the division's cases. In 1940, division psychologists added an additional category for pupils recommended for special help in an ordinary class ("SH, Ord"), which received a 3.4 per cent share of cases that year and 8.8 per cent a year later.[73] It appears that in 1942 the division merged these two distinctive special help categories (SH, Opp and SH, Ord) into a single one ("SH"). The new recommendation rose from 3.8 per cent of cases that year to 10.8 per cent in 1944, falling back to 8.8 per cent in 1945. At all times over the period considered, the percentage of cases that school psychologists recommended for an auxiliary or opportunity class placement without reference to special help ("Opp") remained higher than the percentage of cases they recommended for special help. But the gap narrowed considerably. The Opp recommendation fell from 25 per cent in 1939 – more than ten times the SH, Opp rate – to 15 per cent in 1944, or just twice the SH rate. It jumped back to more than 20 per cent in 1945. In other words, as figure 5.1 illustrates, there was movement from at least 1939 onwards towards recommending special academic help for struggling students, an indication that the division had moved gently away from the position that low IQ – intractable against efforts to remediate it – accounted for these children's learning problems. However, this explanation remained the leading one, applied in the largest number of cases.

Case-by-case examples from pupil records, like the foregoing analysis of division statistics, show that IQ score mattered a great deal to a pupil's diagnosis and ability to obtain remedial instruction. Two different practices were clearly at work. Pupils who had relatively higher IQs and were recommended for auxiliary and opportunity classes by psychologists were identified for special help over a limited time frame – that is, for remedial instruction. But students with relatively lower IQs, the majority of cases, received a second type of recommendation that did not specify the duration of time they would spend in the class and did not prescribe special help, more than likely meaning that remedial lessons were not available to them.[74]

Pupils such as Imogene R. and Augusta T. were subjected to the first practice, and with their relatively high IQs were recommended for remedial instruction. Imogene, a Duke of York PS pupil, scored 83 on an IQ test in 1931, relatively high for an auxiliary class pupil. Lewis

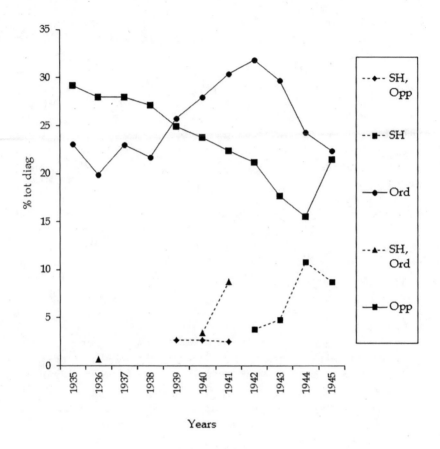

5.1 Toronto Department of Mental Hygiene, Selected Recommendations, 1935–45. As percentage of total diagnoses made (*y*–axis), by year (*x*–axis). Legend, recommendations: SH, Opp (diamond marker, dashed line) = special help in auxiliary/opportunity class; SH (square marker, dashed line) = special help; Ord (circle marker, solid line) = ordinary class; SH, Ord (triangle marker, dashed line) = special help in ordinary class; Opp (square marker, solid line) = opportunity class. Source: CTA. Fonds 200, Series 365, Department of Public Health City of Toronto, selected monthly reports and annual statements, 1931–45. Note: some data is missing in the original source.

diagnosed her as dull-normal, writing in his report that she would benefit from instruction in an auxiliary class "for a time," a placement that would give her "the benefit of more individual teaching."[75] Augusta T. at Hester How registered an IQ of 84 in 1939. Stogdill, then the director of the Mental Hygiene Division, diagnosed Augusta as dull-normal and recommended her for an "auxiliary class for a time." In 1941, Lewis, who had returned to the director's job to replace Stogdill, re-examined Augusta. Her IQ had risen to 94; he diagnosed her as "normal." The school promoted her to grade 5 at the beginning of the new term. Sadly, Augusta, who was sick for large stretches of her childhood, died less than a year later at the age of fourteen.[76]

In contrast to Augusta or Imogene, who registered relatively high IQs for auxiliary pupils, Stogdill and Lewis still frequently recommended lower-scoring children for an auxiliary or opportunity class indefinitely, not merely "for a time," and made no recommendation for these pupils for special help in any subject area. These were youngsters who fell under the second practice. Stogdill tested Rupert C.'s IQ in 1933 – it was 62 – and diagnosed him as subnormal, recommending an auxiliary class with no reference to a time limit or to special help.[77] He took the exact same course of action with Alexandra J. – IQ 63 – in 1940.[78] Even with the changes special-subject disability brought, a diagnosis of subnormality still seems to have defined a child as virtually hopeless, and to have figuratively displaced these youngsters to the far corners of the auxiliary or opportunity class where remedial help was hardest to come by and where the possibility of a return to mainstream grades was slimmest. Estelle E. (IQ 71) was placed in an auxiliary class at Hester How on an indefinite basis in October 1934 at the age of eight, and would stay in it until a few weeks after her sixteenth birthday.[79]

Sometimes the two practices blended. Young people could occasionally find themselves staying indefinitely, or for a very long time, in an auxiliary or opportunity class even if initially the psychologist had recommended only a brief remedial placement. Stogdill recommended Henry V., a Duke of York pupil, for an auxiliary class in 1932. He wrote on Henry's Psychiatric examination report (PER): "We feel that it would be worth while [sic] to give this boy individual attention for a few months in the auxiliary class, until he learns to read. His new glasses may make a big improvement. Recommend auxiliary class till June and special help in reading." Henry stayed in the class for nearly two years, far longer than the few months Stogdill had recommended. By 1938, he was sixteen and in grade 6. Probably frustrated at being left behind with much younger pupils, he asked the principal at Duke of York to move up a grade. The principal recorded the details of their tense conversation on the back of Henry's Office record card (ORC). He denied the request and placed him last on the promotion list, with "no chances." Henry gave the principal the impression that – in the principal's words – the "school ha[d] let him down." The principal's thinking was that Henry was "not honest with himself."[80]

Seemingly, on rarer occasions in the 1930s and early 1940s, adults used the auxiliary and opportunity classes to accommodate pupils whose learning problems they attributed to lack of familiarity with English, poor attendance, or other factors that they could not lay at the feet of low IQ. This reprised a practice they had occasionally employed in the early 1920s (see chapter 2). Edward B.'s case serves as an illustration. Tested by Stogdill in 1934, Edward scored an IQ of just 71. Stogdill wrote on his PER that "in appearance and general manner, [Edward] appears to be fairly bright. The test shows definite mental retardation but to just what extent it is impossible to say in view of his language handicap and lack of average opportunity in school." Edward had been born to Greek parents in Montreal and knew Greek and French but struggled with English: "He seems to understand English fairly well, but has great difficulty in expressing himself. This boy is greatly in need of the special help which could be gained in an auxiliary class." Stogdill recommended Edward for that class and for a reassessment in two years' time.[81]

Auxiliary and Opportunity Class Demographics in the 1930s and Early 1940s

Regardless of changes to theories about learning problems or to policy, auxiliary and opportunity classes in Toronto continued to enrol disproportionate numbers of youngsters from some groups throughout the 1930s and early 1940s. Let us look first at ethnic origin in auxiliary and opportunity classes at Hester How, the most diverse school in this study and probably in the entire TBE (see table 5.1). Jewish pupils were overrepresented in the school's auxiliary classes in the 1920s (see chapter 2). This pattern persisted. Between 1930–1 and 1944–5, Jewish pupils – now just 8 per cent of the school population – still represented 14 per cent of the auxiliary, later opportunity, class roll. Another group was also significantly over-represented: at the time people called them "Gypsies," although today it is more common and more accurate to refer to the

5.1 Hester How PS by top four ethnic origins, in auxiliary/opportunity classes
and in school as a whole, 1930–1 to 1944–5 school years

	% of Aux./Opp. Class for Subn. Pop.	% of School Pop. as a Whole[a]
Anglo-Canadian	25.8 (n = 31)	23.0
Roma ("Gypsies")	17.5 (n = 21)	9.0
Jewish	14.2 (n = 17)	8.0
Italian	10.8 (n = 13)	7.5
All others	31.7 (n = 38) (15 other groups)	52.5 (22 other groups)

[a] Based on a representative sample of pupil records from the school, discussed
in appendix A.

group as "Roma" (and using the adjective "Romani").[82] Romani children were 9 per cent of the Hester How population, and yet were more than 17 per cent of auxiliary or opportunity class pupils.

Accounting for ethnic and racial group over-representation in auxiliary programs after 1930 is just as complicated as accounting for it in the period before that is discussed in chapter 2. There are different potential explanations, for instance, for the over-representation of Roma in auxiliary or opportunity classes. One explanation could easily lie with culture-loaded IQ tests. A language difference, prejudice against Roma, which was pervasive, and the group's tendency to self-segregate extremely, could have made them much less familiar with the IQ testing idiom than other children, contributing to lower scores. True, most Toronto Roma, including those attending auxiliary programs, were born in the city and fluent in English even though they also spoke their own languages, the "Vlach" or "Vlax" dialects.[83] But many Roma practiced elaborate "marime" (or purity) rules, some of which enforced a strict division and distance between them and the "gadje" (or non-Roma). They regarded gadje practices and ideas as impure or suspect, avoided them or treated them very skeptically, and typically, as a result, strictly segregated themselves from mixing with gadje.[84] The fierce discrimination that they often encountered in Canada – a suspicious or leering public, experiences of outright violence, and police harassment – reinforced the tendency to stay away from others.[85]

Intelligence testers in the 1910s and 1920s believed that all practically all deficiency was hereditary. As we saw in chapters 2 and 3, they also believed that members of some racial or ethnic groups were deficient at least in part on account of the inferior characteristics their entire group possessed and passed on from generation to generation.[86] By the 1930s, when Romani children were over-represented in Toronto auxiliary and opportunity classes, this sort of view, though certainly still present in some circles, had fallen out of favour in many others. The decline of this type of thinking matched the fall of the theory that all learning difficulties were innate, the notion that we have seen remedial educators and special-subject disability proponents rejected. Education historian Thomas D. Fallace writes, "by the 1930s, scholars more or less overturned the idea that non-White social groups were innately, cognitively, biologically, or anatomically inferior."[87] However, educators at times replaced biological deficiency theories with a "cultural deficiency" explanation that, Fallace writes, "became the new approach to educating non-Whites." In the United States, such educators thought along the lines of the eventual "culture of poverty" argument that Oscar Lewis would make several decades later. In this argument, it was not so much white discrimination and lack of opportunity in the moment that suppressed African American educational outcomes, but a cultural deficit African Americans had inherited from their forefathers.[88] A cultural deficiency theory appeared in Canadian quarters, too, supported by psychologists such as Florence Dunlop (see chapter 6).[89]

No direct evidence exists that Toronto educators by the 1930s believed that Romani children suffered from cultural deprivation. In fact I have not been able to find anything that Canadian educators wrote about Roma as a group. Yet it would not be surprising to learn that they held views consistent with the cultural deprivation theory and applied these to the Roma, a group that Torontonians generally stereotyped as poor and "exotic" outsiders.[90] Without direct evidence, explanations for the over-representation of Romani youngsters in auxiliary and opportunity classes can again be only speculation, though that over-representation undeniably existed.

Auxiliary and opportunity classes at Hester How after 1930 also continued to enrol relatively large numbers of working-class students (see table 5.2), as had been the case in the 1920s. The same classes at Duke of York had their share of these students as well (see table 5.3).[91] This is to be expected given that both schools were overwhelmingly working-class. A noticeably over-represented group in the auxiliary and opportunity classes at Duke of York and Hester How were pupils who came from families in which the head had no occupation. In tables 5.2 and 5.3, they are represented by the category "none/not

5.2 Occupational group and class of Hester How PS pupils,
1930–1 to 1944–5 school years

	% of Aux./Opp. Class for Subn. Pop.	% of School Pop. as a Whole[a]
Owners and managers	2.5 (n = 3)	5.7
Agents on commission	0 (n = 0)	3.4
Self-employed	7.5 (n = 9)	11.4
Middle class	1.7 (n = 2)	4.0
Working class (subtotal of three categories below)	71.7 (n = 86)	70.3
Skilled and semi-skilled	39.2 (n = 47)	45.1
Unskilled	32.5 (n = 39)	24.0
White collar	0 (n = 0)	1.1
None/not available	12.5 (n = 15)	2.9
Miscellaneous (cannot be classified)	4.2 (n = 5)	2.3

[a] Based on a representative sample of pupil records from the school, discussed in appendix A.

5.3 Occupational group and class of Duke of York PS pupils,
1930–1 to 1944–5 school years

	% of Aux./Opp. Class for Subn. Pop.	% of School Pop. as a Whole[a]
Owners and managers	0.7 (n = 1)	1.1
Agents on commission	4.9 (n = 7)	5.0
Self-employed	4.9 (n = 7)	9.5
Middle class	2.1 (n = 3)	4.1
Working class (subtotal of three categories below)	68.5 (n = 98)	72.2
Skilled and semi-skilled	24.5 (n = 35)	36.6
Unskilled	44.1 (n = 63)	33.4
White collar	0 (n = 0)	2.2
None/not available	18.9 (n = 27)	5.4
Miscellaneous (cannot be classified)	0 (n = 0)	2.8

[a] Based on a representative sample of pupil records from the school, discussed in appendix A.

available." (I explain this category in detail in appendix A.) At Duke of York, youngsters from the category were three-and-a-half times more present in auxiliary or opportunity classes than in the general school population. At Hester How in the same period, the rate was over four times more present. Relatively elevated numbers of young people from families where the head was in the "none/not available" category represent continuity from the 1920s. They occur in statistics for auxiliary classes in that decade (see chapter 2) and in junior vocational school statistics for the 1920s to mid-1930s (see chapter 3).

What is more, at both schools the "none/not available" group represented in the auxiliary and opportunity classes seems to have included high proportions of single mothers who did not report remunerative work. The Duke of York auxiliary/opportunity class "none/not available" group, for example, includes six single women who reported no occupation and account for more than 20 per cent of the "none/not available" group's total of twenty-seven. By contrast, auxiliary class children of single mothers who were working (primarily in domestic cleaning and waitressing) represent just 6 per cent of the unskilled worker group. Thus children of single, non-waged mothers seem also to have been over-represented in auxiliary and opportunity classes by the 1930s.[92]

In contrast to class and ethnic origin, which can only be reconstructed from pupil records on a school-by-school basis, the TBE reported system-wide statistics on the number of boys and girls attending auxiliary and opportunity classes for the entire period 1930 to 1945. It reported these statistics on gender to the DOE, which included them in its annual reports. Those reports show that until about 1936–7, boys constituted about 60 per cent and girls roughly 40 per cent of enrolments in auxiliary/opportunity classes. The gap widened afterwards, rising to around 65 per cent boys versus 35 per cent girls (see table 5.4).

It is not clear why the ratio shifted slightly but perceptibly. However, there was heightened interest in Toronto in the mid-1930s in programs for boys with lower than normal IQs and boys who struggled academically. The TBE opened Church Street School for Boys, and an Academic Vocational Class for boys at Maurice Cody PS, during this decade. Neither of these was an auxiliary program, because the boys who attended had IQs that were too high to qualify them for auxiliary education. Nevertheless, the creation of two new programs like these may suggest that people in the 1930s were more acutely aware of boys with academic difficulties than in the past, and became more likely to

5.4 Enrolment in TBE auxiliary/opportunity classes, girls and boys, 1930–1 to 1944–5 school years

	Girls	%	Boys	%	Tot.
1930–1	353	40.5	519	59.5	872
1931–2	347	38.6	551	61.4	898
1932–3	378	40.4	558	59.6	936
1933–4	385	41.2	549	58.8	934
1934–5	423	41.9	587	58.1	1010
1935–6	385	38.5	614	61.5	999
1936–7	327	34.3	627	65.7	954
1937–8	324	34.5	616	65.5	940
1938–9	336	37.2	568	62.8	904
1939–0	313	33.1	634	67.0	947
1940–1[a]	n/a	–	n/a	–	n/a
1941–2	274	36.1	485	63.9	759
1942–3	262	34.1	506	65.9	768
1943–4	273	35.0	506	65.0	779
1944–5	253	33.9	494	66.1	747

[a] The DOE did not report auxiliary education statistics in 1940–1.

Source: Ontario, Legislative Assembly, *Report of the Minister of Education Province of Ontario*, Report of the Inspector of Auxiliary Classes (Toronto: various publishers, various years).

recommend these boys for all sorts of programs, including auxiliary and opportunity classes as well. Church Street School for Boys opened in 1934 when the TBE converted a regular elementary school, Church Street PS, into this school for twelve-year-olds with IQs in the 75–90 range who were labelled non-academic.[93] Shortly after, Maurice Cody PS inaugurated its Academic Vocational Class. It was for boys only as well and enrolled struggling early adolescents who, like those at Church Street School, had a minimum IQ of 75. To enter the Academic Vocational Class, pupils were also required to have reached grade 5. "The aim of the class is readjustment of the boy, educationally and so-cially," Murray E. Steele, the school's principal, wrote. The classes were partly remedial, and Steele noted that "we aim to give every boy who remains in the class a grade VII standing." But other ends were served as well: "Boys who do good work remain two years in the shop and are then ready for the preparatory class at vocational school. Some return to the regular grades much improved because they have learned the value of work. Others go directly to work from the class."[94] The Church Street and Maurice Cody programs also absorbed slightly younger boys who were eligible for the junior vocational school, but that it could no longer accommodate as its enrolment grew considerably during the first half of the 1930s (see chapter 4).

Pedagogy and Curriculum in Auxiliary and Opportunity Classes, 1930–1945

Auxiliary and opportunity class teachers in the 1930s and early 1940s refocused on individualized and remedial instruction and, in particular, on teaching reading. A few of them even questioned directly the idea, predominate in the 1920s, that their pupils should receive largely manual training and could acquire only very basic reading and writing skills. In 1930, an author using only the initials J.M. wrote an article entitled "Are the Three 'R's Being Neglected?" for *The Bulletin*, a publication of the Auxiliary Class Teachers' Section of the Ontario Educational Association (OEA). "With the great growth of the movement toward giving special attention and teaching to the mentally backward, or mentally different as some would call them," J.M. wrote, "there has been a corresponding increase in manual work as related to this teaching." The author found this emphasis unsatisfactory. "Is it more important," J.M pondered, "that a subnormal child should know how to weave a basket than that he should know how to read, and use the simple elements of arithmetic?" Auxiliary pupils were capable of learning to "both read and measure, after considerable instruction, of course, but leaving no room for doubt." J.M. wished to change the popular perception of the "auxiliary classes as those in which children make brightly painted wooden toys, weave raffia and fashion book covers."[95]

The Bulletin's editors printed a reply in the next issue. In "The Question Answered," an unnamed author remarked that J.M.'s article had "provoked many comments." Differences of opinion existed "on the relative value of so-called 'hand-work' and academic work and to the time that should be devoted to each." But many auxiliary education teachers agreed that more reading instruction was both possible and necessary: "Speaking generally, every pupil who is properly placed in an Auxiliary class, and who has no special disability, can be taught to read." Teaching reading should become more of a focus, as should "writing and number work." "After all," this author wrote, "when a child has learned to make *one* basket successfully then basketry has ceased to have an educational value for that pupil, and if we insist on keeping him making baskets, we are turning the classroom into a factory."[96] DeLaporte, as well, wanted to enhance academic instruction in auxiliary education. In a 1941 article in *Special Class Teacher* – the publication that succeeded *The Bulletin* – she admitted that auxiliary educators "have learned that we can go far in reading and arithmetic, farther than we had previously thought possible."[97]

By the 1930s, innovations such as diagnostic tests and materials such as basal readers also made it much more practical for auxiliary or opportunity class teachers to carry out remedial instruction and individualize the program in their classrooms. Provincial authorities encouraged them to use the new tools. "The catch phrase 'individual instruction' is forever heard in connection with retarded pupils," Stothers observed. "It is gratifying to report that the practice of using diagnostic tests and techniques, while still comparatively rare, is increasing – among auxiliary educators."[98] To help auxiliary education teachers take up diagnostic tests, in 1941 *Special Class Teacher* commissioned a set of articles by experienced auxiliary educator Marian K. Harvie. She explained step-by-step how to use "Gates' Reading Diagnosis Test" and "Gray's Standardized Oral Reading Paragraphs" in auxiliary work.[99] On the staff of Toronto's Bolton School for Girls at the time she wrote the articles, Harvie had taught previously at the provincial custodial institution, the Ontario Hospital, Orillia, and had also served as principal of the institution's school section.[100]

The development of basal readers further favoured the expansion of individualized remedial instruction in auxiliary education. Basal readers, increasingly common by the mid-1920s, make it easier for a single teacher to have varied materials for a mixed-ability class. The vocabulary that each book in a set of basal readers uses is carefully controlled. The words used in any given book are limited to those selected from a pre-determined vocabulary list. These are words that have been shown to be familiar to readers at the level at which the book is pitched. The frequency of new words is controlled as well, such that the next reader in the series recycles the same words from the one before and adds a limited number of new ones. This way basal readers build serially on an expanding foundation, or base, adding vocabulary that becomes more varied and difficult as pupils progress from reader to reader.[101]

With sets of readers, each child in a classroom can have a reader at her or his level, reducing the burden on teachers to produce the voluminous amount of materials that would be required to teach each child uniquely, a particular issue in auxiliary or opportunity classes with children of sometimes wildly varying abilities. In the early 1930s, a few Toronto auxiliary class teachers, such as Bessie Kellaway at Kent PS and Ethel L. Cairns at Duke of Connaught PS, compiled and typed copies of their own special primers with controlled vocabulary for their pupils.[102]

By the later 1930s and early 1940s, basal readers with controlled vocabulary and teacher manuals for those readers that stated the frequency of repeated and new words in them were much more common, and teachers no longer had to produce vocabulary lists themselves. In 1933, provincial education authorities authorized a new primer, *Mary, John, and Peter*, for use in the early grades. With its carefully controlled vocabulary, bright colours, beautiful illustrations, and mostly child-centred stories, the primer was similar to new American basal readers and primers of that era, such as the Elson-Gray Readers and Curriculum Foundation Series (Dick and Jane books).[103] By 1944, J.A. Long, the research director of the Ontario College of Education in Toronto, reported that "so much interest has been evidenced in our collection of graded reading textbook series, and remedial reading texts for both the elementary and secondary school levels, that we have extended it considerably during the year, and now have over 425 books on display, including a special section on remedial reading." Meanwhile, his department's "test construction program" was churning out "diagnostic and achievement tests in both reading and arithmetic for the elementary school" and planning "the preparation of complete sets of remedial materials and exercises to accompany all our diagnostic tests."[104]

The new progressive curriculum for the elementary grades that Ontario introduced, the *Programme of Studies for Grades I to VI of the Public and Separate Schools, 1937*, also made remedial education in opportunity classes more practical. This curriculum, notes the historian Theodore Christou, "embodied all three of the core progressive principles, making provisions for individual learners, active learning, and studies of relevance to contemporary society."[105] Amoss – who implemented the name change to "opportunity classes" the same year the DOE released the new program of studies – applauded the "'direct learning,' 'active learning,' and 'attitudinal training'" in the "new course."[106] In fact, he claimed credit for auxiliary programs as the "experimental laboratories" that had "assisted in establishing the value" of the new curriculum's progressives principles. The new program would make it easier for the opportunity classes to return pupils to the grades. "In the past," Amoss wrote, "one of the chief difficulties to be surmounted in returning a pupil to grade has been the knowledge requirements in history and geography. Even after a pupil had been re-adjusted in the fundamentals, reading, writing, and arithmetic, and re-habilitated in his attitude towards school and society, the grade teacher would sometimes object to his return on the ground of his ignorance of townships and post offices, counties and country towns, etc."[107]

The new subject of social studies was a hallmark of progressive edu-cation, as historians such as Christou and Amy von Heyking argue.[108] Amoss was confident that this "social science" curriculum's change of emphasis "from knowledge to interest" would be a great help to auxiliary education. Now that social science, or studies, had supplanted history and geography in the elementary grades, he wrote, "it is hoped that readjustment may become an increasingly important function of the special class."[109] Amoss's views by the 1930s about the program of stud-ies for opportunity classes represented something of an about-face from his views in the 1920s, when he had suggested that IQ studies showed that subnormal auxiliary pupils had a different, more concrete form of intelligence and required a different and less taxing curriculum.[110]

In the 1940s, DeLaporte as well promoted reforming the opportu-nity class curriculum by adding social studies and literature. To en-courage studies in the latter, she prepared, and published in *Special Class Teacher*, a levelled reading list for "non-academic or dull-normal" learners that listed abridgements and simplified retellings of literary classics: "There are gaps in the knowledge of those children whose reading skills have not enabled them to know David Copperfield or Ben Hur, who have never shuddered through Macbeth, laughed with Tom Sawyer, nor thrilled through Treasure Island." Teachers could fill these holes through "judicious manipulation of texts." That way, "the non-academic child will feel at home among his companions and gain some significance from allusions to famous characters and stories which he hears from time to time at the movies or among his friends, or sees in the daily papers."[111] She provided several dozen titles with the name of the publishing house and grade level of each text's vocabulary. Her idea for the list came from a similar document the Los Angeles City School District had produced in several editions since the 1930s.[112]

Like Amoss, DeLaporte advocated for social studies in auxiliary pro-grams. "As backward children usually grow up, live and die within the radius of a few miles," she wrote in yet another article in *Special Class Teacher* in 1941, "we have not burdened children in Opportunity and Handicraft Classes with any great detailed knowledge of Geography or the History of other peoples." But with the Second World War, DeLaporte believed, special class pupils needed to know more: "World events, the radio and newspapers have completely changed the picture. Many graduates of our classes, or the brothers or fathers of our pupils are in the army, away in strange and unfamiliar places." What was more, she contended, research advances and accomplishments in teaching remedial reading and arithmetic demonstrated that auxiliary pupils were more capable in many academic areas than educators had previously believed. "Special effort may take us equally far in Social Studies," she wrote.[113] F. Pearl Malloy, the editor-in-chief of *Special Class Teacher*, had experimented with social studies in her special class at St Helen's School for Boys in the Toronto Catholic separate school system. In a 1944 article for *The School*, she related her great success teaching the subject using the progressive enterprise method, a child-centred approach in which the class chose a thematic topic and then carried out coordinated activities that formed a unit teaching them about it from the perspectives of various curriculum areas, such as science, mathematics, social studies, literature, and so on.[114]

Curriculum changes that paralleled what was occurring in elementary school auxiliary and opportunity classes unfolded in the handicraft schools for adolescents as well. In the early 1940s, Koerber and his teaching colleague John McGivney administered diagnostic reading tests to all students who entered Jarvis Junior Vocational School. The tests revealed that as many as 25 to 35 per cent of them were effectively "non-readers." Some could not read at all, while others could read at only a grade 1 level.[115] To compensate, by 1944 all pupils at the school spent an average of seventy minutes every day in reading instruction. Each incoming boy was enrolled in a reading class at his individual level. The diagnostic tests for new pupils sorted them into five ability groups that used three different course outlines. All outlines contained three basic elements: reading and discussion of literature; mechanics, especially "word attack" strategies; and psychologically adjusting pupils' attitudes towards reading. The most advanced groups concentrated the least on mechanics. The least advanced group spent "the bulk" of their time figuring out a word attack strategy that worked for them, with considerable individual instruction from Koerber and McGivney.[116] Like DeLaporte, McGivney worried that there was a lack of suitable and interesting materials for the older struggling readers he taught: "He is an adolescent, and the fact that he does not read is not an indication that he has an extremely low I.Q. or childish tastes." His older students branded phonics "a baby's game," although McGivney continued to teach with it, and he reported that it was "difficult to get books simple enough in material that they are not too juvenile for our young men."[117]

Adolescents who attended Edith L. Groves School for Girls also had remedial reading instruction by 1945, if not earlier. Teacher Stella Webb was in charge of a program that seems similar to Koerber and McGivney's, in which she diagnosed girls' "reading ills" and attempted to correct them. There was also individual teaching at the school for girls who had difficulty with arithmetic.[118]

Conclusion

In the 1930s and early 1940s, teachers and other educators seemed to gain new confidence in the educability of auxiliary pupils, particularly youngsters diagnosed with special-subject disabilities. New developments, first in brain injury science and later in reading instruction and remedial education, helped to change conventional thinking that just a decade earlier, under the sway of IQ testers, had attributed just about all learning difficulties to low innate intelligence. Responding to these developments, Toronto public schools and the DOE instituted new remedial programs. While some historians, such as Franklin, view the changes of this period as part of an arc of medicalization in auxiliary education, they are better understood as a changing mood that moved auxiliary education away from an over-reliance on IQ theories of learning problems as fixed and resistant to instruction. With the treatment of special-subject disabilities now a possibility, Ontario's inspector of auxiliary classes, Amoss, promised in 1937 that the door to the renamed opportunity class would serve as an exit as well as an entrance. Diagnostic tests and basal and graded primers and readers supported individualized instruction in auxiliary and opportunity classes and junior vocational and handicraft schools. The new special class curriculum included more reading instruction and subjects such as literature and social studies.

Like the orthopaedic, sight-saving, deaf and hard-of-hearing, and speech correction classes (see chapter 4), remedial instruction portended that disabled children had greater potential than was previously believed. In auxiliary and opportunity classes and in junior vocational and handicraft schools, it promised greater mental equality for young- sters whose learning difficulties the schools could diagnose, treat, and remediate sufficiently in order for the child to re-enter the education- al mainstream. This was a significant change, one that generated the kind of excitement from school officials that is captured in Inspector Munro's account of the "remarkable Mabel" and her progress under remedial instruction. However, remedial instruction was never avail- able to all auxiliary and opportunity class pupils. School psychologists such as Stogdill still made extensive use of IQ tests to diagnose and make placement recommendations. Pupils with the lowest IQ scores were the least frequently recommended for remedial help, and aux- iliary and opportunity classes continued to disproportionately enrol boys, working-class and poor pupils, and members of specific ethnic groups, such as Roma.

Many of the changes of the 1930s and early 1940s, especially the rise of special-subject disabilities, were also related to innovations in educa- tional psychology. The area of personality adjustment grew enormous- ly in importance in the 1930s and early 1940s, in school psychology and in auxiliary education. The next chapter examines that growth.

Chapter Six

Changing Ideas in a Changing Environment: The Impact of Personality Adjustment and Child Guidance

In 1940, Dr Florence Dunlop, the psychologist at the Ottawa Public School Board, summarized her profession's evolving role: "The true psychological approach to education is to prevent disabilities from arising in academic subjects and in personality adjustments; failing this prevention, to detect, diagnose and correct maladjustments as soon as they arise."[1] Two central developments Dunlop names helped to refashion auxiliary education in the 1930s and early 1940s. The first was the rise of special-subject disabilities (see chapter 5). The second, which I will examine in this chapter, was the influence on auxiliary education of mental hygiene, psychological theories about personality adjustment, and child guidance clinics. The psychological concept of maladjustment that mental hygienists introduced both shaped and was shaped by a continuing shift in ideas about disability and educational difficulties and disadvantages.

At their outset in the 1910s, auxiliary classes identified and segregated so-called mental defectives who reformers believed should be in custodial institutions for life. Auxiliary education was heavily influenced by eugenicists and their ideas. With the transformation of thinking about children's learning and psychological difficulties that I describe in this and the previous chapter, eugenics' influence over auxiliary education waned. Mona Gleason writes in *Small Matters: Canadian Children in Sickness and Health* that "doctors, nurses, teachers, and curriculum specialists contributed in important and decisive ways to a eugenic-infused pedagogy of failure regarding disability into the 1940s and indeed beyond."[2] She is indisputably correct that eugenics greatly influenced the outlook on disabled children in the twentieth century. Nevertheless, I would argue for a slightly different periodization than this for auxiliary education. After 1930, special-subject disabilities, remedial education, and, as we shall now see, mental hygiene significantly remade auxiliary education and in the process all but eliminated eugenics' influence in it by about 1945. True, an evolving eugenics may have continued to influence other aspects of public policy long after 1930, as Erika Dyck and others credibly claim.[3] Its influence on auxiliary education, however, declined markedly.

Auxiliary education was quickly evolving from a novel reform to an institutionalized feature of the school system. Auxiliary programs would weather the Great Depression that threatened to slow the expansion of city school systems for the first time in decades. Toronto's auxiliary programs emerged from the tumultuous 1930s in a position of strength. I conclude this chapter by looking at a final development that occurred in auxiliary education in the 1940s. If it was not directly the result of the ascendance of mental hygiene and special-subject disabilities, it nevertheless – like these developments – signalled a more hopeful attitude towards the capacities of young people with disabilities. This development was an expanding curriculum in handicraft schools, bolstered, it turns out, by the contributions that current and former pupils made to society, industry, and combat during the Second World War.

The Rise of Mental Hygiene in Education

Appearing initially in the 1920s, mental hygiene – a new type of psychology – devoted attention to what its practitioners described as "personality adjustment." It would shortly also spawn child guidance clinics for treating emotional and behavioural problems. Within a decade's time, mental hygiene had become representative of the view that mental states were built in environments and that changing a person's surroundings could change their mental condition. Because they believed in malleability, many mental hygienists by this time rejected the hereditarian doctrine that personality and mental capacity were innate and impervious to change.[4] In fact, quite like remedial educators, they had a committed interest in the improvability of mental conditions. As Gleason argues in *Normalizing the Ideal: Psychology, Schooling, and the Family in Postwar Canada*, by the 1930s, "the future of psychology as a vibrant and viable social science depended on its movement away from the hereditary, and therefore unchangeable, basis for mental hygiene to the environmental, and therefore treatable and pliable, basis."[5]

One of the earliest experiments in mental hygiene and child guidance anywhere in North America was the Canadian National Committee for Mental Hygiene (CNCMH) five-year study (1924–9) of Regal Road Public School (PS) in Toronto.[6] Like many early mental hygiene projects, it was funded by the Rockefeller family fortune through the Laura Spelman Rockefeller Memorial.[7] The CNCMH was also heavily involved in eugenics and in the first intelligence quotient (IQ) surveys of Toronto schools in the late 1910s and early 1920s (see chapter 2). Before mental hygiene had fully branched off in the 1930s into environmental explanations for mental problems, the CNCMH in the 1920s was Canada's leading eugenics lobby *and* its leading proponent of mental hygiene – two creeds that at that time could coexist within one organization.[8] As Angus McLaren writes about the CNCMH in this era: "It is important not to exaggerate the gap that separated the eugenicists and the environmentalists. Although their methods differed, their goals of efficient social management were similar."[9]

W.E. Blatz directed the Regal Road mental hygiene study. A psychologist in the functionalist school that presupposed the adaptability of the mind, he was from the side of the CNCMH that held environmentalist views, which defined his clinical work and his special expertise in adjustment theory.[10] The well-adjusted child that Blatz and others envisioned was self-confident, cheerful, well-behaved, and got along well with others.[11] At Regal Road, Blatz observed and catalogued the causes of misbehaviour and maladjustment in schoolchildren and attempted to systematically develop treatments that he hoped would bring about positive changes in conduct and demeanour.[12] Blatz would gain international celebrity in the 1930s from his work with the famous Dionne quintuplets.[13] By decade's end, "Blatzian security," Theresa Richardson writes, had risen to prominence in Canadian child guidance circles. A theory of adjustment, it referred to not "a static state of safety but a state of mind characterized by serenity, meaning a faith in one's own ability to successfully deal with future events."[14] Adjustment theory was an early sign of the "turn to personality," or the drift in culture and educational institutions that Catherine Gidney describes from Victorian character formation and its ideals of self-sacrifice towards a modern psychology of individual self-fulfilment.[15]

Offered a chance in 1930 to extend Blatz's Regal Road study at taxpayer expense, Toronto Board of Education (TBE) trustees considered, and declined.[16] The end of the study, however, did not spell the end of mental hygiene in Toronto public schools. By the mid-1930s, the expanding child guidance movement gave mental hygienists across Canada and the United States regular opportunities to bring adjustment and personality theories to bear on schools.[17] In Toronto, this was apparent in the efforts of C.G. Stogdill, the director of the municipal Department of Public Health's Mental Hygiene Division, to reallocate a portion of the division caseload from IQ testing and mental disability diagnosis to child guidance work treating behaviour and adjusting personality.[18] Appointed director in 1931, he had taught at Jarvis Junior Vocational School in the 1920s before returning to university to become a medical doctor.[19] Under him, the division hired a psychiatric children's worker, Isabel Dalzell, who handled cases of "anti-social conduct" at school and in pupils' homes.[20] In 1938, the medical officer of health reported on the division's work: "The development of socially satisfactory personalities and the prevention of mental disabilities in later life is a primary function of mental hygiene, as part of our public health programme."[21] Dunlop, who described her work in Ottawa in similar terms, would have approved.

Alongside the shift towards personality, psychologists in child guidance clinics cultivated a new clientele. Kathleen Jones argues that in the 1920s and 1930s, the "everyday child," a universalizing category that covered youngsters from all classes, became an important clinic user. With this expanded category, child guidance experts brought the concept of maladjustment to families in every part of town, slums and suburbs included. At the same time, they redefined maladjustment as having more to do with normal children and emotions than with inherent badness and "delinquency and degeneracy."[22] They no longer clung to the old explanations related to working-class status and degeneration, originated in eugenics, that they had once used to account for many children's instabilities.[23] As class- and low-IQ-based explanations of bad behaviour declined in clinical work (although they never disappeared totally), explanations of maladjustment that mentioned gender and age increased. Jones argues that by the mid-1930s, growth in the numbers of middle-class children who visited child guidance clinics, children whose IQs were (or were presumed to be) average, propelled this difficult-to-perceive but nonetheless important transition.[24] Indeed, the interest of Toronto's middle class in child guidance grew to the extent that by the late 1930s, more than twenty child study groups existed in the city. These groups were organized for middle-class women through partnerships between Blatz's Institute of Child Study at the University of Toronto and the Toronto Home and School Councils.[25]

Adjustment in Auxiliary Education

The heightening attention paid to supposedly normal children in child guidance activities, along with lessening emphasis on degeneration and mental deficiency, did not mean that children with disabilities went overlooked. "Modern education takes as its aim the helping of children to make a wholesome adjustment to life and to develop well-integrated, socially effective personalities," Samuel R. Laycock reminded auxiliary educators in 1943. "This is the goal of *all* teachers, whether they teach in elementary schools, high schools or special schools." Laycock was an educational psychologist and, with Blatz, the nation's foremost child guidance expert.[26] Many of the things that marked a child as well-adjusted – body free of deformities, scholastic capability, and emotional security – were implicitly not available to disabled children, Gleason argues.[27] To psychologists such as Laycock, this placed young people with disabilities at a much greater risk of maladjustment than their non-disabled peers. Adjustment was thoroughly shaped by ability and disability (as well as by gender). Yet, with the exception of Gleason, scholars have not looked expressly at the adjustment-disability relationship, and have focused instead on the concept as it related to non-disabled children.[28]

However, child guidance experts could and often did attribute maladjustment to an unconventional body or disability. "It is a well known fact," Laycock wrote, "that nothing is so likely to cause a sense of inferiority in boys as lack of adequate size and strength or the presence of deformities." As for girls, Laycock stated that they became discouraged on account of "unattractive appearance, obesity or the presence of physical blemishes."[29] Disabled children, Laycock believed, were especially likely to be victimized by their own substandard bodies or minds: "It is the frustration of this kind that faces many types of exceptional children – the blind, the deaf, the crippled, the epileptic, the cardiac, the tuberculous, and so forth." Laycock thought that children whom educators designated subnormal or "dumb" became frustrated by their incapacities as well.[30]

Gendered notions about children's bodies played a particularly important part in the adjustment of young people with disabilities and other exceptional youngsters.[31] Jones argues that boys used an arsenal of gendered insults, such as "pansy," "fairy," or "sissy," against peers with physical differences. Boys on the receiving end of these taunts were thought to be vulnerable to maladjustment. A lad's physical disabilities signified to others "a lack of the stuff it took to be a real boy."[32]

The proper answer to such an insult – that is, the response signalling adjustment to child guidance professionals – was for the boy to fight for his boyhood. Daisy Hally, a psychiatric social worker at Toronto's Hospital for Sick Children, described a case exemplifying this thinking when she addressed the Ontario Educational Association (OEA) in 1934. The case involved "John J.," age fourteen, "a stockily built youngster with a high colour and rather feminine contour." She described John's problems with bullies and commented approvingly on him finally getting the courage to fight back and "lick" a boy who had called him a "fatty." Formerly sullen and dejected, John's rough defence of his boyhood indicated to Hally that he was taking responsibility for himself and progressing towards an appropriate adjustment.[33] Boys who were exceptional because they were intellectually gifted were thought susceptible to gendered threats to their adjustment as well. "Strangely enough," Laycock wrote, "the gifted, too, often have acute problems of adjustment in achieving a sense of personal worth. The desire not to be different and not to be thought a *pansy* drives many a gifted child [*sic*] to the level of mediocrity in mental tests."[34]

Adjusting a child often signified to adherents of adjustment theory that they should re-align the child's expectations to better fit them with her or his physical or mental abilities. This represented the adult guiding the young person towards an appreciation of the truth about their particular situation in life.[35] This element of adjustment especially affected children with disabilities. In their mental hygiene manual for teachers, for example, J.D.M. Griffin, Laycock, and William Line wrote the following about crippled children: "Too often these children, through the optimistic attitudes and encouragement of enthusiastic teachers, come to feel they can get a job and be completely self-supporting. While in some cases this is true, most of the children who are badly crippled must eventually be content with employment in some sheltered workshop or in their own home; and this is often disappointing in its remuneration."[36]

Laycock especially, it seems, emphasized teaching children with disabilities to accept and adjust to their situation, though by no means does this indicate that he thought the outlook for them was hopeless: "They should be led to frankly assess their own handicaps and limitations as well as their assets and talents." But adults should never allow disabled children's reach to exceed their grasp. "The Pollyanna mechanism is not a sound adjustment," Laycock wrote. The fictional Pollyanna, who looked for the bright side in even the worst situation, was no role model for real children with disabilities, he thought: "It is *not* nicer to be blind or deaf or crippled or to be a slow learner or have a weak heart. It is the part of mental health to frankly face situations – not only the liabilities but also the assets and then determine on wise courses of action."[37] Educators of disabled children, he believed, ought to instil in them the vital qualities of self-reliance and mature emotional independence that they would need in their later lives as independent disabled adults.[38]

Adults who tended to the psychological adjustment of young people with disabilities played a challenging game. An overly commiserating attitude could lead just as soon to maladjustment as an overly expectant one. "Unwise parents," Laycock said, overprotected disabled children: "Lavishing undue pity and sympathy on the handicapped child may result in the child feeling insecure since he senses in his parents the feeling that he is inferior."[39] Gender mattered here, too. Child guidance experts blamed mothers for many forms of insecurity but in particular for maladjustments that they said resulted from overprotective parenting. As Gleason and Jones show, they went as far as to develop pathological profiles of the overprotective, nagging, or, by contrast, emotionally unstable and distant mother who impeded her child's normal adjustment and indeed required diagnosis and treatment at the guidance clinic herself.[40] With their routine and candid style, Laycock and other mental hygienists added a new tone to the solicitous and pitying one often used around children with physical disabilities.[41]

Gradually, mental hygiene seeped into other areas of auxiliary education. If the school did not meet the individual pupil's needs, mental hygienists warned, it could actually produce maladjusted, emotionally handicapped children. Laycock argued that a program of studies that was not adapted progressively to the pupil's ability was "likely to cause a sense of frustration and thereby create a problem for adjustment." The effects of a mismatch were compounded for children with disabilities: "If, therefore, exceptional children appear to have more problems in attaining a sense of personal worth in mental tasks than is the case with more typical children, it is because curricula and teaching procedures have been better adapted to the latter, rather than for any other reason."[42] Laycock, Blatz, and other "child study progressivists," Theodore Christou notes, were highly attuned to child-centred development. Programs of study should be adapted to the healthy development of a child's personality, they believed, instead of focused on conveying particular subject matter. This type of curriculum would supposedly nurture a young person's complete intellectual, physical, psychological, and emotional profile. Ontario's new progressive *Programme of Studies for Grades I to VI of the Public and Separate Schools*, introduced in 1937, sought this balance with its holistic philosophy, child-centred approach, and focus on producing emotionally secure children.[43]

A few proponents of adjustment theory even proposed that maladjustment was the underlining cause of special-subject disabilities. Paul Witty of the School of Education at Northwestern University made this argument in an article for a 1938 issue of the child guidance practitioner publication *Understanding the Child*. He wrote that "a considerable portion of remedial work is limited in value since it attempts to help children who *have failed* rather than to correct the conditions which produce failure." These conditions included "personality aberrations and emotional frustrations" that caused special-subject disabilities. "Mechanical, routine" remedial pedagogy could not hope to address adequately what Witty claimed was in reality a psychological problem.[44] Elsewhere in the same issue, Stogdill wrote that most "so-called special disabilities" should in fact be blamed on children's personality problems or on poorly adapted curricula: "In the writer's opinion, 'special disabilities' are most fruitfully regarded as indicating inadequacies of the educational program on the one hand and aspects of the child's emotional and interest life on the other."[45] Speech teachers, in a similar manner, blamed stuttering on psychological maladjustment. Toronto teacher Bessie Bowling, who we first encountered in chapter 1 and whose career in auxiliary education spanned decades, wrote in *The School* in 1941 that stuttering "has to do with the whole personality, for it is a symptom of some emotional difficulty or conflict. Stuttering indicates that the person is not making a satisfactory adjustment to the group."[46]

Reading experts and remedial educators, however, disagreed with Stogdill and others who ascribed most reading or special-subject disabilities to maladjustment. They were more likely to view personality troubles as symptoms of a learning problem than as a cause. "Everyone who has worked with children who have failed to learn the ordinary things that others learn admits that emotion is part of the total complex in these cases," Grace Fernald wrote in *Remedial Techniques in Basic School Subjects*. But in a large majority of the cases of "extreme disability" she had treated over the years at her Los Angeles clinic, "emotional instability" followed a reading disability instead of the other way around: "The child began his school life joyfully, eager to learn to read and write, ... the emotional upset occurred only as the child's desire was thwarted by his inability to learn as other children did."[47] Emmett A. Betts, citing other remedial experts such as Leo Brueckner and Donald D. Durrell, characterized "an emotional reaction" as often "only a symptom of reading disability." Like his warning about the over-attribution of reading problems to low IQ, Betts believed that "too frequently have the causes of reading difficulties been ascribed to emotional instability, lack of confidence, inability to concentrate, unwillingness, and the like."[48]

Adjusting Toronto's Auxiliary Pupils

Mental Hygiene Division directors and school psychologists Stogdill and E.P. Lewis treated maladjusted Toronto schoolchildren in the 1930s and 1940s, attempting through different interventions in their schooling to guide them towards a better adjustment. The girls and boys they saw included pupils attending or recommended for auxiliary programs. A small number of these youngsters' pupil records can be found in the archival collections for Hester How, Duke of York, and Coleman public schools. The records illustrate the ways that psychologists handled different adjustment issues that auxiliary class pupils and other exceptional children faced. More often than not, the recommended remedy was changing a student's academic placement to be more in line with her or his abilities and needs. The psychologist determined these remedies, often using IQ tests to assess the child's level. Like remedial and reading experts such as Marion Monroe or Fernald, who used intelligence tests as part of their diagnostic process, mental hygienists did not dismiss IQ outright – they simply did not consider low intelligence an adequate explanation for every learning or psychological problem they encountered. Stogdill and Lewis's clinical practice of identifying mismatches between general ability and grade level in struggling Toronto schoolchildren was consistent with the theory that the former – and Blatz as well – advanced in scientific papers about improper school placements as responsible for many psychological maladjustments.[49] Stogdill and Lewis, in their clinical work, applied that theory most frequently to older pupils who had repeated grades and to girls and boys who misbehaved in school and were physically or socially awkward.

Stogdill determined that frustration brought on by improper school placement had caused Daisy T.'s maladjustment when he examined her in the late 1930s. She was fifteen and only in grade 5 at Duke of

York. Her "marked limitation of ability with resultant unsatisfactory school progress has no doubt caused [the] girl much unhappiness and is at the root of her defensive attitudes toward and unwillingness to continue longer in school," he wrote. Yet he also thought that if Daisy entered an academic program better suited to her abilities – he diagnosed her as subnormal – she could become adjusted: "Attractive in appearance and apparently a likeable sort of person when on her own and relieved of undue strain, [Daisy] has much in her favor." Stogdill recommended a girls' handicraft school. But instead, Daisy stayed in grade 5 at Duke of York. She subsequently left school permanently less than two weeks before her sixteenth birthday.[50]

Yvonne T. was an eight-year-old Coleman pupil who was misbehaving in school. "[Yvonne] is a big, sturdy-looking girl with a rather brusque aggressive manner," Lewis wrote in her Psychiatric examination report (PER) in the early 1940s. "School reports she bullies other children and is generally making a poor social adjustment." Lewis surmised that her problems were her size, lack of ability, and placement in the wrong program: "Child has dull normal ability to which she is not working up and she is very much overage and big for the grade." He was concerned as well about her "home conditions," which he said warranted follow-up, although he did not specify why. (Yvonne was being raised by a single mother, which may be why he thought she was vulnerable.) He recommended her for an ordinary class placement and later review. Early in the following school year, the principal "whipped" Yvonne for being a "continued nuisance." Two and half years later, Lewis examined her a second time and interviewed her mother. Little had changed: "[Yvonne] is a very big aggressive girl. Who is likely to get her way by force rather than tactful ways. She is of dull normal intelligence with low average social sense." Lewis recommended a handicraft school placement, in which she "would of course be happier." He also suggested that her teacher engage her in "occasional heart to heart talks," and that she join the Girl Guides. At the end of the school year, Yvonne finished grade 5, the highest grade at Coleman, and like other students at her school moved on to grade 6 at nearby Gledhill PS.[51]

Like Yvonne, Wendell A. was suffering because of an academic program that was poorly suited to his needs. But unlike Yvonne's, Wendell's personality adjustment had yet to be negatively affected, although Lewis believed it was under threat. Wendell "is a pleasant, good appearing lad, who is desirous of getting along and will do everything in his power," he wrote. "In so far as this involves good academic work, however, he cannot reach the goal since he lacks the capacity. He is disturbed about that now." In order to "preserve his good qualities of personality," Lewis recommended Wendell – whose IQ of 82 was too high for an auxiliary class placement – attend the non-academic program at Church Street School for Boys.[52]

Not every child who was in what a psychologist considered the wrong program, however, was thought to be at risk. As long as the youngster was agreeable and reasonably well-behaved, like Wendell, she or he could still be considered well-adjusted. Stogdill examined Bruce D. in 1931 after the boy scored poorly on a group IQ test: "He is overage for his grade and is mentally retarded three years." Bruce, however, was "cooperative throughout the test," and his school reported no discipline problems. Despite believing that he "would make better progress in an auxiliary class than he will in an ordinary grade," Stogdill nonetheless reported that "he appears to be a contented, well-adjusted boy."[53] In another case, Bonnie C., like Bruce, performed poorly on the intelligence test. Stogdill administered it to her to assess her suitability for Bolton School for Girls. Despite the fact that she was nearly sixteen and still in grade 6, he did not consider her maladjusted. She was "a very pleasant, friendly girl. She seemed very happy and well adjusted and thoroughly enjoyed the test situation, having a good sense of humour."[54]

In his clinical work, Stogdill sometimes attributed learning difficulties to personality maladjustment, the connection he theorized in his article in *Understanding the Child*. Ella V. was a Duke of York pupil he examined in the early 1930s. Her IQ was 95, within the normal range, yet she had been failing grades and was still in junior fourth at nearly sixteen years of age. "[Ella] has average mental ability with very good memory, especially for numbers – a fair vocabulary and a fair comprehension of words. The difficulty seems to one of personality. The girl has become discouraged with her progress," he reported. "She is sensitive and nervous about making an error and would rather give up than be wrong." Stogdill thought that Ella should attend one of the city's technical schools. Instead, she stayed for a third year in a row in junior fourth at Duke of York. She left school at age sixteen with less than a complete elementary school education.[55]

Teachers at junior vocational and handicraft schools devoted particular attention to their pupils' vocational guidance needs[56] and, increasingly from the 1930s onwards, to their personality adjustment needs as well. They believed that students who attended these schools were more likely than other young people of the same age to have problems adjusting.[57] Jarvis Junior Vocational implemented a guidance program in 1931 based on adjustment principles. Regarding the program, the school's principal, W.J. Tamblyn, boasted that "inferiority complexes, fears, emotions, prejudices, outbursts of temper are treated as carefully and it is hoped that some day it may be said as scientifically – as is indigestion or another physical disability." Treatment involved assigning each boy to a carefully selected homeroom. "Teachers of different personality traits are chosen [for each homeroom]," Tamblyn said, "because it has been found that a teacher of one personality will not appeal to certain children, while those of a different disposition will appeal to others."[58]

John McGivney and Walter Koerber, reading teachers at Jarvis Junior Vocational, subscribed to psychological adjustment theories, along with theories of special-subject disabilities and remedial instruction. Both attributed non-reading in at least some pupils to adjustment issues. A past school trauma surrounding the boy's very first attempts to learn to read – perhaps he did not like his teacher or his teacher did not like him – caused non-reading boys to establish "a compensating withdrawal mechanism," McGivney argued, meaning that they would avoid reading at all costs to conceal their difficulty. This explained, he claimed, why any non-reading boy at Jarvis Junior Vocational would, in order to learn to read, "give his right arm or his left leg or a million dollars (if he had it) but he would not freely put forward an extra ounce of energy."[59] Adjustment was behind the homeroom system at Bolton and Edith L. Groves schools for girls as well. Both used a "Receiving Room" to assess each new student's level before placing her in a class group.[60] At Bolton, homerooms were "elastic," and teachers could transfer girls between them. Personality adjustment assumed a greater importance than IQ in assembling the groupings. "For instance," Principal Mackenzie wrote,

> a sensitive girl with a high I.Q. quite often obtains the confidence she needs by working with a group where she can lead; while on the other hand, a girl with a low I.Q., who is inclined to parade her accomplishments would be checked by association with a superior group. The social adjustments made in these ways are of infinitely greater importance both to the girl and to her prospective employer than the additional academic, or vocational work she might receive through a very accurately graded system.[61]

Weathering the Great Depression

Auxiliary education costs money. From the 1900s to the 1920s, among Canadian schooling's most exhilarating expansionary decades, enrolments in regular grades and auxiliary classes surged and dollars often flowed freely, even during economic downturns.[62] In times like these, Toronto school officials easily justified the expense of auxiliary programs, even when acknowledging that they came at a higher per-pupil cost than regular classes. In 1928, Chief Inspector D.D. Moshier did a detailed accounting of auxiliary program costs. The TBE spent just shy of $400,000 yearly, he reported, to educate approximately 2,500 pupils "who are labouring under some disability."[63] (Total TBE expenditures for 1928–9 amounted to about $11.6 million.[64]) In the TBE in 1928, the per-pupil cost for an "ordinary public school pupil" was $91, while an "auxiliary class pupil" was $243. The discrepancy was due to the higher "average registration" in the ordinary classes. There, the average was forty-three pupils per class; in auxiliary classes, the average was just fifteen. The per-pupil cost for students in commercial, technical, and collegiate institute programs – that is, regular high schools – ranged from about $140 to $185. A junior vocational school pupil cost the board $230 (if male) or $244 (if female). Classes for the deaf and hard-of-hearing and sight-saving classes were even more costly and ranged from $250 to $290 per pupil. The most expensive program was the orthopaedic class, at $540 per pupil.[65] The provincial government's grant under the Auxiliary Classes Act defrayed only a tiny portion of the cost of auxiliary education. The government allocated the board $13,000 in 1928–9 for elementary auxiliary programs. It also granted, for junior vocational schools, an unspecified amount, possibly around $10,000.[66]

The Great Depression that began in late 1929 squeezed educational finances, and placed auxiliary programs under fiscal scrutiny for virtually the first time.[67] Toronto experienced tough times through most of the 1930s, though the city as a whole did not fare as badly as some other centres.[68] Two factors appear to have saved Toronto auxiliary education from suffering the cuts imposed on such programs in other cities during the decade. The first was the relative, and perhaps surprising, fiscal buoyancy of Toronto's entire public school system. The TBE had stable revenues during the depression. The board took in a low of $9.3 million from property taxes in 1930 and a high of $10.8 million in 1938.[69] True, not all of a school system's revenues come from property taxes; another funding source is provincial transfers, and the province cut cash transfers to school boards deeply in the 1930s.[70] But Toronto, which raised 95 per cent of its budget from its own property tax base even before the depression, received little from the province to begin with, and thus provincial cuts did not hurt it significantly.[71] The matter of expenditures also enters into the budgeting picture, and the TBE also managed to keep its spending in check. Naturally, the best way for any school board to do this is to belt-tighten on its largest expense: teacher salaries. The TBE reportedly made "deductions from the salary Schedules to ease the burden of taxes." These pay cuts, applied across the board to teachers, were in the amounts of 3.5 per cent in 1935 and 6.3 per cent in 1936.[72]

In jurisdictions less fiscally fortunate than Toronto, however, auxiliary education often went on the chopping block alongside other "fads and frills." This is what happened in numerous US cities. A 1933 National Education Association survey showed that nearly 10 per cent of American city school systems had already either partly or entirely cut classes for children with physical disabilities and almost 16 per cent (about fifty cities and towns) had made similar cuts to their classes for "mentally handicapped children." Still, auxiliary education was not hit as hard as other programs. Night schools and adult classes were cut back or eliminated totally in 43 per cent of cities surveyed; summer schools suffered this fate in more than 41 per cent of the cities the National Education Association polled. [73]

In addition to the shielding effects of the TBE's financial good fortune, interested organizations continued to support auxiliary programs during the depression. Old and new allies – the National Council of Women, the Women Teachers' Association, the Big Sisters (Jewish, Protestant, and Roman Catholic branches), and the Home and School Association – rallied to the cause and probably also helped to insulate Toronto auxiliary programs against cost-cutting.[74] A sympathetic article clipped from a local newspaper and pasted in the Bolton School for Girls scrapbook in this period contains one reply of auxiliary education proponents to their cost-cutting critics: "How many folk who pay school taxes know that in the city girls are learning hair-cutting, manicuring ... which ordinarily belong to the 'beauty parlor'? ... Frills? Perhaps, but made of 'whole cloth' by 'real girls.'"[75]

Toronto's auxiliary programs were in good enough condition for the board to show them off to visitors. In 1934, the International Council for Exceptional Children held its annual meeting in the city. American and other foreign delegates attended and were treated to a tour of TBE auxiliary programs, with stops at the Hester How sight-saving classes, the Clinton PS oral classes for the deaf, the three junior vocational schools, and other programs. A main event of the conference was an afternoon panel discussion that seated American dignitaries with their Canadian hosts. Notable heads of special education services in American cities – Newark's Meta L. Anderson, Detroit's Alice Metzner, and Wilmington, Delaware's J.E. Wallace Wallin, who was also a psychologist and internationally recognized author of books about exceptional children – were on the panel. So were influential Canadians Harry Amoss and Helen MacMurchy, although the latter had been heard from only very little in auxiliary education circles for more than a decade.[76]

Handicraft School Pupils during the Second World War

As they had during the Great Depression, national and world events during the Second World War changed the context of education in Toronto's schools, and auxiliary classrooms were also affected. Historically, educators saw few prospects for the young people who attended handicraft schools (or what originally were called junior vocational schools; the program was renamed in 1935). However, these meagre expectations rose noticeably during the first half of the 1940s. New employment and educational opportunities during the war, as well as service in the armed forces, enabled current and former handicraft school students to join the workforce and contribute to the fight against fascism. Through these activities, they demonstrated to educators their capabilities and potential to participate in their communities. One result was a new childcare curriculum at the girls' handicraft schools. Along with other changes, the new program implied a growing spirit of optimism about handicraft pupils as closer to equals to other youth.

The founders of junior vocational schools in the early 1920s believed in the intellectual inferiority of a subgroup of the adolescent population that compulsory attendance laws forced to stay in school to age sixteen. They sometimes harboured eugenics-based fears about these adolescents' lack of sexual restraint as well. They believed that they – especially the ones labelled subnormal – would require significant vocational and moral training to compensate for their deficiencies. Only then would they be qualified to hold even menial positions in the industrial workforce or, in the case of girls, to work as domestic servants in the homes of others. The Second World War, however, created fresh demand for workers and new employment opportunities for youth, including adolescents eligible for handicraft schools. Historians such as Ruth Pierson and Jennifer Stephen have shown how an insatiable wartime Canadian labour market demanded all available workers.[77] In 1942, the federal government established the National Selective Service to tap incompletely mobilized labour pools, especially the portion of the female population that was not yet working outside the home.[78] Youth were mobilized as well. High schools in many parts of Ontario closed early in the spring and opened late in the fall so that students could work in agriculture. There was a sixfold increase in the number of employment certificates that the province's schools issued to fourteen- and fifteen-year-olds. Educational institutions also became involved, reluctantly at first, in labour force and army recruitment.[79] Early efforts should be expanded, TBE superintendent C.C. Goldring argued in 1943, to teach students about "the special training available in the various branches of the armed forces. Both boys and girls," he continued, "need to know a great deal about working in war industries, the type of jobs available, the duties, the kind of work needed, the training necessary and where it can be secured."[80]

The demands of the wartime economy placed handicraft school girls in an unprecedented position in which there was a strong call for their labour. The nature of that demand caught their teachers off guard. Although John Allison has noted the explosion in demand for young adult and older Toronto female technical school graduates to work in war industries at companies such as Small Arms Limited, it was not solely industrial workers and soldiers who were needed and who would come from the city's schools.[81] As early as 1939, the year hostilities broke out in Europe, Edith L. Groves School had begun to receive requests for its students to work as childminders for youngsters whose regular caregivers – their mothers, siblings, and other kin – were employed outside the home in the city's mushrooming defence industries. The school "had never recommended our students as nursemaids," Principal Jane Little would later write in an article in *Special Class Teacher* in 1942. Staff admitted that they were surprised to learn that many of the school's graduates "were holding these positions successfully."[82] In fact, Little noted, "since the establishment of the school in 1923, pupils had been trained in homemaking, domestic science, sewing, and power operating, but it had been considered unwise to train our type of pupil (retarded girls) to accept complete responsibility for infants and pre-school children."[83]

By 1941, staff at Edith L. Groves School were ready to change the training the school afforded. At first the motive was to address labour force demands in a time of war, but eventually staff recognized that in defiance of what auxiliary educators had previously believed, handicraft school girls were capable of working in areas such as childcare. The staff started a special course that year, a childcare class that would serve "as part of our defence program," teaching adolescent girls at the school to care for infants.[84] At first, they moved ahead cautiously, their apprehensiveness reflecting a lack of conviction that these girls could successfully look after young children. They did not allow students younger than fifteen to enrol. "Undesirables" who were without proper "character, appearance, and good manners" and who lacked experience caring for younger siblings were also barred. But well-adjusted adolescent girls, staff began to think, might in fact possess qualities making them employable as nursemaids: "It was felt that what these girls lacked in mental equipment they might make up to the children by their extraordinary kindness, good manners, and good character."[85] Moreover, Little observed, many of the girls already had experience minding their own siblings and their neighbours' children.[86]

Although the childcare course was initiated to answer the emergency call for daycare, as the expectations of Little and other educators grew, it expanded to include training adolescent handicraft pupils to take up childcare work later as a career. In 1942, Little remarked: "After the war, nursemaids who have had special training will be in demand and in this way we are preparing them for post-war conditions."[87] The same year, Principal Mackenzie introduced the course at her Bolton School for Girls. By 1945, the burgeoning Bolton program had a space of its own, a nursery located in a "large, sunny room on the second floor." Girls taking the course were responsible for the care of twenty children aged two to five.[88]

As the handicraft school child-care course expanded, it acquired a fuller and more sophisticated curriculum. Pupils listened to talks on topics such as "parent education," delivered by a psychologist and other "outsider lecturers."[89] Josephine Budden, a Bolton teacher, described a program of studies in 1945 that "taught the fundamentals of child training," apparently influenced by child development principles and adjustment theory. The course covered "both theoretically and practically, the type of discipline best suited to the young child, the kind of play equipment which is of the most interest and value, the kind of social life he enjoys and the satisfaction a child receives in doing things himself."[90] Four senior girls completed a three-week training stint in which each in turn was "placed in charge of the Nursery," carefully observed by a staff member who had graduated from the University of Toronto's Institute of Child Study, which was under Blatz's leadership.[91] The childcare course became one of the TBE's most successful secondary school programs of the 1940s. Goldring, in his wartime pamphlet *A Forward Look at the Toronto School System*, commended Edith L. Groves and Bolton schools for "pioneer work" in the nursery training course and in their day nurseries.[92]

"The performance during the war of people with mental retardation and other disabilities," Margret Winzer argues, "created a new level of confidence and expectancy and justified the notion that special children could learn more than just fundamental skills." As a result, auxiliary educators expanded special class curricula for older children to better coordinate programs of study with "national defense priorities" and to provide students with skills that they could actually use to live independently in the community.[93] Pupils at Groves and Bolton who took the childcare course were not the only young people with disabilities or learning difficulties to contribute to Canada's war effort. The Canadian armed forces may have screened out more than 10,000 men and 775 women "for medical reasons" – including 387 men and forty-nine women rejected from service after 1941 for "nervous and mental disorders."[94] Yet significant numbers of former pupils of Jarvis Junior Vocational made it into the armed forces. (Graduates of the girls' schools may have as well, though unlike at Jarvis Junior Vocational, no record of their enlistments survives in the school board's archives.) The Jarvis Junior Vocational log of "Graduate Visitors" for the 1941 to 1944 period includes approximately 150 names, and slightly less than one-third of this number were serving, or had served, in the armed forces. Two brothers who visited their former school in 1942 were in the army. Other visitors that year included several past pupils who had enlisted in the air force. One alumnus visiting in 1943 had served overseas, attaining the rank of sergeant, and was back in Canada to train personnel. A "negro" former student was posted to western Canada in the Army Service Corps.[95] In his 1947 study of 1,000 graduates of the school, W.J. McIntosh observed with brimming pride that 270 graduates had served their King. Eight were killed in action. Other Jarvis Junior Vocational alumni who did not serve in the armed forces worked in factories, in delivery, or as skilled tradesmen during the war years.[96]

Conclusion

Mental hygiene, personality adjustment theories, and child guidance, as well as new theories of special-subject disabilities, all helped to improve auxiliary educators' outlook on the possibilities and potential of young people with disabilities and learning difficulties. The environmentalist views of the 1930s and early 1940s presupposed that the mind's condition was not immutable but was moulded by external factors that could be controlled. Consequently, diagnosis, treatment, and appropriate training in the correct educational setting could improve personality or learning problems or prevent them from appearing at all.

As they began to address maladjustment in all children, mental hygiene experts in the 1930s and 1940s still paid specific attention to how they believed the condition affected children with disabilities. Unconventional physical appearance, disability, or deformity signalled to them a possible maladjustment. Mental hygienists recommended parents and teachers conduct treatment with caution. Responsible adults did not pity disabled children but did not adopt a Pollyannaish attitude either. Instead, they encouraged disabled children to confront their situation without illusions, even if this meant lowering expectations – which in practice it often did. Stogdill and Lewis on many occasions recommended that a maladjusted child switch to a program better suited to her or his abilities, which could entail an auxiliary placement. Junior vocational and handicraft schools for adolescents took adjustment into consideration when they placed students in ability groups.

By the 1930s and early 1940s, auxiliary education was established enough to endure crisis events in the society that surrounded the schools. Toronto's auxiliary programs survived the depression well enough that the TBE confidently showed them off at the International Council for Exceptional Children conference in 1934. The conditions of the Second World War and the response of handicraft school pupils and their teachers to those conditions further showcased the solidity of the auxiliary class system, as well as its adaptability. During the war, adolescent girls attending handicraft schools and participating in the child-care training program pushed auxiliary education towards new ideas about learning potential and further away from a mindset influenced by the limiting eugenics of an earlier day.

Conclusion

In 1910 auxiliary education was a novelty, but over a few short decades it evolved into an entrenched feature of urban schooling. How did this happen? I have argued that auxiliary education defies an easy classification as either unimpeachable altruism or malevolent and naked social control. Satisfying accounts of its origins and development must discard such singular and over-determining arguments and instead embrace complexities and contradictions in order to explore the many vying interests involved. Changes to auxiliary education policy, teaching practice, and curricula have often come with subtle shifts in notions about the cause, nature, and treatment of disabilities and learning problems. Psychologists, remedial specialists, eugenicists, teachers, and other authorities have largely been responsible for those shifts. Yet it is impossible to fully appreciate the meaning of auxiliary education without also considering the complete range of reactions that pupils and parents had to its classes and programs. They greeted auxiliary education sometimes with hope, other times with trepidation. It had the power to meet their expectations and to dash them; to create opportunities and to deny them. In adapting to auxiliary education, Toronto's public school system resembled, admired, copied, and from time to time inspired forward-looking systems like those in Pittsburgh, Cleveland, Boston, New York, Vancouver, Ottawa, and Los Angeles. An account of auxiliary education in Toronto public schools tells us much about what transpired in other urban systems as well.

Toronto's eugenicists were some of the earliest supporters of auxiliary classes. They proposed them as a "clearing house" for a custodial farm colony that they could wield as a weapon in their fight against feeblemindedness.[1] School officials also had lofty hopes for auxiliary education. R.H. Cowley was chief inspector during most of the 1910s and 1920s when the Toronto Board of Education (TBE) completed the most significant expansion of its auxiliary programs. He believed, characteristically of administrative progressives of his generation, that educational science in the form of innovations such as intelligence quotient (IQ) testing would help schools to channel each pupil to her or his proper place in a system increasingly differentiated by function. Programs for pupils labelled disabled, deaf, or in some way or another disadvantaged were absolutely crucial to the differentiation on which administrative progressives, like Cowley, believed modern and efficient school systems depended.[2] Special classes for backward children had the added benefit of dealing immediately with what was then called retardation, which referred to the large number of schoolchildren who were over-age for the grades they were in.

Along with eugenicists and administrative progressives, child savers were the third group whose ideas were responsible for bringing auxiliary education to Toronto initially. The forest schools and open-air classes they supported were supposed to improve the sad lot of disadvantaged and sickly urban children by exposing them to the fresh air that helped ward off tuberculosis and by soothing the disabling effects of poor health and malnutrition. Another type of program, special foreign classes, was intended to ensure that the inability to speak English was only a temporary handicap for immigrant children. Unlike the other programs I have examined, which stood the test of time, forest schools reached their apex in the 1910s. They then declined with the diminishing tuberculosis threat. Victoria Park Forest School closed for good in 1934.[3] High Park Forest School hung on for several more decades, but by the end it was more akin to a summer camp than an auxiliary program. It finally shut down in 1964 when the Toronto Board of Health declared there was "no justification, on health grounds" for it to continue.[4] As immigration slowed from the outbreak of the First World War until the late 1940s, there was less need for the foreign classes that had proliferated in Toronto in the early 1910s when immigration reached record heights.[5] This program, however, would be revived in the 1950s as "new Canadian classes."[6]

By the end of the 1910s, stubbornly high numbers of over-age pupils appeared to underscore policy failure and the need to re-evaluate the causes of learning problems. The American inventor of mass IQ testing for public schools, Lewis Terman, announced that "the retardation problem is exactly the reverse of what it is popularly supposed to be," and argued that most children who failed to learn lacked the necessary mental capacity. They did not fail because of poor teaching, ill health, or other external factors that educationists such as Leonard Ayres had previously said were responsible for the greatest proportion of retardation.[7] Terman's view – that intelligence was inborn and intractable – dominated policy in Toronto in the 1920s. The TBE hired its first school psychologist, Eric Kent Clarke. Under his guidance, the board abolished separate auxiliary classes for backward and mentally defective children, merging both types into auxiliary classes for subnormals. An IQ test score in the 50 to 75 range became the main entry to auxiliary classes during this decade. The curriculum was redesigned as well, expertly planned to fit what were perceived to be the limited abilities of subnormal students. The science of IQ set expectations for what and how much these pupils could learn.

In 1923, the TBE established junior vocational schools for adolescent subnormals (later known as handicraft schools). With vocationalism ascendant and juvenile employment opportunities in decline, educators, employers, and families turned to schools to prepare adolescents more directly for work. Beginning in 1920, Ontario raised the regular school-leaving age from fourteen to sixteen. Secondary school enrolments in Toronto more than doubled over the next ten years. Officials struggled to keep pace with a population that had become more diverse as well as larger. Former auxiliary class pupils and other adolescents with low IQs were a particular source of concern. In the mid-1920s, after visiting similar schools in Pittsburgh, Toronto school officials expanded the junior vocational program to take in adolescents labelled dull-normal (IQ 75 to 90). Junior vocational and handicraft schools prepared boys for unskilled industrial labour and girls for domestic service. Authorities at the schools for girls, fearing that their pupils were especially vulnerable to moral ruination, hired a social worker, Helen Robinson, who tried to channel pupils' extracurricular interests into what she believed were wholesome activities, such as swimming lessons and summer camps, and away from morally suspect popular amusements. Even though most working-class youngsters did not attend them, and indeed were more likely to attend collegiate institutes or technical and commercial high schools, junior vocational and handicraft schools helped forge an early association between special and vocational education at the secondary school level that has proved stubbornly persistent over time.[8]

The TBE added a final slate of auxiliary programs in the 1920s. These were the classes for children with physical disabilities; those who were partially sighted, deaf, and hard-of-hearing; and those with speech difficulties. The board was remarkably forward-looking in its accommodations for pupils in these programs. It modified the Wellesley PS plant, installing ramps and handrails for children in wheelchairs or who used crutches. Sight-saving programs employed special materials, such as large-type textbooks. All of the programs just mentioned were designed to give the youngsters who attended them access to as much of the mainstream curriculum as possible. Supported by developments in surgery and rehabilitation therapy, the programs pushed past Victorian notions of infirmity to adopt modern ideas about disabled people's capacity to surmount handicaps. But this focus on typicality came at a high price. One example is the controversial pure oralist method in day-school classes for deaf children at Clinton PS, which forbade students from using sign language. Oralists, such as Toronto's Imogen Palen, believed with great conviction that deaf children would only truly become part of the community by learning to read lips and to speak. Yet speech and lip-reading were very difficult to learn, especially for children deafened at a young age. Moreover, even when students did learn them, they often proved of limited use in daily life.

The financial calamity of the 1930s failed to wipe out auxiliary education. Toronto's programs emerged from the decade as strong as ever. But this did not mean that auxiliary education stood still. In the 1930s and early 1940s, significant changes occurred to theories about learning difficulties; to the psychology of exceptionality; and to auxiliary programs, policies, and curriculua. Clinicians working in the area of brain injury, psychologists studying specific learning problems, and remedial educators developed the concept of special-subject disability. It signified that – contrary to what IQ testers such as Terman had argued in the 1920s – low innate intelligence was not the cause of every child's learning difficulty. Special-subject disability created the possibility that children of normal IQ could experience a disability in just one area, such as reading. In Toronto, school inspector P.F. Munro, taken with the success of a student he referred to as "Mabel," heralded special-subject disabilities as an innovatory approach to auxiliary education. Remedial treatment in auxiliary classes would enable some of their pupils to rejoin mainstream grades. Teachers adopted the concept. While the TBE hired new remedial teachers, the province, in 1937 – recognizing the shifting purpose of auxiliary classes – changed the name of this program to opportunity classes. And yet the new policy was narrowly applied. IQ testing continued, with students who received the highest scores the only ones gaining access to the special-subject disability diagnosis and to remedial instruction.

At about the same time that special-subject disability emerged, mental hygiene experts were at work on theories about adjustment and exceptionality. They thought that children with disabilities were at greater risk for maladjustment because their disabled bodies did not meet gender and other norms of appearance. Yet they had faith that they could still treat and mitigate these children's psychological problems. The application of mental hygiene and special-subject disability theories in auxiliary programs challenged the pessimism of eugenicists and IQ testers that had dominated a decade earlier. Their views fell into decline as auxiliary classes after 1930 began to reflect the belief that mental states were malleable and that remedial education and psychological treatment could improve the learning chances of at least some young people.

As we have seen throughout this book, young people with disabilities and learning difficulties were historical actors who interacted with auxiliary education. So were their parents. Both could only seldom prevail against inspectors, provincial officials, and trustees who set auxiliary education policies; teachers who taught the classes; and psychologists and principals who could recommend and place students. Especially in the 1920s, IQ spoke loudly and decisively. It usually dictated diagnosis and placement, regardless of other struggles a child might be facing, including frequent absences, illness, lack of aptitude for one but not all forms of academic work, lack of effort, or bad teaching, which would then go unaddressed. It was unusual for young people to gain much control over their circumstances in the IQ testing moment, though a rare few did. Even after 1930 and the rise of special-subject disability, auxiliary classes were still limiting for many who attended them. So were junior vocational and handicraft schools. Youth voted with their feet, fleeing these schools when employment beckoned. A much smaller number of girls and boys, with their parents' help, at times refused to attend auxiliary programs for various reasons.

In other cases, however, auxiliary education brought benefits, or families sought out the classes, and sometimes even petitioned the board to admit their children. Some children who attended orthopaedic, sight-saving, and hearing or speech classes (see chapter 4) said that they had benefited educationally from that attendance and from being in a program that separated them, and other children like them, from mainstream classes. When IQ's dominance receded in the 1930s, a few children received teaching in auxiliary classes that addressed a special-subject disability. One group of immigrant parents may have embraced the junior vocational schools as a gender-segregated option with a domestic science curriculum that would enable them to further their daughters' education along lines that met with their traditions. Adolescent girls at Toronto handicraft schools used the unprecedented conditions of the Second World War to change some terms of their schooling to somewhat better reflect their needs.

From Auxiliary to Special Education

Auxiliary education in the first half of the twentieth century laid the foundation for special education today. Special education enrolments scaled dramatically upwards in the 1950s and 1960s. Reliable, school board-specific statistics tracking expansion over the years are difficult to locate, but I was able to assemble the following haphazard but indicative figures. In 1956, 3,500 TBE students in a total pupil population of 83,000 were enrolled in special classes. They represented about 4.2 per cent of the total TBE student population.[9] In 1974, special class pupils' share of that total population had risen to 7.2 per cent.[10]

By the late 1960s, however, serious cracks had begun to appear in the previously practically foundational reasoning that more special class services and more students accessing them were indisputably positive developments. In 1970, parents and community activists in the inner-city Toronto neighbourhood of Trefann Court formally accused the TBE's special programs of pervasive bias. "The school system directly discriminates against the poor and immigrant, and ... the streaming of children into technical and special education is part of that discriminatory process," a brief the group prepared alleged.[11] "Our general impression, then, from seeing our own children and from the reports of their success in getting jobs, is that they don't learn much in Opportunity Class and in the Special Education high schools which follow."[12]

The TBE commissioned its first-ever systematic study of student demographics in response to the Trefann Court controversy.[13] The findings of the Every Student Survey largely confirmed the charge parents and activists had laid. The survey exposed rates of special education attendance for children of lower income families that were from twenty to more than sixty times higher than rates for children of professionals. Indeed, 4.1 per cent of pupils in the "lowest" occupational group, consisting of households headed by labourers and others with

similar working-class occupations, were enrolled in opportunity classes and other special programs. Yet in the "highest" occupational group,
households headed by professionals, just 0.2 per cent of children were
enrolled in these programs. In the single-mother occupational group,
7.1 per cent of pupils were enrolled in opportunity programs; in the unemployed group, the figure was 8.7 per cent; in the group in which the
head received "welfare" or mother's allowance, it was 13.4 per cent.[14]
These findings share many similarities with some of the auxiliary education demographics of Toronto for the 1920–45 period.[15]

The consequence of the Trefann Court challenge, the Every Student
Survey that followed it, and similar developments in places beyond
Toronto was a serious reassessment of separate special education settings. The questions people asked were not totally new. Educators,
policy-makers, and others have debated setting for quite a long time.[16]
In the 1900s and 1910s, long before anyone used the terms "mainstreaming" or "inclusion" – even before separate special classes were
firmly established, for that matter – some systems, school leaders, and
educators embraced inclusive or semi-inclusive alternative settings for
educating backward children. The rise of auxiliary education from the
1910s to the 1940s slowly closed off those other paths.[17] But the politi-
cization of setting remerged with a vengeance in the 1970s, followed
quickly by relatively radical policy change.[18]

In 1970, the TBE adopted the continuum of services model based on
the revolutionary cascade of services approach designed by the University of Minnesota's Evelyn Deno, which was then gaining popularity across Canada and the United States. By this time, most exceptional
students in both countries were in totally segregated settings. Only a
small number were in integrated classrooms. Deno's model inverted
this placement pyramid. It advocated placing the largest number of
special class pupils possible in the most integrated programs for as
much of their school day as possible. The most segregated programs
were to be reserved for the smallest number of pupils.[19] This became
known as "mainstreaming." In 1975, the United States Congress passed
the Education for All Handicapped Children Act (PL 94–142), effectively making mainstreaming legally compulsory.[20] Ontario passed similar legislation in 1980. Bill 82 mandated public education for virtually
all school-age youngsters in the province and integrated some existing separate programs for mentally retarded children into mainstream
school buildings. But it stopped short of PL 94–142's "least restrictive

environment" language. It did not require boards to include exceptional students in regular graded classrooms. A requirement for integrated placements in regular classrooms would not appear in Ontario schools until further legislative changes forced the issue in the early 1990s.[21]

Despite the reforms of this period, special education continued to grow unabated right through the 1980s and 1990s. By 1982, 19 per cent of TBE elementary students received special education services in segregated or semi-integrated settings like pull-out classes; 3.7 per cent of secondary school students received these services as well.[22] The 1997 Every Secondary Student Survey asked TBE pupils to report on special education services they had received at any point in their high school careers. Nearly one in five replied that they had participated in a "gifted/enrichment" program; 8 per cent had received learning disabilities services, including attending learning centres (withdrawal classes); 2 and 3 per cent of students, respectively, had attended reading clinics or participated in special education programs for students with behavioural problems.[23] The Every Secondary Student Survey was the last survey that the TBE would carry out as a school board. In 1997, the Ontario government forced it to amalgamate with surrounding public school boards, creating the mega-sized Toronto District School Board (TDSB).[24]

In the 2000s, the TDSB, like other jurisdictions, moved from mainstreaming towards inclusion. The difference between the two is important. Mainstreaming merely placed disabled children within regular classrooms, with little thought to how they might participate meaningfully. Inclusion, however, "instead of focusing on instructional needs alone," treats disabled children in schools as another "equity-seeking group – not unlike racialized or lesbian and gay students."[25] Touching on more than setting, inclusion cuts across educational policy areas. It attempts to ensure that disabled students have access to playgrounds and play equipment, that they will not be unfairly targeted by safe schools policies, and that they will see other disabled people in the curriculum, on the teaching staff, and in other places in the school.[26]

Inclusion, like mainstreaming before it, did not seem to impede the expansion of special education. Now special education grew through the number of identified pupils, not necessarily through the number of separate programs offered. By the 2011–12 school year, in the amalgamated TDSB, 46,000 youngsters had "Special Education Needs." This represented 18 per cent of students across both the elementary and secondary panels. Nearly half of this total, however, were students who possessed an Individual Education Plan (IEP) but had yet to be "formally identified" with a specific special educational need through the Identification, Placement, and Review Committee (IPRC) process.[27]

With growth comes increased spending. In 1998, the final year before the province took over educational finance for all of its school boards, and drastically changed the special education funding formula in the process, the TDSB's expenditures on special education totalled $213 million.[28] Projected 2017–18 operating expenditures show special education on pace to hit a much higher figure. Special education will cost the TDSB $373.7 million, or 11.3 per cent, of its colossal $3.29 billion operating budget.[29] This is a far cry from what the last available figures for the period of study in this book show. In 1943, the TBE spent about $550,000 on auxiliary education, or 5 per cent of the total board budget of $10.7 million. The biggest share was for the handicraft schools, which ate $230,000.[30]

From Special Education to Inclusion?

Today calls for inclusion are intensifying. "Policy talk" in Toronto's public school system strongly favours inclusion. However, the reality is that the continuum of services model from the 1970s still dominates practice in schools.[31] In 2013, approximately 13,200 TDSB students labelled exceptional attended segregated classes for more than 50 per cent of the school day. Fewer exceptional students – 9,400 – attended mainstream classes for more than 50 per cent of the day.[32]

The debate about inclusion therefore is ongoing and demonstrates that a historical absence of consensus between and among parents, educators, and policy-makers on the way to educate exceptional children is alive and well. Many teachers support inclusion in principle, but study after study has found that large numbers of them, even the ones who are sympathetic, worry that it is difficult to put into practice.[33] Parents have been the main proponents for mainstreaming and inclusion, and have used lobbying and even litigation to win significant policy changes in Canada and the United States since the 1970s at least.[34] But parents do not speak in one voice either. Some have vocally opposed the closure of their children's special programs and the planned integration of these girls and boys into mainstream settings.[35] As recently as 2012, the Learning Disabilities Association of Canada heralded the Supreme Court decision in *Moore v. British Columbia* as a victory for "a cascade or continuum" model of special education services over "current interpretations of inclusive practice." Moore's parents brought a complaint against School District No. 44, North Vancouver, to the British Columbia Human Rights Commission in 1994 after the district closed the separate special class that their son attended. The Supreme Court ruled that the district had discriminated against Moore by offering him only an inclusive placement.[36]

Or consider what some disabled and deaf adults have to say about special and inclusive education. Edna Barg was the sight-saving pupil in the 1930s whose experiences we looked at in chapter 4. "Frequently today," she wrote in the 1980s, "we hear of parents who want their handicapped child to be allowed to enter the neighbourhood school with his friends. Is this really the best way to educate these children? I think it is not." Her grandson, who was "perceptually handicapped," struggled in the regular classroom, just as she had five decades earlier, until he was moved to a separate special class. "Now he is in a class with other bright, but handicapped children and is doing very well, and he is happy at school. What a tragedy if he had been kept in the neighbourhood school and allowed to fail."[37] Members of the deaf community in the United States have responded with "dismay, if not outrage" to inclusive education policies they believe are a fresh attempt to rob deaf children of a separate linguistic and cultural heritage to which they are entitled.[38]

Is educational policy, at this present moment, moving relentlessly towards inclusion, as some have suggested?[39] If history is an indication, nothing in the form exceptional children's education will take is inevitable. Its future will be determined by the same swirling educational, social, political, scientific, and individual human factors that, as we have seen, defined its past. A class by themselves? A still-unsettled issue.

Pupil Record Cards

The Toronto Board of Education (TBE) began to use pupil record cards in 1916, around the same time that other large urban school systems in Canada and the United States adopted them as part of modern pupil accounting practices.[1] This book draws on two types of pupil record the TBE used in the 1916–45 period: the Office record card (ORC) (see figure A1) and the Admission-discharge-promotion (ADP) (see figure A2). The single-sided ORC is a 3"-by-5" index card. The ADP card is larger (5"-by-8") and is two-sided. The same basic pupil information – e.g., name, address, birth date, birthplace, father's occupation – can be found on both types of record. There is, however, a great deal of evidence on ADPs that is not present on ORCs. Every time a TBE pupil was examined through the school system by a nurse, doctor, dentist, or psychologist, the examining party carefully recorded on the child's ADP the type and date of the examination and any diagnosis and treatment recommendations stemming from it. ADPs also record the grades students passed or failed, their marks, and their attendance.

Throughout this book, I have replaced pupils' given names and surnames, which appear on their records, with ecumenical-sounding pseudonyms that I have chosen randomly.[2]

The most significant difference between the two types of card was that the ADP followed the child from school to school, while the ORC did not. ORCs were a sort of registration card, retained in a school as a permanent catalogue of all the pupils who had ever attended.[3] (Prior to 1916, the TBE used register books for this purpose.)[4] When a child left a school, the ORC remained behind, and the child's new school started a fresh one. The ADP was different in that it functioned as the child's permanent record. Printed on it are instructions stating that it "must follow the pupil from room to room and school to school." An ADP went out of circulation only when the system "discharged" the student. This happened when he or she moved on to a secondary school, reached the school leaving age of sixteen while still in elementary school and quit, left elementary school at age fourteen or fifteen with an employment certificate or home permit, or transferred to a different city or to a Catholic separate or a private school. After discharge, the ADP remained at the last TBE elementary school the student had attended. There was one exception: If the student went to a junior vocational or handicraft school, the ADP card went, too. (This exception is significant to some of my conclusions in chapter 3, as I will explain in more detail below.)

I also drew on other records and information associated with ADPs and ORCs when this evidence was available to me. For some children who met with the school psychologist (later this person doubled as director of the Toronto Department of Public Health's Division of Mental Hygiene), the school system also generated a Psychiatric examination report (PER) (see figure A3). (In fact, these forms are misidentified as "psychiatric," since the information, such as intelligence quotient (IQ) score, diagnosis, and placement recommendation, is chiefly psychological.) The psychologist or mental hygiene division director used this form every time he (in Toronto they were all men) examined a child. After the examination, he completed the PER and also marked his initials on the child's ADP next to where on that card he entered the child's IQ and his diagnosis and placement recommendation from the examination. In the "Report" section of the PER, he filled in a brief description of the child's school background and home life, IQ test performance, and educational prospects. A carbon copy of the PER is pinned to some children's ADPs or sometimes to an ORC instead. Just as often, however, the PER is missing, even though the ADP indicates that an examination took place. I cannot account for the whereabouts of these missing forms.

Very rarely, other ephemera could also be found carefully folded and pinned to an ADP or ORC, such as correspondence with parents, a slip admitting the child to a new school, and report cards. As well, some principals recorded the child's disciplinary infractions and punishments on the blank reverse side of the ORC, even though it included no official space for that information.

Hester How, Coleman, and Duke of York

This book draws on the ORC and ADP collections of three former TBE elementary schools: Hester How PS (closed in 1953), Coleman PS

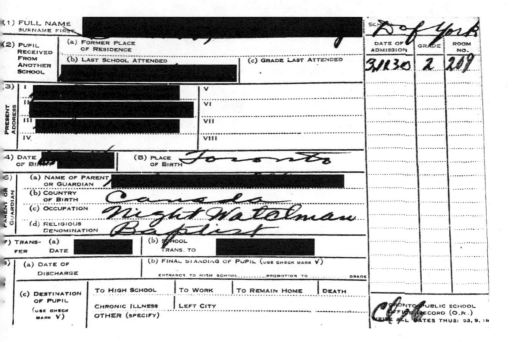

A.1 3″ x 5″ Office record card (ORC), single-sided, used by TBE schools ca. 1916–. Black boxes indicate personal identifying information removed. Credit author and Toronto District School Board Archives.

(closed in 1965), and Duke of York PS (amalgamated with Regent Park PS in 1980).[5] The collections are housed at the Toronto District School Board Archives. There are separate sets of ORCs and of ADPs for each school. Cards in each set are stored alphabetically by student surname in separate boxes and drawers. In the 1970s, the TBE microfilmed the Coleman ORCs and ADPs, along with the collections of several other schools that I did not consult. I used the Coleman microfilms instead of the originals.[6]

No strict criteria guided my choice to use records from these three schools and not from other schools instead. One reason that I chose the schools I did was that there were both ORC and ADP collections for all three of them. (This is not the case for every school for which pupil records are in the archives.) I also selected these schools because they were open during the entire period that this study covered, or much

A.2 5"x 8" Admission-discharge-promotion (ADP) card, sides one and two, used by TBE schools ca. 1916–. Black boxes indicate personal identifying information removed. Credit author and Toronto District School Board Archives.

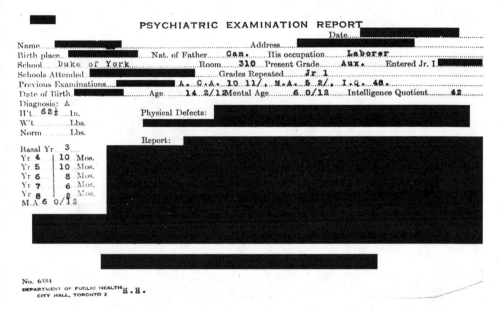

A.3 Psychiatric examination report (PER) used by TBE schools ca. 1916–.
Black boxes indicate personal identifying information and psychologist's
remarks removed. Credit author and Toronto District School Board Archives.

of it in the Duke of York case. To achieve the broadest perspective possible, I tried as well to choose schools that were of different sizes and that were located in different types of neighbourhoods. Every school has a unique personality – and because schools are often microcosms of their neighbourhood, that personality reflects a neighbourhood's faces. A few details about the three schools I selected and the neighbourhoods they served will help the reader to better situate the pupils whose records I drew upon in this study.

Hester How was a twelve-room school built in 1912 to replace the old Elizabeth Street building that had stood on the site since 1868. The trustees named the new building after the old school's long-serving principal, Hester How.[7] How devoted her teaching career to the part of Toronto that became known as "the Ward."[8] Hester How PS was a neighbourhood landmark. It stood adjacent to the famous Elizabeth Street Playground, just south of Toronto General Hospital and just north of where Elizabeth bisected Elm Street.[9]

A.4 "Hester How Public School," 1920s. Elizabeth Street. City of Toronto Archives, Alexandra Studio Fonds, Alexandra Studio commissioned photographs, item 220.

The Ward's particular characteristics were mirrored in Hester How's population. Its official attendance boundaries (as reported in 1930) covered a long, thin strip of central Toronto that encompassed a residential zone, as well as the sprawling manufacturing, mail order, and retail operations of Eaton's department store. The school's catchment stretched from University Avenue on its west side to Yonge Street on its east side and south from College Street all the way to Lake Ontario.[10] For decades, the area served as Toronto's main immigrant reception zone. By 1900, it was the "chief Jewish ghetto."[11] In 1913, only one of every six Hester How pupils claimed Canadian birth. More than half of the student body had been born in Russia. (Nearly all of these students would have been Jewish.) Other pupils at the school were Austro-Hungarian, Chinese, English, Italian, Roumanian, and Scottish.[12] As the Ward's Jewish population migrated west over time, the neighbourhood continued to serve as an immigrant area, hosting a Little Italy and a Chinatown.[13]

The Ward was a lightning rod for municipal reformers' anxieties about urban decay. In 1918, the Toronto Bureau of Municipal Research published *What Is "the Ward" Going to Do with Toronto?*, a dire warning about slum conditions "'boiling over' into adjacent areas."[14] The Hester How teaching staff was devoted tirelessly to changing and, as most of them would have seen it, improving the hardscrabble lives of immigrant pupils. Their teaching zeal at times shaded into outright religious proselytization.[15] The bureau identified the Ward's immigrants as a source of feeblemindedness.[16] The old Elizabeth Street school was one of the first four in the city to acquire an auxiliary class for mental defectives in 1910.[17] Until as late as 1930, Hester How did not offer junior or senior fourth forms, with students stopping at senior third or moving on to a different school to complete the elementary grades.[18]

The second school whose records I drew upon was Coleman, located in Toronto's far east end where the city's boundary snaked back and forth with suburban East York and Scarborough Township.[19] Pupils lived on streets such as Coleman Avenue and Barrington Avenue or Guest Avenue where it abutted the Canadian National Railway tracks. A casual look at *Might's* city directory for "Little York" in 1921 reveals mostly Anglo surnames and a mixture of skilled, semi-skilled, and unskilled blue-collar occupations for residents who could afford the modest but well-kept homes on these streets.[20] In 1923, Ford Motor Co built a plant nearby, just over the city limit in East York, which would employ 500 workers.[21] A tiny, old school building with just four rooms, Coleman did not go past junior third and did not have an auxiliary class of its own.[22] Coleman pupils over the years were transferred to auxiliary programs at nearby Gledhill PS. Others were sent to the city's junior vocational and handicraft schools when they became too old for Coleman.

Around the midway point of the 1929–30 school year, the TBE opened Duke of York to replace four old, smaller schools in the Moss Park vicinity of the city's eastern core.[23] Large and modern, the school had eighteen rooms.[24] The attendance area was a quadrant bounded by Gerrard to the north, Yonge to the west, Sherbourne to the east, and the lake to the south.[25] The handsome new school stood out in its declin-

A.5 "Coleman Ave. Public School, Coleman Ave., north side, between Barrington Ave. & Dawes Rd., Toronto, Ont.," 1910. Courtesy of Toronto Public Library.

ing neighbourhood that one geographer's 1941 study described as a "fourth-class residential area," the type of older inner-city zone where houses were of "a deteriorated and overcrowded appearance," sitting on small properties blighted by a lack of any space "upon which grass can grow."[26] This part of Toronto was only slightly better off than the Ward, though not nearly as ethnically diverse – its residents were mostly Anglo-Canadians.[27]

Method

In the archives, there are an estimated 2,000 ORCs and 1,200 ADPs for Hester How pupils who attended in the 1916–45 period, 1,000 ORCs and 400 ADPs for Coleman pupils who attended in the same period, and 8,500 ORCs and 3,900 ADPs for Duke of York pupils in the 1929–45 period, dating from its opening. I searched these cards – 17,000 of

A.6 "Duke of York Public School, Pembroke St, w. side, n. of Shuter St," 1939.
James Victor Salmon photographer. Courtesy of Toronto Public Library.

them all told – for the records of every pupil I could find who at any time between September 1916 and June 1945:

- attended an auxiliary/opportunity class;
- transferred from one of the schools to a junior vocational or handi-craft school or other auxiliary program (e.g., forest school, sight-saving class, etc.);
- had an ADP or ORC with a PER pinned to it, even if she or he never attended an auxiliary program;[28]
- and, because Coleman did not have an auxiliary/opportunity class, who were sent from that school to an auxiliary/opportunity class at another school.

I searched the ORCs first. Every ORC that I found for a pupil meeting at least one of the above criteria I tried to match with the pupil's corresponding ADP from the same school. I then searched the ADP collections for any auxiliary students who had an ADP but not an ORC. Most pupils have both cards; a smaller number have only one or the other, in this case usually just the ORC.[29] When the information differed from one type of card to the other (e.g., by giving a different birth-date), I relied on the ADP. I reasoned that because it fulfilled the role of a permanent record it was more likely to contain the most accurate information. In this manner, I eventually located some 1,350 pupils who met the criteria above.

Note on Two-Parent Families and Single Mothers

In most cases, ADPs and ORCs carry details only about the pupil's father – e.g., his birthplace and occupation – and say nothing about the pupil's mother. In a second, more rare type of case, details about the pupil's father and mother appear on the card. In these cases, to stay consistent – because the large majority of records do not have maternal information – I used only the father's information to classify students by occupation and class, ethnic origin, and the like. In a third type of case, only the mother's information is available. In these cases, I have made an assumption: the mother was a single parent. I have therefore used her information (e.g., occupation, birthplace) to classify her children by class, ethnic origin, etc.[30]

Note on Representative Samples

To create representative samples against which to compare the auxiliary pupil records, research assistants working on the project sampled records from the ADP collections of Hester How and Duke of York randomly. They selected the ADP of every seventh pupil at Duke of York who attended at any point between September 1929 and June 1945 and of every third pupil at Hester How between September 1916 and June 1945. This yielded samples of 558 pupils for the first school and 404 for the second.[31] Because I was interested in variables that should normally be identical on ADPs and ORCs (e.g., birthplace, father's occupation), the representative samples are based on the ADP collections only.

Included in the archival ADP collection of a school are ADPs for every student who attended it as the last public elementary school they went to in Toronto. The one exception to this rule was the ADPs of pupils transferring to junior vocational and handicraft schools, which it appears were forwarded to those schools with them. I realized this only after research assistants had collected the data. Consequently, the representative samples unfortunately omit this subgroup, which has a skewing effect. Because, however, only a small percentage of students actually attended junior vocational and handicraft schools (accounting for just 3 to 6 per cent of all Toronto secondary students; see appendix B), I believe that effect is of relatively minor significance, though it

does involve some of the questions that interest me that compare auxiliary education populations to general school populations. I have, for
that reason, refrained in chapter 3 from comparing the records of pupils
transferring to junior vocational and handicraft schools to a representative sample for the school that does not contain these students.

The historian G. Kitson Clark once wrote: "Do not guess, try to count,
and if you can not count admit that you are guessing."[32] I have tried
my best to follow this advice. The representative data is very basic and
imperfect, built on information that is quite old and comes with inherent deficiencies (e.g., the aforementioned lack of junior vocational and
handicraft school students). Yet I feel that this rare evidence is useful as
a baseline that we would not otherwise have, for a period about which
we know little regarding the relative representation of various groups
in special programs.

Occupation and Class and Ethnic Origin in Pupil Records

Toronto schools never asked for a child's class or ethnic origin directly, but they did keep track of parental occupation and birthplace and
child's birthplace and religion. I used this information to assign pupils
to categories representing class and ethnic origin.

Occupation and Class

Historians who sort occupations into class categories quickly discover
how tricky this seemingly simple task really is.[33] Canadian educational
historians who have developed occupational classifications for their
studies, such as Paul Axelrod and R.D. Gidney and W.P.J. Millar, adh-
dere to similar methodological conventions. Though these procedures
remain relatively informal, they may be described and summarized
as follows. Classifications reflect historical context and the historians
avoid superimposing presentist understandings of class on the past.
Historians employ carefully selected categories and subcategories that
enable them to test the specific historical claims that interest them. They
also freely adapt and modify classification schemes belonging to other
historians or social scientists to suit these purposes.[34] In designing my
occupational classification scheme, I have attempted to stick closely to
these basic and informal conventions.

My study of three largely working-class schools in Toronto in the first
half of the twentieth century called for an occupational classification

Table A.1 Occupational classification, Toronto

Group (x) and (xy) subgroup	Examples of most common occupations in this group in my study
1. Owners and managers	Merchant, manager
2. Agents on commission	Salesman, insurance agent
3. Self-employed	Storekeeper, pedlar, barber
4. Middle class	Engineer, foreman, accountant
5. Working class, i.e.,	
(5a) skilled or semi-skilled blue collar	Mechanic, driver, painter, tailor
(5b) unskilled blue collar	Labourer, factory worker, soldier
(5c) white collar	Clerk, bookkeeper, telegraph or telephone operator
6. Miscellaneous	E.g., "Safety league," "Commercial trains," "Press," "Shoe handler"
7. None or not available	Left blank, "None," "Unemployed," "Pensioner"

Adapted from Harris, *Unplanned Suburbs* (1996).

capable of representing class differences in this sort of urban, industrial environment. The Canadian historical geographer Richard Harris designed just such a classification for his first-rate study of Toronto's metropolitan social history in this period, *Unplanned Suburbs: Toronto's American Tragedy 1900–1950*.[35] I have turned to Harris's design for a model, modifying it somewhat to better suit my study.[36]

A few comments on the classifications in table A.1 follow. Some readers might be tempted to think of the "5c white collar" group as more correctly belonging to the "4 middle class" group. In status and income, however, Harris argues (and I concur) that wage-earning white-collar workers were by this time most definitely part of the working class. They shared with wage-dependent people a deteriorating control over their work processes.[37]

"3 Self-employed workers" occupied an ambiguous class position. Some were former wage workers who subsequently started their own businesses and passed from the less favourable employee to the usually more favourable small employer status.[38] Other self-employed workers were not employers and fitted instead into the low-remuneration, sometimes fringe niches of the urban economy – rag collectors, pedlars,

and the like. Often immigrants, they were no better off than the majority of working-class people and sometimes fared worse.[39]

On a few pupil record cards, an employer is recorded instead of an
occupation. When, for example, "city employee," or a large private
enterprise or corporation – e.g., "Canada Malting" or "C.P.R." (Canadian Pacific Railway) – was stated and no other indicator about the
person's work was present, I classified the occupation as "5b Unskilled
blue-collar." The assumption seems warranted, given that when a person who worked for a large outfit held a skilled position, that position
seems to have been recorded (e.g., "Mechanic – Bell Tel. Co."). Quite
frequently in pupil records from the years 1939–45, the father's occupation was given as an armed services branch – e.g., "Army," or "Air
Force." Following the same reasoning I applied to other large organizations, I classified these as "5b Unskilled blue collar." I did so unless the
person held a specific occupation – for example, "Army-Steamfitter,"
in which case I classified according to that occupation ("5a Skilled or
semi-skilled blue collar" in this instance).

Occasionally, a job or its description is peculiar enough to defy classification. These I placed in the "6 Miscellaneous" group. Table A.1 provides examples.

Women's occupations are incorporated into my classification scheme,
but only when the woman listed on the child's pupil record meets the
criteria for a single mother. The most common single-mother occupations in my study are housekeeper, domestic, and waitress, which
are working-class occupations I have classified under "5b Unskilled
blue collar."[40]

Lastly, I used the group "7 None/not available" for pupil records
in which the occupation box was left blank or read "unemployed,"
"none," or "pensioner." Blank entries could represent a lack of occupation, or they could indicate that the person completing the card did
not know what occupation to write. It is impossible to know which is
which, or to what degree, and for that reason "7 None/not available"
may almost invariably overstate the number of heads without occupation. Some of them had occupations, I just do not know what those
were. The "7 None/not available" category also includes the peculiar
case of a handful of pupil record cards where only the mother's occupation is present and is listed as a "housewife." It is possible that these are
married women whose husbands' occupations were not recorded, and
therefore are unknown. But it is also possible that they are single mothers and household heads who offered "housewife" as their occupation

to keep up respectability, even though they must have had other employment or recieved a mother's allowance. In both cases, however, the occupation is still either unknown or none, therefore the "7 None/not available" designation seemed the most appropriate selection for every case of this type.

Harris in his book calculated the proportions of household heads that fell into each class group represented in table A.1 city-wide to give a sense of Toronto's overall class structure. (The calculations are based on the census year 1921, which he uses as a baseline.) More than 60 per cent of households were "5 Working class"; approximately 14 per cent were "4 Middle class"; approximately 7 per cent were in the "1 Owners and managers" group. The remainder fell into the groups "2 Agents on commission" (5.5 per cent) and "3 Self-employed" (12.5 per cent). These percentages take into account only the occupations Harris considered "classifiable" – that is, groups one through five only and excluding the groups "Miscellaneous" and "None/not available."[41]

Ethnic Origin

Classifying students by ethnic origin is every bit as complicated as classifying them by occupation and class. Pupil record cards did not call for school officials to write down a child's ethnic origin (or race). Ethnic origin must instead be inferred from other information that is present on the records and then assigned by the historian.

Ethnic origin is a function, among many other facts,[42] of a person's and their parents' birthplace, which are not always the same. In my study, if a child was born in a country other than Canada, I classified the child's ethnic origin by her or his place of birth. For example, a child born in Italy is classified as Italian. To reflect the often cross-generational nature of ethnic origin, if the child's parent was born in a country other than Canada, I classified that child according to the father's country of birth (or the mother's, if the father's was not available). To continue with the same example, a child whose father was born in Italy is classified as Italian, even if the child was born in Canada. I reasoned that this approach better represented ethnic origin than counting only foreign-born children as ethnic. That would have obscured the ethnic identities of second-generation immigrants that were often palpable to them, to other Torontonians, and, not least of all, to the schools that tried to assimilate them to dominant Canadian ways.[43]

One exception to my classification regards US-born children. I extended the same reasoning about second-generation ethnicity to them that I did to Canadian-born children. If a US-born child's father was born in a country other than the United States, then I classified the child according to the father's birthplace. Accordingly, a child born in the United States, whose father was born in Italy, is classified as Italian. If the father and the child were both born in the United States, only then did I classify the child as American.

It was also necessary to make exceptions to my approach to properly account for Jews and "Gypsies" (Roma) as groups.

When a child's religion on her or his pupil record was given as Jewish, I classified that child as Jewish, irrespective of birthplace. Again, my goal was to capture ethnic origin rather than religion or nationality.[44] For instance, a Jewish child whose father was born in Poland I classified as Jewish, not Polish. A Jewish child born in Canada, whose father was also born in Canada, is likewise classified as Jewish in my study.

Classifying Roma, or "Gypsies" as Torontonians then called them, also required special considerations.[45] The history of Canadian Roma is poorly documented.[46] There are three ways to identify them from pupil record cards. Often, their religion was recorded as "Gypsy" – but this did not capture all Roma, because the schools sometimes recorded them as belonging to other creeds. They can also be identified by their father's or mother's occupations. Toronto's Roma participated in two very unusual lines of work. Fathers of Romani schoolchildren were repeatedly identified in pupil records as coppersmiths. Copper-plating was a known Romani ethnic employment ghetto, practiced by the men who belonged to several different Romani "unions" (at that time the organizational unit of Romani society) in Canadian and American cities. Similarly, Romani women worked together in fortune-telling; pupil records identified them as "palmists."[47] Of course, not all coppersmiths or palmists whose children attended Toronto public schools were Romani, though most seem to have been. Third, Roma routinely held one of several quite unique surnames, which I have relied on to identify them as well.[48] By triangulating religion, occupation, and surname, I am confident that it is possible to identify most Romani children in the records. Chad Gaffield, in his study of Franco-Ontarians, successfully employed a similar method of triangulating religion, surname, and birthplace to identify French Canadians in the 1851 and 1861 censuses when these sources did not include ethnic origin explicitly either.[49]

Auxiliary Program Enrolments

Tables show enrolments in selected Toronto Board of Education (TBE) auxiliary programs from the 1920s (when statistics became available) to the 1940s. (Enrolment statistics for forest schools, foreign classes, and open-air classes discussed in chapter 1 are not included.)

Table B.1 Auxiliary/opportunity classes and enrolment, TBE schools, 1920–1 to 1944–5 school years[a]

Year[b]	Classes[c]	Students	% of tot. enrol. (elem.)	Tot. enrol. (elem.)	Year	Classes	Students	% of tot. enrol. (elem.)	Tot. enrol. (elem.)
1920–1	13	271[d]	.4	72,104	1933–4	54	934	1.0	97,177
1921–2	24	378	.5	74,823	1934–5	55	1,010	1.0	97,288
1922–3	38	590	.8	77,301	1935–6	54	999	1.2	82,411
1923–4	42	697	.9	77,941	1936–7	52	954	1.2	82,453
1924–5	47	701	.8	92,065	1937–8	52	940	1.2	81,263
1925–6	46	754	.8	90,937	1938–9	51	904	1.2	80,465
1926–7	49	775	1.0	76,299	1939–40	51	947	1.2	76,519
1927–8	41	849	1.1	77,358	1940–1	48	886	1.2	74,030
1928–9	47	761	.8	93,552	1941–2	43	759	1.0	73,134
1929–30	47	760	.8	94,837	1942–3	40	768	1.1	71,797
1930–1	53	872	.9	96,077	1943–4	40	779	1.1	72,998
1931–2	53	898	.9	96,301	1944–5	41	747	1.1	70,113
1932–3	54	936	1.0	97,049					

[a] The first statistics available are from 1920–1. Auxiliary classes were renamed opportunity classes in 1937.
[b] Statistics for 1920–1 to 1927–8 school years are based on the month of December; 1940–1 is based on June. The Ontario Department of Education (DOE), the source for the other years, did not indicate what month it used for its statistics.
[c] Does not include regular classes at the Hospital for Sick Children and the Shelter sometimes listed as auxiliary classes.
[d] Estimate based on reported class average of twenty-one pupils.

Sources: *TBE Annual Report 1920...1928*, Attendance Report; Ontario, Legislative Assembly, *Report of the Minister of Education Province of Ontario* (Toronto: various publishers, various years); TDSBA, TDSB 2003–0375, TBE Attendance Statistics 1933–1943, "Toronto Public School Summary of Enrolment – June 1941."

Table B.2 Junior vocational and handicraft school enrolment, Toronto, 1925–6 to 1944–5 school years[a]

	Jarvis Jr. Vocational Boys	Groves and Bolton Girls	Total[b]	% of sec. enrol.	Sec. enrol.[c]
1925–6	244	249	493	3.2	15,505
1926–7	473	296	769	4.7	16,544
1927–8	470	349	819	4.6	17,802
1928–9	518	369	887	4.3	20,786
1929–30	537	475	1,012	4.7	21,492
1930–1	607	513	1,120	5.0	22,592
1931–2	638	565	1,203	4.8	24,943
1932–3	622	585	1,207	4.6	26,191
1933–4	696	767	1,463	6.0	24,413
1934–5	704	680	1,384	5.9	23,612
1935–6	614	588	1,202	5.2	23,203
1936–7	609	589	1,198	5.2	22,944
1937–8	624	545	1,169	4.7	24,955
1938–9	624	545	1,169	4.6	25,167
1939–40	541	592	1,133	4.5	25,376
1940–1	471	553	1,024	4.3	24,066
1941–2	441	434	875	3.9	22,353
1942–3	430	537	967	4.7	20,578
1943–4[d]	250	571	821	3.8	21,853
1944–5[e]	n/a	n/a	n/a	n/a	21,525

[a] The first statistics available are from 1925–6. Junior vocational schools were renamed handicraft schools in 1935.
[b] Based on enrolment at inspection date.
[c] Based on complete enrolment (part- and full-time) in May of that school year.
[d] May enrolment not available. Based on net enrolment for the year.
[e] Enrolment statistics for handicraft schools in 1944–5 were combined with a non-auxiliary-education vocational program and cannot be distinguished.

Source: Ontario, Legislative Assembly, *Report of the Minister of Education Province of Ontario* (Toronto: various publishers, various years).

Table B.3 Sight-saving classes and enrolment, TBE schools, 1922–3 to 1944–5 school years

Year[a]	Classes	Students	Year	Classes	Students
1922–3	1	17	1934–5	5	78
1923–4	3	41	1935–6	5	76
1924–5	3	45	1936–7	5	67
1925–6	3	41	1937–8	5	72
1926–7	3	38	1938–9	5	65
1927–8	3	46	1939–40	5	77
1928–9	4	57	1940–1[b]	5	65
1929–30	4	59	1941–2	5	73
1930–1	5	70	1942–3	5	91
1931–2	5	75	1943–4	5	67
1932–3	5	68	1944–5	5	65
1933–4	5	81			

[a] Statistics for 1922–3 to 1927–8 school years are based on the month of December; 1940–1 is based on June. The DOE did not indicate what month it used for its statistics.
[b] DOE statistics not available. TBE attendance statistics are substituted instead.

Sources: *TBE Annual Report 1922*, 119; *TBE Annual Report 1923*, 100; *TBE Annual Report 1924 ... 1927*, Attendance Report; Ontario, Legislative Assembly, *Report of the Minister of Education Province of Ontario*, Report of the Inspector of Auxiliary Classes (Toronto: various publishers, various years); TDSBA, TDSB 2003–0375, TBE Attendance Statistics 1933–1943, "Toronto Public School Summary of Enrolment – June 1941."

Table B.4 Wellesley PS orthopaedic classes and enrolment, 1926–7 to 1944–5 school years

Year[a]	Classes	Students	Year	Classes	Students
1926–7	2	33	1936–7	5	75
1927–8	3	44	1937–8	5	70
1928–9	3	48	1938–9[b]	5	181
1929–30	4	49	1939–40	5	75
1930–1	4	59	1940–1[c]	4	69
1931–2	5	62	1941–2	5	68
1932–3	5	73	1942–3	5	95
1933–4	5	76	1943–4	5	88
1934–5	5	73	1944–5	5	88
1935–6	5	73			

[a] Statistics for 1926–7 and 1927–8 school years are based on the month of December; 1940–1 is based on June. The DOE did not indicate what month it used for its statistics.
[b] Polio outbreak in Toronto, fall 1937 (see chapter 4).
[c] DOE statistics not available. TBE attendance statistics are substituted instead.

Sources: *TBE Annual Report*, 1927, 1928, Attendance Report; Ontario, Legislative Assembly, *Report of the Minister of Education Province of Ontario,* Report of the Inspector of Auxiliary Classes (Toronto: various publishers, various years); TDSBA, TDSB 2003–0375, TBE Attendance Statistics 1933–1943, "Toronto Public School Summary of Enrolment – June 1941."

Table B.5 Hard of hearing classes and enrolment, TBE schools,
1924–5 to 1944–5 school years

Year	Classes	Students
1924–5[a]	1	11
1925–6	1	13
1926–7	1	13
1927–8	2	22
1928–9 to 1938–9[b]		
1939–40	4	61
1940–1	n/a	n/a
1941–2	4	61
1942–3	4	62
1943–4	4	56
1944–5	4	59

[a] Statistics for 1924–5 to 1927–8 school years are based on the month of December.
The DOE did not indicate what month it used for its statistics.
[b] Statistics for 1928–9 to 1938–9 combine hard-of-hearing classes, oral day school
classes for the deaf, and speech correction classes

Sources: *TBE Annual Report 1924 ... 1927*, Attendance Report; Ontario, Legislative
Assembly, *Report of the Minister of Education Province of Ontario* (Toronto: various
publishers, various years).

Table B.6 Oral day school deaf classes and enrolment, TBE schools, 1924–5 to 1944–5 school years

Year[a]	Classes	Students
1924–5	1	11
1925–6	2	15
1926–7	3	25
1927–8	3	28
1928–9 to 1938–9[b]		
1939–40	3	23
1940–1	n/a	n/a
1941–2	3	32
1942–3	3	30
1943–4	3	30
1944–5	4	38

[a] Statistics for 1924–5 to 1927–8 school years are based on the month of December. The DOE did not indicate what month it used for its statistics.
[b] Statistics for 1928–9 to 1938–9 combine hard-of-hearing classes, oral day school classes for the deaf, and speech correction classes

Sources: *TBE Annual Report 1924 ... 1927*, Attendance Report; Ontario, Legislative Assembly, *Report of the Minister of Education Province of Ontario* (Toronto: various publishers, various years).

Table B.7 Speech correction classes and enrolment, TBE schools,
1924–5 to 1944–5 school years

Year[a]	Classes	Students
1924–5	n/a	90
1925–6	n/a	100
1926–7	n/a	n/a
1927–8	n/a	n/a
1928–9 to 1938–9[b]		
1939–40	6	1,214
1940–1	n/a	n/a
1941–2	6	1,122
1942–3	6	1,114
1943–4	6	1,090
1944–5	6	1,094

[a] Statistics for 1924–5 to 1925–6 school years are based on the month
of December. The DOE did not indicate what month it used for its statistics.
[b] Statistics for 1928–9 to 1938–9 combine hard-of-hearing classes
oral day school classes for the deaf, and speech correction classes

Sources: *TBE Annual Report 1924*, 67; *TBE Annual Report 1925*, 78; Ontario,
Legislative Assembly, *Report of the Minister of Education Province of Ontario*
(Toronto: various publishers, various years); TDSBA, TDSB 2003–0375, TBE Attendance
Statistics 1933–1943, "Toronto Public School Summary of Enrolment – June 1941."

Notes

Introduction

1 Helen MacMurchy, *To Inspectors, Principals, and Teachers* (Toronto: DOE, 1919).

2 The landmark report of the 1930 White House Conference on Child Health and Protection contains the modern usage "special education." See "F. Special Classes," in *White House Conference on Child Health and Protection. Preliminary Committee Reports* (New York: The Century Co, 1930), 314–43.

3 James W. Trent, Jr, *Inventing the Feeble Mind: A History of Mental Retardation in the United States* (Berkeley: University of California Press, 1994), 165.

4 Erika Dyck, *Facing Eugenics: Reproduction, Sterilization, and the Politics of Choice* (Toronto: University of Toronto Press, 2013), 3–4. A note about the terms "deaf" and "Deaf" as well: some deaf people today, and a few historians and other scholars (though not all), prefer the capital-"D" "Deaf" over "deaf." The former usage was developed in the 1970s to signal that Deaf people are a distinctive linguistic and cultural group. See Douglas C. Baynton, *Forbidden Signs: American Culture and the Campaign Against Sign Language* (Chicago: University of Chicago Press, 1996), 11–12. While I do not disagree with the usage, I have preferred "deaf" throughout my text, as Baynton does in his. My reasons for this are the same as the ones I have given for preferring historical disability terminology over modern, scrubbed alternatives.

5 This book is about the city's public school system. I do not cover the Roman Catholic separate school system, which in the period of this study was a little larger than one-tenth the size of the public system. Auxiliary classes and programs did exist in that system after 1923. See R.T. Dixon, *We Remember, We Believe: A History of Toronto's Catholic Separate School*

Boards, 1841 to 1997 (Toronto: Toronto Catholic District School Board, 2007), 132–3, 147.

6 *TBE Minutes 1919*, appendix no. 112, Report of Trustee (Mrs) Groves on her visit to Special Auxiliary Classes in American Cities, 19 June 1919, Referred to Special Committee appointed by the Board re Auxiliary Classes, 19 June 1919, 749–55.

7 David B. Tyack, *The One Best System: A History of American Urban Education* (Cambridge, MA: Harvard University Press, 1974).

8 At least three historians of Canadian education have made this point recently. See Amy von Heyking, "Ties that Bind? American Influences on Canadian Education," *Education Canada* 44, no. 4 (fall 2004): 30–4; Kerry Alcorn, *Border Crossings: US Culture and Education in Saskatchewan, 1905–1937* (Montreal: McGill-Queen's University Press, 2013); Anthony Di Mascio, "The Emergence of Academies in the Eastern Townships of Lower Canada and the Invisibility of the Canada-US Border," *Historical Studies in Education/Revue d'histoire de l'éducation* 27, no. 2 (fall 2015): 78–94.

9 For comparisons, see case studies of cities, such as Robert L. Osgood, *For "Children Who Vary from the Normal Type": Special Education in Boston, 1838–1930* (Washington: Gallaudet University Press, 2000); Barry M. Franklin, "Progressivism and Curriculum Differentiation: Special Classes in the Atlanta Public Schools," *History of Education Quarterly* 29, no. 4 (winter 1989): 571–93; Barry M. Franklin, *From "Backwardness" to "At-Risk": Childhood Learning Difficulties and the Contradictions of School Reform* (Albany: SUNY Press, 1994); Gerald Thomson, "Remove from Our Midst These Unfortunates': A Historical Inquiry into the Influence of Eugenics, Educational Efficiency as Well as Mental Hygiene upon the Vancouver School System and Its Special Classes, 1910–1969" (PhD diss., University of British Columbia, 1999); E. Anne Bennison, "Creating Categories of Competence: The Education of Exceptional Children in the Milwaukee Public Schools, 1908–1917" (PhD diss., University of Wisconsin-Madison, 1988). See also school surveys from the period that list an even greater number of urban centres with similar classes: Robert W. Kunzig, "Public School Education of Atypical Children," United States Office of Education, Bulletin no. 10 (Washington: Government Printing Office, 1931); Arch O. Heck, *Special Schools and Classes in Cities of 10,000 Population and More in the United States*, United States Office of Education Bulletin, 1930, no. 7 (Washington: Government Printing Office, 1930); David H. Russell and Fred T. Tyler, "Special Education in Canada," *The School* (elem. ed.) 30, no. 10 (June 1942): 882–9. True, there were regional variations, with some cities adopting later than others. Sherman Dorn, in a case study of

Nashville, argues that cities in the American South were late to the auxiliary education game in "Public-Private Symbiosis in Nashville Special
Education," *History of Education Quarterly* 42, no. 3 (autumn 2002): 368–94.
In the Kunzig survey (62–3), however, Nashville was only one of two cities
(with San Antonio) not to have auxiliary classes for subnormals in a list
of Southern metropolises exceeding 100,000 persons. That list includes
centres in the Deep South that did have classes, such as Birmingham and
New Orleans, and cities in states and districts farther north that did as
well, such as Baltimore, Washington, and Wilmington.

   If there was one area where Toronto did not keep up, it was gifted
education. The city experimented with gifted classes for two years during
the early 1930s at Howard Park PS, but did not subsequently adopt them
permanently. O.O. Worden, "A Comparative Experimental Study of Two
Similar Groups of Super-Normal Elementary School Children" (DPaed
thesis, University of Toronto, 1936). However, separate special classes for
gifted children were not especially common in the first half of the twentieth century. In Canada, only London, Oshawa, and Saskatoon had them.
In the United States, only two major cities, Cleveland and Los Angeles,
appear to have had them in 1930, although they existed in several smaller
centres. Jason Ellis, "Brains Unlimited: Giftedness and Gifted Education
Canada before *Sputnik*," *Canadian Journal of Education/Revue canadienne
de l'éducation* 40, no. 2 (2017): 1–26; George F. Rogers, "The Enrichment
of Courses in the Elementary Schools," *Proceedings of the Seventy-First
Convention of the OEA* (Toronto: OEA, 1932), 170; Samuel R. Laycock,
"Special Classes for Gifted Children in a Small City," *Understanding the
Child* 9, no. 1 (April 1940): 3; Kunzig, "Public School Education of Atypical
Children," 61–3.
10 Osgood, For *"Children Who Vary from the Normal Type"*; Robert L. Osgood,
    *The History of Special Education: A Struggle for Equality in American Public
    Schools* (Westport, CT: Praeger, 2008); Robert L. Osgood, *The History of
    Inclusion in the United States* (Washington: Gallaudet University Press,
    2005); Franklin, *Backwardness to At-Risk*; Scot Danforth, *The Incomplete Child:
    An Intellectual History of Learning Disabilities* (New York: Peter Lang, 2009).
11 See chapter 1.
12 Marvin Lazerson, "The Origins of Special Education," in Jay G. Chambers
    and William T. Hartman, eds., *Special Education Policies: Their History,
    Implementation, and Finance* (Philadelphia: Temple University Press, 1983),
    15–46.
13 For additional examples of this approach, see Adam R. Nelson, "Equity
    and Special Education: Some Historical Lessons from Boston," in Kenneth

K. Wong and Robert Rothman, eds., *Clio at the Table: Using History to Inform and Improve Education Policy* (New York: Peter Lang, 2009), 157–79; Jason Ellis and Paul Axelrod, "Continuity and Change: Special Education Policy Development in Toronto Public Schools, 1945 to the Present," *Teachers College Record* 118, no. 2 (February 2016): 1–42, http://www.tcrecord. org/Content.asp?ContentId=18228; Felicity Armstrong, "The Historical Development of Special Education: Humanitarian Rationality or 'Wild Profusion of Entangled Events'?" *History of Education* 31, no. 2 (2002): 437–56; Ted Cole, *Apart or a Part? Integration and the Growth of British Special Education* (Milton Keynes: Open University Press, 1989); Seymour B. Sarason and John Doris, *Educational Handicap, Public Policy, and Social History: A Broadened Perspective on Mental Retardation* (New York: The Free Press, 1979).

14 See Kimberly Kode, *Elizabeth Farrell and the History of Special Education*, ed. Kristin E. Howard (Arlington, VA: Council for Exceptional Children, 2002).

15 Margret A. Winzer, *The History of Special Education: From Isolation to Integration* (Washington: Gallaudet University Press, 1993); Margret A. Winzer, *From Integration to Inclusion: A History of Special Education in the 20th Century* (Washington: Gallaudet University Press, 2009). Some accounts by university practitioners contain both this tendency and the one mentioned in the previous sentence. See Judy Lupart and Charles Webber, "Canadian Schools in Transition: Moving from Dual Education Systems to Inclusive Schools," *Exceptionality Education International* 22, no. 2 (2012): 8–37.

16 Joseph L. Tropea, "Bureaucratic Order and Special Children: Urban Schools, 1890s–1940s," *History of Education Quarterly* 27, no. 1 (1987): 29–53; Joseph L. Tropea, "Bureaucratic Order and Special Children: Urban Schools, 1950s–1960s," *History of Education Quarterly* 27, no. 3 (1987): 339–61; Franklin, *From "Bacwkardness" to "At-Risk."* See also Ann Gibson Winfield, *Eugenics and Education in America: Institutionalized Racism and the Implications of History, Ideology, and Memory* (New York: Peter Lang, 2007). The author claims that eugenics historically exerted, and continues to hold, enormous influence over American education. But peculiarly she makes very little direct reference to special education, the area where eugenics has arguably influenced it the most.

17 Mona Gleason, *Small Matters: Canadian Children in Sickness and Health* (Montreal: McGill-Queen's University Press, 2013); Cynthia Comacchio, *The Dominion of Youth: Adolescence and the Making of a Modern Canada, 1920–50* (Waterloo, ON: Wilfrid Laurier University Press, 2006); Tamara

Myers, *Caught: Montreal's Modern Girls and the Law, 1869–1945* (Toronto: University of Toronto Press, 2006); Veronica Strong-Boag, *Fostering Nation? Canada Confronts Its History of Childhood Disadvantage* (Waterloo, ON: Wilfrid Laurier University Press, 2011).

18 On "the new disability history," see Paul K. Longmore and Lauri Umansky, eds., *The New Disability History: American Perspectives* (New York: New York University Press, 2001); Kim. E. Nielsen, *A Disability History of the United States* (Boston: Beacon Press, 2012). On this point about people with disabilities as historical actors specifically, see Paul K. Longmore and David Golberger, "The League of the Physically Handicapped and the Great Depression: A Case Study in the New Disability History," *Journal of American History* 87, no. 3 (December 2000): 888–922; Richard J. Altenbaugh, "Where Are the Disabled in the History of Education? The Impact of Polio on Sites of Learning," *History of Education* 35, no. 6 (2006): 705–30. See also general historiographical essays by Catherine L. Kudlick, "Disability History: Why We Need Another 'Other,'" *American Historical Review* 108, no. 3 (June 2003): 763–93; Kate Rousmaniere, "Those Who Can't, Teach: The Disabling History of American Educators," *History of Education Quarterly* 53, no. 1 (February 2013): 90–103.

19 Douglas C. Baynton, "Disability and the Justification of Inequality in American History," in Longmore and Umansky, *The New Disability History*, 33–57, makes this point about disability "being everywhere in history, once you begin looking for it, but conspicuously absent in the histories we write" (53), a lacuna that historians are addressing. See Geoffrey Reaume, *Remembrance of Patients Past: Patient Life at the Toronto Hospital for the Insane, 1870–1940* (Don Mills, ON: Oxford University Press, 2000); Geoffrey Reaume, *Lyndhurst: Canada's First Rehabilitation Centre for People with Spinal Cord Injuries, 1945–1988* (Montreal: McGill-Queen's University Press, 2007); Veronica Strong-Boag, "Children of Adversity': Disabilities and Child Welfare in Canada from the Nineteenth to the Twenty-First Century," *Journal of Family History* 32, no. 4 (October 2007): 413–32; Veronica Strong-Boag, "'Forgotten People of All the Forgotten': Children with Disabilities in English Canada from the Nineteenth Century to the New Millennium," in Mona Gleason, Tamara Myers, Leslie Paris, and Veronica Strong-Boag, eds., *Lost Kids: Vulnerable Children in Twentieth-Century Canada and the United States* (Vancouver: UBC Press, 2010), 33–50; Nic Clarke, *Unwanted Warriors: The Rejected Volunteers of the Canadian Expeditionary Force, 1914–18* (Vancouver: UBC Press, 2015); Dustin Galer, "A Friend in Need or a Business Indeed? Disabled Bodies and Fraternalism in Victorian Ontario," *Labour/Le Travail* 66 (fall 2010):

9–36; Joanna L. Pearce, "Not for Alms but Help: Fund-Raising and Free
Education for the Blind," *Journal of the Canadian Historical Association*
23, no. 1 (2012): 131–55. See also David Wright, *Downs: The History of a
Disability* (Oxford: Oxford University Press, 2011); Gleason, *Small Matters*,
119–46; Lykke de la Cour, "From 'Moron' to 'Maladjusted': Eugenics,
Psychiatry, and the Regulation of Women, Ontario, 1930s–1960s"
(PhD diss., University of Toronto, 2013); Claudia Malacrida, *A Special Hell:
Institutional Life in Alberta's Eugenic Years* (Toronto: University of Toronto
Press, 2015); Natalie Spagnuolo, "Defining Dependency, Constructing
Curability: The Deportation of 'Feebleminded' Patients from the Toronto
Asylum, 1920–1925," *Histoire sociale/Social History* 49, no. 98 (May 2016):
125–53. An overview of an evidently burgeoning field is Geoffrey Reaume,
"Disability History in Canada: Present Work in the Field and Future
Prospects," *Canadian Journal of Disability Studies* 1, no. 1 (2012): 35–81.

20 TDSBA, ADP, Hester How PS, drawers A–L, M–Z, 1923–4; ORC, Hester
How PS, drawers A–D, E–I, J–M, Mc–Si, Sh–Z; ADP, Duke of York PS,
TDSB 2003–0834 (2 boxes), TDSB 2003–0835, TDSB 2003–0836, TDSB 2003–
0837; ORC, Duke of York PS, TDSB 2003–1307, box 1–4, TDSB 2003–1308,
box 5–7, TDSB 2003–1309, box 8–11; ADP, Coleman PS, microfilm reel 11;
ORC, Coleman PS, microfilm reel 10.

I received permission from TDSB staff to use these records and to name
the three schools on condition that I not name or identify pupils whose
record cards I examined, or their teachers. I have also chosen not to name
principals. I am quite confident that in the cases where I discuss an individual child in any detail, I have held back enough to prevent that person,
or her or his kin, from identifying her or him through my work. I would
like to thank the TDSBA for access to this source.

Other historians have used pupil records to look at the history of special
classes but either have not drawn upon nearly the number of records that
I consulted for this book or have not covered as long a time period as I do.
See Franklin, *Backwardness to At-Risk*, 43–7; Bennison, "Creating Categories
of Competence."

21 Franca Iacovetta and Wendy Mitchinson, "Introduction: Social History
and Case Files Research," in Iacovetta and Mitchinson, eds., *On the Case:
Explorations in Social History* (Toronto: University of Toronto Press, 1998),
5–6.

22 Ibid., 13. I have also profiled a limited number of other youngsters and
their families using memoirs, recollections, or other similar sources. I have
not withheld the names of educators, parents, and even a few pupils who
are named, or who name themselves, in published sources. Historians of

childhood have raised considerations regarding the fallibility of memory in recollections and memoirs, which researchers must also treat judiciously. See Neil Sutherland, "When You Listen to the Winds of Childhood, How Much Can You Believe?" *Curriculum Inquiry* 22, no. 3 (autumn 1992): 235–56; Mona Gleason, "Disciplining the Student Body: Schooling and the Construction of Canadian Children's Bodies, 1930–1960," *History of Education Quarterly* 41, no. 2 (summer 2001): 189–215.

23 *TBE Annual Report 1912*, Medical Inspector's Report, 22.
24 *TBE Annual Report 1911*, Medical Inspector's Report, 33.
25 Paul Davis Chapman, *Schools as Sorters: Lewis M. Terman, Applied Psychology, and the Intelligence Testing Movement, 1890–1930* (New York: New York University Press, 1988).
26 Bruce Curtis, D.W. Livingstone, and Harry Smaller, *Stacking the Deck: The Streaming of Working-Class Kids in Ontario Schools* (Toronto: Our Schools/ Our Selves, 1992); Jeannie Oakes, *Keeping Track: How Schools Structure Inequality*, 2nd ed. (New Haven: Yale University Press, 2005).
27 Amy von Heyking, *Creating Citizens: History and Identity in Alberta's Schools, 1905–1980* (Calgary: University of Calgary Press, 2006), 29–53; Theodore Michael Christou, *Progressive Education: Revisioning and Reframing Ontario's Public Schools, 1919–1942* (Toronto: University of Toronto Press, 2012), 69–87; Herbert Kliebard, *The Struggle for the American Curriculum, 1893–1958* (New York: Routledge, 1987), 89–122.
28 This is not saying that eugenics in general necessarily declined in this period, only that its influence on auxiliary education waned considerably.
29 R.D. Gidney and W.P.J. Millar, *How Schools Worked: Public Education in English Canada, 1900–1940* (Montreal: McGill-Queen's University Press, 2012), 199.
30 Ibid., 187.

1 Eugenics Goes to School

1 Paul Rutherford, "Introduction," in Paul Rutherford, ed., *Saving the Canadian City: The First Phase 1880–1920* (Toronto: University of Toronto Press, 1974), xi–xix.
2 Paul Rutherford, "Tomorrow's Metropolis: The Urban Reform Movement in Canada, 1880–1920," in Gilbert A. Stelter and Alan F.J. Artibise, eds., *The Canadian City: Essays in Urban and Social History* (Montreal: McGill-Queen's University Press, 1984), 439.
3 Christopher Armstrong and H.V. Nelles, "The Rise of Civic Populism in Toronto 1870–1920," in Victor L. Russell, ed., *Forging a Consensus: Historical*

Essays on Toronto (Toronto: University of Toronto Press, 1984), 192–237; Roger E. Riendeau, "Servicing of the Modern City 1900–1930," in Russell, *Forging a Consensus*, 157–70. See Horatio Hocken, "The New Spirit in Municipal Government (1914)," in Rutherford, *Saving the Canadian City*, 195–208.

4 Neil Sutherland, *Children in English-Canadian Society: Framing the Twentieth-Century Consensus* (Toronto: University of Toronto Press, 1976), 47.

5 J.M.S. Careless, *Toronto to 1918: An Illustrated History* (Toronto: J. Lorimer, 1984), 149; James T. Lemon, *Toronto since 1918: An Illustrated History* (Toronto: James Lorimer and Company and National Museums of Canada, 1985), 194.

6 Robert F. Harney, "Ethnicity and Neighbourhoods," in Robert F. Harney, ed., *Gathering Place: Peoples and Neighbourhoods of Toronto, 1834–1945* (Toronto: Multicultural History Society of Ontario, 1985), 1–24.

7 That is, in 1921. Lemon, *Toronto since 1918*, 196.

8 Michael J. Piva, *The Condition of the Working Class in Toronto, 1900–1921* (Ottawa: University of Ottawa Press, 1979), 3.

9 Ibid., 18–20; Ruth Frager, *Sweatshop Strife: Class, Ethnicity, and Gender in the Jewish Labour Movement of Toronto, 1900–1939* (Toronto: University of Toronto Press, 1992), 10–34. For their children's school experiences, see Robert C. Vipond, *Making a Global City: How One Toronto School Embraced Diversity* (Toronto: University of Toronto Press, 2017), 22–76.

10 Piva, *Condition of the Working Class*. See also Bryan D. Palmer and Gaetan Heroux, "'Cracking the Stone': The Long History of Capitalist Crisis and Toronto's Dispossessed, 1830–1930," *Labour/Le Travail* 69 (spring 2012): 9–62.

11 C.S. Clark, *Of Toronto the Good: The Queen City of Canada as It Is* (Montreal: The Toronto Publishing Company, 1898).

12 Riendeau, "Servicing the Modern City," 173; John C. Weaver, "'Tomorrow's Metropolis' Revisited: A Critical Assessment of Urban Reform in Canada, 1890–1920," in Stelter and Artibise, *The Canadian City*, 456.

13 Rutherford, "Introduction," xiii.

14 Armstrong and Nelles, "The Rise of Civic Populism."

15 John C. Weaver, "The Modern City Realized: Toronto Civic Affairs, 1880–1915," in Alan F.J. Artibise and Gilbert A. Stelter, eds., *The Usable Urban Past: Planning and Politics in the Modern Canadian City* (Montreal: McGill-Queen's University Press, 1979), 63–4.

16 J.O. McCarthy, "Municipal Responsibility," *Public Health Journal* 5, no. 4 (April 1914): 234.

17 Dianne Dodd, "Helen MacMurchy, MD: Gender and Professional Conflict in the Medical Inspection of Toronto Schools, 1910–1911," *Ontario History* 93, no. 2 (2001): 131. On the National Council of Women, see Veronica Strong-Boag, *The Parliament of Women: The National Council of Women of Canada, 1893–1929* (Ottawa: National Museums of Canada, 1976); Carol Lee Bacchi, *Liberation Deferred? The Ideas of English-Canadian Suffragists, 1877–1918* (Toronto: University of Toronto Press, 1983).

18 Toronto Bureau of Municipal Research, "The Bureau of Municipal Research" (Toronto: Bureau of Municipal Research, 1919).

19 Weaver, "The Modern City Realized," 59.

20 Toronto Bureau of Municipal Research, "Measurement of Educational Waste in the Toronto Public Schools" (Toronto: Bureau of Municipal Research, 1920), 3.

21 David B. Tyack, *The One Best System: A History of American Urban Education* (Cambridge, MA: Harvard University Press, 1974), 30–59, 177–216. See also R.D. Gidney and W.P.J. Millar, *How Schools Worked: Public Education in English Canada, 1900–1940* (Montreal: McGill-Queen's University Press, 2012), 80–123, though only the sections in these pages about urban schooling pertain; Robert M. Stamp, "The Response to Urban Growth: The Bureaucratization of Public Education in Calgary, 1884–1914," in David C. Jones, Nancy M. Sheehan, and Robert M. Stamp, eds., *Shaping the Schools of the Canadian West* (Calgary: Detselig, 1979), 109–23. On auxiliary education specifically as a form of curriculum differentiation, see Barry M. Franklin, "Progressivism and Curriculum Differentiation: Special Classes in the Atlanta Public Schools," *History of Education Quarterly* 29, no. 4 (winter 1989): 571–93.

22 E.A. Hardy and Honora M. Cochrane, *Centennial Story: The Board of Education for the City of Toronto, 1850–1950* (Toronto: Thomas Nelson & Sons, 1950), 72–87. Age-grading is, simply, the practice of placing students in grades by their age. Now ubiquitous, it was far from universal practice a century or more ago.

23 Ibid., 117–20; Ontario, *Public and Separate Schools and Teachers in the Province of Ontario for the Year Ending 1913* (Toronto: L.K. Cameron, 1913), 17–29.

24 Calculated from DOE reports, various years (1910–20), "Detailed statistics." For 1916 to 1919, some secondary enrolments were taken from *TBE Minutes 1916*, appendix no. 66, Technical and High School Report no. 5, 703; *TBE Minutes 1917*, appendix no. 103, Technical and High School Report no. 5, 649; *TBE Minutes 1918*, appendix no. 97, Technical and High School Report no. 5, May 1918, 644.

25 Ontario, *Public and Separate Schools and Teachers in the Province of Ontario* (Toronto: A.T. Wilgress, 1919), 21–37; TBE, *Board of Education Toronto, Handbook Nineteen-Nineteen* (Toronto: J.R. Irving, 1919).

26 See William Leeds Richardson, *The Administration of Schools in the Cities of the Dominion of Canada* (Toronto: J.M. Dent, 1922), 208. Montreal was Canada's largest city, but its denominational and linguistic division into Catholic and Protestant boards split the school population. A similar split pertained in Toronto as well, but with much less equilibrium, making the public by the far the larger of the two boards.

27 Ontario, Legislative Assembly, *Report of the Minister of Education Province of Ontario for the Year 1920* (Toronto: Clarkson W. James, 1921), 131, 242, 250, 259; H.H. Bonner, *Statistics of City School Systems, 1919–20*, United States Bureau of Education Bulletin, 1922, no. 17 (Washington: Government Printing Office, 1922), 38, table 10.

28 Tyack, *One Best System*, 177–216.

29 William J. Reese, *Power and the Promise of School Reform: Grassroots Movements during the Progressive Era* (Boston: Routledge & Kegan Paul, 1986), xxiii–xxiv.

30 Kathleen McConnachie, "Methodology in the Study of Women in History: A Case Study of Helen MacMurchy, MD," *Ontario History* 75, no. 1 (1983): 61–70; Dodd, "Helen MacMurchy, MD."

31 Veronica Strong-Boag, "Taking Stock of the Suffragists: Personal Reflections on Feminist Appraisals," *Journal of the Canadian Historical Association* 21, no. 2 (2010): 76–89. See also Janice Fiamengo, "Rediscovering Our Foremothers Again: Racial Ideas of Canada's Early Feminists, 1885–1914," in Mona Gleason and Adele Perry, eds., *Rethinking Canada: The Promise of Women's History*, 5th ed. (Don Mills, ON: Oxford University Press, 2006), 144–62.

32 Dodd, "Helen MacMurchy, MD," 128–30.

33 Ibid., 129; Angus McLaren, *Our Own Master Race: Eugenics in Canada, 1885–1945* (Toronto: Oxford University Press, 1990), 30–1, 49–51, 56–67.

34 Hardy and Cochrane, *Centennial Story*, 143; Dodd, "Helen MacMurchy, MD," 130.

35 Hardy and Cochrane, *Centennial Story*, 69; Dodd, "Helen MacMurchy, MD," 134.

36 Dodd, "Helen MacMurchy, MD," 130. See also Veronica Strong-Boag, "Canada's Women Doctors: Feminism Constrained," in Linda Kealey, ed., *A Not Unreasonable Claim: Women and Reform in Canada, 1880s–1920s* (Toronto: Women's Educational Press, 1979), 109–29.

37 Dodd, "Helen MacMurchy, MD," 128–31.

38 Strong-Boag, "Canada's Women Doctors," 203; Wayne Roberts, "'Rocking the Cradle for the World': The New Woman and Maternal Feminism, Toronto 1877–1914," in Kealey, *A Not Unreasonable Claim*, 22; Joyce Goodman, "Pedagogy and Sex: Mary Dendy (1855–1933), Feeble-Minded Girls and the Sandlebridge Schools, 1902–33," *History of Education* 34, no. 2 (2005): 171–87.

39 Dodd, "Helen MacMurchy, MD," 131.

40 McLaren, *Our Own Master Race*, 14–16.

41 See Diane B. Paul, *Controlling Human Heredity: 1865 to the Present* (Atlantic Highlands, NJ: Humanities Press, 1995), 18; Stephen J. Gould, *The Mismeasure of Man* (New York: W.W. Norton, 1981), 21–3; McLaren, *Our Own Master Race*, 128–36.

42 Carolyn Strange and Jennifer A. Stephen, "Eugenics in Canada: A Checkered History, 1850s–1990s," in Alison Bashford and Phillipa Levine, eds., *The Oxford Handbook of the History of Eugenics* (Oxford: Oxford University Press, 2010), 524.

43 Erika Dyck, *Facing Eugenics: Reproduction, Sterilization, and the Politics of Choice* (Toronto: University of Toronto Press, 2013), 3–26. See also McLaren, *Our Own Master Race*; Joanna Schoen, *Choice & Coercion: Birth Control, Sterilization, and Abortion in Public Health and Welfare* (Chapel Hill: University of North Carolina Press, 2005); Paul A. Lombardo, ed., *A Century of Eugenics in America: From the Indiana Experiment to the Human Genome Era* (Bloomington: Indiana University Press, 2008).

44 McLaren, *Our Own Master Race*, 17.

45 Ontario, Legislative Assembly, *Sixth Report upon the Care of the Feeble-Minded in Ontario, 1911*, Toronto: 1912 (Sessional Papers 1912, no. 23), 26.

46 Ontario, Legislative Assembly, *Report upon the Care of the Feeble-Minded in Ontario, 1907*, Toronto: 1907 (Sessional Papers 1907, no. 63), 3; Trent, Jr, *Inventing the Feeble Mind*, 159–63.

47 Trent, Jr, *Inventing the Feeble Mind*, 161.

48 Mark Jackson, *The Borderland of Imbecility: Medicine, Society and the Fabrication of the Feeble Mind in Late Victorian and Edwardian England* (Manchester: Manchester University Press, 2000), 29–31.

49 Ontario, Legislative Assembly, *Report upon the Care of the Feeble-Minded in Ontario, 1907*, 3.

50 Wendy Kline, *Building a Better Race: Gender, Sexuality, and Eugenics from the Turn of the Century to the Baby Boom* (Berkeley: University of California Press, 2001), 23–9; McLaren, *Our Own Master Race*, 39–41; Ontario, Legislative Assembly, *Fourth Report of the Feeble-Minded in Ontario, 1909*, Toronto: 1910 (Sessional Papers 1910, no. 23), 46–8. On recapitulation theory as a

prime influence on progressive education, see Thomas D. Fallace, *Race and the Origins of Progressive Education, 1880–1929* (New York: Teachers College Press, 2015).

51 Ontario, Legislative Assembly, *Report upon the Care of the Feeble-Minded in Ontario, 1908,* Toronto: 1909 (Sessional Papers 1909, no. 58), 41.

52 Clarence M. Hincks, "The Scope and Aims of the Mental Hygiene Movement in Canada," *Canadian Journal of Mental Hygiene* 1, no. 1 (April 1919): 24–7.

53 Ontario, Legislative Assembly, *Sixth Report upon the Care of the Feeble-Minded in Ontario, 1912,* 6. See also Harvey G. Simmons, *From Asylum to Welfare* (Toronto: National Institute on Mental Retardation, 1982), 50–85; Mona Gleason, *Small Matters: Canadian Children in Sickness and Health* (Montreal: McGill-Queen's University Press, 2013), 123–7; Trent, Jr, *Inventing the Feeble Mind,* 141–83; Jackson, *Borderland of Imbecility,* 146–50.

54 Alberta passed its sexual sterilization act in 1928, followed by British Columbia in 1933. A number of American states also had sexual sterilization acts. McLaren, *Our Own Master Race,* 90–106; Dyck, *Facing Eugenics,* 5–9.

55 Ontario, Legislative Assembly, *Report upon the Care of the Feeble-Minded in Ontario, 1908,* 39. See also Ontario, Legislative Assembly, *Fourth Report of the Feeble-Minded in Ontario, 1909,* 45; Ontario, Legislative Assembly, *Sixth Report upon the Care of the Feeble-Minded in Ontario, 1912,* 17.

56 Seymour B. Sarason and John Doris, *Educational Handicap, Public Policy, and Social History: A Broadened Perspective on Mental Retardation* (New York: The Free Press, 1979), 266; Robert L. Osgood, *For "Children Who Vary from the Normal Type": Special Education in Boston, 1838–1930* (Washington: Gallaudet University Press, 2000), 58; Jackson, *Borderland of Imbecility,* 65–9; Goodman, "Pedagogy and Sex," 171–87.

57 Ontario, Legislative Assembly, *Report upon the Care of the Feeble-Minded in Ontario, 1908,* 17–18. Detroit had classes as well. Sarason and Doris, *Educational Handicap,* 266.

58 Miss Dendy, "Types of Feebleminded Children," *Report of the International Congress of Women, Held in Toronto Canada, June 24th–30th, 1909* (Toronto: The National Council of Women of Canada, 1910), 45.

59 Jackson, *Borderland of Imbecility,* 64–74.

60 *TBE Minutes 1909,* 18 June 1909, 108 (the TBE minutes incorrectly identify Dendy as "Benby"); "Didn't Appoint 4th Inspector," *Toronto Daily Star,* 19 June 1909, 3; Ontario, Legislative Assembly, *Fourth Report of the Feeble-Minded in Ontario, 1909,* 3–5.

61 *TBE Minutes 1909*, 18 June 1909, 109.

62 Gene Homel, "James Simpson and the Origins of Canadian Social Democracy" (PhD diss., University of Toronto, 1978), 436–7.

63 Mark Jackson makes the same argument about Dendy's appeal to a wide swath of British reformers of varied political views. Jackson, *Borderland of Imbecility*, 69.

64 *TBE Minutes 1910*, appendix no. 6, Management Report no. 2, 27 January 1910, adopted as amended 3 February 1910, 33, 37; Ontario, Legislative Assembly, *Fifth Report upon the Care of the Feeble-Minded in Ontario, 1910*, Toronto: 1911 (Sessional Papers 1911, no. 23), 46.

65 Ontario, Legislative Assembly, *Fifth Report upon the Care of the Feeble-Minded in Ontario, 1910*, 46–51; "Sad Cases of Dull Children," *Toronto Daily Star*, 6 May 1910, 12.

66 Ontario, Legislative Assembly, *Fifth Report upon the Care of the Feeble-Minded in Ontario, 1910*, 46–50.

67 *TBE Minutes 1910*, 5 May 1910, 74; appendix no. 29, Management Report no. 11, 9 June 1910, adopted 16 June 1910, 398; Ontario, Legislative Assembly, *Fifth Report upon the Care of the Feeble-Minded in Ontario, 1910*, 52.

68 Simmons, *From Asylum to Welfare*, 90.

69 Toronto Bureau of Municipal Research, *What Is "the Ward" Going to Do with Toronto?* (Toronto: Bureau of Municipal Research, 1918).

70 TDSBA, *TBE Handbook 1911*, 41–2, 44; *TBE Minutes 1912*, appendix no. 69; R.H. Cowley, "Report on the Public Schools of Toronto," 7 June 1912, 585.

71 *TBE Annual Report 1892*, 43; *TBE Annual Report 1893*, 66.

72 *TBE Minutes 1910*, appendix no. 34, Management Report no. 12, 23 June 1910, 425.

73 Hardy and Cochrane, *Centennial Story*, 247.

74 Susan E. Houston, "Victorian Origins of Juvenile Delinquency: A Canadian Experience," in Michael B. Katz and Paul H. Mattingly, eds., *Education and Social Change: Themes from Ontario's Past* (New York: New York University Press, 1975), 86.

75 John Bullen, "Hidden Workers: Child Labour and the Family Economy in Late Nineteenth-Century Urban Ontario," *Labour/Le Travail* 18 (fall 1986): 175–7.

76 Ibid., 177–80.

77 TDSBA (VF), TBE – Schools – Elementary – Hester How PS, C.C. Goldring, "History of Hester How Public School," *TBE Minutes 1953*, appendix, 258. See also TDSBA (VF), TBE – Schools – Elementary – Hester How PS; James L. Hughes, "Hester How," *The School* (December 1915), 300–5.

78 Hughes, "Hester How," 301.
79 Goldring, "History of Hester How Public School," 258–9.
80 Bullen, "Hidden Workers," 178. Bullen gives the date as 1892. Goldring gave it as 1890. Goldring, "History of Hester How Public School," 258.
81 See TDSBA, *TBE Handbook 1918*, 108.
82 Osgood, *For "Children Who Vary from the Normal Type,"* 82–92; Joseph L. Tropea, "Bureaucratic Order and Special Children: Urban Schools, 1890s–1940s," *History of Education Quarterly* 27, no. 1 (spring 1987): 30–5; Sarason and Doris, *Educational Handicap*, 262–4, 275–6.
83 Osgood, *For "Children Who Vary from the Normal Type,"* 78–9. Osgood introduces the terminology "differentiated" and "undifferentiated" in his later book: Robert L. Osgood, *The History of Special Education: A Struggle for Equality in American Public Schools* (Westport, CT: Praeger, 2008), 41–4.
84 Osgood, *For "Children Who Vary from the Normal Type,"* 90–2.
85 Osgood, *The History of Special Education*, 41–54.
86 *TBE Minutes 1911*, appendix no. 42, Management Report no. 10, 25 May 1911, adopted 1 June 1911, 399.
87 Sarason and Doris, *Educational Handicap*, 316–19.
88 See *TBE Minutes 1913*, appendix no. 8, Management Report no. 2, 30 January 1913, adopted 6 February 1913, 53; "The Defectives Neglected While City and Province Disagree over Their Duty," *Toronto Daily Star*, 9 May 1912, 3. See also Osgood, *For "Children Who Vary from the Normal Type,"* 138.
89 E.R. Johnstone, "The Summer School for Teachers of Backward Children," *Journal of Psycho-Asthenics* 13 (1908): 127.
90 Ibid., 122–30; Trent, Jr, *Inventing the Feeble Mind*, 156–61.
91 Trent, Jr, *Inventing the Feeble Mind*, 166–74.
92 Johnstone, "The Summer School for Teachers of Backward Children," 126.
93 Gerald T. Hackett, "The History of Public Education for Mentally Retarded Children in the Province of Ontario 1867–1964" (EdD diss., University of Toronto, 1969), 395. On Sandiford and eugenics, see McLaren, *Our Own Master Race*, 61–3.
94 Helen MacMurchy, *Organization and Management of Auxiliary Classes*, Educational Pamphlets no. 7 (Toronto: Department of Education, Ontario, 1915), 3.
95 Ibid., 111. See also Helen MacMurchy, *To Inspectors, Principals, and Teachers* (Toronto: Ontario Department of Education, 1919).
96 MacMurchy, *To Inspectors, Principals, and Teachers*, 8.
97 *TBE Annual Report 1913*, 39–41.
98 *TBE Annual Report 1911*, 8.

99 Leonard P. Ayres, *Laggards in Our Schools: A Study of Retardation and Elimination in City School Systems* (New York: Russell Sage Foundation, 1909), 1.

100 MacMurchy, *To Inspectors, Principals, and Teachers*, 8.

101 *TBE Annual Report 1911*, 43.

102 Ayres, *Laggards in Our Schools*, 3.

103 See the end of this book's introduction for an explanation of junior and senior forms, the grading system Ontario schools used until about 1937, when the modern language of "grades" replaced it.

104 *TBE Annual Report 1916*, 41.

105 Ayres, *Laggards in Our Schools*, 3.

106 Ibid., 5.

107 Ibid., 4, 8.

108 See, e.g., OHEC, S.J. Radcliffe, *Retardation in the Schools of Ontario* (Toronto: author, n.d. [1922]).

109 Ayres, *Laggards in Our Schools*, 2.

110 Tyack, *One Best System*, 202. See also Gidney and Millar, *How Schools Worked*, 20–7; Lynn Trethewey, "Producing the Over-Aged Child in South Australian Primary Schools," *Historical Studies in Education/Revue d'histoire de l'éducation* 10, no. 1–2 (1998): 179.

111 Tyack, *One Best System*, 177–98.

112 *TBE Annual Report 1913*, 23–58. In addition to retardation being a problem in Canadian and American education, reformers in the state of South Australia also tackled it in the 1910s and defined it in much the same way as their Canadian and American counterparts. Trethewey, "Producing the Over-Aged Child," 159–79.

113 *TBE Annual Report 1913*, 47–8.

114 Ibid., 40.

115 Toronto Bureau of Municipal Research, "Measurement of Educational Waste," 15.

116 CTA, fonds 1003, series 973, subseries 2, item 4, "Are All Children Alike?" Bureau of Municipal Research, white paper 4, 28 May 1915.

117 *TBE Minutes 1912*, appendix no. 100, Management Report no. 18, 31 October 1912, adopted 7 November 1912, 828; appendix no. 106, Management Report no. 19, 14 November 1912, adopted 21 November 1912, 833. It is sometimes difficult to determine whether these classes were for backward children, foreign children (discussed in a subsequent section of this chapter), or a combination of both. See TDSBA, *TBE Handbook 1914* to *TBE Handbook 1921*; *TBE Minutes 1913*, appendix no. 13, Management Report no. 3, 13 February 1913, adopted 20 February 1913, 101; appendix no. 39,

Management Report no. 7, 10 April 1913, adopted 17 April 1913, 384; appendix no. 86, Management Report no. 15, 25 September 1913, adopted 2 October 1913, 819; *TBE Minutes 1914,* Management Report no. 3, 12 February 1913, adopted 19 February 1914, 102.

118 *TBE Annual Report 1913,* 43–4.

119 TDSBA (VF), TBE Depts. Special Education, Auxiliary Classes, History, memorandum, "Re Education of Defectives," Superintendent of Education [John Seath] to the Minister of Education, 22 December 1913.

120 TDSBA (VF), memorandum, "Re Education of Defectives," addendum, "Statement Regarding Classes for Backward and Foreign Children, n.d. [1914]."

121 *TBE Annual Report 1914,* 15.

122 *TBE Annual Report 1918,* 100. See also TDSBA, memorandum, "Re Education of Defectives."

123 MacMurchy, *To Inspectors, Principals, and Teachers,* 3; TDSBA, memorandum, "Re Education of Defectives."

124 Gidney and Millar, *How Schools Worked,* 22.

125 OHEC, *Regulations for Auxiliary Classes,* DOE Circular no. 22 (Toronto: King's Printer, 1917).

126 Gleason, *Small Matters,* 131.

127 *TBE Minutes 1912,* appendix no. 54, Management Report no. 10, 30 May 1912, adopted 6 June 1912, 441; Neil S. MacDonald, *Open-Air Schools* (Toronto: McClelland, 1918), 51.

128 *TBE Minutes 1918,* appendix no. 143, R.H. Cowley Report to the Board of Education on Dr Noble's Motion, 23 October 1918, 948–9.

129 MacDonald, *Open-Air Schools,* 9–59; Robert Stamp, *The Schools of Ontario, 1876–1976* (Toronto: University of Toronto Press, 1982), 68.

130 MacDonald, *Open-Air Schools,* 36.

131 Heather MacDougall, *Activists and Advocates: Toronto's Health Department, 1883–1983* (Toronto: Dundurn Press, 1990), 126–30.

132 *TBE Annual Report 1911,* 29–30.

133 Sutherland, *Children in English Canadian Society,* 49–50; Osgood, *For "Children Who Vary from the Normal Type,"* 152–5.

134 MacDonald, *Open-Air Schools,* 78; *TBE Annual Report 1915,* 4.

135 TDSBA (VF), TBE Schools – Elementary – High Park Forest School, W.A. Craick, "The Forest School in High Park Builds up Health of Delicate Children by Life in Open," *Toronto Star Weekly,* 30 June 1917, n.p.

136 Fred S. Dent, "Toronto's Open-Air School," *The School* 2, no. 9 (1914): 535.

137 *TBE Annual Report 1919,* 107.

138 W.E. Struthers, "The Open-Air School," in *Proceedings of the Fifty-Third Annual Convention of the OEA* (Toronto: William Briggs, 1914), 286–7; Dent, "Toronto's Open-Air School," 535–6; *TBE Annual Report 1912*, 15.

139 MacDonald, *Open-Air Schools*, 52–3; *TBE Annual Report 1915*, 5–6.

140 *TBE Minutes 1914*, appendix no. 2, "Inaugural Address of W.O. McTaggart, B.A.," 8.

141 *TBE Minutes 1916*, appendix no. 118, Management Report no. 21, 30 October 1916, adopted 2 November 1916, 1,083; MacDonald, *Open-Air Schools*, 116.

142 Struthers, "The Open-Air School," 286.

143 *TBE Annual Report 1913*, 7.

144 MacDougall, *Activists and Advocates*, 193.

145 MacDonald, *Open-Air Schools*, 62.

146 *TBE Annual Report 1915*, 4.

147 Ibid.

148 Stephen A. Speisman, *The Jews of Toronto: A History to 1937* (Toronto: McClelland and Stewart, 1979), 81–90.

149 See Mariana Valverde, *The Age of Light, Soap, and Water: Moral Reform in English Canada, 1885–1925* (Toronto: McClelland and Stewart, 1991), 15–16; Rutherford, "Introduction," xvii–xviii; Kari Dehli, "For Intelligent Motherhood and National Efficiency: The Toronto Home and School Council, 1916–1930," in Ruby Heap and Alison Prentice, eds., *Gender and Education in Ontario* (Toronto: Canadian Scholars Press, 1991), 147–63; Gleason, *Small Matters*, 90–3.

150 MacDonald, *Open-Air Schools*, 60.

151 William J. Reese, "After Bread, Education: Nutrition and Urban School Children, 1890–1920," *Teachers College Record* 81, no. 4 (1980): 496; A.R. Ruis, "'The Penny Lunch has Spread Faster than the Measles': Children's Health and the Debate over School Lunches in New York City, 1908–1930," *History of Education Quarterly* 55, no. 2 (May 2015): 195–7.

152 Marta Danylewycz, "Domestic Science Education in Ontario, 1900–1940," in Heap and Prentice, *Gender and Education in Ontario*, 130.

153 Dent, "Open-Air Schools," 535.

154 *TBE Annual Report 1916*, 17.

155 *TBE Annual Report 1919*, 107.

156 Struthers, "The Open-Air School," 283.

157 *TBE Annual Report 1912*, 7–8.

158 Michael Piva estimated that in 1921, "the vast majority" of Toronto's male blue-collar workers earned wages that were insufficient to maintain a

family of five. The food budget in this calculation was set at just less than
$12. Unpaid and paid female and juvenile labour was a necessary supple-
ment to the family budget. But even with these crucial additions, funds
were tight. Piva, *The Condition of the Working Class in Toronto, 1900–1921*,
38–43.

159 Gleason, *Small Matters*, 52–3.
160 *TBE Annual Report 1918*, 130.
161 See Gleason, *Small Matters*, 52–3.
162 Reese, "After Bread, Education," 506–9. Socialists, Reese argues, were less
likely to judge working-class food as the problem and called upon the
state to establish universal school lunch programs. Moral reformers in
turn rejected these programs out of a perception that they would pauper-
ize the poor. And, as A.R. Ruis shows, school feeding programs in some
cities in this period, such as New York, rejected Americanization priorities
and "embraced different cultural diets." Choosing to feed Italian children
macaroni, Italian bread, and minestrone "evoked an agenda of health
promotion – getting children to eat nourishing food – over one of cultural
assimilation – getting children to eat more like Americans, which aligned
with national policy recommendations." Ruis, "The Penny Lunch," 198–9.
163 *TBE Minutes 1913*, appendix no. 43, Management Report no. 8, 24 April
1913, adopted 1 May 1913, 412; appendix no. 48, Management Report
no. 9, 8 May 1913, 442; appendix no. 92, Management Report no. 16,
9 October 1913, adopted 16 October 1913, 886; TDSBA (VF), memorandum, "Re Education of Defectives," addendum, "Statement Regarding
Classes for Backward and Foreign Children," n.d. [1914].
164 Robert Craig Brown and Ramsay Cook, *Canada 1896–1912: A Nation
Transformed* (Toronto: McClelland and Stewart, 1974), 79.
165 *TBE Annual Report 1913*, 56.
166 Of 639 students, 432 were born in these countries. *TBE Annual Report
1913*, 56.
167 Ibid., 28.
168 Ibid.; Sarason and Doris, *Educational Handicap*, 302.
169 Leonard P. Ayres, *The Cleveland School Survey: Summary Volume* (Cleveland:
The Survey Committee of the Cleveland Foundation, 1917), 212.
170 Luigi G. Pennacchio, "Toronto's Public Schools and the Assimilation of
Foreign Students, 1900–1920," *Journal of Educational Thought* 20, no. 1
(1986): 38–9; Tyack, *One Best System*, 229–54.
171 Stamp, *Schools of Ontario*, 92–6; Robert F. Harney and Harold Troper,
Immigrants: A Portrait of the Urban Experience, 1890–1930 (Toronto: Van
Nostrand Reinhold, 1975), 109–14.

172 J.T.M. Anderson, *The Education of the New Canadian* (Toronto: J.M. Dent, 1918), 171; R.D. Gidney and W.P.J. Millar, "How to Teach English to Immigrant Children: Canadian Pedagogical Theory and Practice, 1910–1960," *Historical Studies in Education/Revue d'histoire de l'éducation* 26, no. 2 (fall 2014): 100; Tyack, *One Best System*, 232–3.

173 TDSBA, memorandum, "Re Education of Defectives," addendum, "Statement Regarding Classes for Backward and Foreign Children," n.d. [1914]. See also *TBE Annual Report 1914*, 15; *TBE Annual Report 1920*, 115.

174 *TBE Annual Report 1913*, 29.

175 McLaren, *Our Own Master Race*, 47–68.

176 On this issue and other questions of culture and race, schooling, structure, and agency in the education of immigrant children in this period, see an excellent new case study of one Toronto school by Vipond, *Making a Global City*. See also the overview of the American literature by Michael R. Olneck, "American Public Schooling and European Immigrants," in William J. Reese and John L. Rury, eds., *Rethinking the History of American Education* (New York: Palgrave Macmillan, 2008), 103–41. For historical Canadian examples, see Peter Sandiford and Ruby Kerr, "Intelligence of Chinese and Japanese Children," *Journal of Educational Psychology* 17, no. 6 (September 1926): 361–7; P.F. Munro, *An Experimental Inquiry into the Intelligence of the Jew at Ryerson Public School* (Toronto: University of Toronto Press, 1926).

It should also be noted that many other educational policies could be deliberately exclusionary. The Indian Act contributed to the segregation of Indigenous pupils in federal government day and residential schools. Jean Barman, "Schooled for Inequality: The Education of British Columbia Aboriginal Children," in Jean Barman and Mona Gleason, eds., *Children, Teachers, and Schools in the History of British Columbia*, 2nd ed. (Calgary: Detselig, 2003), 55–79. School segregation of Chinese and Japanese (domestic- and foreign-born) children was introduced in Victoria as early as 1902, with Vancouver and several other British Columbia cities following suit. Black children were also segregated at times in British Columbia, Ontario, and Nova Scotia. See Timothy J. Stanley, *Contesting White Supremacy: School Segregation, Anti-Racism, and the Making of Chinese Canadians* (Vancouver: University of British Columbia Press, 2011), 97–104; and Paul Axelrod, *The Promise of Schooling: Education in Canada, 1800–1914* (Toronto: University of Toronto Press, 1997), 78–80.

177 W.A. Craick, "Victoria Street School Building Is Oldest in City – Was Built in 1855," *Toronto Star Weekly*, 16 March 1918, 23. See also Munro, *An Experimental Inquiry*, 9.

178 Norman F. Black, *English for the Non-English* (Regina: Regina Book Shop, 1913), 87; *TBE Minutes 1913*, appendix no. 43, Management Report no. 8, 24 April 1913, adopted 1 May 1913, 412.
179 CTA, "Are All Children Alike?," 4.
180 *Sixth Report upon the Care of the Feeble-Minded in Ontario, 1912*, 50.
181 See Goodman, "Pedagogy and Sex," 177–80.
182 *Report upon the Care of the Feeble-Minded in Ontario, 1908*, 11; Simmons, *From Asylum to Welfare*, 29–35. On the terminology, see Ontario, Legislative Assembly, *Report upon the Care of the Feeble-Minded in Ontario, 1907*, 3.
183 "To Safeguard Those Who Have Weak Minds," *Toronto Daily Star*, 27 March 1912, 10.
184 Simmons, *From Asylum to Welfare*, 73–4.
185 Ibid., 73–9.
186 Vera C. Pletsch, *Not Wanted in the Classroom: Parent Associations and the Education of Trainable Retarded Children in Ontario, 1947–1969* (London, ON: Althouse Press, 1997).
187 See *TBE Minutes 1915*, 30 December 1915, 221. As we shall see shortly, the classes were already closed by the time Fares made this request.
188 "The Mental Defectives," letter to the editor, *Globe*, 7 February 1921, 4.
189 Nic Clarke, "Sacred Daemons: Exploring British Columbian Society's Perceptions of 'Mentally Deficient' Children, 1870–1930," *B.C. Studies* 144 (winter 2004–5): 61–89; Jessa Chupik and David Wright, "Treating the 'Idiot' Child in Early 20th-Century Ontario," *Disability & Society* 21, no. 1 (January 2006): 77–90; Veronica Strong-Boag, "'Children of Adversity': Disabilities and Child Welfare in Canada from the Nineteenth to the Twenty-First Century," *Journal of Family History* 32, no. 4 (October 2007): 420–7.
190 *Fifth Report upon the Care of the Feeble-Minded in Ontario, 1910*, 47–50.
191 CAMHA, Clarke Institute of Psychiatry/Toronto Psychiatric Hospital Fonds, Dr C.K. Clarke Series, "Life and Works of C.K. Clarke, M.D. Psychiatry in the Schools" (ca. 1922), 1.
192 Trent, Jr, *Inventing the Feeble Mind*, 133–5, 163–5.
193 "To Safeguard Those Who Have Weak Minds," *Toronto Daily Star*, 27 March 1912, 10; "Home Proposed for Feeble-Minded," *Globe*, 27 March 1912, 9. The *Star* reporter, unlike the reporter from the *Globe* who had quoted Conboy directly, paraphrased the chairman's remark as these children "could not be instructed in any way."
194 Lillian Carruthers, "Children in Special Classes," letter to the editor, *Toronto Daily Star*, 29 March 1912, 5.

195 Ian Robert Dowbiggin, *Keeping America Sane: Psychiatry and Eugenics in the United States and Canada, 1880–1940* (Ithaca, NY: Cornell University Press, 1997); Douglas C. Baynton, *Forbidden Signs: American Culture and the Campaign against Sign Language* (Chicago: University of Chicago Press, 1996), 56–72.

196 Amy Samson, "Eugenics in the Community: Gendered Professions and Eugenic Sterilization in Alberta, 1928–72," *Canadian Bulletin of Medical History* 31, no. 1 (2014): 143–63.

197 Kate Rousmaniere, *City Teachers: Teaching and School Reform in Historical Perspective* (New York: Teachers College Press, 1997), 2.

198 Miss Blackwell, "Auxiliary Classes in the Public Schools," *Public Health Journal* 5, no. 12 (December 1914): 624; MacMurchy, *To Inspectors, Principals, and Teachers*, 8. See also Mrs Kerr, "Defective Children," *Public Health Journal* 5, no. 12 (December 1914): 621.

199 Carruthers, "Children in Special Classes," 5. See also "Glass of Warm Milk for Weakly Pupils," *Toronto Daily Star*, 17 January 1913, 14; Clarke, "Sacred Daemons." Jane Read, "Fit for What? Special Education in London, 1890–1914," *History of Education* 33, no. 3 (May 2004): 293–7, argues that English special class teachers held distinct and more sympathetic views about mentally defective pupils than did eugenicists in that country.

200 Carruthers, "Children in Special Classes," 5. See also Lillian Carruthers, "How Numerous Are Subnormal Pupils?" *Toronto Daily Star*, 9 November 1912, 8.

201 Gidney and Millar, *How Schools Worked*, 86–7.

202 "Those Needing Most Care Are Neglected," *Toronto Daily Star*, 9 May 1912, 7; Hackett, "The History of Public Education," 115.

203 "Those Needing Most Care Are Neglected," 7.

204 "The Defectives Neglected While City and Province Disagree over Their Duty," *Toronto Daily Star*, 9 May 1912, 3.

205 "Nineteen Inspectors in Schools, and Yet Complaints Are Made," *Toronto Daily Star*, 10 May 1912, 12.

206 *TBE Annual Report 1913*, 55.

207 Charles S. Hartwell, "The Grading and Promotion of Pupils," *Journal of Proceedings and Addresses of the Forty-Eighth Meeting of the National Education Association* (Winona, MN: National Education Association, 1910), 294–305.

208 Ibid., 295–6; John Kennedy, *The Batavia System of Individual Instruction* (Syracuse, NY: C.W. Bardeen, 1914), 9.

209 Kennedy, *The Batavia System*, 9–12.

210 Hartwell, "The Grading and Promotion of Pupils," 295–6.

211 *TBE Annual Report 1916*, 38–9.

212 "Strong Plea Made for Mental Defectives," *Globe*, 6 March 1914, 8.

213 Hackett, "The History of Public Education," 95.

214 Ontario, *The Revised Statutes of Ontario, 1927*, vol. 3, ch. 324, The Auxiliary Classes Act (Toronto: Government of Ontario, 1927). The use of "child of normal mentality at eight years of age" referred to the emerging Binet-Simon intelligence tests, which employed the concept of mental age to assess a child's mental ability. A mental age of eight later came to represent an IQ of 50. See Jason Ellis, "Early Educational Exclusion: 'Idiotic' and 'Imbecilic' Children, Their Families, and the Toronto Public School System, 1914–50," *Canadian Historical Review* 98, no. 3 (September 2017): 483–504.

215 OHEC, *Regulations for Auxiliary Classes*, 3.

216 Ontario, Legislative Assembly, *Report of the Minister of Education for the Province of Ontario for the Year 1920*, appendix H, Report of the Inspector of Auxiliary Classes (Toronto: Clarkson W. James, 1921), 108.

217 OHEC, *Regulations for Auxiliary Classes*, 3–4.

218 Ibid., 4.

219 Ontario, *The Revised Statutes of Ontario, 1927*, vol. 3, ch. 324, The Auxiliary Classes Act.

220 Simmons, *Asylum to Welfare*, 79–80.

221 See McLaren, *Our Own Master Race*, 61–3, 82–3.

222 CAMHA, Canadian National Committee for Mental Hygiene (CNCMH) fonds. Eugenical Sterilization, Box 1, "Petition, March 1916. From Canadian Conf. of Charities + Correction to Prime Minister of Canada RE: 'feeble-minded.'"

223 Simmons, *Asylum to Welfare*, 79–85.

224 "Trustees Approve Big Plan to Care for Defectives," *Toronto Daily Star*, 8 December 1916, 21; *TBE Minutes 1916*, 7 December 1916, 199.

225 Simmons, *Asylum to Welfare*, 82–5.

226 Ibid., 80–1.

227 Lemon, *Toronto since 1918*, 17; "T.L. Church Is Mayor by Majority of 6,469," *Globe*, 2 January 1915, 13.

228 Lemon, *Toronto since 1918*, 19–21.

229 Charles M. Johnston, *E.C. Drury: Agrarian Idealist* (Toronto: University of Toronto Press, 1986), 51–98.

230 Ontario, Legislative Assembly, *Report on the Care and Control of the Mentally Defective and Feeble-Minded in Ontario, by the Honourable Frank*

Egerton Hodgins, Toronto: 1919 (Sessional Papers 1920, no. 24, vol. 5, appended), 99.

231 Simmons, *Asylum to Welfare*, 98–100.

232 C. Elizabeth Koester, "An Evil Hitherto Unchecked: Eugenics and the 1917 Ontario Royal Commission on the Care and Control of the Mentally Defective and Feeble-Minded," *Canadian Bulletin of Medical History/ Bulletin canadien d'histoire de la médecine* 33, no. 1 (spring 2016): 59–81.

233 Simmons, *Asylum to Welfare*, 98–100; Dodd, "Helen MacMurchy, MD," 142–4.

234 See Franklin, "Progressivism and Curriculum Differentiation"; Marvin Lazerson, "The Origins of Special Education," in Jay G. Chambers and William T. Hartman, eds., *Special Education Policies: Their History, Implementation, and Finance* (Philadelphia: Temple University Press, 1983), 16–33; Gerald E. Thomson, "'Remove from Our Midst These Unfortunates': A Historical Inquiry into the Influence of Eugenics, Educational Efficiency as Well as Mental Hygiene upon the Vancouver School System and Its Special Classes, 1910–1969" (PhD diss., University of British Columbia, 1999).

2 IQ Testing Transforms Auxiliary Education

1 Lewis Terman, "The Problem," in Lewis Terman et al., eds., *Intelligence Tests and School Reorganization* (Yonkers-on-Hudson: World Book, 1923), 1.

2 Paul Davis Chapman, *Schools as Sorters: Lewis M. Terman, Applied Psychology, and the Intelligence Testing Movement, 1890–1930* (New York: New York University Press, 1988); Judith R. Raftery, "Missing the Mark: Intelligence Testing in Los Angeles Public Schools, 1922–1932," *History of Education Quarterly* 28, no. 1 (1988): 73–93; Ann Marie Ryan and Alan Stoskopf, "Public and Catholic School Responses to IQ Testing in the Early Twentieth Century," *Teachers College Record* 110, no. 4 (2008): 894–922; Ann Marie Ryan, "From Child Study to Efficiency: District Administrators and the Use of Testing in the Chicago Public Schools, 1899 to 1928," *Paedagogica Historica* 47, no. 3 (2011): 343–51; Gillian Sutherland, *Ability, Merit and Measurement: Mental Testing and English Education 1880– 1940* (Oxford: Clarendon Press, 1984). On IQ testing and streaming in auxiliary education specifically, see Barry M. Franklin, *From "Backwardness" to "At-Risk": Childhood Learning Difficulties and the Contradictions of School Reform* (Albany: SUNY Press, 1994), 43–6; Franklin, "Progressivism and Curriculum Differentiation: Special Classes in the Atlanta Public Schools,"

History of Education Quarterly 29, no. 4 (1989): 586–90. For an article that breaks the mould of sorting-focused studies, see Paula S. Fass, "The IQ: A Cultural Historical Framework," *American Journal of Education* 88, no. 4 (1980): 444–58, in which the author argues for a wider interpretation of the meaning of IQ testing.

3 See also Serge Nicolas, Bernard Andrieu, Jean-Claude Croizet, Raysid B. Sanitioso, and Jeremy Trevelyan Burman, "Sick? Or Slow? On the Origins of Intelligence as a Psychological Object," *Intelligence* 41 (2013): 699–711.

4 Stephen J. Gould, *The Mismeasure of Man* (New York: W.W. Norton, 1981), 148; Alfred Binet, *Les idées modernes sur les enfants* (Paris: Flamarrion, 1909), 124–5.

5 Alfred Binet and Theodore Simon, *A Method of Measuring the Intelligence of Young Children*, trans. Clara Harrison Town (Lincoln, IL: Courier, 1911), 54–5.

6 Gould, *Mismeasure of Man*, 149–54; Leila Zenderland, *Measuring Minds: Henry Herbert Goddard and the Origins of American Intelligence Testing* (Cambridge: Cambridge University Press, 1998), 94–7; Chapman, *Schools as Sorters*, 19–20.

7 Zenderland, *Measuring Minds*, 96–9.

8 Daniel J. Kevles, *In the Name of Eugenics: Genetics and the Uses of Human Heredity* (Berkeley: University of California Press, 1985), 78.

9 Binet and Simon, *A Method of Measuring the Intelligence of Young Children*, 68.

10 Gould, *Mismeasure of Man*, 151–3. See also, Zenderland, *Measuring Minds*, 96.

11 Quoted in Gould, *Mismeasure of Man*, 151.

12 Gould, *Mismeasure of Man*, 158–9.

13 Ibid., 149.

14 Ibid., 149–50. Mental age was a concept devised initially for use with children. To use the scale with adults, IQ testers simply decided that all adults should be considered to have a maximum mental age of sixteen. Terman wrote: "Native intelligence, in so far as it can be measured by tests now available, appears to improve but little after the age of 15 or 16 years. It follows that in calculating the IQ of an adult subject, it will be necessary to disregard the years he has lived beyond the point where intelligence attains its final development." Lewis M. Terman, *The Measurement of Intelligence* (Boston: Houghton-Mifflin, 1916), 79.

15 Chapman, *Schools as Sorters*, 27–9.

16 Terman, *Measurement of Intelligence*, 79.

17 Chapman, *Schools as Sorters*, 28; Gould, *Mismeasure of Man*, 160–3.

18 Terman, *Measurement of Intelligence*, 91–2. Thomas D. Fallace, *Race and the Origins of Progressive Education, 1880–1929* (New York: Teachers College Press, 2015), 90–1.

19 Gould, *Mismeasure of Man*, 192–9.

20 Quoted in Kevles, *In the Name of Eugenics*, 82–3. This classification consisting of "multiple White races" relied on the earlier work of William Z. Ripley and Madison Grant. Fallace, *Race and the Origins of Progressive Education*, 87–8.

21 N.J. Block and Gerald Dworkin, "IQ, Heritability, and Inequality," in Block and Dworkin, eds., *The IQ Controversy: Critical Readings* (New York: Pantheon, 1976), 457–62; Gould, *Mismeasure of Man*, 199–222.

22 Theodore Christou, *Progressive Education: Revisioning and Reframing Ontario's Public Schools, 1919–1942* (Toronto: University of Toronto Press, 2012), 16–17; Jennifer A. Stephen, *Pick One Intelligent Girl: Employability, Domesticity, and the Gendering of Canada's Welfare State, 1939–1947* (Toronto: University of Toronto Press, 2007), 68–70; Angus McLaren, *Our Own Master Race: Eugenics in Canada 1885–1945* (Toronto: University of Toronto Press, 1990), 60–3; "'U' Professor, P. Sandiford, Dies, Aged 59," *Globe and Mail*, 13 October 1941, 4. See also Peter Sandiford, *The Mental and Physical Life of Schoolchildren* (London: Longmans, Green, and Co, 1919).

23 Kevles, *In the Name of Eugenics*, 83.

24 Chapman, *Schools as Sorters*, 84. See also Terman et al., eds., *Intelligence Tests and School Reorganization*.

25 Lewis M. Terman, *The Intelligence of Schoolchildren* (Boston: Houghton-Mifflin, 1919), 7.

26 Peter Sandiford, "Examinations or Intelligence Tests?" *The School* 7, no. 10 (1919): 641–4.

27 *TBE Annual Report 1921*, 57–8; C.C. Goldring, *Intelligence Testing in a Toronto Public School* (DPaed thesis, published, University of Toronto, n.d., [ca. 1924]); C.K. Clarke, "What Is Your Child's IQ?," *Maclean's Magazine* 35, no. 2 (15 January 1922): 13–15, 36–8.

28 Terman, *Measurement of Intelligence*, xi.

29 At the "Year IX" and "X" levels (testing mental ages nine and ten), two tests call for external materials – a "Healy-Fernald Construction Puzzle" and set of weighted cubes – which the book gives directions for ordering from a Chicago company. However, the book also includes alternative tests that could be substituted for the external materials should the examiner not wish to send away for them. A scoring booklet was also available from Houghton-Mifflin, but like the cubes and puzzle, it was not required either. Terman, *Measurement of Intelligence*, 121–41.

30 Ibid., 127.
31 Block and Dworkin, *The IQ Controversy*, 4–44. There were other opponents as well. Ann Marie Ryan and Alan Stoskopf have shown how American Catholic educators were quicker than their public schools counterparts to question the IQ tests because Catholic educators were more inclined to be suspicious of the undue influence of modern science and eugenics in education, two trends to which IQ testers were tied. Ryan and Stoskopf, "Public and Catholic School Reponses to IQ Testing in the Early Twentieth Century," 905–15. Judith Raftery argues in her study of Los Angeles public schools in the 1920s that many of the city's educators quickly discovered, after IQ tests were introduced to sort students for ability streams, that the tests were particularly ineffective at accurately measuring the ability of the system's many Mexican American students, who often spoke Spanish as a first language. Instead of streaming by IQ scores, Los Angeles officials sought other means of slotting children into the various programs. This, however, did not prevent race from becoming the basis for segregating Mexican American and African American students in separate streams from white students. Judith R. Raftery, "Missing the Mark." See also Fallace, *Race and the Origins of Progressive Education*, 96–7; Chapman, *Schools as Sorters*, 29–30. Criticism of IQ testing in education in Canada was much sparser, but see Alice Willson, "Intelligence Tests and Classification," *The School* 10, no. 8 (April 1922): 472–4. As we shall see, the chief inspector of Toronto schools, R.H. Cowley, would briefly raise concerns about IQ tests as well.
32 Chapman, *Schools as Sorters*, 81–106.
33 See also ibid., 84–5; Raftery, "Missing the Mark," 77; Fallace, *Race and the Origins of Progressive Education*, 83–93.
34 Chapman, *Schools as Sorters*, 29.
35 Terman probably also refuted Ayres because Ayres had been an early critic of intelligence testing and Terman had a reputation for intellectual defensiveness. Chapman, *Schools as Sorters*, writes that "Terman was extremely sensitive to ... criticism of testing" (30) and was known to respond aggressively.
36 Terman, *The Intelligence of Schoolchildren*, 24–5.
37 Ibid., 73.
38 *TBE Minutes 1919*, appendix no. 140, Report no. 1. of the Committee Appointed by the Board re Auxiliary Classes, 28 July 1919, adopted as amended 28 August 1919, 873; *TBE Minutes 1920*, appendix no. 10, "Auxiliary Classes. Special Report Dr Helen MacMurchy to the TBE," 9 January 1920, 13–14.

39 Eric Keith (*sic*) Clarke, "Some Phases of the Mental Hygiene Problem," *Public Health Journal* 14, no. 10 (1923): 536.

40 CAMHA, Eric K. Clarke biography file.

41 Ian Robert Dowbiggin, *Keeping America Sane: Psychiatry and Eugenics in the United States and Canada, 1880–1940* (Ithaca, NY: Cornell University Press, 1997), 158–62.

42 McLaren, *Our Own Master Race*, 59–63.

43 Eric Kent Clarke, "The Mental Health of the Coming Generation," *Social Welfare* 7, no. 10 (July 1925): 196.

44 Though Pratt was a Newfoundlander by birth. On his early life and career, see the first of David Pitt's two-volume biographical treatment: *E.J. Pratt: The Truant Years 1882–1928* (Toronto: University of Toronto Press, 1984).

45 Eric Kent Clarke, "Survey of the Toronto Public Schools," *Canadian Journal of Mental Hygiene* 2, no. 2 (1920): 182–5; *TBE Annual Report 1921*, 74–7.

46 Clarke, "Survey of the Toronto Public Schools," 182–5.

47 See Terman, *Measurement of Intelligence*, 79–80.

48 I arrived at the number by tallying separate statistics that Clarke reported to the TBE in 1920 and 1921. It is not clear how Clarke calculated, and the tally could account for some of the same children examined more than once. See *TBE Annual Report 1920*, 55–7; *TBE Annual Report 1921*, 75.

49 Eric Clarke, "Mental Hygiene in the Public Schools," *Proceedings of the Fifty-Ninth Annual Convention of the OEA* (Toronto: OEA, 1920), 202.

50 Clarke, "Survey of the Toronto Public Schools," 184.

51 Ibid.

52 *TBE Minutes 1919*, appendix no. 195, 1,163; appendix no. 207, Report no. 2 of Committee re Auxiliary Classes, 2 December 1919, adopted 4 December 1919, 1,258.

53 Clarke, "Survey of the Toronto Public Schools," 184.

54 *TBE Annual Report 1919*, 91. See Terman, *Measurement of Intelligence*, 4.

55 *TBE Annual Report 1919*, 64.

56 Clarke, "Survey of the Toronto Public Schools," 185.

57 *TBE Annual Report 1920*, 53–6.

58 *TBE Annual Report 1924*, 67.

59 The 1930 version has the same wording as the 1925 version. OHEC, *Regulations for Auxiliary Classes*, DOE Circular no. 22 (Toronto: various publishers, 1917, 1922, 1925, 1930).

60 Jason Ellis, "'Inequalities of Children in Original Endowment': How Intelligence Testing Transformed Early Special Education in a North American City School System," *History of Education Quarterly* 53, no. 4 (November 2013): 414–21.

61 School surveys completed at the time showed that by the mid-1920s, hundreds of US city school systems were using IQ tests. Of the systems that used individual tests, as Toronto did, the most common reason was to set up classes for "subnormals." See Chapman, *Schools as Sorters*, 153–66. On Vancouver's similarly established mental testing department, see Gerald E. Thomson, "'Remove from Our Midst These Unfortunates': A Historical Inquiry into the Influence of Eugenics, Educational Efficiency as Well as Mental Hygiene upon the Vancouver School System and Its Special Classes, 1910–1969" (PhD diss., University of British Columbia, 1999).

62 Heather MacDougall, *Activists and Advocates: Toronto's Health Department, 1883–1983* (Toronto: Dundurn Press, 1990), 194–5; CAMHA, Canadian Mental Health Association Fonds, Bio Files People – Misc. Lewis, Edmund Percival (1883–1949).

63 CAMHA, Provincial Psychiatric Clinics: lectures [B.T. McGhie (ed.)] May 1930, Burdett McNeel Fonds, F. 17.1.8, E.P. Lewis, "Psychiatric Clinics in the Toronto Public Schools" (19 May 1930).

64 Chapman, *Schools as Sorters*, 153–8.

65 CAMHA, Lewis, "Psychiatric Clinics"; Gerald T. Hackett, "The History of Public Education for Mentally Retarded Children in the Province of Ontario 1867–1964" (EdD diss., University of Toronto, 1969), 245, 253. It was only in 1939 that a Canadian pencil-and-paper version similar to the NIT became available. C.G. Stogdill and Harry Amoss developed and published it as the *Canadian Intelligence Examination* using Canadian statistical norms and idiom.

66 CAMHA, Lewis, "Psychiatric Clinics."

67 See appendix A.

68 TDSBA, Hester How PS, ORC drawer Mc–Si, ADP drawer M–Z, "David P.," ORC, ADP.

69 TDSBA, Hester How PS, ORC drawer A–D, ADP drawer A–L, "Emily L.," ORC, ADP.

70 See TDSBA, Hester How PS, ADP drawers A–L, M–Z, 1923–4, and ORC drawers A–D, E–I, J–M, Mc–Si, Sh–Z. These are students for whom ADP cards have survived in the archives. ADP cards contain both a record of the form/grade or special class the child attended in a given year, as well as the results of IQ tests the child took and the dates on which the tests occurred. The other type of record my study uses, ORCs, do not report the IQ tests. See appendix A for more information. I have ORCs only for another sixty-seven pupils who attended the auxiliary class at Hester How in this period.

71 TDSBA, Hester How PS, ADP drawers A–L, M–Z, 1923–4 and ORC drawers A–D, E–I, J–M, Mc–Si, Sh–Z. Five of the seven pupils placed this way entered in that early timeframe. Two others, Aaron N. and James B., were placed in the auxiliary class in autumn 1926. See TDSBA, Hester How PS, ORC drawer A–D, ADP drawer A–L, "Aaron N.," ORC, ADP; ORC drawer J–L, ADP drawer A–L, "James B.," ORC, ADP.

72 TDSBA, Hester How PS, ORC drawer A–D, ADP drawer A–L, "George W.," ORC, ADP. It is not clear why George W. attended the auxiliary class and not the foreign class, although it is possible there was no foreign class at Hester How in 1922. See also TDSBA, "James B."

73 TDSBA, "Aaron N."

74 Terman, *The Measurement of Intelligence*, 152–4.

75 TDSBA, Hester How PS, ORC drawer A–D, ADP drawer A–L, "Bessie L.," ORC, ADP; ORC drawer A–D, ADP drawer A–L, 'Simon G.,' ORC, ADP.

76 TDSBA, "Bessie L." See also TDSBA, Hester How PS, ORC drawer A–D, ADP drawer A–L, "Willie F.," ORC, ADP, and "Simon G."

77 TDSBA, "David P."

78 Ellis, "'Inequalities of Children in Original Endowment,'" 414–23.

79 Mona Gleason writes that "how children interacted with medical experts and educational systems designed to increase, safeguard, and promote their health remains largely unexplored" by historians. Gleason, "Size Matters: Medical Experts, Educators, and the Provision of Health Services to Children in Early to Mid-twentieth Century English Canada," in Cynthia Comacchio, Janet Golden, and George Weisz, eds., *Healing the World's Children: Interdisciplinary Perspectives on Child Health in the Twentieth Century* (Montreal: McGill-Queen's University Press, 2008), 177. Though see the former and Gleason, *Small Matters*.

80 Kathleen Jones, *Taming the Troublesome Child: American Families, Child Guidance, and the Limits of Psychiatric Authority* (Cambridge, MA: Harvard University Press, 1999), 148–56. See also Mona Gleason, "'Lost Voices, Lost Bodies?' Doctors and the Embodiment of Children and Youth in English Canada from 1900 to the 1940s," in Gleason, Tamara Myers, Leslie Paris, and Veronica Strong-Boag, eds., *Lost Kids: Vulnerable Children and Youth in Twentieth-Century Canada and the United States* (Vancouver: University of British Columbia Press, 2010), 136–7.

81 Terman, *Measurement of Intelligence*, 278–9.

82 TDSBA, Duke of York PS, ORC TDSB 2003–1307, box 8, ADP, TDSB 2003–0834b, box 2 of 2, "Emma C.," ORC, ADP.

83 Terman, *Measurement of Intelligence*, 124–6.

84 TDSBA, Hester How PS, ORC drawer A–D, ADP drawer A–L, "Katie L.,"
    ORC, ADP.
85 TDSBA, Hester How PS, ORC drawer A–D, ADP drawer A–L, "Jack L.,"
    ORC, ADP.
86 TDSBA, Hester How PS, ADP drawer A–L, "Ida L.," ADP.
87 TDSBA, Duke of York PS, ORC TDSB 2003–1307, box 1, ADP TDSB
    2003–0835, "Fred V.," ORC, ADP.
88 Will was Jewish, and his father was born in England, thus I inferred that
    the other language Lewis referred to was Yiddish. TDSBA, Hester How
    PS, ORC drawer A–L, "Will C.," ORC.
89 Clarke, "Some Phases of the Mental Hygiene Movement," 538.
90 CAMHA, Lewis, "Psychiatric Clinics."
91 The discrepancy, the zero in the right-hand column, might seem illogical,
    but recall that the data in the right-hand column are from a representative,
    random sample. The data in the left-hand column are from a complete
    group. See appendix A for further explanation.
92 R.D. Gidney and W.P.J. Millar, *How Schools Worked: Public Education in
    English Canada, 1900–1940* (Montreal: McGill-Queen's University Press,
    2012), 42–5.
93 In chapter 3, I take up the similarly puzzling case of Jewish pupils over-
    represented in the ranks of young people discharged to junior vocational
    schools. In that case, I am able to offer a somewhat satisfying explanation.
94 Historians have documented, and sometimes have attempted to explain
    Jewish academic exceptionalism. See Gidney and Millar, *How Schools
    Worked*, 43–7; W.P.J. Millar, "'We Wanted Our Children Should Have It
    Better': Jewish Medical Students at the University of Toronto, 1910–51,"
    Journal of the Canadian Historical Association 11, no. 1 (2000): 113–18; Michael
    R. Olneck and Marvin Lazerson, "The School Achievement of Immigrant
    Children, 1900–1930," *History of Education Quarterly* 14, no. 4 (winter 1974):
    453–82; Joel Perlmann, *Ethnic Differences: Schooling and Social Structure
    among the Irish, Italians, Jews, and Blacks in an American City, 1880–1935*
    (Cambridge, MA: Cambridge University Press, 1988), 122–62.
95 P.F. Munro, *An Experimental Investigation of the Mentality of the Jew in Ryerson
    Public School Toronto* (Toronto: University of Toronto Press, 1926), 53–4.
96 Ibid., 23.
97 E.N. Wright, *Student's Background and Its Relationship to Class and
    Programme in School*, Research Department, TBE (Toronto: TBE, 1970); Janis
    Gershman, *The Evaluation of Special Education Programs: Past Attempts and
    Present Directions*, Research Department, TBE (Toronto: TBE, 1975).

98 Ontario, Legislative Assembly, *Report of the Minister of Education Province of Ontario for the Year 1929* (Toronto: Herbert H. Ball, 1930), 30; Ontario, Legislative Assembly, *Report of the Minister of Education Province of Ontario for the Year 1930* (Toronto: Herbert H. Ball, 1931), 27.

99 See TDSBA, Hester How PS, ADP drawers A–L, M–Z, 1923–4 and ORC drawers A–D, E–I, J–M, Mc–Si, Sh–Z.

100 Julia Grant, *The Boy Problem: Educating Boys in Urban America, 1870–1970* (Baltimore: Johns Hopkins University Press, 2014), 96–7; Ayres, *Laggards in Our Schools*, 150–8; Terman, *The Measurement of Intelligence*, 69–70.

101 Ayres, *Laggards in Our Schools*, 157–8.

102 E.D. MacPhee, "Behaviour in Auxiliary Classes," *Proceedings of the Sixty-Sixth Annual Convention of the OEA* (Toronto: OEA, 1927), 132.

103 Grant, *The Boy Problem*, 94–5.

104 Joseph L. Tropea, "Bureaucratic Order and Special Children: Urban Schools, 1890s–1940s," *History of Education Quarterly* 27, no. 1 (spring 1987): 29–30.

105 Based on data from the representative sample. See appendix A. Boys, n=15; girls, n=6.

106 Ayres, *Laggards in Our Schools*, 150–60. The TBE's age-grade tables in the 1920s were not broken down by gender. R.D. Gidney and W.P.J. Millar's analysis of other age-grade tables from the period that are broken down this way concludes that larger numbers of over-age boys were a Canada-wide fact in the 1920s. See Gidney and Millar, *How Schools Worked*, 40–2. See also – not included in their published volume – "Appendices for How Schools Worked," 7–10, 59–60, http://www.mqup.ca/HowSchoolsWorkedAppendices.pdf.

107 Herbert Kliebard, *The Struggle for the American Curriculum, 1893–1958* (New York: Routledge, 1987), 89–122; Amy von Heyking, *Creating Citizens: History and Identity in Alberta's Schools, 1905–1980* (Calgary: University of Calgary Press, 2006), 29–53; Christou, *Progressive Education*, 69–87.

108 E.T. Seaton, "Classification and Time-Table in Auxiliary Classes," Auxiliary Class Teachers' Section, *Proceedings of the Sixty-Fourth Annual Convention of the OEA* (Toronto: OEA, 1925), 179.

109 See Ontario, *Suggestions for Teachers of Subnormal Children* (Toronto: C.W. James, 1925).

110 Peter Sandiford, "Technical Education and the I.Q.," *Proceedings of the Sixty-Eighth Annual Convention of the OEA* (Toronto: OEA, 1929), 155. See also Harry Amoss, "The Abnormal Pupil," *Proceedings of the Sixty-Second*

Annual Convention of the OEA (Toronto: OEA, 1923), 418–29; Ontario, *Suggestions for Teachers of Subnormal Children*, 6.

111 Sandiford, "Technical Education and the I.Q.," 155–6.
112 Amoss, "The Abnormal Pupil," 423. On Amoss's career, see Hackett, "The History of Public Education for Mentally Retarded Children," 183–8.
113 Amoss, "The Abnormal Pupil," 423. See also Terman, *The Intelligence of School Children*, 127.
114 Seaton, "Classification and Time-Table in Auxiliary Classes," 181. See also "Minutes," Auxiliary Class Teachers' Section, *Proceedings of the Sixty-Fourth Annual Convention of the OEA* (Toronto: OEA, 1925), 57–9.
115 *TBE Annual Report 1921*, 105. See also Ontario, *Suggestions for Teachers of Subnormal Children*, 5–6.
116 Seaton, "Classification and Time-Table in Auxiliary Classes."
117 *TBE Annual Report 1928*, 94. See also courses of study that are described in *TBE Annual Report 1920*, 59–61; *TBE Minutes 1929*, appendix no. 178, 1,557–8.
118 Ontario, Legislative Assembly, *Report of the Minister of Education Province of Ontario for the Year 1920*, appendix H, Report of the Inspector of Auxiliary Classes (Toronto: Clarkson W. James, 1921), 108.
119 Hackett, "The History of Public Education," appendix J, 400.
120 David Tyack, *The One Best System: A History of American Urban Education* (Cambridge, MA: Harvard University Press, 1974), 185–6. For a partial list of the different types of Ontario certificates, see *Public and Separate Schools in the Province of Ontario, November 1923* (Toronto: Clarkson W. James, 1923), 3.
121 Ontario, Legislative Assembly, *Report of the Minister of Education Province of Ontario for the Year 1929*, appendix G, Report of the Inspector of Auxiliary Classes, 33.
122 See appendix B.

3 Auxiliary Education for Adolescents

1 E.A. Hardy and Honora M. Cochrane, *Centennial Story: The Board of Education for the City of Toronto* (Toronto: Thomas Nelson & Sons, 1950), 150; Ontario, *Schools and Teachers in the Province of Ontario*, part 2: *Collegiate Institutes, High Schools, Continuation Schools, Vocational Schools, Normal Schools and Technical Institues* (Toronto: Baptist Johnson, 1950), 202.
2 Robert Stamp, *The Schools of Ontario, 1876–1976* (Toronto: University of Toronto Press, 1982), 83.

3 See Ontario, Legislative Assembly, *Report of the Minister of Education Province of Ontario for the Year 1920* to *Report of the Minister of Education Province of Ontario for the Year 1930* (Toronto: various publishers), Detailed Statistics, Secondary Schools; Hardy and Cochrane, *Centennial Story*, 150–4.

4 Ontario, Legislative Assembly, *Report of the Minister of Education of the Province of Ontario for the Year 1920* (Toronto: C.W. James, 1921), 242–3, 252–3, 259.

5 Ontario, Legislative Assembly, *Report of the Minister of Education of the Province of Ontario for the Year 1929* (Toronto: H.H. Ball, 1930), 202, 308–9.

6 Stamp, *Schools of Ontario*, 111; Cynthia Comacchio, *The Dominion of Youth: Adolescence and the Making of Modern Canada* (Waterloo, ON: Wilfrid Laurier University Press, 2006), 99–106. There was more diversity, but R.D. Gidney and W.P.J. Millar, *How Schools Worked: Public Education in English Canada, 1900–1940* (Montreal: McGill-Queen's University Press, 2012), 29–32, warn against historians forming the mistaken impression that this meant high school had become a common denominator experience for Canadian youth. This would not occur until much later.

7 Clara Thomas (York University) Archives and Special Collections, MRP 240; Lynne Marks, "New Opportunities within the Separate Sphere" (MA major research paper, York University, 1984), 51. Marks's calculations are based on DOE reports, a source that the wise Gidney and Millar caution historians to approach with care. The DOE's statistics-gathering methods were rudimentary. The figures "are flawed by crude groupings of occupational categories and by the substantial numbers who were categorized as 'other' or unknown." Yet Gidney and Millar do employ the DOE data to present some quite reasonable hypotheses about class and secondary schooling and so can others. Gidney and Millar, *How Schools Worked*, 73–4.

8 Harvey G. Simmons, *From Asylum to Welfare* (Toronto: National Institute on Mental Retardation, 1982), 121–8; James W. Trent, Jr, *Inventing the Feeble Mind: A History of Mental Retardation in the United States* (Berkeley: University of California Press, 1994), 204–15.

9 Stamp, *Schools of Ontario*, 107.

10 Ibid., 107–9.

11 Ontario, *The Revised Statutes of Ontario, 1927*, vol. 3, ch. 333, The Adolescent School Attendance Act (Toronto: Government of Ontario, 1927); Stamp, *Schools of Ontario*, 107–9.

12 Craig Heron, "The High School and the Household Economy in Working-Class Hamilton, 1890–1940," *Historical Studies in Education/Revue d'histoire*

de l'éducation 7, no. 2 (1995): 224–5; Rebecca Coulter, "The Working Young of Edmonton, 1921–1931," in Joy Parr, ed., *Childhood and Family in Canadian History* (Toronto: McClelland and Stewart, 1982), 147–9.

13 Heron, "The High School and the Household Economy," 246–51.

14 Coulter, "The Working Young of Edmonton," 144.

15 Heron, "The High School and the Household Economy," 229–31; Gidney and Millar, *How Schools Worked*, 66–72.

16 Gidney and Millar, *How Schools Worked*, 66–7.

17 R.D. Gidney and W.P.J. Millar, *Inventing Secondary Education: The Rise of the High School in Nineteenth-Century Ontario* (Montreal: McGill-Queen's University Press, 1990), 304–12.

18 See Marvin Lazerson and Norton W. Grubb, "Introduction," in *American Education and Vocationalism: A Documentary History* (New York: Teachers College Press, 1974), 1–56; Marvin Lazerson and Timothy Dunn, "Schools and the Work Crisis: Vocationalism in Canadian Education," in Hugh A. Stevenson and J. Donald Wilson, eds., *Precepts, Policy and Process: Perspectives on Contemporary Canadian Education* (London, ON: Alexander, Blake Associates, 1980), 287–8.

19 Stamp, *Schools of Ontario*, 74–83.

20 Lazerson and Dunn, "Schools and the Work Crisis," 288.

21 Lazerson and Grubb, "Introduction," 18–23.

22 David B. Tyack, *The One Best System: A History of American Urban Education* (Cambridge, MA: Harvard University Press, 1974), 182–216; Herbert Kliebard, *The Struggle for the American Curriculum, 1893–1958* (New York: Routledge, 1987), 128–52; Gidney and Millar, *How Schools Worked*, 200–2.

23 Marvin Lazerson, *Origins of the Urban School: Public Education in Massachusetts, 1870–1915* (Cambridge, MA: Harvard University Press, 1971), 97–201; Tyack, *The One Best System*, 188–91; Theodore Michael Christou, *Progressive Education: Revisioning and Reframing Ontario's Public Schools* (Toronto: University of Toronto Press, 2012), 76–82.

24 *TBE Annual Report 1922*, 58–9.

25 Timothy A. Dunn, "Teaching the Meaning of Work: Vocational Education in British Columbia, 1900–1929," in David C. Jones, Nancy M. Sheehan, and Robert M. Stamp, eds., *Shaping the Schools of the Canadian West* (Calgary: Detselig, 1979), 236–56. See also David John Hogan, *Class and Reform: School and Society in Chicago, 1880–1930* (Philadelphia: University of Pennsylvania Press, 1985), 138–93.

26 Christou, *Progressive Education*, 93–7.

27 Jennifer Stephen, "Unemployment and the New Industrial Citizenship: A Review of the Ontario Unemployment Commission, 1916," in Robert

Adamoski, Dorothy E. Chunn, Robert Menzies, eds., *Contesting Canadian Citizenship: Historical Readings* (Peterborough, ON: Broadview Press, 2002), 169.

28 E.A. Bott, "Studies in Industrial Psychology. I. Point of View and II. Juvenile Employment in Relation to Public Schools and Industries in Toronto" (Toronto: University Library, 1920); Stephen, "Unemployment and the New Industrial Citizenship," 155–77.

29 Stephen, "Unemployment and the New Industrial Citizenship," 155–77; Christou, *Progressive Education*, 93–7.

30 *TBE Annual Report 1920*, 121–2.

31 *TBE Annual Report 1922*, 83.

32 Eric Keith [sic] Clarke, "Some Phases of the Mental Hygiene Problem," *Public Health Journal* 14, no. 10 (October 1923): 541; AO, Ontario Government Record Series, "Auxiliary Education Services correspondence files," RG 2–59, box 1, file Toronto, 1924–30. Memorandum, W.W. Pearse, TBE Business Administrator and Secretary Treasurer, to S.B. Sinclair, Inspector of Auxiliary Classes, January 6th, 1928, encl. "Report of Work by S.B. Sinclair in Connection with Auxiliary Classes."

33 *TBE Minutes 1923*, appendix no. 28, Advisory Industrial Report no. 3, 6 February 1923, adopted 15 February 1923, 131.

34 *TBE Minutes 1923*, appendix no. 46, Advisory Industrial Report no. 5, 6 March 1923, adopted 15 March 1923, 388; appendix no. 55, Advisory Vocational Report no. 6, 27 March 1923, adopted 5 April 1923, 426. Mary E. James, "Edith Groves School to Continue," *Globe and Mail*, 17 March 1951, 14. As historian Susan Gelman argues, these gender-segregated schools provided one of the few opportunities for Toronto women to advance to leadership positions in secondary schools. Groves and Bolton were the only two Toronto high schools with female principals as late as 1930, despite women representing a significant and growing percentage of secondary school teachers. Susan Gelman, "'The "Feminization" of the High Schools'? Women Secondary School Teachers in Toronto: 1871–1930," *Historical Studies in Education/Revue d'histoire de l'éducation* 2, no. 1 (1990): 119–48.

35 *TBE Minutes 1923*, appendix no. 55, Advisory Vocational Report no. 6, 27 March 1923, adopted 5 April 1923, 426.

36 AO, Ontario Government Record Series, "Auxiliary Education Services correspondence files," RG 2–59, box 1, file Toronto, 1924–30. Memorandum, W.W. Pearse, TBE Business Administrator and Secretary Treasurer, to S.B. Sinclair, Inspector of Auxiliary Classes, January 6th, 1928, encl. "Report of Work by S.B. Sinclair in Connection with Auxiliary

Classes"; Ontario, Legislative Assembly, *Report of the Minister of Education Province of Ontario for the Year 1924* (Toronto: C.W. James, 1925), 50.

37 Jane Little, "The History of the Edith L. Groves School," *Special Class Teacher* 18, no. 1 (November 1943): 15; *TBE Minutes 1923*, appendix no. 28, Advisory Industrial Report no. 3, 6 February 1923, adopted 15 February 1923, 131.

38 *TBE Minutes 1926*, 2 September 1926, 189; *TBE Minutes 1927*, Advisory Industrial Report no. 14, 30 June 1927, adopted 1 September 1927, 883.

39 *TBE Minutes 1923*, appendix no. 67, Advisory Industrial Report no. 7, 10 April 1923, adopted 19 April 1923, 504–5.

40 Gidney and Millar, *How Schools Worked*, 248 and 448–9, n20–1.

41 Ontario, *Recommendations and Regulations for the Establishment, Organization, and Management of Commercial High Schools and Commercial Departments in High and Continuation Schools* (Toronto: L.K. Cameron, 1915).

42 Gidney and Millar, *How Schools Worked*, 448n20.

43 There are occasional references in the junior vocational schools' reports to different levels of classes in this program, although these levels seem to have been informally or sporadically applied and seem as well to have been differentiated by ability as much as by age. See *TBE Annual Report 1929*, 108.

44 *TBE Annual Report 1928*, 154.

45 Lewis Terman, *The Measurement of Intelligence* (Boston: Houghton Mifflin, 1916), 92–3.

46 Ibid., 92.

47 See also Alexandra Minna Stern, *Eugenic Nation: Faults and Frontiers of Better Breeding in America*, 2nd ed. (Berkeley: University of California Press, 2016), 92–100.

48 Terman, *Measurement of Intelligence*, 87.

49 Ibid., 91–2. See also Thomas D. Fallace, *Race and the Origins of Progressive Education, 1880–1929* (New York: Teachers College Press, 2015), 90–1.

50 E.P. Lewis, "The Non-academic Child," *Proceedings of the Sixty-Ninth Annual Convention of the OEA Conference* (Toronto: OEA, 1930), 125–6.

51 *TBE Minutes 1928*, appendix no. 176, Report no. 1 of Special Committee of the Board on "Dull Normal" and "Retarded" Pupils in the Public Schools, 17 December 1928, adopted 20 December 1928, 1,413.

52 Hardy and Cochrane, *Centennial Story*, 267.

53 *TBE Minutes 1927*, appendix no. 196, Report of the Visit to Pittsburgh to Study Work in Connection with Dull Normal Pupils, n.d., 1,367. Moshier replaced Cowley in 1927 and served until 1932. Hardy and Cochrane, *Centennial Story*, 140.

54 *TBE Minutes 1927*, appendix no. 196, Report of the Visit to Pittsburgh, 1,366.

55 Ibid., 1,364. On Leavitt, see Hogan, *Class and Reform*, 165.

56 *TBE Minutes 1927*, appendix no. 196, Report of the Visit to Pittsburgh, 1,367–8.

57 The survey – which inquired about special education provisions only – asked school systems to report on various "special classes for children who are deviates from the normal physically, socially, and mentally" (1). This included "trade schools for deviates," which the survey defined as schools "for children of secondary grade for instruction in the fundamentals underlying the practice of the more common trades and occupations for both sexes." Classes for younger children were reported on elsewhere in the survey. To specifically exclude academic high schools and regular commercial schools or technical schools, the survey instructed respondents not to report on a school in this response "when the school or class covered a course of study which was part of the regular school curricula." The author further added: "*Only when the schools and classes are especially organized to care for those children who are deviates, were these schools and classes to be reported*" (emphasis original). Thus, it is reasonable, I think, to assume close similarities between these "trade schools for deviates," the Pittsburgh trade schools, and Toronto's junior vocational schools. See Arch O. Heck, *Special Schools and Classes in Cities of 10,000 Population and More in the United States*, United States Office of Education Bulletin, 1930, no. 7 (Washington: Government Printing Office, 1930), 12–14.

58 *TBE Minutes 1928*, appendix no. 176, Report no. 1 of Special Committee of the Board on "Dull Normal" and "Retarded" Pupils in the Public Schools, 1,412.

59 Ibid., 1,413.

60 Ibid., 1,417.

61 In fact, the committee recommended two possible models. The other was a very similar "post-primary" approach, used in England, that would have placed vocational education in an elementary school program that was terminal after the intermediate grades "for pupils not fitted for secondary education." *TBE Minutes 1928*, appendix no. 176, Report no. 1 of Special Committee of the Board on "Dull Normal" and "Retarded" Pupils in the Public Schools, 1,417–18. The post-primary possibility would not have worked, mainly for political reasons. It was derived from Ontario Premier Howard Ferguson's ill-fated plan to reorganize Ontario's schools into three divisions: "primary" (ages seven to eleven), "intermediate" (ages eleven to sixteen), and "secondary" for older pupils. Ferguson peddled

that plan to public audiences as early as the mid-1920s, but it foundered for numerous reasons, although most notably because it posed a major threat to the provision of education beyond the primary level in Roman Catholic separate schools, a white-hot political issue. Stamp, *Schools of Ontario*, 148–53.

62 CAMHA, Lewis, "Psychiatric Clinics." This was on a total of 1,927 examinations and recommendations for everything ranging from continued placement in a regular classroom, to an auxiliary class placement, to a junior vocational school placement, and so on.

63 CTA, fonds 200, series 365, file 48, box 224904, folio 2, Department of Public Health City of Toronto, "Annual Statement" 1935, 29. This was on 1,947 examinations. The Mental Hygiene Division statistics are available in these "annual statements" for 1935 onwards.

64 TDSBA, Duke of York PS, ORC TDSB 2003–1307, box 2, "Andrew H.," ORC.

65 TDSBA, Hester How PS, ORC drawer Sh-Z, "Maxine F.," ORC.

66 TDSBA, Hester How PS, ORC drawer A–D, "Herman I.," ORC.

67 TDSBA, Duke of York PS, ORC TDSB 2003–1307, box 4, "Sarah B.," ORC.

68 TDSBA, Duke of York PS, ORC TDSB 2003–1307, box 4, ADP 2003–0384, box 1 of 2, "Donald R.," ORC, ADP.

69 Duke of York did not open until September 1929.

70 *TBE Annual Report 1932*, 66. In a later study, Walter Koerber, a teacher at Jarvis Junior Vocational, found a smaller number of junior vocational school pupils transferring from the grades, although these students still were numerous. Koerber reported that in 1944, 60.1 per cent of the students in the Jarvis Junior Vocational first-year program came directly from an "opportunity class" (the name for auxiliary classes in the elementary schools after 1937). Walter F. Koerber, "An Evaluation of Some Methods of and Procedures in the Teaching of Reading to Non-academic Adolescent Boys" (DPaed thesis, University of Toronto, 1947), 32–3.

71 See *TBE, Handbook Nineteen-Nineteen* (Toronto: J.R. Irving, 1919), 44.

72 TDSBA, Coleman PS, ORC microfilm reel 10, "Fiona N," ORC.

73 TDSBA, Coleman PS, ORC microfilm reel 10, "Vernon N," ORC.

74 I cannot say for certain what the Mental Hygiene Division's role was in their cases, because most of these children's ADP cards, which record mental examinations, did not survive alongside their ORCs.

75 See Bruce Curtis, D.W. Livingstone, and Harry Smaller, *Stacking the Deck: The Streaming of Working-Class Kids in Ontario Schools* (Toronto: Our Schools/Our Selves, 1992); David Clandfield et al., *Restacking the Deck: Streaming by Class, Race, and Gender in Ontario Schools* (Ottawa: Our Schools/Our Selves, 2014). See also James G. Carrier, *Learning Disability:*

Social Class and the Construction of Inequality in American Education (New York: Greenwood Press, 1986); Beth A. Ferri and David J. Connor, "In the Shadow of Brown: Special Education and Overrepresentation of Students of Color," *Remedial and Special Education* 26, no. 2 (March–April 2005): 93–100; Adam Nelson, "Equity and Special Education: Some Historical Lessons from Boston," in Kenneth K. Wong and Robert Rothman, eds., *Clio at the Table: Using History to Inform and Improve Education Policy* (New York: Peter Lang, 2009), 158–62; Jeannie Oakes, *Keeping Track: How Schools Structure Inequality*, 2nd ed. (New Haven: Yale University Press, 2005); and, on the United Kingdom, Sally Tomlinson, *A Sociology of Special Education* (London: Routledge, 1982), 155–71.

76 Curtis, Livingstone, and Smaller, *Stacking the Deck*, 90–2.

77 Compare, e.g., Gidney and Millar's discussion in *How Schools Worked*, 260–3, to David L. Angus and Jeffrey E. Mirel's analysis in *The Failed Promise of the American High School, 1890–1995* (New York: Teachers College Press, 1999), especially, appendix A, table A.1 (203).

78 See table 3.4 in this volume and Gidney and Millar, *How Schools Worked*, 260–3.

79 See Curtis, Livingstone, and Smaller, *Stacking the Deck*, 83–98.

80 See appendix A for an explanation of the occupational classification.

81 See *supra* n7.

82 See Marcus Aurelius Klee, "Between the Scylla and Charybdis of Anarchy and Despotism: The State, Capital, and the Working Class in the Great Depression, Toronto, 1929–1940" (PhD diss., Queen's University, 1998); Lara Campbell, *Respectable Citizens: Gender, Family, and Unemployment in Ontario's Great Depression* (Toronto: University of Toronto Press, 2009).

83 See appendix A for how I arrived at these categories.

84 There are a number of studies by different historians that address continuity and adaptation, part of what J.D. Wilson in the mid-1980s referred to as a "family strategies" theory of immigrants, class, culture, and Canadian education. J. Donald Wilson, "Some Observations on Recent Trends in Canadian Educational History," in Wilson, ed., *An Imperfect Past: Education and Society in Canadian History* (Vancouver: Centre for the Study of Curriculum and Instruction, University of British Columbia, 1984); J. Donald Wilson, "'The Picture of Social Randomness': Making Sense of Ethnic History and Educational History," in David C. Jones, Nancy M. Sheehan, Robert M. Stamp, and Neil G. MacDonald, eds., *Monographs in Education V: Approaches to Educational History* (Winnipeg: University of Manitoba, 1981), 32–7. See more recently Robert C. Vipond, *Making a Global City: How One Toronto School Embraced Diversity* (Toronto: University

of Toronto Press, 2017). The quintessential study is not about immigrants but rather French Canadians. Chad Gaffield, *Language, Schooling, and Cultural Conflict: The Origins of the French-Language Controversy in Ontario* (Montreal: McGill-Queen's University Press, 1987). As Wilson also says, there is a serious lacuna in the Canadian scholarship on immigrant families' educational choices and strategies in the twentieth century, although see Lynne Marks, "Kale Meydelach or Shulamith Girls: Cultural Change and Continuity among Jewish Parents and Daughters – A Case Study of Toronto's Harbord Collegiate Institute in the 1920s," *Canadian Woman Studies/Les cahiers de la femme* 7 no. 3 (1986): 85–9; W.P.J. Millar, "'We Wanted Our Children Should Have It Better': Jewish Medical Students at the University of Toronto, 1910–51," *Journal of the Canadian Historical Association* 11, no. 1 (2000): 109–24; as well as some chapters in David C. Jones, Nancy M. Sheehan, and Robert M. Stamp, eds., *Shaping the Schools of the Canadian West* (Calgary: Detselig, 1979); Nancy M. Sheehan, J. Donald Wilson, and David C. Jones, *Schools in the West: Essays in Canadian Educational History* (Calgary: Detselig, 1986); and Gidney and Millar, *How Schools Worked*, 42–50, 69–70.

85 Marks, "Kale Meydelach."

86 Ibid., 85.

87 Ibid., 87. Modifications in attitudes towards girls' education in the 1920s in Toronto were the result of a culmination of a long series of events, stretching over two continents, that originated as early as the 1880s when reforms swept Jewish life in Eastern Europe. See Gerald Tulchinsky, *Taking Root: The Origins of the Canadian Jewish Community* (Toronto: Lester, 1982), 179–80.

88 It should be noted (although Marks does not note it) that by comparison, in 1923 approximately 57 per cent of all form one pupils (the most junior class) at Harbord were boys and 43 per cent were girls. In 1925, the numbers were 62 per cent male and 38 per cent female. These are my calculations from DOE reports. See Ontario, Legislative Assembly, *Report of the Minister of Education Province of Ontario for the Year 1923* (Toronto: Clarskon W. James 1924), 248–9; and Ontario, Legislative Assembly, *Report of the Minister of Education Province of Ontario for the Year 1925* (Toronto: Clarkson W. James, 1925), 200–1. Of course, pupils entering (Marks's measure) and pupils attending the first form (mine) are not totally congruent measures, although they are close. Incongruity would arise from students repeating the first form and from students entering at a higher form than the first. See also Millar, "We Wanted Our Children Should Have It Better," which shows enormous disparity between the much higher numbers of Jewish

men than Jewish women attending medical school at the University of Toronto. But that gulf was no less wide than the gap between non-Jewish men and women.

89 Historians such as Marks and Joel Perlmann, *Ethnic Differences: Schooling and Social Structure among the Irish, Italians, Jews, and Blacks in an American City, 1880–1935* (Cambridge, MA: Cambridge University Press, 1988) have focused overwhelmingly on modification as the *taking up* of new values towards schooling. They have overlooked, however, the extent to which we can measure modification by looking at which values immigrants *did not give up*, including allowing schooling for girls but not surrendering that it should be academic. Other historians have displayed a gender bias when talking about Jewish families' educational decisions that erases vocational schooling from the list of their choices. They look only at immigrants' rejection of vocational education as unsuitable for boys, but do not consider what they thought about girls attending vocational programs. See, e.g., Stephan F. Brumberg, *Going to America, Going to School: The Jewish Immigrant Public School Encounter in Turn-of-the-Century New York City* (New York: Praeger, 1986), 144–6.

90 *TBE Annual Report 1932*, 56.

91 *TBE Annual Report 1930*, 46.

92 Ontario, Legislative Assembly, *Report of the Minister of Education Province of Ontario for the Year 1930* (Toronto: H.H. Ball, 1931), 354–61.

93 See *TBE Minutes 1926*, appendix no. 123, Advisory Industrial Report no. 11, 8 June 1926, adopted 17 June 1926, 850; appendix no. 162, Advisory Industrial Report no. 15, 28 September 1926, adopted 7 October 1926, 1,112; appendix no. 114, Advisory Vocational Report no. 10, 26 May 1926, adopted 7 June 1926, 795; *TBE Minutes 1930* appendix no. 36, Advisory Vocational Report no. 5, 25 February 1930, adopted 6 March 1930, 205.

94 Girls in secondary school, regardless of program, generally had fewer course options than boys did. David Tyack and Elisabeth Hansot, *Learning Together: A History of Co-education in American Public Schools* (New York: Russell Sage, 1990), 210–11; Veronica Strong-Boag, *The New Day Recalled: Lives of Girls and Women in English Canada, 1919–1939* (Markham, ON: Penguin, 1988), 19–22.

95 Grace I. MacKenzie, "Vocational Training for the Adolescent Girl," *Proceedings of the Sixty-Ninth Annual Convention of the OEA* (Toronto: OEA, 1930), 84.

96 See the DOE annual reports for lists of subjects and enrolments, e.g., Ontario, Legislative Assembly, *Report of the Minister of Education Province of Ontario for the Year 1930*, 354–6.

97 *TBE Annual Report 1929*, 121.

98 See Strong-Boag, *New Day Recalled*, 51–62.

99 Tyack and Hansot, *Learning Together*, 210–11. See also Strong-Boag, *New Day Recalled*, 42–7.

100 MacKenzie, "Vocational Training for the Adolescent Girl," 83.

101 *TBE Annual Report 1929*, 120–1.

102 Carolyn Strange, *Toronto's Girl Problem: The Perils and Pleasures of the City, 1880–1930* (Toronto: University of Toronto Press, 1995), 23–39, 116–24; Strong-Boag, *The New Day Recalled*, 51–4.

103 *TBE Annual Report 1930*, 62.

104 Strange, *Toronto's Girl Problem*, 23. See also Tamara Myers, *Caught: Montreal's Modern Girls and the Law, 1869–1945* (Toronto: University of Toronto Press, 2006), 57–70, and Jennifer Stephen, "The 'Incorrigible,' the 'Bad,' and the 'Immoral': Toronto's 'Factory Girls' and the Work of the Toronto Psychiatric Clinic," in Louis A. Knaffa and Susan W.S. Binnie, eds., *Law Society and the State: Essays in Modern Legal History* (Toronto: University of Toronto Press, 1995), 405–39.

105 Comacchio, *Dominion of Youth*, 112–20.

106 *TBE Minutes 1927*, appendix no. 4, Advisory Industrial Report no. 1, 11 January 1927, adopted 20 January 1927, 6; Helen Caister Robinson, *Decades of Caring: The Big Sister Story* (Toronto: Dundurn Press, 1979), 72–4.

107 MacKenzie, "Vocational Training for the Adolescent Girl," 81.

108 Strange, *Toronto's Girl Problem*, 117–24; Stephen, "The 'Incorrigible'," 413–18.

109 *TBE Annual Report 1929*, 120; Robinson, *Decades of Caring*, 72–4. Jarvis Junior Vocational School had no social worker. When in 1929 a few pupils got into trouble after school, school staff made extracurricular activities mandatory for boys who did not have after-school jobs, even though over half of the boys at the school did work. The boys were provided with supervised gym, use of the school "swimming tank," and structured activities in the reading room and assembly hall. *TBE Annual Report 1929*, 109–10; *TBE Annual Report 1930*, 47. Moral reformers were usually more concerned with wage-earning young women than with men, Strange argues. Strange, *Toronto's Girl Problem*, 23. This is not to say that moral and sexual regulation was not applied at all to Toronto boys at this time. See Bryan Hogeveen, "'The Evils with which We Are Called to Grapple': Elite Reformers, Eugenicists, Environmental Psychologists, and the Construction of Toronto's Working-Class Boy Problem, 1860–1930," *Labour/Le Travail* 55 (spring 2005): 37–68; Steven Maynard, "'Horrible

Temptations': Sex, Men, and Working-Class Male Youth in Urban Ontario, 1890–1935," *Canadian Historical Review* 78, no. 2 (June 1997): 191–235.

110 Little, "The History of the Edith L. Groves School," 16. See also "Ross Cottage Holds 'Open House' Fete," *Toronto Daily Star*, 20 May 1935, 29; E.P. Lewis and A. Mildred Jeffrey, "Ross Cottage – A Special Foster Home," *American Journal of Mental Deficiency* 49, no. 3 (January 1945): 377–82.

111 On Lorimer Lodge, see Mildred A. Jeffrey, "A Follow-up Study on the Re-establishment of Mentally Defective Girls in Domestic Science in an Urban Centre under Colony House Supervision," *American Journal of Mental Deficiency* 48, no. 1 (July 1943): 96–100; John R. Graham, "The Haven, 1878–1930: A Toronto Charity's Transition from a Religious to a Professional Social Work Ethos," in John Coates, John R. Graham, Barbara Swartzentruber, et al., eds., *Spirituality and Social Work: Selected Canadian Readings* (Toronto: Canadian Scholars Press, 2007), 55–61.

112 Jeffrey, "A Follow-up Study on the Re-establishment of Mentally Defective Girls," 96.

113 See Stephen, "Unemployment and the New Industrial Citizenship," 156–67; Lazerson and Grubb, "Introduction," 22–3.

114 *TBE Annual Report 1929*, 118.

115 Hogan, *Class and Reform*, 181.

116 Florence S. Dunlop, *Subsequent Careers of Non-academic Boys* (Ottawa: National Printers Limited, 1935), 21–7.

117 S.B. Sinclair, *Backward and Brilliant Children* (Toronto: Ryerson Press, 1931), 13–14.

118 Ibid., 14.

119 Ibid.

120 *TBE Annual Report 1930*, 50–1.

121 *TBE Annual Report 1922*, 111.

122 Mona Gleason, *Small Matters: Canadian Children in Sickness and Health, 1900–1940* (Montreal: McGill-Queen's University Press, 2013), 133.

123 *TBE Annual Report 1929*, 117. See also: *TBE Annual Report 1930*, 47.

124 *TBE Annual Report 1929*, 122.

125 TDSBA, Hester How PS, ORC drawer A–D, "Marvin K.," ORC.

126 Michael J. Piva, *The Condition of the Working Class in Toronto, 1900–1921* (Ottawa: University of Ottawa), 38–47. See also Heron, "The High School and the Household Economy," 244–5.

127 Ontario, *Revised Statutes of Ontario, 1927*, ch. 333, The Adolescent School Attendance Act.

128 *TBE Annual Report 1932*, 70.
129 TDSBA, [unaccessioned material], box marked "TBE Records, Archives & Museum, Parkview S.S.," The Junior Vocational School Home & School Club Minute Book, April 1927, First Meeting 1929–30, n.d., 42–3.
130 TDSBA, [unaccessioned material], box marked "TBE Records, Archives & Museum, Parkview S.S.," The Junior Vocational School Home & School Club Minute Book, April 1927, Informal Executive Meeting, 11 May 1927, 11; Meeting, 30 November 1933, 133.
131 TDSBA, [unaccessioned material], box marked "TBE Records, Archives & Museum, Parkview S.S.," The Junior Vocational School Home & School Club Minute Book, April 1927, First Meeting 1929–30, n.d., 42–3.
132 TDSBA, [unaccessioned material], box marked "TBE Records, Archives & Museum, Parkview S.S.," The Junior Vocational School Home & School Club Minute Book, April 1927, Annual Report, Junior Vocational School Home & School Club, 1934–5, n.p.
133 TDSBA, [unaccessioned material], box marked "TBE Records, Archives & Museum, Parkview S.S.," The Junior Vocational School Home & School Club Minute Book, April 1927, Executive Meeting, 5 November 1934, 161–2.
134 School board minutes reveal instances as well when a parent petitioned the school board against a placement. See TDSBA, Advisory Vocational Committee Minutes, 1924–6 (unpublished), 26 September 1926, Item 275, n.p.
135 TDSBA, Hester How PS, ORC drawer J–M, ADP drawer M–Z, "Ruthie S.," ORC, ADP.
136 Gidney and Millar, *How Schools Worked*, 17.
137 *TBE Annual Report 1929*, 116–17.
138 *TBE Annual Report 1929*, 110.
139 Veronica Strong-Boag, "'Wages for Housework': Mothers' Allowances and the Beginnings of Social Security in Canada," *Journal of Canadian Studies* 14, no. 1 (1979): 32.
140 *TBE Annual Report 1929*, 116–17.
141 Patricia T. Rooke and R.L. Schnell, *Discarding the Asylum: From Child Rescue to the Welfare State in English Canada (1800–1950)* (Lanham, MD: University Press of America, 1983), 274–5.
142 James Struthers, *The Limits of Affluence: Welfare in Ontario* (Toronto: University of Toronto Press, 1994), 34–8.
143 See also *TBE Annual Report 1930*, Attendance Officer's Report, 186.
144 Stamp, *Schools of Ontario*, 159; Gidney and Millar, *How Schools Worked*, 62–6.

145 *TBE Minutes 1935,* appendix no. 24, Advisory Vocational Report no. 3,
12 February 1935, adopted 21 February 1935, 152; Ontario, Legislative
Assembly, *Report of the Minister of Education Province of Ontario for the Year
1936* (Toronto: T.E. Bowman, 1937), 43.

146 Jason Ellis and Paul Axelrod, "Continuity and Change: Special Education
Policy Development in Toronto Public Schools, 1945 to the Present,"
Teachers College Record 118, no. 2 (February 2016): 1–42, http://www
.tcrecord.org/Content.asp?ContentId=18228.

4 Sight-Saving, Speech and Hearing, and Orthopaedic Classes

1 *TBE Annual Report 1920,* 54.
2 Brad Byrom, "A Pupil and a Patient: Hospital-Schools in Progressive
America," in Paul K. Longmore and Lauri Umansky, eds., *The New
Disability History: American Perspectives* (New York: New York University
Press, 2001), 133–7; Laurie Block, "Cure and the Contempt of Goodwill:
Reason and Feeling in Disability Narratives, 1850–1950," in Cynthia
Comacchio, Janet Golden, and George Weisz, eds., *Healing the World's
Children: Interdisciplinary Perspectives on Child Health in the Twentieth
Century* (Montreal: McGill-Queen's University Press, 2008), 127–32.
3 Byrom, "A Pupil and a Patient," 133–5; Seth Koven, "Remembering and
Dismemberment: Crippled Children, Wounded Soldiers, and the Great
War in Great Britain," *American Historical Review* 99, no. 4 (October 1994):
1,167–202; Henri-Jacques Stiker, *A History of Disability,* trans. William
Sayers (Ann Arbor: University of Michigan Press, 1999), 123–38. On these
developments in Canada, see Ruby Heap, "'Salvaging War's Waste':
The University of Toronto and the 'Physical Reconstruction' of Disabled
Soldiers during the First World War," in Edgar-André Montigny and Lori
Chambers, eds., *Ontario since Confederation: A Reader* (Toronto: University
of Toronto Press, 2000), 214–34; Judith Friedland, *Restoring the Spirit:
The Beginnings of Occupational Therapy in Canada, 1890–1930* (Montreal:
McGill-Queen's University Press, 2011), esp. 85–113; Jennifer Stephen,
"Unemployment and the New Industrial Citizenship: A Review of the
Ontario Unemployment Commission, 1916," in Robert Menzies, Robert
Adamoski, Dorothy E. Chunn, eds., *Contesting Canadian Citizenship:
Historical Readings* (Toronto: Broadview Press, 2002), 174–5; Joanna L.
Pearce, "Not for Alms but Help: Fund-Raising and Free Education for
the Blind," *Journal of the Canadian Historical Association* 23, no. 1 (2012):
133–41. See also Catherine Gidney, *Tending the Student Body: Youth, Health,
and the Modern University* (Toronto: University of Toronto Press, 2015),

52–76, for a sense of how spiritual and secular notions of health could coexist in educational institutions.

4 Daniel J. Wilson, "Psychological Trauma and Its Treatment in the Polio Epidemics," *Bulletin of the History of Medicine* 82, no. 4 (winter 2008): 867–70. See also Mona Gleason, *Small Matters: Canadian Children in Sickness and Health* (Montreal: McGill-Queen's University Press 2013), 120–1.

5 H.J. Prueter, "The Care and Education of Crippled Children in Ontario" (DPaed thesis, University of Toronto, 1936), 8.

6 Jean Hampson, "Occupational Treatment at Crippled Children's School, Toronto," *Occupational Therapy and Rehabilitation* 12, no. 1 (1933): 57–8.

7 Even if subnormal young children had a need for the classes's services, they were not to be integrated into sight-saving or orthopaedic classes, because, it was claimed, they would impede progress there. See Harry Amoss and L. Helen DeLaporte, *Training Handicapped Children* (Toronto: Ryerson Press, 1933), 227; Prueter, "The Care and Education of Crippled Children in Ontario," 141. In Amoss and DeLaporte's manual, the authors do not specifically proscribe subnormal children's attendance in speech and hearing classes. However, the manual implies that these classes were only intended for intellectually normal children. See 261–308.

8 Donald D. MacDonald, "Sight-Saving Classes in the Public Schools" (DPaed thesis, University of Toronto, 1923), 36.

9 Ibid., 63, 72.

10 Ibid., 44.

11 *TBE Minutes 1927*, appendix no. 167, Report of the Special Committee Reported to Investigate the Equipment in Sight-Saving Classes, 18 October 1927, adopted 3 November 1927, 1,204–5.

12 *TBE Annual Report 1931*, 83.

13 "Red Tape Cut by Board to Aid Eyes of Pupils," *Toronto Daily Star*, 3 December 1938, 26.

14 Frederick Aylesworth, "Defective Vision in School-Age Children," *Proceedings of the Sixty-Fifth Annual Convention of the OEA* (Toronto: OEA, 1926), 211–15; *TBE Annual Report 1930*, 93.

15 *TBE Annual Report 1930*, 93.

16 *TBE Annual Report 1922*, 116; "Lip-Reading Classes Now in Eight Schools," *Toronto Daily Star*, 26 January 1922, 7; *TBE Annual Report 1924*, 74–5; *TBE Annual Report 1925*, 84; *TBE Annual Report 1928*, 165; "Pioneer Teacher of Deaf and Dumb," *Globe and Mail*, 4 September 1945, 4; "Deaf Work Pioneer Miss I. Palen, Dead," *Toronto Daily Star*, 4 September 1945, 11.

17 Imogen B. Palen, "Stammering," *The School* 17, no. 7 (March 1929): 635. See also Imogen B. Palen, "Correction of Speech Defects," *The School* 16, no. 5 (January 1928): 438.

18 Jason A. Ellis, "'All Methods – And Wedded to None': The Deaf Education Methods Debate and Progressive Educational Reform in Toronto, Canada, 1922–1945," *Paedagogica Historica* 50, no. 3 (2014): 379.

19 Douglas C. Baynton, *Forbidden Signs: American Culture and the Campaign against Sign Language* (Chicago: University of Chicago Press, 1996), 3–4.

20 Alexander Graham Bell, *Memoir upon the Formation of a Deaf Variety of the Human Race* (National Academy of Sciences, 1884), 48. Canadian Institute for Historic Microreproduction no. 08831; Baynton, *Forbidden Signs*, 30–3; Susan Burch, *Signs of Resistance: American Deaf Cultural History, 1900 to World War II* (New York: New York University Press, 2002), 7–11; Iain Hutchison, "Oralism: A Sign of the Times? The Contest for Deaf Communication in Education Provision in Late Nineteenth-Century Scotland," *European Review of History* 14, no. 4 (2007): 481–3; Ellis, "All Methods," 377–80.

21 *TBE Annual Report 1925*, 83 (emphasis original).

22 E.A. Hardy and Honora M. Cochrane, *Centennial Story: The Board of Education for the City of Toronto 1850–1950* (Toronto: Thomas Nelson & Sons, 1950), 139. Moshier's title was chief inspector; with Goldring's appointment, the title changed to superintendent.

23 TDSBA, Goldring, Cecil Charles, Papers (box 1 of 2), TDSB 2003–0568, C.C. Goldring, "Radio Talk: The Education of Underprivileged and Handicapped Children in Toronto Schools," 10 March 1935.

24 Baynton, *Forbidden Signs*, 10. See also, on the enduring use of sign language in Canadian institutions, Alessandra Iozzo, "'Silent Citizens': Citizenship Education, Disability and d/Deafness at the Ontario Institution of the Deaf, 1870–1914" (PhD diss., University of Ottawa, 2015), 106–12; Sandy R. Barron, "'The World Is Wide Enough for Us Both': The Manitoba School for the Deaf at the Onset of the Oralist Age, 1889–1920," *Canadian Journal of Disability Studies* 6, no. 1 (2017): 63–84.

25 Osgood, *The History of Special Education*, 57. It was allowable, by legislation, for Ontario city school systems to assume from the OSD responsibility for educating local deaf children. Amoss and DeLaporte, *Training Handicapped Children*, 238.

26 "Sign Language Needed by Deaf," *Globe*, 5 July 1922, 2; Clifton H. Carbin, *Deaf Heritage in Canada: A Distinctive, Diverse, and Enduring Culture*, Dorothy L. Smith, ed. (Toronto: McGraw-Hill Ryerson, 1996), 188–90. See also Iozzo-Duval, "Silent Citizens," 100–3, on deaf opposition to pure oralism at the OSD going back to 1907.

27 The Scottish Rite Masons donated the TBE's first hearing aids, which it put into use in Rosedale's hard-of-hearing classes in the late 1930s. Ontario, Legislative Assembly, *Report of the Minister of Education Province of Ontario*

for the Year 1939 (Toronto: T.E. Bowman, 1940), 69. On hearing aids and oralism see, R.A.R. Edwards, "Sound and Fury; or, Much Ado about Nothing? Cochlear Implants in Historical Perspective," *Journal of American History* 92, no. 3 (December 2005): 902–7.

28 TDSBA (VF), TBE – Biography – Goldring, Cecil Charles, "Education of the Deaf Child or the Child with Impaired Hearing" (TBE: 1946), 11.

29 *TBE Minutes 1926*, 18 March 1926, 78–81; 15 April 1926, 95.

30 S.B. Sinclair, "Miss H.D. Milne, an Appreciation," *The Bulletin* 8, no. 2 (November 1931): 7–8; *TBE Annual Report 1930*, 85–6. Even before the TBE established the extramural program, however, evidence shows that physically disabled and impaired pupils went to school. A few could not reach the school on their own. Family members carried or pulled them there in makeshift "go-carts or children's express waggons." *TBE Minutes 1920*, appendix no. 10, "Auxiliary Classes. Special Report Dr Helen MacMurchy to the TBE," 9 January 1920, 21–2.

31 *TBE Annual Report 1930*, 84–5. On causes of "crippling" conditions, see also Prueter, "The Care and Education of Crippled Children in Ontario," 25–32. On "spastic paralysis" in this period, see Edwin Warner Ryerson, "Cerebral Spastic Paralysis in Children," *Journal of the American Medical Association* 98, no. 1 (2 January 1932): 43–5. On the 1937 polio epidemic's effect on Toronto schools, see *TBE Minutes 1937*, appendix no. 154, Retiring Address of W.R. Shaw, Chairman of Board of Education, in 1937, at Final Meeting of Board on 16 December 1937, 675; and Bruce Vance, ed., *The Schools and the Polio Epidemic*, Education in TBE Public Schools, A Series of Historical Sketches, 2 (Toronto: TBE Sesquicentennial Museum and Archives, 1994). See also Christopher J. Rutty, "The Middle-Class Plague: Epidemic Polio and the Canadian State, 1936–37," *Canadian Bulletin of Medical History/Bulletin canadien d'histoire de la médecine* 13 (1996): 277–314.

32 R.W. Hopper, "The Rehabilitation of the Crippled Child," *Social Welfare* 14 (February 1932): 89.

33 Prueter, "The Care and Education of Crippled Children in Ontario," 135.

34 Sinclair, "Miss H.D. Milne, an Appreciation," 7; Edith Lelean Groves (posthumous) with an Introduction by Helen MacMurchy, *Everyday Children: A Book of Poems* (Toronto: The Committee in Charge of the Edith L. Groves Memorial Fund for Underprivileged Children, 1932), 17–18. See also *TBE Minutes 1925*, 17 September 1925, 185–6; *TBE Minutes 1926*, 18 March 1926, 78.

35 Groves with MacMurchy, *Everyday Children*, 20.

36 Ibid., 11–29; Mrs W.E. Groves, "Address of Welcome to the Auxiliary Class Teachers of Ontario," *Proceedings of the Sixty-Second Annual Convention of*

the OEA (Toronto: OEA, 1923), 260–1; TDSBA (VF), TBE Biography Groves, Edith, "Officers and Executive of Toronto Committee on Mental Hygiene – Sept. 1923," "Schools Mourn Famed Leader in Mrs Groves," newspaper clipping, n.d; CAMHA, Clarke Institute of Psychiatry/Toronto Psychiatric Hospital Fonds, C.K. Clarke Series, box 10–08, "Toronto Committee on Mental Hygiene."

37 *TBE Minutes 1925*, 17 September 1925, 185–6; *TBE Minutes 1926*, 18 March 1926, 78, 18 November 1926, 252–3, appendix no. 105, Finance Report no. 10, 17 May 1926, adopted 20 May 1926, 728–30. See also TDSBA, Wellesley St PS Scrapbook 1926–30, clipping, "Carried by Buses," dated 14 April 1926.

38 David B. Tyack, *The One Best System: A History of American Urban Education* (Cambridge, MA: Harvard University Press, 1974), 44–5; *TBE Minutes 1920*, appendix no. 10, "Auxiliary Classes. Special Report Dr Helen MacMurchy to the TBE," 9 January 1920, 21–2.

39 H.D. Milne, "Why an Orthopedic School," *The Bulletin* 2, no. 2 (March 1926), 7.

40 TDSBA, Wellesley St PS Scrapbook 1926–30, loose photo numbered 418; clipping, "Carried by Buses," dated 14 April 1926; clipping, "Classes for Cripples Are Opened To-day," dated 14 April 1926.

41 TDSBA, Wellesley St PS Scrapbook 1926–30, clipping, "To Have Fire Drill in Cripples' Class," dated 14 April 1926; Prueter, "The Care and Education of Crippled Children in Ontario," 47. On the 1923 fire, see *TBE Minutes 1923*, 19 April 1923, 95.

42 AO, Auxiliary Education Services correspondence files, RG 2–59, box 1, file Toronto, 1924–1930, Hannah Milne, "Report of Work of Orthopaedic Classes," 27 June 1928, 1–3; *TBE Annual Report 1930*, 84.

43 TDSBA, Wellesley St PS Scrapbook 1926–30, clipping, "Popular Toronto Teacher Goes to Scots Hospital," n.d. (ca. 1939–45).

44 Judith Friedland, *Restoring the Spirit*, 144.

45 Ibid., 114–30.

46 Ontario, Legislative Assembly, *Report of the Minister of the Province Education for Ontario for the Year 1945* (Toronto: T.E. Bowman, 1947), 49.

47 Hampson, "Occupational Treatment at Crippled Children's School," 56–8.

48 Friedland, *Restoring the Spirit*, 200–2.

49 *TBE Annual Report 1930*, 84–5.

50 Amoss and DeLaporte, *Training Handicapped Children*, 220. In fact, like Hampson, DeLaporte also trained as a ward aide around the end of the First World War. Friedland, *Restoring the Spirit*, 144.

51 Prueter, "The Care and Education of Crippled Children in Ontario," 16–22; *TBE Annual Report 1930*, 85; *TBE Minutes 1932*, appendix no. 142,

Management Report no. 17, 12 October 1932, adopted 20 October 1932, 1,373. In encouraging the schools to penetrate so deeply into medical territory, Prueter and Moshier flirted with charged professional debates about separate spheres of influence for physicians, therapists, and auxiliary educators. See TDSBA, Wellesley St PS Scrapbook 1926–30, clipping, "Doctors Disagree on Therapy Work among Children," dated September 1928; clipping, "Says School Usurps Work of Hospitals," dated September 1929; Prueter, "The Care and Education of Crippled Children in Ontario," 138; Amoss and DeLaporte, *Training Handicapped Children*, 187.

52 See Gleason, *Small Matters*, 127.

53 "Dr Goldwin W. Howland," *Canadian Journal of Occupational Therapy* 17, no. 3 (September 1950): 67–70; "Dr R.M. Wansbrough: Surgeon for 28 Years at Children's Hospital," *Globe and Mail*, 25 May 1956, 4. See also Friedland, *Restoring the Spirit*, 185–8.

54 *TBE Annual Report 1930*, 85.

55 Geoffrey Reaume, *Lyndhurst: Canada's First Rehabilitation Centre for People with Spinal Cord Injuries, 1945–1998* (Montreal: McGill-Queen's University Press, 2007), 24–7.

56 TDSBA, Goldring, Cecil Charles, Papers (box 2 of 2), TDSB 2003–0569, C.C. Goldring, "Occupations Available for the Physically Handicapped," 10.

57 "Suitable Occupations for Handicapped Workers," *The Bulletin* 8, no. 2 (November 1931): 17; *TBE Minutes 1936*, appendix no. 163, Management Report no. 19, adopted 17 December 1936, 704–5; Prueter, "The Care and Education of Crippled Children in Ontario," 24–5; TDSBA, Wellesley St PS Scrapbook 1926–30, clipping, "Report Is Presented on Orthopedic Classes," dated September 1928; clipping, "Aim to Help Crippled Children Find Niche in Life," dated September 1929; clipping, "Board Will Plan Jobs for Crippled Children," dated September 1929.

58 Goldring, "Occupations Available for the Physically Handicapped," 10–11.

59 Ibid.

60 *TBE Minutes 1928*, appendix no. 123, Management Report no. 15, 12 September 1928, adopted 20 September 1928, 1,065.

61 *TBE Annual Report 1932*, 108.

62 *TBE Annual Report 1930*, 94; *TBE Annual Report 1932*, 109.

63 *TBE Minutes 1932*, appendix no. 78, Report no. 1 of Special Committee of Board re Orthopedic Classes at Wellesley School, 3 May 1932, adopted as amended 5 May 1932, 619.

64 *Report of the Minister of the Province Education for Ontario for the Year 1934* (Toronto: T.E. Bowman, 1936), 63.

65 TDSBA, TBE – Curric. Dept. Schools – Elem. Christie – Deer Park, TDSB
    2003–0671, Clinton Deaf Classes file, memorandum N.L. Pollard to C.C.
    Goldring, 29 October 1951.
66 Goldring, "Occupations Available for the Physically Handicapped," 2.
67 Ibid.
68 *TBE Minutes 1926*, 18 November 1926, 253–4. There are additional simi-
    lar examples – see *TBE Minutes 1926*, appendix no. 32, 15 February 1926,
    adopted 18 February 1926, 159; appendix no. 213, Finance Report no. 22,
    29 November 1926, adopted 2 December 1926, 1,396; *TBE Minutes 1933*,
    appendix no. 120, Management Report no. 15, 27 September 1933, adopted
    5 October 1933, 1,203.
69 *TBE Annual Report 1928*, 168.
70 TDSBA, Hester How PS, ORC drawer J–M, ADP drawer M–Z, "Catherine
    W.," ORC, ADP.
71 *TBE Minutes 1941*, Finance Report no. 1, part 2, 20 January 1941, adopted
    23 January 1941, 13.
72 TDSBA, Hester How PS, ORC drawer A–D, ADP drawer A–L, "Donnie
    B.," ORC, ADP.
73 Advertisement, "Miss Grace K. Wadleigh Teacher of Lip-Reading,"
    The Bulletin (December 1926).
74 See Tony Shorgan, "It Was a Privilege Having Polio," 39; Charlie Brockle-
    hurst, "Never Give Up," in Sally Aitken, Helen D'Orazio, and Stewart
    Valin, eds., *Walking Fingers: The Story of Polio and Those Who Lived with It*
    (Montreal: Véhicule Press, 2004), 57; Claire Vincent, "La maladie ma privée
    de mon enfance," in Sally Aitken, Pierrette Caron, and Gilles Fournier, eds.,
    Histoire vécue de la polio au Québec (Montreal: Carte blanche, 2001), 87–8.
75 TDSBA, Hester How PS, ORC drawer E–I, ADP drawer A–L, "Pat F.,"
    ORC, ADP. See also Hester How PS, ORC drawer Sh–Z, ADP drawer M–Z,
    "Millie O.," ORC, ADP.
76 MacDonald, "Sight-Saving Classes in the Public Schools," 39.
77 Molly Ladd-Taylor, *Mother-Work: Women, Child Welfare, and the State,
    1890–1930* (Urbana: University of Illinois Press, 1994), 135–8.
78 Baynton, *Forbidden Signs*, 79–81.
79 *TBE Minutes 1922*, 16 November 1922, 242.
80 *TBE Annual Report 1929*, 201.
81 Nellie Y. MacDonald, "Deaf Children in the Public Schools," *The School* 14,
    no. 5 (January 1926): 499–500.
82 TDSBA, TBE – Curric. Dept. Schools – Elem. Christie – Deer Park, TDSB
    2003–0671, Clinton Deaf Classes file, memorandum N.L. Pollard to C.C.
    Goldring, 29 October 1951.

83 TDSBA, TDSB 2003–0671, TBE – Curric. Dept. Schools – Elem. Christie – Deer Park, Clinton Deaf Classes file, letter Nellie Y. MacDonald to C.C. Goldring, 12 February 1945.

84 "To the Parents of Deaf Children," letter to the editor, Owen Elliot, *Toronto Daily Star*, 4 December 1925, 6. See also "Classes for Deaf and Dumb," letter to the editor, Mother of One Afflicted, *Toronto Daily Star*, 22 December 1925, 6.

85 *TBE Minutes 1943*, 21 October 1943, 145–6; 1 April 1943, 71; appendix Management Report no. 17, part 2, 26 October 1943, 437; *TBE Minutes 1944*, Management Report no. 12, part 2, 13 June 1944, adopted 22 June 1944, 195; *TBE Minutes 1945*, Management Report no. 6, part 2, 6 March 1945, adopted 15 March 1945, 82.

86 AO, RG 18–131, Records of the Royal Commission on Education in Ontario, box 9 (briefs 5–25); brief 6, "How the OAD Can Enlist Parents' Co-operation," proceedings 26th Annual Biennial Convention, Ontario Association of the Deaf (Ontario Association of the Deaf, 1944), 17–24.

87 See Burch, *Signs of Resistance*; Baynton, *Forbidden Signs*; R.A.R. Edwards, *Words Made Flesh: Nineteenth-Century Deaf Education and the Growth of Deaf Culture* (New York: New York University Press, 2012).

88 "Education of the Deaf," *Toronto Daily Star*, 31 March 1945, 6.

89 Baynton, *Forbidden Signs*, 108–31; Edwards, *Words Made Flesh*, 6.

90 Burch, *Signs of Resistance*, 9–11; Harlan Lane, *The Mask of Benevolence: Disabling the Deaf Community*, new ed. (San Diego: Dawn Sign Press, 1999), 13–16. Baynton notes that "combined method" is something of an ambiguous and at times anachronistic phrase. This was not always the terminology that people advocating a combined approach used, nor has its meaning stayed fixed over time. It is a helpful phrase, however, for distinguishing different methods that permitted sign language from pure oralism, which always forbid it. Baynton, *Forbidden Signs*, 13–14. See also Ellis, "All Methods," 382–3, on the Ontario deaf community's use of "combined method" by the 1940s.

91 Ellis, "All Methods," 377–8.

92 Ibid., 381–4.

93 "Deaf Body President Praises and Differs," *Toronto Daily Star*, 23 March 1945, 2.

94 "Education of the Deaf," 6. See also "Dr Goldring's Plans for the Deaf," letter to the editor, David Peikoff, *Globe and Mail*, 16 March 1945, 6; Ellis, "All Methods," 381–8.

95 Clara G. Binnie, "Speech Defects and Mental Health," *The School* (elem. ed.) 32, no. 3 (November 1943): 220–1; E. Bowling, "Some Causes and the

Re-education of Speech Defects," in *Proceedings of the Sixty-Eighth Annual Convention of the OEA* (Toronto: OEA, 1929), 95.

96 *TBE Annual Report 1925*, 82.
97 Possibly the author meant Owen Elliot's letter that the paper had published ten days prior.
98 "Instruction for the Deaf," letter to the editor, A Friend of the Deaf, *Toronto Daily Star*, 14 December 1925, 6.
99 Kari Dehli, "For Intelligent Motherhood and National Efficiency: The Toronto Home and School Council, 1916–1930," in Heap and Prentice, *Gender and Education in Ontario*, 147; Gleason, *Small Matters*, 126–7.
100 Julius Wiggins, *No Sound* (New York: The Silent Press, 1970), 10–11.
101 Ibid., 11.
102 MacDonald, "Deaf Children in the Public Schools," 499–500.
103 Ibid.
104 Imogen Palen, "Lip Reading," in *Proceedings of the Sixty-Second Annual Convention of the OEA* (Toronto: OEA, 1923), 265.
105 Ibid., 264–5; *TBE Annual Report 1929*, 201–2.
106 Burch, *Signs of Resistance*, 27.
107 Wiggins, *No Sound*, 66.
108 Ibid., 29.
109 Ibid., 17.
110 Ibid., 52–3.
111 Ibid., 66.
112 Ellis, "All Methods," 385.
113 *TBE Annual Report 1925*, 83.
114 AO, Milne, "Report of Work of Orthopaedic Classes," 27 June 1928, 1.
115 Osgood, *The History of Special Education*, 60.
116 MacDonald, "Sight-Saving Classes in the Public Schools," 42.
117 TDSBA, Hester How PS, ORC drawer Mc–Si, ADP drawer M–Z, "Donald N.," ORC, ADP. See also Jean Little, *Little by Little: A Writer's Education* (Toronto: Viking, 1987).
118 TDSBA, Hester How PS, ORC drawer E–I, ADP drawer A–L, "Florence R.," ORC, ADP.
119 TDSBA, Hester How PS, ORC drawer J–M, ADP drawer A–L, "Franklin C.," ORC, ADP.
120 TDSBA, Hester How PS, ORC drawer E–I, ADP drawer A–L, "Raymond C.," ORC, ADP.
121 TDSBA, Hester How PS, ORC drawer Sh–Z, ADP drawer M–Z, "Shirley T.," ORC, ADP.
122 Prueter, "The Care and Education of Crippled Children in Ontario," 46.

123 *Clinton Public School 1888–1988* (Toronto: TBE, May 1989), 27.

124 Wiggins, *No Sound*, 37–8.

125 Robert C. Vipond, *Making a Global City: How One Toronto School Embraced Diversity* (Toronto: University of Toronto Press, 2017), 36.

126 Karen K. Yoshida, Fady Shanouda, and Jason Ellis, "An Education and Negotiation of Differences: The 'Schooling' Experiences of English-Speaking Canadian Children Growing up with Polio during the 1940s and 1950s," *Disability & Society* 29, no. 3 (2014): 350–4; Gleason, *Small Matters*, 132–3.

127 S.B. Sinclair, *Backward and Brilliant Children* (Toronto: Ryerson Press, 1931), 25.

128 Mona Gleason, "Disciplining the Student Body: Schooling and the Construction of Canadian Children's Bodies, 1930–1960," *History of Education Quarterly* 41, no. 2 (summer 2001): 202–3.

129 Little, *Little by Little*.

130 TDSBA, Duke of York PS, ORC TDSB 2003–1307, box 2, "Ernest S.," ORC.

131 Block, "Cure and the Contempt of Goodwill," 127–45; Martin F. Norden, *The Cinema of Isolation: A History of Physical Disability in the Movies* (New Brunswick, NJ: Rutgers University Press, 1994), 33–6; Paul Longmore and David Goldberger, "The League of the Physically Handicapped and the Great Depression: A Case Study in the New Disability History," *Journal of American History* 87, no. 3 (December 2000): 895–6.

132 AO, Milne, "Report of Work of Orthopaedic Classes," 3.

133 Prueter, "The Care and Education of Crippled Children in Ontario," 46.

134 *TBE Annual Report 1930*, 47.

135 TDSBA (VF), TBE Schools – Elementary – Wellesley PS, Ruth Byrne Dewsbury, "Happy School Days," *Recording Recollections at Ryerson* 4, no. 2 (June 1985): 12.

136 Richard J. Altenbaugh, "Where Are the Disabled in the History of Education? The Impact of Polio on Sites of Learning," *History of Education* 35, no. 6 (November 2006): 720–1; Longmore and Goldberger, "The League of the Physically Handicapped and the Great Depression," 899–905. Historians of deafness have advanced a similar argument about how boarding schools for people who were deaf were the crucibles of deaf cultural identity. See Edwards, *Words Made Flesh*, 11–31.

137 TDSBA (VF), TBE – Curriculum – Special Education, Edna Barg, "Sight Saving Class," *Recording Recollections at Ryerson* 8, no. 3 (December 1989): 7.

138 Ibid.

139 Little, *Little by Little*, 61.

140 *TBE Annual Report 1930*, 85.
141 TDSBA, Duke of York PS, ORC TDSB 2003–1307, box 4, ADP TDSB 2003–0834. "Dick H.," ORC, ADP.
142 TDSBA, Hester How PS, ADP drawer M–Z, "Pauline N.," ADP.
143 TDSBA, Coleman PS, ORC microfilm reel 10, ADP microfilm reel 11, "Gene M.," ORC, ADP.
144 TDSBA, Duke of York PS, ADP box TDSB 2003–0834, box 1 of 2, "Clara T.," ADP.
145 Prueter, "The Care and Education of Crippled Children in Ontario," 90; *TBE Minutes 1928*, appendix no. 75, Management Report no. 10, 25 April 1928, adopted 2 May 1928, 667.
146 TDSBA, Wellesley PS Scrapbook 1926–30, postcard, 15 July 1927.
147 TDSBA, Wellesley PS Scrapbook 1926–30, "Played 138 Numbers," dated March 1928. The Dominion hospital was more commonly known as the Christie Street Hospital. Reaume, *Lyndhurst*, 11–12.
148 TDSBA, Duke of York PS, ORC TDSB 2003–1307, box 1, "Carl F.," ORC.
149 TDSBA, Hester How PS, ORC drawer E–I; ADP drawer A–L, "Albert E.," ORC, ADP. See also Coleman PS, ORC microfilm reel 10, "Doris B.," ORC.
150 TDSBA, Duke of York PS, ORC TDSB 2003–1307, box 4, "Peter O.," ORC.
151 TDSBA, Duke of York PS, ORC TDSB 2003–1307, box 4, "Frankie C.," ORC.
152 Stiker, *A History of Disability*, 135.
153 Paul K. Longmore and Lauri Umansky, "Introduction: Disability History: From the Margins to the Mainstream," in Longmore and Umansky, *The New Disability History*, 8–11.

5 Special-Subject Disabilities and Auxiliary Education

1 Harry Amoss and L. Helen DeLaporte, *Training Handicapped Children* (Toronto: The Ryerson Press, 1933), 12–13; Ontario, Legislative Assembly, *Report of the Minister of Education Province of Ontario for the Year 1945* (Toronto: T.E. Bowman, 1947), 53; E.P. Lewis, "The Non-academic Child," *Proceedings of the Sixty-Ninth Annual Convention of the OEA* (Toronto: OEA, 1930), 125–6.
2 See also Lester Mann, *On the Trail of Process: A Historical Perspective on Cognitive Processes and Their Training* (New York: Grune & Stratton, 1979); E. Anne Bennison, "Before the Learning Disabled There Were Feeble-Minded Children," in Barry M. Franklin, ed., *Learning Disability: Dissenting Essays* (London: The Falmer Press, 1987), 13–28.
3 Franklin, *Backwardness to At-Risk*, 63.

4 Danforth, *The Incomplete Child*, esp. 137–80.
5 Emmett Albert Betts, *The Prevention and Correction of Reading Difficulties* (Evanston, IL: Row, Peterson, and Co, 1936), 3–4.
6 Danforth, *The Incomplete Child*, 28–58.
7 Ibid., 12; Nila Banton Smith, *American Reading Instruction* (Newark: International Reading Association, 1965), 155–6.
8 Franklin, *Backwardness to At-Risk*, 62–3.
9 Helen MacMurchy, *Organization and Management of Auxiliary Classes*, Educational Pamphlets no. 7 (Toronto: DOE, 1915), 27–33.
10 Franklin, *Backwardness to At-Risk*, 50.
11 Danforth, *The Incomplete Child*, 61–7.
12 Ibid., 69–70.
13 Ibid., 81–5. Psychologists Seymour Sarason and Leo Kanner would later, in the 1940s, criticize Werner and Strauss's method of inferring brain injuries from their patients' symptoms without possessing empirical evidence from patient histories that an injury had ever occurred. Franklin, *Backwardness to At-Risk*, 50–9.
14 Danforth, *The Incomplete Child*, 152; Jane H. Catterson and Lisa Durrell, "Chapter One: The Background," *Journal of Education* 182, no. 1 Durrell's One-Minute Philosophy of Education (2000): 5.
15 Danforth, *The Incomplete Child*, 138.
16 Augusta F. Bronner, *The Psychology of Special Abilities and Disabilities* (Boston: Little, Brown, and Co, 1917). Perhaps not by coincidence then, Bronner is far better known for her work co-directing the Judge Baker Guidance Clinic for children and youth in Boston with William A. Healy than she is for her earlier work on special disabilities. See Kathleen Jones, *Taming the Troublesome Child: American Families, Child Guidance, and the Limits of Psychiatric Authority* (Cambridge, MA: Harvard University Press, 1999). For other research similar to Bronner's, see a small study by Leta S. Hollingworth (with C. Amelia Winford), *The Psychology of Disability in Spelling*, Teachers College, Columbia University Contributions to Education, no. 88 (New York: Teachers College, 1918); and a larger but slightly later undertaking, Arthur I. Gates, *The Psychology of Reading and Spelling: With Special Reference to Disability*, Teachers College, Columbia University Contributions to Education, no. 129 (Teachers College: New York, 1922).
17 Bronner, *The Psychology of Special Abilities and Disabilities*, 14–15.
18 Grace M. Fernald, *Remedial Techniques in Basic School Subjects* (New York: McGraw-Hill, 1943 [reprint 1971]), 30. For Fernald's career, see Ellen B. Sullivan, Roy M. Dorcus, Bennet M. Allen, and Louis K. Koontz, "Grace

Maxwell Fernald: 1879–1950," *Psychological Review* 57, no. 6 (November 1950): 319–21.

19 Danforth, *The Incomplete Child*, 155. See Marion Monroe, *Children Who Cannot Read: The Analysis of Reading Disabilities and the Use of Diagnostic Tests in the Instruction of Retarded Readers* (Chicago: University of Chicago Press, 1932).

20 Danforth, *The Incomplete Child*, 152–5.

21 Ibid., 156–63. Thorleif (Ted) Hegge, a psychologist at the Wayne County Training School and later frequent collaborator with Kirk, would use Monroe's index to establish that a child who was genuinely intellectually disabled could possibly also have a specific reading disability but that this disability was not necessarily present just because the child had a low IQ.

22 Fernald, *Remedial Techniques in Basic School Subjects*, vii–ix.

23 Betts, *The Prevention and Correction of Reading Difficulties*.

24 Catterson and Durrell, "Chapter One: The Background"; Herbert S. Langfeld, "Walter Fenno Dearborn: 1878–1955," *American Journal of Psychology* 68, no. 4 (December 1955): 679–81.

25 Donald D. Durrell, "The Influence of Reading Ability on Intelligence Measures," *Journal of Educational Psychology* 24, no. 6 (September 1933): 412.

26 Ibid., 416.

27 The word means "twisted symbols." Catterson and Durrell, "Chapter One: The Background," 5; Franklin, *Backwardness to At-Risk*, 62.

28 Catterson and Durrell, "Chapter One: The Background," 5.

29 Franklin, *Backwardness to At-Risk*, 63.

30 Ibid., 140.

31 Betts, *The Prevention and Correction of Reading Difficulties*, 51–9.

32 Danforth, *The Incomplete Child*, 138; Robert McG. Thomas, Jr, "Samuel A. Kirk, 92, Pioneer of Special Education Field," *New York Times*, 28 July 1996, http://www.nytimes.com/1996/07/28/us/samuel-a-kirk-92-pioneer-of-special-education-field.html.

33 Sullivan et al., "Grace Maxwell Fernald"; Smith, *American Reading Instruction*, 258–9.

34 Fernald, *Remedial Techniques in Basic School Subjects*, 32.

35 Monroe, *Children Who Cannot Read*, 111.

36 Ibid., 111–36. For example, stories with only short vowel sounds, emphasizing one vowel in particular – such as a story about (124–5) "B*i*ll" who "must get up at s*i*x" to "br*i*ng in the m*i*lk," and who "s*i*ts on the sw*i*ng," which is intended, obviously, to develop the short "i" vowel sound (emphasis mine).

37 He had been a schoolteacher in Saskatchewan in the 1920s, before taking a PhD at Teachers College, Columbia, in the 1930s under the psychologist and reading and spelling difficulties expert Gates. From Teachers College, Harris went to Saskatoon to fill an appointment at the University of Saskatchewan. He moved next to the University of British Columbia for a brief stint (1940–2) as an associate professor before going to Berkeley. See Fred T. Tyler, "David H. Russell, Past-President, APA Division 15 1906–1965," *Educational Psychologist* 2, no. 2 (April 1965): 1.

38 David H. Russell, "The Prevention and Remedy of Reading Difficulties in Smaller Schools" (part 2), *The School* (elem. ed.) 28, no. 6 (February 1940): 485. The first half of this two-part article is Russell, "The Prevention and Correction of Reading Difficulties in Smaller Schools," *The School* (elem. ed.) 28, no. 5 (January 1940): 387–92. See also David H. Russell, *Children Learn to Read* (Boston: Ginn, 1949), in which he states (346), "The diagnostic point of view suggests that behavior is caused and that the teacher attempt to understand, rather than blame, poor behavior or inadequate performance. If a child is a poor reader, the thoughtful teacher does not describe his behavior as 'lazy 'or label him as 'dumb.' Rather she seeks to understand the causes behind the inadequate reading. The modern teacher's point of view is not unlike that of a good physician diagnosing a patient who is physically ill." See also Betts, *The Prevention and Correction of Reading Difficulties*, 77–9.

39 George K. Sheane, "Diagnostic and Remedial Teaching in Arithmetic," *The School* (elem. ed.) 26, no. 9 (May 1938): 776.

40 Leo J. Brueckner, *Diagnostic and Remedial Teaching in Arithmetic* (Philadelphia: The John C. Winston Co, 1930), iii. See Leo J. Brueckner and G.K. Sheane, *Mathematics for Everyday Use* (Toronto: Winston, 1937).

41 Betts, *The Prevention and Correction of Reading Difficulties*, 78–115.

42 See Theodore Michael Christou, *Progressive Education: Revisioning and Reframing Ontario's Public Schools 1919–1942* (Toronto: University of Toronto Press, 2012), 6.

43 P.F. Munro, "The Case of Mabel Helen B – – ," *The School* (elem. ed.) 24, no. 4 (December 1935): 275. Parts of this article reprint Munro's 1931 inspector's report. *TBE Annual Report 1931*, 97–8.

44 Munro, "The Case of Mabel Helen B – – ," 276.

45 Ibid., 277.

46 *TBE Annual Report 1931*, 97 (emphasis original).

47 Munro, "The Case of Mabel Helen B – – "; *TBE Annual Report 1931*, 98–9.

48 P.F. Munro, *An Experimental Investigation of the Mentality of the Jew in Ryerson Public School Toronto* (Toronto: University of Toronto Press, 1926); see chapter 2.

49 *TBE Annual Report 1931*, 99 (emphasis original).

50 *TBE Annual Report 1932*, 110. For MacDonald's earlier views, see *TBE Annual Report 1919*, 90–1.

51 *TBE Annual Report 1932*, 110–12.

52 Ontario, Legislative Assembly, *Report of the Minister of Education Province of Ontario for the Year 1941* (Toronto: T.E. Bowman, 1943), 57–8; Ontario, Legislative Assembly, *Report of the Minister of Education Province of Ontario for the Year 1942* (Toronto: T.E. Bowman, 1944), 48.

53 Ontario, Legislative Assembly, *Report of the Minister of Education Province of Ontario for the Year 1942*, 47–8.

54 Walter F. Koerber, "An Evaluation of Some Methods and Procedures in the Teaching of Reading to Non-academic Adolescent Boys" (DPaed thesis, University of Toronto, 1947), 2.

55 Larry Cuban, *How Teachers Taught: Constancy and Change in American Classrooms, 1890–1990*, 2nd ed. (New York: Teachers College Press, 1993), 19.

56 TDSBA, Goldring, Cecil Charles, Papers (box 2 of 2), TDSB 2003–0569, "Preliminary Investigation Prevalent Attitudes of Teachers towards Handicaps to Learning."

57 See *TBE Annual Report 1930*, 110–12.

58 Ontario, Legislative Assembly, *Report of the Minister of Education Province of Ontario for the Year 1935* (Toronto: T.E. Bowman, 1936), 38–9; Gerald T. Hackett, "The History of Public Education for Mentally Retarded Children in the Province of Ontario 1867–1964" (EdD diss., University of Toronto, 1969), 206.

59 Amoss and DeLaporte, *Training Handicapped Children*, 7.

60 Ibid., 12–13.

61 Ontario, Legislative Assembly, *Report of the Minister of Education Province of Ontario for the Year 1937* (Toronto: T.E. Bowman, 1938), 47.

62 Ontario, Legislative Assembly, *Report of the Minister of Education Province of Ontario for the Year 1939* (Toronto: T.E. Bowman, 1940), 66.

63 TDSBA, TBE – Curriculum Development – General Files – 1907–72, TDSB 2003–0653, Inspectors' Meetings – PS – 1933–60, Minutes of Meeting of the Public School Inspectors, 8 November 1935.

64 TDSBA, TBE – Curriculum Development – General Files – 1907–72, TDSB 2003–0653, Inspectors' Meetings – PS – 1933–60, Minutes of the Meeting of [the] Public School Inspectors, 16 March 1945.

65 *TBE Minutes 1945*, Management Report no. 7, part 2, 27 March 1945, adopted as amended, 5 April 1945, 98–9.

66 TDSBA, TBE – Curriculum Development – General Files – 1907–72, TDSB 2003–0653, Inspectors' Meetings – PS – 1933–60, Minutes of Public School

Inspectors' Meeting, 27 April 1945; Minutes of Public School Inspectors' Meeting, 19 December 1945.

67 TDSBA, Management Committee Minutes, 1944–5 (unpublished), 27 March 1945, 43.

68 *TBE Annual Report 1945*, appendix, Management Report no. 12, part 2, 19 June 1945, adopted as amended, 28 June 1945, 199–200.

69 TDSBA, TBE – Curriculum Development – General Files – 1907–72, TDSB 2003–0653, Inspectors' Meetings – PS – 1933–60, Minutes of Public School Inspectors' Meeting, 27 April 1945; Minutes of Public School Inspectors' Meeting, 19 December 1945.

70 C.G. Stogdill, "Mental Hygiene in Toronto Schools," *The Bulletin* 9, no. 2 (November 1932): 4.

71 CTA, fonds 200, series 365, file 48, box 224904, folio 2, Department of Public Health City of Toronto, Annual Statement 1935; folio 3, Annual Statement 1936.

72 The sources for these statistics are the monthly reports and annual statements of the public health department. CTA, fonds 200, series 365, Department of Public Health City of Toronto, selected monthly reports and annual statements, 1931–45.

73 The category was briefly included in 1936, but discontinued for reasons that I do not know.

74 The following are selected cases. Because I do not have enough cases from pupil records that would enable me to look systematically at IQ score, diagnosis, placement recommendation, and eventual actual placement, I have refrained from attempting a thoroughgoing analysis here. My impression, however, from a small number of cases is that this is what occurred.

75 TDSBA, Duke of York PS, ORC TDSB 2003–1308, box 6, ADP TDSB 2003–0835, "Imogene R.," ORC, ADP.

76 TDSBA, Hester How PS, ORC drawer A–D, ADP drawer A–L, "Augusta T.," ORC, ADP.

77 TDSBA, Duke of York PS, ORC TDSB 2003–1309, box 10, ADP TDSB 2003–0837, "Rupert C.," ORC, ADP.

78 TDSBA, Hester How PS, ORC drawer Mc–Si, ADP drawer M–Z, "Alexandra J.," ORC, ADP.

79 TDSBA, Hester How PS, ORC drawer A–D, ADP drawer A–L, "Estelle E.," ORC, ADP.

80 TDSBA, Duke of York PS, ORC TDSB 2003–1307, box 2, ADP TDSB 2003–0835, "Henry V.," ORC, ADP.

81 TDSBA, Duke of York PS, ORC TDSB 2003–1309, box 8, ADP TDSB 2003–0834b, box 2 of 2, "Edward B.," ORC, ADP.

82 See appendix A for an important note on this group's history in Toronto and how I identified them in the pupil record card sample.

83 Matt T. Salo, "Gypsies/Rom," in Paul Robert Magosci, ed., *Encyclopedia of Canada's Peoples* (Toronto: Published for the Multicultural History Society of Ontario by the University of Toronto Press, 1999), 642–3; Cynthia Levine-Rasky, *Writing the Roma: Histories, Policies, and Communities in Canada* (Halifax: Fernwood Publishing, 2016), 52. According to their pupil records, practically all of the Romani children in Hester How special classes whose birthplace is known were born in Canada, and more than half of their parents were as well.

84 Salo, "Gypsies/Rom," 645–7; Levine-Rasky, *Writing the Roma*, 52–60. Levine-Rasky warns against regarding all Roma as practicing "Romani orthodoxy," because in reality individuals and families identified to varying degrees with Romani rites and customs and often intermixed them with non-Romani religious observances and identities.

85 Levine-Rasky, *Writing the Roma*, 33–8.

86 Lewis Terman, *The Measurement of Intelligence* (Boston: Houghton Mifflin, 1916), 91–2.

87 Thomas D. Fallace, *Race and the Origins of Progressive Education, 1880–1929* (New York: Teachers College Press, 2015), 145.

88 Ibid.

89 Florence S. Dunlop, "The Identification, Description and Development of the Intellectually Gifted," n.d., 5.

90 Levine-Rasky, *Writing the Roma*, 36–8; Jennifer Bonnell, *Reclaiming the Don: An Environmental History of Toronto's Don River Valley* (Toronto: University of Toronto Press, 2014), 99–104; Robert F. Harney and Harold Troper, *Immigrants: A Portrait of the Urban Experience, 1890–1930* (Toronto: Van Nostrand Reinhold, 1975), 38; Julianna Beaudoin, "Challenging Essentialized Representations of Romani Identities in Canada" (PhD diss., The University of Western Ontario, 2014), 88–90.

91 Duke of York opened only in 1929–30.

92 In keeping with the working-class and blue-collar character of both schools, I found no examples at all in pupil records of single mothers employed in white collar work – e.g., in offices – or in middle-class occupations such as teaching.

93 *TBE Minutes 1934*, 18 April 1934, 81; appendix no. 59, Management Report no. 9, 11 April 1934, adopted 18 April 1934, 265. See also TDSBA (VF), TBE

– Schools – Elem. – Church, Private TBE Minutes, 11 April 1934, 63–6; W.L. Bryan, "Church Street School: A Non-academic School for Boys," *Special Class Teacher* 12, no. 3 (February 1938): 12–13, 26.

94   Murray E. Steele, "An Academic Vocational Class for Boys," *The School* (elem. ed.) 31, no. 6 (February 1943): 495–9.

95   J.M., "Are the Three 'R's' Being Neglected?" *The Bulletin* 7, no. 2 (December 1930): 4.

96   "The Question Answered," *The Bulletin* 7, no. 3 (March 1931): 7–8.

97   L. Helen DeLaporte, "Are We Part of the World?" *Special Class Teacher* 15, no. 3 (May 1941): 68–9.

98   "Individual Instruction," *Special Class Teacher* 15, no. 2 (February 1941): 36.

99   Marian K. Harvie, "Oral Reading Tests," *Special Class Teacher* 16, no. 1 (November 1941): 15–19; Marian K. Harvie, "Oral Reading Tests," *Special Class Teacher* 16, no. 3 (May 1942): 74–5, 89–90.

100 On Harvie's career, see Hackett, "The History of Public Education for Mentally Retarded Children in the Province of Ontario 1867–1964," 178.

101 Smith, *American Reading Instruction*, 216–17.

102 Ontario, Legislative Assembly, *Report of the Minister of Education Province of Ontario for the Year 1936* (Toronto: T.E. Bowman, 1937), 48.

103 *Mary, John, and Peter: The Ontario Readers Primer* (Toronto: T. Eaton Co, 1933); Robert Stamp, *The Schools of Ontario, 1876–1976* (Toronto: University of Toronto Press, 1982), 168; Smith, *American Reading Instruction*, 212–29. See, e.g., William S. Gray and May Arbuthnot, *Fun with Dick and Jane* (Toronto: Gage & Co, 1940), in the Curriculum Foundation Series.

104 J.A. Long, "Department of Educational Research Ontario College of Education, Report of Activities, 1943–44," *The School* (elem. ed.) 32, no. 10 (June 1944): 848.

105 Christou, *Progressive Education*, 117.

106 Ontario, Legislative Assembly, *Report of the Minister of Education Province of Ontario for the Year 1937*, 47.

107 Ibid.

108 Christou, *Progressive Education*, 66–7; Amy von Heyking, *Creating Citizens: History and Identity in Alberta's Schools, 1905–1980* (Calgary: University of Calgary Press, 2006), 69–71.

109 Ontario, Legislative Assembly, *Report of the Minister of Education Province of Ontario for the Year 1937*, 47.

110 See chapter 2.

111 L.H. DeLaporte, "Books for Retarded Adolescents," *Special Class Teacher* 19, no. 1 (November 1944): 5.

112 Ibid., 8.

113 DeLaporte, "Are We Part of the World?," 68–9.

114 F. Pearl Malloy, "Devices in Enterprise Work for Auxiliary Classes," *The School* (elem. ed.) 2, no. 7 (1944): 622–4. On the enterprise, see von Heyking, *Creating Citizens*, 67–8.

115 J. McGivney, "Teaching Reading to Non-academic Adolescents Who Have Not Completed Grade I of the Primary School," part 1, *Special Class Teacher* 19, no. 2 (February 1945): 51. See also J. McGivney, "Teaching Reading to Non-academic Adolescents Who Have Not Completed Grade I of the Primary School," part 2, *Special Class Teacher* 19, no. 3 (May 1945): 93–5.

116 Koerber, "An Evaluation of Some Methods and Procedures in the Teaching of Reading to Non-academic Adolescent Boys," 2, 138–42.

117 J. McGivney, "Teaching Reading," part 2, 93–5.

118 TDSBA, TDSB 2003–0534, Scrapbook, vol. 3 (1944–7), "Parents' Day," September 1945.

6 Changing Ideas in a Changing Environment

1 Florence S. Dunlop, "The School Psychologist," *The School* (elem. ed.) 28, no. 9 (May 1940): 753.

2 Mona Gleason, *Small Matters: Canadian Children in Sickness and Health* (Montreal: McGill-Queen's University Press, 2013), 122.

3 Erika Dyck, *Facing Eugenics: Reproduction, Sterilization, and the Politics of Choice* (Toronto: University of Toronto Press, 2013); Wendy Kline, *Building a Better Race: Gender, Sexuality, and Eugenics from the Turn of the Century to the Baby Boom* (Berkeley: University of California Press, 2001); Alexandra Minna Stern, *Eugenic Nation: Faults and Frontiers of Better Breeding in America*, 2nd ed. (Berkeley: University of California Press, 2016).

4 Mona Gleason, *Normalizing the Ideal: Psychology, Schooling, and the Family in Postwar Canada* (Toronto: University of Toronto Press, 1999), 23–4; Hans Pols, "Divergences in American Psychiatry during the Depression: Somatic Psychiatry, Community Mental Hygiene, and Social Reconstruction," *Journal of the History of the Behavioral Sciences* 37, no. 4 (fall 2001): 369–88; Kathleen W. Jones, *Taming the Troublesome Child: American Families, Child Guidance, and the Limits of Psychiatric Authority* (Cambridge, MA: Harvard University Press, 1999), 1–3. See also Sol Cohen, "The Mental Hygiene Movement, the Development of Personality and the School: The Medicalization of American Education," *History of Education Quarterly* 23, no. 2 (summer 1983): 128; Theresa Richardson, *The Century of the Child:*

The Mental Hygiene Movement and Social Policy in the United States and Canada (Albany: SUNY Press, 1989), 87–127.

5   Gleason, *Normalizing the Ideal*, 23–4. See also Catherine Gidney, *Tending the Student Body: Youth, Health, and the Modern University* (Toronto: University of Toronto Press, 2015), 150–61.

6   *TBE Annual Report 1925*, 91–5; Richardson, *The Century of the Child*, 118–19.

7   Richardson, *The Century of the Child*, 117–23.

8   Angus McLaren, *Our Own Master Race: Eugenics in Canada, 1885–1945* (Toronto: Oxford University Press, 1990), 109–13.

9   Ibid., 111–12.

10   Richardson, *The Century of the Child*, 117–23; McLaren, *Our Own Master Race*, 111; Hans Pols, "Between the Laboratory and Life: Child Development Research in Toronto, 1919–1956," *History of Psychology* 5, no. 2 (2002): 135–6.

11   Jones, *Taming the Troublesome Child*, 72–3; Gleason, *Normalizing the Ideal*, 28–31; Pols, "Between the Laboratory and Life," 136–45.

12   *TBE Annual Report 1925*, 91–5; Richardson, *The Century of the Child*, 118–19.

13   Richardson, *The Century of the Child*, 121.

14   Ibid.

15   Gidney, *Tending the Student Body*, 164–72.

16   *TBE Minutes 1930*, 2 October 1930, 197–8.

17   Gleason, *Normalizing the Ideal*, 24–31; Cohen, "The Mental Hygiene Movement, the Development of Personality and the School," 134–9; Gerald E. Thomson, "'Not an Attempt to Coddle Children': Dr Charles Hegler Gundry and the Mental Hygiene Division of the Vancouver School Board, 1939–1969," *Historical Studies in Education/Revue d'histoire de l'éducation* 14, no. 2 (fall 2002): 247–78.

18   See C.G. Stogdill, "Mental Hygiene in Toronto Schools," *The Bulletin* 9, no. 2 (November 1932): 4–6; CTA, fonds 200, Department of Public Health Reports, file 16, box 224909, folio 1, "Monthly Reports of the Medical Officer of Health, 1932," Report no. 11 of the Medical Officer of Health, October 1932, 2.

19   A. Buie, "Dr Charles G. Stogdill Appointed Director, Division of Mental Hygiene," *The Bulletin* 8, no. 2 (November 1931): 10.

20   Isabel J. Dalzell, "Psychiatric Social Work with the Maladjusted Child of Normal Intelligence," *Canadian Public Health Journal* 25, no. 12 (January 1934): 602.

21   CTA, fonds 200, Department of Public Health Reports, file 16, box 224909, folio 7, "Monthly Reports of the Medical Officer of Health, 1938," Monthly Report of the Medical Officer of Health, March 1938, 2.

22 Jones, *Taming the Troublesome Child*, 94.
23 Ibid.
24 Ibid., 150–2.
25 Kari Dehli, "Women and Class: The Social Organization of Mothers' Relations to Schools in Toronto, 1915–1940" (PhD diss., University of Toronto, 1988), 354–64.
26 S.R. Laycock, "Meeting the Needs of Children in Special Classes," *Special Class Teacher* 17, no. 2 (February 1943): 43. See also S.R. Laycock, "Mental Hygiene in Special Education," *Journal of Exceptional Children* (October 1936): 2. On Laycock's career, see Gleason, *Normalizing the Ideal*, 37–51.
27 Gleason, *Normalizing the Ideal*, 4–5; Gleason, *Small Matters*, 133–5.
28 Gleason, *Small Matters*, 120–7.
29 Samuel R. Laycock, "The Mental Hygiene of Exceptional Children" (part 1), *Special Class Teacher* 15, no. 3 (May 1941): 75; Laycock, "Mental Hygiene in Special Education," 3. See also J.D.M. Griffin, S.R. Laycock, and W. Line, *Mental Hygiene: A Manual for Teachers* (New York: American Book, 1940), 151.
30 Laycock, "Mental Hygiene of Exceptional Children" (part 1), 75–6.
31 Jones, *Taming the Troublesome Child*, 150.
32 Ibid., 164–5.
33 Daisy Hally, "Mental Hygiene Approach to a Better Understanding of Children's Reactions," *Proceedings of the Seventy-Third Convention of the OEA* (Toronto: OEA, 1934), 76–8.
34 Laycock, "Mental Hygiene of Exceptional Children," 76 (emphasis original).
35 Richardson, *The Century of the Child*, 89.
36 Griffin et al., *Mental Hygiene*, 156.
37 Laycock, "Mental Hygiene in Special Education," 5. See also, Griffin et al., *Mental Hygiene*, 154–5.
38 Laycock, "Mental Hygiene in Special Education," 5.
39 Laycock, "Meeting the Needs of Children in Special Classes," 65–8.
40 Jones, *Taming the Troublesome Child*, 174–88; Gleason, *Normalizing the Ideal*, 30–1.
41 See also J.D.M. Griffin, "Educating the Victim of Polio," *Special Class Teacher* 12, no. 3 (February 1938): 20. See chapter 4 of this book for a description of the pitying approach.
42 Laycock, "Mental Hygiene of Exceptional Children" (part 1), 75–6. See also Stogdill, "Mental Hygiene in Toronto Schools," 6.
43 Theodore Michael Christou, *Progressive Education: Revisioning and Reframing Ontario Public Schools, 1919–1942* (Toronto: University of Toronto Press, 2012), 71–6, 126–8.

44 Paul Witty, "Diagnostic Testing and Remedial Teaching," *Understanding the Child* 7, no. 1 (April 1938): 3.

45 C.G. Stogdill, "Subject Disabilities: A Symptom," *Understanding the Child* 7, no. 1 (April 1938): 8–9.

46 Elizabeth Bowling, "The Stutterer," *The School* (elem. ed.) 29, no. 10 (June 1941): 934–6. See also Ruth Lewis, "Speech Defects and the Classroom Teacher," *The School* (elem. ed.) 33, no. 1 (September 1944): 47–9.

47 Grace M. Fernald, *Remedial Techniques in Basic School Subjects* (New York: McGraw-Hill, 1943 [reprint 1971]), 7–8.

48 Emmett Albert Betts, *The Prevention and Correction of Reading Difficulties* (Evanston, IL: Row, Peterson, and Co, 1936), 231–2.

49 See also Richardson, *The Century of the Child*, 118.

50 TDSBA, Duke of York PS, ORC TDSB 2003–1307, box 1, ADP TDSB 2003–0835, "Daisy T.," ORC, ADP.

51 TDSBA, Coleman PS, ORC microfilm reel 10, "Yvonne T.," ORC. Only Yvonne's mother's information is present on her ORC, which suggests that her mother was raising her without her father.

52 TDSBA, Coleman PS, ORC microfilm reel 10, "Wendell A.," ORC.

53 TDSBA, Duke of York PS, ORC TDSB 2003–1309, box 10, ADP TDSB 2003–0835, "Bruce D.," ORC, ADP.

54 TDSBA, Duke of York PS, ORC TDSB 2003–1308, box 7, ADP TDSB 2003–0834, box 1 of 2, "Bonnie C.," ORC, ADP.

55 TDSBA, Duke of York PS, ORC TDSB 2003–1309, box 10, ADP TDSB 2003–0834, box 1 of 2, "Ella V.," ORC, ADP.

56 See chapter 3.

57 Jane Little, "Vocational Guidance in the Edith L. Groves School," *Special Class Teacher* 13, no. 3 (February 1939): 90; CAMHA, Burdett McNeel Fonds, Provincial Psychiatric Clinics: Lectures. B.T. McGhie (ed.), W.J. Tamblyn, "The Junior Vocational School," n.d.

58 CAMHA, Tamblyn, "The Junior Vocational School."

59 J. McGivney, "Teaching Reading to Non-academic Adolescents Who Have Not Completed Grade I of the Primary School" (part 1), *Special Class Teacher* 19, no. 2 (February 1945): 52. See also Walter F. Koerber, "An Evaluation of Some Methods and Procedures in the Teaching of Reading to Non-academic Adolescent Boys" (DPaed thesis, University of Toronto, 1947), 2–3.

60 *TBE Annual Report 1930*, 55–6.

61 Grace I. Mackenzie, "Vocational Training for the Adolescent Girl," *Proceedings of the Sixty-Ninth Convention of the OEA* (Toronto: OEA, 1930),

80–1. See also Marjorie Larkin, "A Social Worker Discusses 'Backward' Children," *Special Class Teacher* 13, no. 2 (September 1938): 50.

62 R.D. Gidney and W.P.J. Millar, *How Schools Worked: Public Education in English-Canada* (Montreal: McGill-Queen's University Press), 169–78. This is not saying that the occasional eyebrow was not raised about spending.

63 *TBE Annual Report 1928*, 406.

64 Ontario, Legislative Assembly, *Report of the Minister of Education Province of Ontario for the Year 1929* (Toronto: Herbert H. Ball, 1930), 133, 241, 333. To arrive at this total, I summed figures from three different columns in the report – instructional expenses, maintenance expenses, and debt charges – across the separate tables for elementary schools, collegiate institutes, and technical and commercial schools (day and night programs and the college of art included).

65 *TBE Annual Report 1928*, 408.

66 Moshier's figures for the TBE's elementary school auxiliary programs include approximately $34,000 in expenditures for two forest schools. The provincial auxiliary class grant did not cover this program. Moshier's figures are for 1928, presumably for the calendar year. The province tracked its figures though by school year. The first school year for which the inspector of auxiliary classes provided figures in his report is 1928–9, the school year that I have used everywhere in this paragraph. See Ontario, Legislative Assembly, *Report of the Minister of Education Province of Ontario for the Year 1929*, 30. The amount of Toronto's grant for junior vocational schools, which the DOE called "Promotion and Special Industrial Classes" (ibid., 31), was not reported. Hamilton, however, received $2,600 for classes of this sort with an enrolment about one-quarter that of Toronto's classes. This would suggest that the TBE would have been in line for about $10,400, although the sources I have at hand do not allow me to confirm this figure.

67 "Retire Women Early Compared to Men," *Toronto Daily Star*, 8 April 1938, 8; TDSBA, box 2003–0534, Scrapbook, vol. 2, clipped letter, "Soaring Costs of Education. Big Sums Spent on Certain of the Schools in Toronto," *Toronto Telegram*, n.d., n.p. See also *TBE Minutes 1938*, 7 April 1938, 117.

68 James T. Lemon, *Toronto since 1918: An Illustrated History* (Toronto: James Lorimer and Company and National Museums of Canada, 1985), 59–79.

69 Ontario, Legislative Assembly, *Report of the Minister of Education Province of Ontario for the Year 1931* to *Report of the Minister of Education Province of Ontario for the Year 1940* (Toronto: various publishers), Financial Statistics.

The mill rate is the standard unit used to levy local property taxes across Canada and the United States. It typically has a municipal portion, which goes to local services such as sewer, water, fire, police, and the like, and an education portion that funds local schools. One "mill" is 1/1,000th of a property's value. See Gidney and Millar, *How Schools Worked*, 152–62, for further explanation.

Why was the TBE able to remain solvent? A complete answer would require more thorough investigation than is possible here. A partial, but I hope still convincing, one follows. It managed to keep amassing funds without significantly raising the education portion of the mill rate, or local property tax rate. The rate remained stable at around 10 mills from 1929 through to about 1936. It was, for instance: 10.2 mills in 1929; 10.45 mills in 1931; 10.3 mills in 1933; and 10.5 mills in 1935. See "School Budget down Salaries left Alone," *Toronto Daily Star*, 12 February 1935, 23; TDSBA, *TBE Annual Financial Statement and Statistics 1939*, 23. The board raised the rate to 11.45 mills in 1937 and again to 11.55 mills in 1938. Even the approximately one-mill increase in the latter period, adding around 10 per cent to every taxpayer's bill, was not exorbitant after years of stable rates. Property taxes remained low largely because Torontonians continued to pay them. If they had fallen into arrears, revenues would have declined. Trustees then would have had to choose between cutting services to reduce expenditures or drastically increasing the mill rate to recoup the shortfall from the ratepayers who still were paying. This vicious cycle of arrears, spending cuts, and rate increases is precisely what transpired in the Toronto suburbs and in other suburbs, small towns, and rural townships across the country, plunging them into crisis conditions. See "School Tax Rates Generally Lower," *Toronto Daily Star*, 15 March 1933, 16; Ontario, Legislative Assembly, *Report of the Minister of Education Province of Ontario for the Year 1935* (Toronto: T.E. Bowman, 1936), 121; Gidney and Millar, *How Schools Worked*, 183–6. However, Toronto residents were better positioned than others. Job losses in the city (though bad) were not as severe as in the suburbs. City homeowners were more established in their houses, and less likely to carry mortgages than suburbanites. The latter, caught between paying the bank or the tax collector, reasonably saw fore-closure as the bigger threat and paid the bank first; sometimes they paid only the bank. City tenants doubled and tripled-up in existing housing. More people living in a unit meant a greater likelihood that they could together make the rent and the building owner could in turn pay the taxes. Richard Harris, *Unplanned Suburbs: Toronto's American Tragedy, 1900 to 1950* (Baltimore: Johns Hopkins University Press, 1996), 234–56.

70 Robert M. Stamp, *The Schools of Ontario, 1876–1976* (Toronto: University of Toronto Press, 1982), 143.

71 *TBE Annual Report 1929*, 388.

72 TDSBA, *TBE Annual Financial Statement and Statistics 1939*. However, while teachers' salaries dropped, so did prices, which meant their purchasing power remained level. See Stamp, *Schools of Ontario*, 147. The TBE even had sufficient resources to spend $1 million on new capital projects between 1934 and 1938. See TDSBA, *TBE Annual Financial Statement and Statistics 1939*. In this respect, Toronto fared about as well as the seven other Canadian cities that, Gidney and Millar note, also rather surprisingly increased educational spending despite the depression: Halifax, Saint John, Quebec City, Toronto, Hamilton, Ottawa, London, and Edmonton all spent more in 1933 than they had in 1929. See Gidney and Millar, *How Schools Worked*, 181.

73 David Tyack, Robert Lowe, and Elisabeth Hansot, *Public Schools in Hard Times: The Great Depression and Recent Years* (Cambridge, MA: Harvard University Press, 1984), 39–40.

74 TDSBA, box TDSB 2003–0534, Scrapbook, vol. 1, clipping, "1,000 Girls Guests of Toronto Women," 4 Dec 1930, n.p.; "Women of Toronto Tender Reception to School Pupils," *Globe*, 8 December, n.p. See also *TBE Annual Report 1930*, 60–1.

75 TDSBA, box TDSB 2003–0534, Scrapbook, vol. 2, clipping, "Bolton School Open House an Eye-opener for Many."

76 Charles M. Elliott, "The Toronto Meeting," *International Council for Exceptional Children Review* 1, no. 1 (May 1934): 4–5, 9, 25; TDSBA, box TDSB 2003–0534, Bolton Avenue School for Girls Photographs, "International Council for Exceptional Children. Visiting Programme, Thursday, February 22nd, 1934."

77 Ruth Roach Pierson, *"They're Still Women After All": The Second World War and Canadian Womanhood* (Toronto: McClelland and Stewart, 1986), 49–61; Jennifer Stephen, *Pick One Intelligent Girl: Employability, Domesticity, and the Gendering of Canada's Welfare State, 1939–1947* (Toronto: University of Toronto Press, 2007), 18–65.

78 Stephen, *Pick One Intelligent Girl*, 25–6.

79 Stamp, *The Schools of Ontario*, 171–4; John Allison, "Technical Schooling in Toronto: Growing up in the Trades during the Second World War," *Historical Studies in Education/Revue d'histoire de l'éducation* 28, no. 1 (spring 2016): 53–72.

80 TDSBA (VF), TBE – Biography – Goldring, Cecil Charles, C.C. Goldring, "A Forward Look at Toronto School System" (Toronto: TBE, 1943), 17–19.

81 Allison, "Technical Schooling in Toronto," 64–5.

82 "Nursery Training Course in the Edith L. Groves School, Toronto, Canada," *Special Class Teacher* 16, no. 2 (February 1942): 42. The author of this article, although unnamed, would seem to be Jane Little. A remarkably similar article that Little did claim authorship for appeared in *The School* a few months afterwards. Jane Little, "The Nursery Training Course in the Edith L. Groves School for Girls," *The School* (elem. ed.) 31, no. 2 (October 1942): 110–12.

83 Little, "The Nursery Training Course," 110.

84 Ibid.

85 Little, "Nursery Training Course," 42.

86 Little, "The Nursery Training Course," 110.

87 Little, "Nursery Training Course," 42.

88 Josephine Budden, "Boulton Avenue Nursery School," *Special Class Teacher* 19, no. 3 (May 1945): 114–15.

89 Little, "The Nursery Training Course," 111–12.

90 Budden, "Boulton Avenue Nursery School," 114–15.

91 Ibid.

92 TDSBA (VF), TBE – Biography – Goldring, Cecil Charles, C.C. Goldring, "A Forward Look at Toronto School System" (Toronto: TBE, 1943), 26–7.

93 Margret A. Winzer, *From Integration to Inclusion: A History of Special Education in the 20th Century* (Washington: Gallaudet University Press, 2009), 99–100.

94 Gleason, *Normalizing the Ideal*, 32.

95 TDSBA, [unaccessioned material], box marked "TBE Records, Archives & Museum, Parkview S.S.," spiral-bound notebook, "Record of Graduate Visitors."

96 TDSBA (VF), TBE Schools – Sec. – Jarvis C.I.; J.W. McIntosh, "Follow-up Study of One Thousand Non-academic Boys," *Journal of Exceptional Children* 15 (March 1949): 166–70, 191.

Conclusion

1 Ontario, Legislative Assembly, *Third Report upon the Care of the Feeble-Minded in Ontario, 1908*, Toronto: 1909 (Sessional Papers 1912, no. 58), 25.

2 David B. Tyack, *The One Best System: A History of American Urban Education* (Cambridge, MA: Harvard University Press, 1974), 177–216.

3 TDSBA (VF), TBE Schools – Elementary – High Park Forest School, C.C. Goldring memorandum to the Chairman and Members of the Board of Education, 19 April 1944.

4 *TBE Minutes 1964*, 6 February 1964, 20–1.
5 James T. Lemon, *Toronto since 1918: An Illustrated History* (Toronto: James Lorimer and Company and National Museums of Canada, 1985), 70.
6 See TDSBA, historical collection, C.G. Stogdill, "Special Education Facilities in Public and Secondary Schools Operated by the TBE," 1 October 1956, 6.
7 Lewis M. Terman, *The Intelligence of Schoolchildren* (Boston: Houghton-Mifflin, 1919), 24–5.
8 See Bruce Curtis, D.W. Livingstone, and Harry Smaller, *Stacking the Deck: The Streaming of Working-Class Kids in Ontario Schools* (Toronto: Our Schools/ Our Selves, 1992), 83–98.
9 TDSBA, historical collection, Stogdill, "Special Education Facilities in Public and Secondary Schools Operated by the TBE."
10 Janis Gershman, "The Evaluation of Special Education Programs: Past Attempts and Present Directions," Report no. 134 (Toronto: TBE, 1975), 2.
11 TDSBA, Director of Education Miscellaenous Files, box 9, file Reply to Trefann Court Brief, "A Response to the Report of N.A. Sweetman and G.A. Gore on Opportunity Classes," 10 February 1970, 4.
12 Ibid., 6.
13 Jason Ellis and Paul Axelrod, "Continuity and Change: Special Education Policy Development in Toronto Public Schools, 1945–present," *Teachers College Record* 118, no. 2 (February 2016): 12–15, http://www.tcrecord. org/Content.asp?ContentId=18228. This sort of study of the over-representation of working-class and minority pupils, as well as boys, in special education became quite popular in the late 1960s and early 1970s. This probably had to do with that era's intensive critique of urban schooling as bureaucratic, cold, repressive of minority students, and limiting of their opportunities. For an overview of the United States, in which the authors trace the identification of these issues back to Lloyd Dunn's 1968 "classic critique of the field" (265), see Russell J. Skiba, Ada B. Simmons, Shana Ritter, et al., "Achieving Equity in Special Education: History, Status, and Current Challenges," *Exceptional Children* 74, no. 3 (2008): 264–88. The original sources are Lloyd M. Dunn, "Special Education for the Mildly Retarded: Is Much of It Justifiable?" *Exceptional Children* 35, no. 1 (September 1968): 5–22; and for a similar critique, Jane R. Mercer, *Labelling the Mentally Retarded: Clinical and Social System Perspectives on Mental Retardation* (Berkeley: University of California Press, 1973). See also, more recently, James G. Carrier, *Learning Disability: Social Class and the Construction of Inequality in American Education* (Westport, CT: Greenwood Press, 1986); Sally Tomlinson, *A Sociology of Special Education* (London: Routledge, 1982). Dunn, who was born and taught in Saskatchewan,

influenced Canadian special education as well. See Ellis and Axelrod, "Continuity and Change," 15; and Cheryl Hanley-Maxwell and Lana Collet-Klingenberg, "Chapter 4: Biographies of Key Contributors in the Field," in Hanley-Maxwell and Collet-Klingenberg, eds., *Education*, the Sage Reference Series on Disability Key Issues and Future Directions (Los Angeles, CA: Sage, 2011), 153–4.

On the history of over-representation in Canadian schools specifically, see Curtis, Livingstone, and Smaller, *Stacking the Deck*; and, more recently, David Clandfield et al., *Restacking the Deck: Streaming by Class, Race, and Gender in Ontario Schools* (Toronto: Our Schools/Our Selves, 2014).

There are also several historical case studies of the United States. See Ferri and Connor, "In the Shadow of Brown," 96–9; David J. Connor and Beth A. Ferri, "Integration and Inclusion – A Troubling Nexus: Race, Disability, and Special Education," *Journal of African American History* 90, no. 1/2 (winter 2005): 107–27; Adam R. Nelson, "Equity and Special Education: Some Historical Lessons from Boston," in Kenneth K. Wong and Robert Rothman, eds., *Clio at the Table: Using History to Inform and Improve Education Policy* (New York: Peter Lang, 2009), 157–79.

14 E.N. Wright, "Student's Background and its Relationship to Class and Programme in School, the Every Student Survey" (Toronto: TBE Research Service, 1970), 34–5.

15 Data that predates the 1950s is almost impossible to come by, although see E. Anne Bennison, "Creating Categories of Competence: The Education of Exceptional Children in the Milwaukee Public Schools, 1908–1917" (PhD diss., University of Wisconsin-Madison, 1988), 328–49. She was able to reconstruct the ethnic and occupational and class origins of upwards of 200 pupils who attended Milwaukee auxiliary classes from 1908 to 1917. She found that (345) "a majority of exceptional children students were first-generation Americans from working-class backgrounds."

16 Sherman Dorn, Douglas Fuchs, and Lynn S. Fuchs, "A Historical Perspective on Special Education Reform," *Theory into Practice* 35, no. 1 (1996): 12–19; Robert L. Osgood, *The History of Inclusion in the United States* (Washington: Gallaudet University Press, 2005), 1.

17 See chapter 1 of this book; Charles S. Hartwell, "The Grading and Promotion of Pupils," *Journal of Proceedings and Addresses of the Forty-Eighth Meeting of the National Education Association* (Winona, MN: National Education Association, 1910), 294–305; John Kennedy, *The Batavia System of Individual Instruction* (Syracuse, NY: C.W. Bardeen, 1914).

18 Bruce Uditsky, "From Integration to Inclusion: The Canadian Experience," in Roger Slee, ed., *Is There a Desk with My Name on It? The Politics of*

Integration (London: Falmer, 1993), 81–2; Osgood, *The History of Inclusion in the United States*, 85–109.

19 Ellis and Axelrod, "Continuity and Change," 16–17; Osgood, *The History of Inclusion in the United States*, 92–3.

20 Osgood, *The History of Inclusion in the United States*, 100–6.

21 Ellis and Axelrod, "Continuity and Change," 18–22.

22 The TBE reported that it "served" 8,225 special education students out of a total elementary enrolment of 43,734 and 1,245 students in a secondary enrolment of 33,361. *TBE Annual Report 1982*, 14.

23 Maisy Cheng and Maria Yau, "Every Secondary Student Survey, 1997: Detailed Findings," report no. 230 (Toronto: TDSB, 1999), 6, 43.

24 Ellis and Axelrod, "Continuity and Change," 23–6.

25 Ibid., 27.

26 Ibid. See also Uditksy, "From Integration to Inclusion," 86–90; Osgood, *The History of Inclusion in the United States*, 183–7.

27 Robert S. Brown and Gillian Parekh, "The Intersection of Disability, Achievement, and Equity: A System Review of Special Education in the TDSB," Research Report no. 12–13-12 (Toronto: TDSB, 2013), 16. This phenomenon of students receiving services prior to diagnosis and placement has increased dramatically in the 2010s. Ellis and Axelrod, "Continuity and Change," 28–9.

28 *Minutes of the* TDSB *1998*, report no. 2, Special Education Advisory Committee, 9 April 1998, 267, http://www.tdsb.on.ca/Leadership/Boardroom/Agenda-Minutes.

29 TDSB, TDSB *Financial Facts: Revenue and Expenditure Trends* (Toronto: TDSB, 2018), 25, http://www.tdsb.on.ca/Portals/0/AboutUs/docs/FinancialFacts_April2018.pdf.

30 TBE, *Annual Financial Statement 1943*. Net expenditures (less government grants worth about 5 per cent of total expenditures) for instruction, operations, maintenance, administration, and capital costs. Later figures are not available.

31 Ellis and Axelrod, "Continuity and Change," 31.

32 Ibid., 28–9.

33 Thomas E. Scruggs and Margo A. Mastropieri, "Teacher Perceptions of Mainstreaming/Inclusion, 1958–1995: A Research Synthesis," *Exceptional Children* 63, no. 1 (October 1996): 59–74; Anne Jordan, Christine Glenn, and Donna McGhie-Richmond, "The Supporting Effective Teaching (SET) Project: The Relationship of Inclusive Teaching Practices to Teachers' Beliefs about Disability and Ability, and about Their Roles as Teachers," *Teaching and Teacher Education* 26, no. 2 (February 2010): 259–66.

34 Pletsch, *Not Wanted in the Classroom: Parent Associations and the Education of Trainable Retarded Children in Ontario: 1947–1969* (London, ON: Althouse Press, 1997); Uditsky, "From Integration to Inclusion," 81–2; Osgood, *The History of Inclusion in the United States*, 100–6.
35 Ellis and Axelrod, "Continuity and Change," 26–7.
36 David Philpott and Christina Fiedorowicz, "The Supreme Court of Canada Ruling on Learning Disabilities" (Learning Disabilities Association of Canada, 2012), http://www.ldac-acta.ca/downloads/pdf/advocacy/Education%20Implications%20-%20Moore%20Decision.pdf.
37 TDSBA (VF), TBE – Curriculum – Special Education, Edna Barg, "Sight Saving Class," *Recording Recollections at Ryerson* 8, no. 3 (December 1989): 7.
38 Osgood, *The History of Inclusion in the United States*, 179.
39 Judy Lupart and Charles Webber, "Canadian Schools in Transition: Moving from Dual Education Systems to Inclusive Schools," *Exceptionality Education International* 22, no. 2 (2012): 8–37.

Appendix A

1 *TBE Minutes 1916*, appendix no. 61, Management Report no. 14, 31 May 1916, adopted 8 June 1916, 621; Roy Reynolds and Donald J. Netherty, *An Annotated Guide to the Manuscripts in the Historical Collection of the TBE*, Educational Records series, OISE, no. 13 (Toronto: TBE, 1977), 84. On the introduction of pupil record card systems, see American Association of School Administrators, *Committee on Uniform Records and Reports of the National Education Association. Final Report of the Committee on Uniform Records and Reports to the National Council at the St Louis Meeting* (Chicago: University of Chicago Press, 1912); *School Management*, Ontario Normal School Manuals (Toronto: William Briggs, 1915), 195–201.
2 See the introduction of this book for a discussion of this point.
3 See also Robert C. Vipond, *Making a Global City: How One Toronto School Embraced Diversity* (Toronto: University of Toronto Press, 2017), 19. Vipond also used ORCs, in this case from Clinton PS. He writes that "there are, presumably, other complete sets of registration cards for other schools both in Toronto and elsewhere." A few sets for Toronto are in fact listed in Reynolds and Netherty, *An Annotated Guide*.
4 Reynolds and Netherty, *An Annotated Guide*, 84.
5 TDSBA, "Brief Chronological History of TBE Schools No Longer in Existence," typescript, 1984, 10–16. Duke of York's original site closed in 1980 to vacate the building for the French-language public school

Gabrielle Roy. The school was relocated and amalgamated with Regent Park, and the Regent Park/Duke of York school was ordered closed in 2011. "Duke of York to Be French School," *Globe and Mail*, 16 May 1980, 5; *TDSB minutes*, 16 November 2011, 53, http://www.tdsb.on.ca/Leadership/Boardroom/Agenda-Minutes.

6 TDSBA, ADP, Hester How PS, drawers A–L, M–Z, 1923–4; ORC, Hester How PS, drawers A–D, E–I, J–M, Mc–Si, Sh–Z; ADP, Duke of York PS, TDSB 2003–0834 (2 boxes), TDSB 2003–0835, TDSB 2003–0836, TDSB 2003–0837; ORC, Duke of York PS, TDSB 2003–1307, box 1–4, TDSB 2003–1308, box 5–7, TDSB 2003–1309, box 8–11; ADP, Coleman PS, microfilm reel 11; ORC, Coleman PS, microfilm reel 10. By using the Coleman microfilm, I hoped to contribute to the long-term preservation of the originals by avoiding adding wear and tear on the brittle paper cards on which they are printed.

7 TDSBA (VF), TBE – Schools – Elementary – Hester How PS, C.C. Goldring, "History of Hester How Public School," *TBE Minutes 1953*, appendix, 257–61.

8 TDSBA (VF), TBE – Schools – Elementary – Hester How PS, James L. Hughes, "Hester How," *The School* (December 1915), 300–5. On the Ward generally, see Toronto Bureau of Municipal Research, *What Is "the Ward" Going to Do with Toronto?* (Toronto: Toronto Bureau of Municipal Research, 1918); several essays in Harney, *Gathering Place*; and John Lorinc, Michael McClelland, Ellen Scheinberg, and Tatum Taylor, eds., *The Ward: The Life and Loss of Toronto's First Immigrant Neighbourhood* (Toronto: Coach House, 2015).

9 Toronto Bureau of Municipal Research, *What Is "the Ward" Going to Do with Toronto?*, 7.

10 *TBE Minutes 1930*, appendix no. 82, Management Report no. 11, 7 May 1930, adopted 15 May 1930, 757–75.

11 Robert F. Harney, "Ethnicity and Neighbourhoods," in Harney, *Gathering Place*, 17.

12 Goldring, "History of Hester How Public School," 259.

13 Harney, "Ethnicity and Neighbourhoods," 17.

14 Toronto Bureau of Municipal Research, *What Is "the Ward" Going to Do with Toronto?*, 5.

15 Luigi G. Pennacchio, "The Defence of Identity: Ida Siegel and the Jews of Toronto versus the Assimilation Attempts of the Public School and Its Allies, 1900–1920," *Canadian Jewish Historical Society Journal* 9, no. 1 (spring 1985): 41–60.

16 Toronto Bureau of Municipal Research, *What Is "the Ward" Going to Do with Toronto?*, 58–60.

17 *TBE Minutes 1910*, appendix no. 34, Management Report no. 12, 23 June 1910, 425.
18 *TBE Minutes 1930*, appendix no. 82, Management Report no. 11, 7 May 1930, adopted 15 May 1930, 757–75.
19 Ibid.
20 *The Toronto City Directory 1921*, vol. 46 (Toronto: Might Directories Limited, 1921). See also Nadine A. Hooper, "Toronto: A Study in Urban Geography" (MA thesis, University of Toronto, 1941), 70 and figure 39, plate 8 of 8.
21 Richard Harris, *Unplanned Suburbs: Toronto's American Tragedy, 1900 to 1950* (Baltimore: Johns Hopkins University Press, 1996), 58–9.
22 TBE, *Board of Education Toronto. Handbook Nineteen-Nineteen* (Toronto: J.R. Irving, 1919), 44.
23 James Lemon, *Toronto since 1918: An Illustrated History* (Toronto: James Lorimer and National Museums of Canada, 1985), 51.
24 *TBE Annual Report 1930*, 106.
25 *TBE Minutes 1930*, appendix no. 82, Management Report no. 11, 7 May 1930, adopted 15 May 1930, 757–75.
26 Hooper, "Toronto: A Study in Urban Geography," 69–71 and figure 39, plate 7 of 8.
27 Lemon, *Toronto since 1918*, 51.
28 I do not count the students who never attended in my statistical tables of auxiliary pupils.
29 There were many fewer instances of ADPs for which the corresponding ORC was missing. At Hester How, for example, this appears to have occurred in approximately 5 per cent of cases. Presumably, in these cases at some point over time the ORC was lost. Even though cards are missing from both types of collection, there is no indication that the missing or remaining cards were in any way selected. The gaps appear to be random.
30 In a few cases, a child's guardian – that is, someone identified as neither of the child's parents – was recorded. I have treated guardian information (e.g., occupation) as though it were for the child's parent.
31 I initially included a representative sample of Coleman pupils as well, but because this school was very small and did not have auxiliary classes, I decided ultimately to omit it in the quantitative dimension of the analysis. I did record in my notes information on seventy-eight Coleman students who, over the years, transferred to auxiliary programs at other schools, the basis of the discussion of individual Coleman pupils in the book.

The samples of 404 pupils for Hester How and 558 pupils for Duke of York cover the entire periods of 1916–45 and 1929–45, respectively. The tables in the chapters, however, are based on shorter periods that align with the periods the chapters examine. I have therefore tailored the representative samples accordingly to include only records from the period corresponding to that of the chapter. This trims the sample sizes in any given chapter to less than 404 or 558.

32 G. Kitson Clark, *The Making of Victorian England* (London, 1962), 14, qtd. in William O. Aydelotte, "Quantification in History," in D.K. Rowney and J.Q. Graham, eds., *Quantitiave History: Selected Readings in the Quantitative Analysis of Historical Data* (Homewood, IL: Dorsey Press, 1969), 3–22.

33 Michael B. Katz, "Occupational Classification in History," *Journal of Interdisciplinary History* 3, no. 1 (summer 1972): 63–4. This approach to class as an ascribed or descriptive category is itself controversial, because some historians instead regard class a historical process or relationship – as in "class formation" or "class consciousness." For useful overviews of the various issues the debate raises for educational historians in particular, see Paul Axelrod, *Making a Middle Class: Student Life in English Canada during the Thirties* (Montreal: McGill-Queen's University Press, 1990), 167–73; David J. Hogan, *Class and Reform: School and Society in Chicago, 1880–1930* (Philadelphia: University of Pennsylvania Press, 1985), xi–xx. For an excessively polemical, though still somewhat useful, essay on the methodological and ideological distinctions between historians approaching class as a process or as a descriptive category, see Bryan D. Palmer, "Emperor Katz's New Clothes; or with the Wizard in Oz," review of Michael B. Katz, Michael J. Doucet, and Mark J. Stern, *The Social Organization of Early Industrial Capitalism* (Cambridge, MA: Harvard University Press, 1982), *Labour/Le Travail* 13 (spring 1984): 190–9.

34 Axelrod, *Making a Middle Class,* 174–7, was guided by the occupational categories developed by Donald Treiman, *Occupational Prestige in Comparative Perspective* (New York: Academic Press, 1977). See also R.D. Gidney and W.P.J. Millar, *Inventing Secondary Education: The Rise of the High School in Nineteenth-Century Ontario* (Montreal: McGill-Queen's University Press, 1990), 340–1. Gidney and Millar adapted an earlier scheme for nineteenth-century occupations and classes that Canadian social scientists Gordon Darroch and Michael Ornstein developed (A. Gordon Darroch and Michael D. Ornstein, "Ethnicity and Occupational Structure in Canada in 1871: The Vertical Mosaic in Historical Perspective," *Canadian Historical Review* 61, no. 3 [1980]: 305–33). Gidney and Millar "modified the original version of this classification scheme somewhat in order to accommodate the needs of our particular study," for instance by adding new categories for "female heads of households" and "gentlemen." Similarly, Gidney

and Millar, in their article "Medical Students at the University of Toronto, 1910–40: A Profile," *Canadian Bulletin of Medical History/Bulletin canadien d'histoire de la médecine* 13 (1996): 34–46, 49n19, borrowed Axelrod's occupational classification from *Making a Middle Class*. Other good examples are: Wyn Millar, Ruby Heap, and Bob Gidney, "Degrees of Difference: The Students in Three Professional Schools at the University of Toronto, 1910 to the 1950s," in Ruby Heap, Wyn Millar, and Elizabeth Smyth, eds., *Learning to Practise: Professional Education in Historical and Contemporary Perspective* (Ottawa: University of Ottawa Press, 2005), 155–87; Charles Morden Levi, *Comings and Goings: University Students in Canadian Society, 1854–1973* (Montreal: McGill-Queen's University Press, 2003); Chad Gaffield, Lynne Marks, and Susan Laskin, "Student Populations and Graduate Careers: Queen's University, 1895–1900," in Paul Axelrod and John G. Reid, eds., *Youth, University and Canadian Society: Essays in the Social History of Higher Education* (Montreal: McGill-Queen's University Press, 1989), 3–25; Malcolm MacLeod, "Parade Street Parade: The Student Body at Memorial University College, 1925–49," in Axelrod and Reid, *Youth, University and Canadian Society,* 64–6, 69–70n42; Clara Thomas (York University) Archives and Special Collections, MRP 240; Lynne Marks, "New Opportunities within the Separate Sphere" (MA major research paper, York University, 1984).

35 Harris, *Unplanned Suburbs.*

36 Ibid., 293–6. Harris is concerned with owner-built houses as part of the suburbanization process. As a result, he found it useful to separate the building trades from the broader umbrella groups of self-employed and blue-collar workers under which they would ordinarily fall. This distinction is not pertinent to my study, and I did not make it.

37 Ibid., 293–4.

38 Ibid., 293.

39 Robert F. Harney and Harold Troper, *Immigrants: A Portrait of the Urban Experience, 1890–1930* (Toronto: Van Nostrand-Reinhold, 1975), 54–5.

40 Veronica Strong-Boag, *The New Day Recalled: Lives of Girls and Women in English Canada, 1919–1939* (Markham, ON: Penguin, 1988), 51–6.

41 Harris, *Unplanned Suburbs,* 294.

42 Used as a descriptive category, or ascribed characteristic, ethnic origin or ethnicity suffers from many of the same limitations that class does when used in this sense. Ethnic groups are not monolithic or static. They shift over time and are internally divided by place of origin, place of residence, class, political preferences, associational life, and other matters. See Harney, "Ethnicity and Neighbourhoods," 2–12.

43 Pennacchio, "The Defence of Identity"; Luigi G. Pennacchio, "Toronto's Public Schools and the Assimilation of Foreign Students, 1900–1920," *Journal of Educational Thought* 20 (1986): 37–48; Shmuel Shammai, "The Jews and the Public Education System: The Students' Strike over the 'Flag Fight' in Toronto after the First World War," *Canadian Jewish Historical Society Journal* 10, no.1 (fall 1988): 46–53; Jean-Philippe Croteau, "Les Commissions scolaires et les immigrants à Toronto et à Montréal (1900–1945): quatre modèles d'intégration en milieu urbain," *Francophonies d'Amérique* 31 (2011): 49–85.

44 There were significant differences, to be sure, between Canadian-born and immigrant Jews and, for that matter, between immigrant Polish and, say, Hungarian Jews. As with many ethnic groups, Jewish ethnicity was stratified and complex. See Gerald Tulchinsky, *Taking Root: The Origins of the Canadian Jewish Community* (Toronto: Lester, 1982); Gerald Tulchinsky, *Branching Out: The Transformation of the Canadian Jewish Community* (Toronto: Stoddart, 1998).

45 Most – but not all – "Gypsies" in Canada in the early twentieth century were Roma. This is because "Gypsy" and Roma are not directly interchangeable terms. There were in fact several groups of Gypsies that did not necessarily identify as Rom/Roma – namely, Sinti, Manouche, Cale (Kaale), and Rudar (Ludar). Matt T. Salo, "Gypsies/Rom," in Paul R. Magocsi, ed., *Encyclopedia of Canada's Peoples* (Toronto: Multicultural History Society of Ontario and University of Toronto Press, 1999), 642–3; and Cynthia Levine-Rasky, *Writing the Roma: Histories, Policies, and Communities in Canada* (Halifax: Fernwood Publishing, 2016), 11–19.

46 Roma were present in colonial Canada as deportees from England. Later a wave of Roma arrived in the country around 1900, largely from Europe. Often misrepresented as inherently peripatetic, they in fact homesteaded in the western provinces, including at Le Duc and High River in Alberta, where their knowledge of Slavic languages enabled them to interact successfully with other European immigrants. Levine-Rasky, *Writing the Roma*, 31–52; Salo, "Gypsies/Rom," 643. By the 1920s, most Roma were based in urban areas, but according to demographer Matt Salo, they "still travelled extensively," moving in a regularized circuit through the same Canadian cities, as well as to cities in the United States. Some Roma were living in Toronto as early as the 1910s, if not before that, and occupied the river valleys of the Don and Humber. By the 1930s, they could consistently be found domiciled in rented apartments and storefronts in the Ward, and their children attended Hester How. See Jennifer Bonnell, *Reclaiming the Don: An Environmental History of Toronto's Don River Valley* (Toronto:

University of Toronto Press, 2014), 98–104; Harney and Troper, *Immigrants*, 38; Hooper, "Toronto: A Study in Urban Geography," 75.

47 One Roma "nation" were known as "Kalderásha," which translates literally to "Coppersmith." Ronald Lee, "The Gypsies in Canada. An Ethnological Study," *Journal of the Gypsy Lore Society* (third series) 46, no. 1–2 (January–April 1967): 42–5. There is an opportunity for some enterprising scholar to write the history of Canadian Roma, whose long origins in the country and continued presence merit a sound historical treatment. Though see anthropological and sociological studies of the topic: Julianna Beaudoin, "Challenging Essentialized Representations of Romani Identities in Canada" (PhD diss., University of Western Ontario, 2014); and Levine-Rasky, *Writing the Roma*.

48 Ronald Lee, "The Gypsies in Canada. An Ethnological Study [Part 2]," *Journal of the Gypsy Lore Society* (third series) 47, no. 1–2 (January–April 1968): 13–14.

49 Chad Gaffield, *Language, Schooling, and Cultural Conflict: The Origins of the French-Language Controversy in Ontario* (Montreal: McGill-Queen's University Press, 1987), 190–1.

Bibliography

Primary Sources

American Association of School Administrators. Committee on Uniform Records and Reports of the National Education Association. *Final Report of the Committee on Uniform Records and Reports to the National Council at the St Louis Meeting*. Chicago: University of Chicago Press, 1912.

Amoss, Harry. "The Abnormal Pupil." In *Proceedings of the Sixty-Second Annual Convention of the OEA*, 418–29. Toronto: OEA, 1923.

Amoss, Harry, and L. Helen DeLaporte. *Training Handicapped Children*. Toronto: Ryerson Press, 1933.

Anderson, J.T.M. *The Education of the New Canadian*. Toronto: J.M. Dent, 1918.

Aylesworth, Frederick. "Defective Vision in School-Age Children." In *Proceedings of the Sixty-Fifth Annual Convention of the OEA*, 211–15. Toronto: OEA, 1926.

Ayres, Leonard P. *The Cleveland School Survey: Summary Volume*. Cleveland: The Survey Committee of the Cleveland Foundation, 1917.

– *Laggards in Our Schools: A Study of Retardation and Elimination in City School Systems*. New York: Russell Sage Foundation, 1909.

Barg, Edna. "Sight Saving Class." *Recording Recollections at Ryerson* 8, no. 3 (December 1989).

Bell, Alexander Graham. *Memoir upon the Formation of a Deaf Variety of the Human Race*. National Academy of Sciences, 1884: Canadian Institute for Historic Microreproduction. No. 08831.

Betts, Emmett Albert. *The Prevention and Correction of Reading Difficulties*. Evanston, IL: Row, Peterson, and Co, 1936.

Binet, Alfred. *Les idées modernes sur les enfants*. Paris: Flammarion, 1909.

Binet, Alfred, and Theodore Simon. *A Method of Measuring the Intelligence of Young Children*. Translated by Clara Harrison Town. Lincoln, IL: Courier, 1911.

Binnie, Clara G. "Speech Defects and Mental Health." *The School* (elem. ed.) 32, no. 3 (November 1943): 219–21.

Black, Norman F. *English for the Non-English*. Regina: Regina Book Shop, 1913.

Blackwell, Miss. "Auxiliary Classes in the Public Schools." *Public Health Journal* 5, no. 12 (December 1914): 622–6.

Bonner, H.H. *Statistics of City School Systems, 1919–20*. United States Bureau of Education Bulletin, 1922, no. 17. Washington: Government Printing Office, 1922.

Bott, E.A. *Studies in Industrial Psychology*. Vol. 1, *Point of View* and vol. 2, *Juvenile Employment in Relation to Public Schools and Industries in Toronto*. Toronto: University Library, 1920.

Bowling, E. "Some Causes and the Re-education of Speech Defects." In *Proceedings of the Sixty-Eighth Annual Convention of the OEA*, 93–8. Toronto: OEA, 1929.

– "The Stutterer." *The School* (elem. ed.) 29, no. 10 (June 1941): 934–6.

Bronner, Augusta F. *The Psychology of Special Abilities and Disabilities*. Boston: Little, Brown, and Co, 1917.

Brueckner, Leo J. *Diagnostic and Remedial Teaching in Arithmetic*. Philadelphia: The John C. Winston Co, 1930.

Brueckner, Leo J., and G.K. Sheane. *Mathematics for Everyday Use*. Toronto: Winston, 1937.

Bryan, W.L. "Church Street School: A Non-academic School for Boys." *Special Class Teacher* 12, no. 3 (February 1938): 12–13, 26.

Budden, Josephine. "Boulton Avenue Nursery School." *Special Class Teacher* 19, no. 3 (May 1945): 114–15.

Buie, A. "Dr Charles G. Stogdill Appointed Director, Division of Mental Hygiene." *The Bulletin* 8, no. 2 (November 1931): 10.

Carruthers, Lillian. "Children in Special Classes." *Toronto Daily Star*, 29 March 1912, 5.

– "How Numerous Are Subnormal Pupils?" *Toronto Daily Star*, 9 November 1912, 8.

City of Toronto, Department of Public Health. Selected monthly reports and annual statements, 1931–45.

Clark, C.S. *Of Toronto the Good: The Queen City of Canada as It Is*. Montreal: The Toronto Publishing Company, 1898.

Clarke, C.K. "What Is Your Child's IQ?" *Maclean's Magazine* 35, no. 2 (15 January 1922): 13–15, 36–8.

Clarke, Eric Kent. "The Mental Health of the Coming Generation." *Social Welfare* 7, no. 10 (July 1925): 196–8.

– "Mental Hygiene in the Public Schools." In *Proceedings of the Fifty-Ninth Annual Convention of the OEA*, 202–5. Toronto: OEA, 1920.

– "Some Phases of the Mental Hygiene Problem." *Public Health Journal* 14, no. 10 (1923): 536–42.

– "Survey of the Toronto Public Schools." *Canadian Journal of Mental Hygiene* 2, no. 2 (1920): 182–5.

Craick, W.A. "The Forest School in High Park Builds up Health of Delicate Children by Life in Open." *Toronto Star Weekly*, 30 June 1917, n.p.

– "Victoria Street School Building Is Oldest in City – Was Built in 1855." *Toronto Star Weekly*, 16 March 1918, 23.

"Classes for Deaf and Dumb." Letter to the editor, Mother of One Afflicted. *Toronto Daily Star*, 22 December 1925, 6.

Dalzell, Isabel J. "Psychiatric Social Work with the Maladjusted Child of Normal Intelligence." *Canadian Public Health Journal* 25, no. 12 (January 1934): 602–4.

"Deaf Body President Praises and Differs." *Toronto Daily Star*, 23 March 1945, 2.

"The Defectives Neglected while City and Province Disagree over Their Duty." *Toronto Daily Star*, 9 May 1912, 3.

DeLaporte, L. Helen. "Are We Part of the World?" *Special Class Teacher* 15, no. 3 (May 1941): 68–9.

– "Books for Retarded Adolescents." *Special Class Teacher* 19, no. 1 (November 1944): 5–8.

Dendy, Miss [Mary]. "Types of Feebleminded Children." *Report of the International Congress of Women. Held in Toronto Canada. June 24th–30th, 1909*, 45–57. Toronto: The National Council of Women of Canada, 1910.

Dent, Fred S. "Toronto's Open-Air School." *The School* 2, no. 9 (1914): 533–6.

Dewsbury, Ruth Byrne. "Happy School Days." *Recording Recollections at Ryerson* 4, no. 2 (1985): 12.

"Didn't Appoint 4th Inspector." *Toronto Daily Star*, 19 June 1909, 3.

"Dr Goldring's Plans for the Deaf." Letter to the editor, David Peikoff. *Globe and Mail*, 16 March 1945, 6.

Dunlop, Florence S. "The Identification, Description and Development of the Intellectually Gifted." n.d.

– "The School Psychologist." *The School* (elem. ed.) 28, no. 9 (May 1940): 753–6.

– *Subsequent Careers of Non-academic Boys*. Ottawa: National Printers Limited, 1935.

Durrell, Donald D. "The Influence of Reading Ability on Intelligence Measures." *Journal of Educational Psychology* 24, no. 6 (September 1933): 412–16.

"Education of the Deaf." *Toronto Daily Star*, 31 March 1945, 6.

Elliott, Charles M. "The Toronto Meeting." *International Council for Exceptional Children Review* 1, no. 1 (May 1934): 4–5, 9, 25.

Fernald, Grace M. *Remedial Techniques in Basic School Subjects*. New York: McGraw-Hill, 1943 [reprint 1971].

Gates, Arthur I. *The Psychology of Reading and Spelling: With Special Reference to Disability*. Teachers College, Columbia University Contributions to Education, no. 129. New York: Teachers College, Columbia University, 1922.

"Glass of Warm Milk for Weakly Pupils." *Toronto Daily Star*, 17 January 1913, 14.

Goldring, Cecil Charles (C.C.). *Education of the Deaf Child or the Child with Impaired Hearing*. Toronto: TBE, 1946.

– "A Forward Look at Toronto School System." Toronto: TBE, 1943.

– *Intelligence Testing in a Toronto Public School*. DPaed, published, University of Toronto, n.d. [ca. 1924].

Gray, William S., and May Arbuthnot. *Fun with Dick and Jane*. Toronto: Gage & Co, 1940.

Griffin, J.D.M. "Educating the Victim of Polio." *Special Class Teacher* 12, no. 3 (February 1938): 7–8, 20.

– S.R. Laycock, and W. Line. *Mental Hygiene: A Manual for Teachers*. New York: American Book, 1940.

Groves, Mrs W.E. "Address of Welcome to the Auxiliary Class Teachers of Ontario." In *Proceedings of the Sixty-Second Annual Convention of the OEA*, 260–3. Toronto: OEA, 1923.

Groves, Edith Lelean (posthumous), with an introduction by Helen MacMurchy. *Everyday Children: A Book of Poems*. Toronto: The Committee in Charge of the Edith L. Groves Memorial Fund for Underprivileged Children, 1932.

Hally, Daisy. "Mental Hygiene Approach to a Better Understanding of Children's Reactions." In *Proceedings of the Seventy-Third Annual Convention of the OEA*, 75–8. Toronto: OEA, 1934.

Hampson, Jean. "Occupational Treatment at Crippled Children's School, Toronto." *Occupational Therapy and Rehabilitation* 12, no. 1 (1933): 55–8.

Hartwell, Charles S. "The Grading and Promotion of Pupils." *Journal of Proceedings and Addresses of the Forty-Eighth Meeting of the National Education Association*, 294–305. Winona, MN: National Education Association, 1910.

Harvie, Marian K. "Oral Reading Tests." *Special Class Teacher* 16, no. 1 (November 1941): 15–19.

– "Oral Reading Tests." *Special Class Teacher* 16, no. 3 (May 1942): 74–5, 89–90.

Heck, Arch O. *Special Schools and Classes in Cities of 10,000 Population and More in the United States*. United States Office of Education Bulletin, 1930, no. 7. Washington: Government Printing Office, 1930.

Hincks, Clarence M. "The Scope and Aims of the Mental Hygiene Movement in Canada." *Canadian Journal of Mental Hygiene* 1, no. 1 (April 1919): 20–9.

Hocken, Horatio. "The New Spirit in Municipal Government (1914)." In Paul Rutherford, ed., *Saving the Canadian City: The First Phase 1880–1920*, 195–208. Toronto: University of Toronto Press, 1974.

Hollingworth, Leta S., with C. Amelia Winford. *The Psychology of Disability in Spelling*. Teachers College, Columbia University Contributions to Education, no. 88. New York: Teachers College, Columbia University, 1918.

"Home Proposed for Feeble-Minded." *Globe*, 27 March 1912, 9.

Hopper, R.W. "The Rehabilitation of the Crippled Child." *Social Welfare* 14 (February 1932): 87–90.

Hughes, James L. "Hester How." *The School* 4, no. 4 (December 1915): 300–5.

"Individual Instruction." *Special Class Teacher* 15, no. 2 (February 1941): 36.

"Instruction for the Deaf." Letter to the editor, A Friend of the Deaf, *Toronto Daily Star*, 14 December 1925, 6.

J.M. "Are the Three 'R's' Being Neglected?" *The Bulletin* 7, no. 2 (December 1930): 4.

Jeffrey, Mildred A. "A Follow-up Study on the Re-establishment of Mentally Defective Girls in Domestic Science in an Urban Centre under Colony House Supervision." *American Journal of Mental Deficiency* 48, no. 1 (July 1943): 96–100.

Johnstone, E.R. "The Summer School for Teachers of Backward Children." *Journal of Psycho-Asthenics* 13 (1908): 122–30.

Kennedy, John. *The Batavia System of Individual Instruction*. Syracuse, NY: C.W. Bardeen, 1914.

Kerr, Mrs. "Defective Children." *Public Health Journal* 5, no. 12 (December 1914): 620–2.

Koerber, Walter F. "An Evaluation of Some Methods and Procedures in the Teaching of Reading to Non-academic Adolescent Boys." DPaed thesis, University of Toronto, 1947.

Kunzig, Robert W. *Public School Education of Atypical Children*. United States Office of Education, Bulletin no. 10. Washington: Government Printing Office, 1931.

Larkin, Marjorie. "A Social Worker Discusses 'Backward' Children." *Special Class Teacher* 13, no. 2 (September 1938): 78–9.

Laycock, Samuel R. "Meeting the Needs of Children in Special Classes." *Special Class Teacher* 17, no. 2 (February 1943): 65–8.

– "Mental Hygiene in Special Education." *Journal of Exceptional Children* (October 1936): 2–9.

– "The Mental Hygiene of Exceptional Children." Part 1. *Special Class Teacher* 15, no. 3 (May 1941): 74–7.

– "Special Classes for Gifted Children in a Small City." *Understanding the Child* 9, no. 1 (April 1940): 3–6.

Lewis, E.P. "The Non-academic Child." In *Proceedings of the Sixty-Ninth Annual Convention of the OEA*, 124–30. Toronto: OEA, 1930.

Lewis, E.P., and A. Mildred Jeffrey. "Ross Cottage – A Special Foster Home." *American Journal of Mental Deficiency* 49, no. 3 (January 1945): 377–82.

Lewis, Ruth. "Speech Defects and the Classroom Teacher." *The School* (elem. ed.) 33, no. 1 (September 1944): 47–9.

"Lip-Reading Classes Now in Eight Schools." *Toronto Daily Star*, 26 January 1922, 7.

Little, Jane. "The History of the Edith L. Groves School." *Special Class Teacher* 18, no. 1 (November 1943): 13–16 .

– "Nursery Training Course in the Edith L. Groves School, Toronto, Canada," *Special Class Teacher* 16, no. 2 (February 1942): 42–4.

– "The Nursery Training Course in the Edith L. Groves School for Girls." *The School* (elem. ed.) 31, no. 2 (October 1942): 110–12.

– "Vocational Guidance in the Edith L. Groves School." *Special Class Teacher* 13, no. 3 (February 1939): 90, 107–8.

Little, Jean, *Little by Little: A Writer's Education*. Toronto: Viking, 1987.

Long, J.A. "Department of Educational Research Ontario College of Education, Report of Activities, 1943–44." *The School* (elem. ed.) 32, no. 10 (June 1944): 847–9.

McCarthy, J.O. "Municipal Responsibility." *Public Health Journal* 5, no. 4 (April 1914): 234–5.

MacDonald, Donald D. "Sight-Saving Classes in the Public Schools." DPaed thesis, University of Toronto, 1923.

MacDonald, Neil S. *Open-Air Schools*. Toronto: McClelland, 1918.

MacDonald, Nellie Y. "Deaf Children in the Public Schools." *The School* 14, no. 5 (January 1926): 499–500.

McGivney, J. "Teaching Reading to Non-academic Adolescents Who Have Not Completed Grade I of the Primary School." Part 1. *Special Class Teacher* 19, no. 2 (February 1945): 51–3.

– "Teaching Reading to Non-academic Adolescents Who Have Not Completed Grade I of the Primary School." Part 2. *Special Class Teacher* 19, no. 3 (May 1945): 93–5.

McIntosh, W.J. "Follow-up Study of One Thousand Non-academic Boys." *Journal of Exceptional Children* 15 (1949): 166–70, 191.

MacKenzie, Grace I. "Vocational Training for the Adolescent Girl." In *Proceedings of the Sixty-Ninth Annual Convention of the OEA*, 80–9. Toronto: OEA, 1930.

MacMurchy, Helen. *Organization and Management of Auxiliary Classes.* Educational Pamphlets no. 7. Toronto: DOE, 1915.

– *To Inspectors, Principals, and Teachers.* Toronto: DOE, 1919.

MacPhee, E.D. "Behaviour in Auxiliary Classes." In *Proceedings of the Sixty-Sixth Annual Convention of the OEA*, 126–34. Toronto: OEA, 1927.

Malloy, F. Pearl. "Devices in Enterprise Work for Auxiliary Classes." *The School* (elem. ed.) 2, no. 7 (1944): 622–4.

Mary, John, and Peter: The Ontario Readers Primer. Toronto: T. Eaton Co, 1933.

"The Mental Defectives." Letter to the editor, *Globe*, 7 February 1921, 4.

Milne, H.D. "Why an Orthopedic School." *The Bulletin* 2, no. 2 (March 1926): 7–9.

"Miss Grace K. Wadleigh Teacher of Lip-Reading." Advertisement. *The Bulletin* (December 1926): n.p.

Monroe, Marion. *Children Who Cannot Read: The Analysis of Reading Disabilities and the Use of Diagnostic Tests in the Instruction of Retarded Readers.* Chicago: University of Chicago Press, 1932.

Munro, P.F. "The Case of Mabel Helen B------." *The School* (elem. ed.) 24, no. 4 (December 1935): 275–7.

– *An Experimental Investigation of the Mentality of the Jew in Ryerson Public School Toronto.* Toronto: University of Toronto Press, 1926.

"Nineteen Inspectors in Schools, and Yet Complaints Are Made." *Toronto Daily Star*, 10 May 1912, 12.

Ontario. *Revised Statutes of Ontario, 1927.* Vol. 3, ch. 324, The Auxiliary Classes Act. Toronto: Government of Ontario, 1927.

– *Revised Statutes of Ontario, 1927.* Vol. 3, ch. 333, The Adolescent School Attendance Act. Toronto: Government of Ontario, 1927.

– *Schools and Teachers in the Province of Ontario.* Part 2: *Collegiate Institutes, High Schools, Continuation Schools, Vocational Schools, Normal Schools and Technical Institues.* Toronto: Baptist Johnson, 1950.

– *Public and Separate Schools and Teachers in the Province of Ontario for the Year Ending 1913.* Toronto: L.K. Cameron, 1913.

- *Public and Separate Schools and Teachers in the Province of Ontario.* Toronto: A.T. Wilgress, 1919.
- *Public and Separate Schools in the Province of Ontario, November 1923.* Toronto: Clarkson W. James, 1923.
- *Recommendations and Regulations for the Establishment, Organization, and Management of Commercial High Schools and Commercial Departments in High and Continuation Schools.* Toronto: L.K. Cameron, 1915.
- *Regulations for Auxiliary Classes.* Toronto: various publishers, 1917, 1922, 1925, 1930.
- *Suggestions for Teachers of Subnormal Children.* Toronto: C.W. James, 1925.

Ontario, Legislative Assembly. *Report upon the Care of the Feeble-Minded in Ontario, 1907.* Sessional Papers 1907, no. 63. Toronto: 1907.
- *Third Report upon the Care of the Feeble-Minded in Ontario, 1908.* Sessional Papers 1909, no. 58. Toronto: 1909.
- *Fourth Report of the Feeble-Minded in Ontario, 1909.* Sessional Papers 1910, no. 23. Toronto: 1910.
- *Fifth Report upon the Care of the Feeble-Minded in Ontario, 1910.* Sessional Papers 1911, no. 23. Toronto: 1911.
- *Sixth Report upon the Care of the Feeble-Minded in Ontario, 1911.* Sessional Papers 1912, no. 23. Toronto: 1912.
- *Report on the Care and Control of the Mentally Defective and Feeble-Minded in Ontario, by the Honourable Frank Egerton Hodgins.* Sessional Papers 1920, no. 24, vol. 5, appended. Toronto: 1919.
- *Report of the Minister of Education Province of Ontario.* Toronto: various publishers, 1920 to 1945.

OEA. "Minutes." Auxiliary Class Teachers' Section. In *Proceedings of the Sixty-Fourth Annual Convention of the OEA.* Toronto: OEA, 1925.

Palen, Imogen B. "Correction of Speech Defects." *The School* 16, no. 5 (January 1928): 434–8.
- "Lip Reading." In *Proceedings of the Sixty-Second Annual Convention of the OEA,* 264–5. Toronto: OEA, 1923.
- "Stammering." *The School* 17, no. 7 (March 1929): 631–6.

Prueter, H.J. "The Care and Education of Crippled Children in Ontario." DPaed thesis, University of Toronto, 1936.

"The Question Answered." *The Bulletin* 7, no. 3 (March 1931): 7–8.

Radcliffe, S.J. *Retardation in the Schools of Ontario.* Toronto: author, n.d. [1922].

"Red Tape Cut by Board to Aid Eyes of Pupils." *Toronto Daily Star,* 3 December 1938, 26.

"Retire Women Early Compared to Men." *Toronto Daily Star,* 8 April 1938, 8.

Richardson, William Leeds. *The Administration of Schools in the Cities of the Dominion of Canada*. Toronto: J.M. Dent, 1922.

Rogers, George F. "The Enrichment of Courses in the Elementary Schools." In *Proceedings of the Seventy-First Annual Convention of the OEA*, 169–76. Toronto: OEA, 1932.

"Ross Cottage Holds 'Open House' Fete." *Toronto Daily Star*, 20 May 1935, 29.

Russell, David H. *Children Learn to Read*. Boston: Ginn, 1949.

– "The Prevention and Correction of Reading Difficulties in Smaller Schools." *The School* (elem. ed.) 28, no. 5 (January 1940): 387–92.

– "The Prevention and Remedy of Reading Difficulties in Smaller Schools." Part 2. *The School* (elem. ed.) 28, no. 6 (February 1940): 485–9.

Russell, David H., and Fred T. Tyler. "Special Education in Canada." *The School* (elem. ed.) 30, no. 10 (June 1942): 882–9.

Ryerson, Edwin Warner. "Cerebral Spastic Paralysis in Children." *Journal of the American Medical Association* 98, no. 1 (2 January 1932): 43–5.

"Sad Cases of Dull Children." *Toronto Daily Star*, 6 May 1910, 12.

Sandiford, Peter. "Examinations or Intelligence Tests?" *The School* 7, no. 10 (1919): 641–4.

– *The Mental and Physical Life of Schoolchildren*. London: Longmans, Green, and Co, 1919.

– "Technical Education and the I.Q." In *Proceedings of the Sixty-Eighth Annual Convention of the OEA*, 151–8. Toronto: OEA, 1929.

Sandiford, Peter, and Ruby Kerr. "Intelligence of Chinese and Japanese Children." *Journal of Educational Psychology* 17, no. 6 (September 1926): 361–7.

"School Budget down Salaries Left Alone." *Toronto Daily Star*, 12 February 1935, 23.

School Management. Ontario Normal School Manuals. Toronto: William Briggs, 1915.

"School Tax Rates Generally Lower." *Toronto Daily Star*, 15 March 1933, 16.

Seaton, E.T. "Classification and Time-Table in Auxiliary Classes." Auxiliary Class Teachers' Section. In *Proceedings of the Sixty-Fourth Annual Convention of the OEA*, 179–82. Toronto: OEA, 1925.

Sheane, George K. "Diagnostic and Remedial Teaching in Arithmetic." *The School* (elem. ed.) 26, no. 9 (May 1938): 775–9.

"Sign Language Needed by Deaf." *Globe*, 5 July 1922, 2.

Sinclair, S.B. *Backward and Brilliant Children*. Toronto: Ryerson Press, 1931.

– "Miss H.D. Milne, an Appreciation." *The Bulletin* 8, no. 2 (November 1931): 7–8.

Steele, Murray E.. "An Academic Vocational Class for Boys." *The School*
    (elem. ed.) 31, no. 6 (February 1943): 495–9.
Stogdill, C.G. "Mental Hygiene in Toronto Schools." *The Bulletin* 9, no. 2
    (November 1932): 4–6.
– "Subject Disabilities: A Symptom." *Understanding the Child* 7, no. 1 (April
    1938): 7–9.
"Strong Plea Made for Mental Defectives." *Globe*, 6 March 1914, 8.
Struthers, W.E. "The Open-Air School." In *Proceedings of the Fifty-Third Annual
    Convention of the OEA*, 281–7. Toronto: William Briggs, 1914.
"Suitable Occupations for Handicapped Workers." *The Bulletin* 8, no. 2
    (November 1931): 17.
TBE. *Annual Financial Statement and Statistics 1939*.
– *Annual Financial Statement 1943*.
– *Annual Report*, 1892, 1893, 1911–16, 1918–32, 1982.
– *Handbook*, 1911, 1914–21.
– *Minutes*, 1909–16, 1918–20, 1922–3, 1925–30, 1932–8, 1941, 1943–5, 1964.
TDSB. *Minutes 1998*. Report no. 2, Special Education Advisory Committee,
    9 April 1998. http://www.tdsb.on.ca/Leadership/Boardroom/Agenda-
    Minutes.
– *Minutes*. 16 November 2011. http://www.tdsb.on.ca/Leadership/
    Boardroom/Agenda-Minutes.
– *TDSB Financial Facts: Revenue and Expenditure Trends*. Toronto: TDSB, April
    2018. http://www.tdsb.on.ca/Portals/0/AboutUs/docs/FinancialFacts_
    April2018.pdf.
Toronto Bureau of Municipal Research. "Are All Children Alike?" White paper
    4. Toronto: Toronto Bureau of Municipal Research: 1915.
– "The Bureau of Municipal Research." Toronto: Bureau of Municipal
    Research, 1919.
– *Measurement of Educational Waste in the Toronto Public Schools*. Toronto:
    Toronto Bureau of Municipal Research, 1920.
– *What Is "the Ward" Going to Do with Toronto?*. Toronto: Toronto Bureau of
    Municipal Research, 1918.
"Those Needing Most Care Are Neglected." *Toronto Daily Star*, 9 May 1912, 7.
"T.L. Church Is Mayor by Majority of 6,469." *Globe*, 2 January 1915, 13.
"To Safeguard Those Who Have Weak Minds." *Toronto Daily Star*, 27 March
    1912, 10.
"To the Parents of Deaf Children." Letter to the editor, Owen Elliot. *Toronto
    Daily Star*, 4 December 1925, 6.
Terman, Lewis M. *The Intelligence of Schoolchildren*. Boston: Houghton-Mifflin,
    1919.

- *The Measurement of Intelligence.* Boston: Houghton-Mifflin, 1916.
- "The Problem." In Lewis Terman, Virgil E. Dickson, A.H. Sutherland, Raymond H. Franzen, C.R. Tupper, and Grace Fernald, eds., *Intelligence Tests and School Reorganization,* 1–32. Yonkers-on-Hudson, NY: World Book, 1923.

The Toronto City Directory 1921. Vol. 46. Toronto: Might Directories Limited, 1921.

"Trustees Approve Big Plan to Care for Defectives." *Toronto Daily Star,* 8 December 1916, 21.

White House Conference on Child Health and Protection. Preliminary Committee Reports. New York: The Century Co, 1930.

Vincent, Claire. "La maladie ma privée de mon enfance." In Sally Aitken, Pierrette Caron, and Gilles Fournier, eds., *Histoire vécue de la polio au Québec,* 86–92. Montreal: Carte blanche, 2001.

Wiggins, Julius. *No Sound.* New York: The Silent Press, 1970.

Willson, Alice. "Intelligence Tests and Classification." *The School* 10, no. 8 (April 1922): 472–4.

Witty, Paul. "Diagnostic Testing and Remedial Teaching." *Understanding the Child* 7, no. 1 (April 1938): 3–6.

Worden, O.O. "A Comparative Experimental Study of Two Similar Groups of Super-Normal Elementary School Children." DPaed thesis, University of Toronto, 1936.

Secondary Sources

Aitken, Sally, Helen D'Orazio, and Stewart Valin, eds. *Walking Fingers: The Story of Polio and Those Who Lived with It.* Montreal: Véhicule Press, 2004.

Alcorn, Kerry. *Border Crossings: U.S. Culture and Education in Saskatchewan, 1905–1937.* Montreal: McGill-Queen's University Press, 2013.

Allison, John. "Technical Schooling in Toronto: Growing up in the Trades during the Second World War." *Historical Studies in Education/Revue d'histoire de l'éducation* 28, no. 1 (spring 2016): 53–72.

Altenbaugh, Richard J. "Where Are the Disabled in the History of Education? The Impact of Polio on Sites of Learning." *History of Education* 35, no. 6 (November 2006): 705–30.

Angus, David L., and Jeffrey E. Mirel. *The Failed Promise of the American High School, 1890–1995.* New York: Teachers College Press, 1999.

Armstrong, Christopher, and H.V. Nelles. "The Rise of Civic Populism in Toronto 1870–1920." In Victor L. Russell, ed., *Forging a Consensus: Historical Essays on Toronto,* 192–237. Toronto: University of Toronto Press, 1984.

Armstrong, Felicity. "The Historical Development of Special Education: Humanitarian Rationality or 'Wild Profusion of Entangled Events'?" *History of Education* 31, no. 2 (2002): 437–56.

Axelrod, Paul. *Making a Middle Class: Student Life in English Canada during the Thirties*. Montreal: McGill-Queen's University Press, 1990.

– *The Promise of Schooling: Education in Canada, 1800–1914*. Toronto: University of Toronto Press, 1997.

Bacchi, Carol Lee. *Liberation Deferred? The Ideas of English-Canadian Suffragists, 1877–1918*. Toronto: University of Toronto Press, 1983.

Barman, Jean. "Schooled for Inequality: The Education of British Columbia Aboriginal Children." In Jean Barman and Mona Gleason, eds., *Children, Teachers, and Schools in the History of British Columbia*, 2nd ed., 55–79. Calgary: Detselig, 2003.

Barron, Sandy R. "'The World Is Wide Enough for Us Both': The Manitoba School for the Deaf at the Onset of the Oralist Age, 1889–1920." *Canadian Journal of Disability Studies* 6, no. 1 (2017): 63–84.

Baynton, Douglas C. "Disability and the Justification of Inequality in American History." In Longmore and Umansky, *The New Disability History*, 33–57.

– *Forbidden Signs: American Culture and the Campaign against Sign Language*. Chicago: University of Chicago Press, 1996.

Beaudoin, Julianna. "Challenging Essentialized Representations of Romani Identities in Canada." PhD diss., University of Western Ontario, 2014.

Bennison, E. Anne. "Before the Learning Disabled There Were Feeble-Minded Children." In Barry M. Franklin, ed., *Learning Disability: Dissenting Essays*, 13–28. London: The Falmer Press, 1987.

– "Creating Categories of Competence: The Education of Exceptional Children in the Milwaukee Public Schools, 1908–1917." PhD diss., University of Wisconsin-Madison, 1988.

Block, Laurie. "Cure and the Contempt of Goodwill: Reason and Feeling in Disability Narratives, 1850–1950." In Cynthia Comacchio, Janet Golden, and George Weisz, eds., *Healing the World's Children: Interdisciplinary Perspectives on Child Health in the Twentieth Century*, 125–57. Montreal: McGill-Queen's University Press, 2008.

Block, N.J., and Gerald Dworkin. "IQ, Heritability, and Inequality." In Block and Dworkin, eds., *The IQ Controversy: Critical Readings*, 410–540. New York: Pantheon, 1976.

Bonnell, Jennifer. *Reclaiming the Don: An Environmental History of Toronto's Don River Valley*. Toronto: University of Toronto Press, 2014.

Brown, Robert Craig, and Ramsay Cook. *Canada 1896–1912: A Nation Transformed*. Toronto: McClelland and Stewart, 1974.

Brown, Robert S., and Gillian Parekh. *The Intersection of Disability, Achievement, and Equity: A System Review of Special Education in the TDSB*. Research report no. 12–13–12. Toronto: TDSB, 2013.

Brumberg, Stephan F. *Going to America, Going to School: The Jewish Immigrant Public School Encounter in Turn-of-the-Century New York City*. New York: Praeger, 1986.

Bullen, John. "Hidden Workers: Child Labour and the Family Economy in Late Nineteenth-Century Urban Ontario." *Labour/Le Travail* 18 (fall 1986): 163–87.

Burch, Susan. *Signs of Resistance: American Deaf Cultural History, 1900 to World War II*. New York: New York University Press, 2002.

Byrom, Brad. "A Pupil and a Patient: Hospital-Schools in Progressive America." In Longmore and Umansky, *The New Disability History*, 133–56.

Campbell, Lara. *Respectable Citizens: Gender, Family, and Unemployment in Ontario's Great Depression*. Toronto: University of Toronto Press, 2009.

Carbin, Clifton H. *Deaf Heritage in Canada: A Distinctive, Diverse, and Enduring Culture*. Edited by Dorothy L. Smith. Toronto: McGraw-Hill Ryerson, 1996.

Careless, J.M.S. *Toronto to 1918: An Illustrated History*. Toronto: J. Lorimer, 1984.

Carrier, James G. *Learning Disability: Social Class and the Construction of Inequality in American Education*. Westport, CT: Greenwood Press, 1986.

Catterson, Jane H., and Lisa Durrell. "Chapter One: The Background." In "Durrell's One-Minute Philosophy of Education," *Journal of Education* 182, no. 1 (2000): 1–10.

Chapman, Paul Davis. *Schools as Sorters: Lewis M. Terman, Applied Psychology, and the Intelligence Testing Movement, 1890–1930*. New York: New York University Press, 1988.

Cheng, Maisy, and Maria Yau. *Every Secondary Student Survey, 1997: Detailed Findings*. Report no. 230. Toronto: TDSB, 1999.

Christou, Theodore Michael. *Progressive Education: Revisioning and Reframing Ontario Public Schools, 1919–1942*. Toronto: University of Toronto Press, 2012.

Chupik, Jessa, and David Wright. "Treating the 'Idiot' Child in Early 20th-Century Ontario." *Disability and Society* 21, no. 1 (January 2006): 77–90.

Clandfield, David, Bruce Curtis, Grace-Edward Galabuzi, Alison Gaymes San Vincente, D.W. Livingstone, and Harry Smaller. *Restacking the Deck: Streaming by Class, Race, and Gender in Ontario Schools*. Toronto: Our Schools/Our Selves, 2014.

Clarke, Nic. "Sacred Daemons: Exploring British Columbian Society's Perceptions of 'Mentally Deficient' Children, 1870–1930." *B.C. Studies* 144 (winter 2004–5): 61–89.

– *Unwanted Warriors: The Rejected Volunteers of the Canadian Expeditionary Force, 1914–18.* Vancouver: University of British Columbia Press, 2015.

Clinton Public School 1888–1988. Toronto: TBE, May 1989.

Cohen, Sol. "The Mental Hygiene Movement, the Development of Personality and the School: The Medicalization of American Education." *History of Education Quarterly* 23, no. 2 (summer 1983): 123–49.

Cole, Ted. *Apart or a Part? Integration and the Growth of British Special Education.* Milton Keynes, UK: Open University Press, 1989.

Comacchio, Cynthia. *The Dominion of Youth: Adolescence and the Making of a Modern Canada, 1920–50.* Waterloo, ON: Wilfrid Laurier University Press, 2006.

Connor, David J., and Beth A. Ferri. "Integration and Inclusion – A Troubling Nexus: Race, Disability, and Special Education." *Journal of African American History* 90, no. 1/2 (winter 2005): 107–27.

Coulter, Rebecca. "The Working Young of Edmonton, 1921–1931." In Joy Parr, ed., *Childhood and Family in Canadian History*, 143–59. Toronto: McClelland and Stewart, 1982.

Croteau, Jean-Philippe. "Les commissions scolaires et les immigrants à Toronto et à Montréal (1900–1945): quatre modèles d'intégration en milieu urbain." *Francophonies d'Amérique* 31 (2011): 49–85.

Cuban, Larry. *How Teachers Taught: Constancy and Change in American Classrooms, 1890–1990.* 2nd ed. New York: Teachers College Press, 1993.

Curtis, Bruce, D.W. Livingstone, and Harry Smaller. *Stacking the Deck: The Streaming of Working-Class Kids in Ontario Schools.* Toronto: Our Schools/Our Selves, 1992.

Danforth, Scot. *The Incomplete Child: An Intellectual History of Learning Disabilities.* New York: Peter Lang, 2009.

Danylewycz, Marta. "Domestic Science Education in Ontario, 1900–1940." In Ruby Heap and Alison Prentice, eds., *Gender and Education in Ontario*, 127–45. Toronto: Canadian Scholars Press, 1991.

Darroch, A. Gordon, and Michael D. Ornstein. "Ethnicity and Occupational Structure in Canada in 1871: The Vertical Mosaic in Historical Perspective." *Canadian Historical Review* 61, no. 3 (1980): 305–33.

"Deaf Work Pioneer Miss I. Palen, Dead." *Toronto Daily Star*, 4 September 1945, 11.

Dehli, Kari. "For Intelligent Motherhood and National Efficiency: The Toronto Home and School Council, 1916–1930." In Ruby Heap and Alison Prentice, eds., *Gender and Education in Ontario*, 147–63. Toronto: Canadian Scholars Press, 1991.

- "Women and Class: The Social Organization of Mothers' Relations to Schools in Toronto, 1915–1940." PhD diss., University of Toronto, 1988.

de la Cour, Lykke. "From 'Moron' to 'Maladjusted': Eugenics, Psychiatry, and the Regulation of Women, Ontario, 1930s–1960s." PhD diss., University of Toronto, 2013.

Di Mascio, Anthony. "The Emergence of Academies in the Eastern Townships of Lower Canada and the Invisibility of the Canada–U.S. Border." *Historical Studies in Education/Revue d'histoire de l'éducation* 27, no. 2 (fall 2015): 78–94.

Dixon, R.T. *We Remember, We Believe: A History of Toronto's Catholic Separate School Boards, 1841 to 1997*. Toronto: Toronto Catholic District School Board, 2007.

Dodd, Dianne. "Helen MacMurchy, MD: Gender and Professional Conflict in the Medical Inspection of Toronto Schools, 1910–1911." *Ontario History* 93, no. 2 (2001): 127–49.

Dorn, Sherman. "Public–Private Symbiosis in Nashville Special Education." *History of Education Quarterly* 42, no. 3 (autumn 2002): 368–94.

Dorn, Sherman, Douglas Fuchs, and Lynn S. Fuchs. "A Historical Perspective on Special Education Reform." *Theory into Practice* 35, no. 1 (1996): 12–19.

Dowbiggin, Ian Robert. *Keeping America Sane: Psychiatry and Eugenics in the United States and Canada, 1880–1940*. Ithaca, NY: Cornell University Press, 1997.

"Dr Goldwin W. Howland." *Canadian Journal of Occupational Therapy* 17, no. 3 (September 1950): 67–70.

"Dr R.M. Wansbrough: Surgeon for 28 Years at Children's Hospital." *Globe and Mail*, 25 May 1956, 4.

"Duke of York to Be French School." *Globe and Mail*, 16 May 1980, 5.

Dunn, Lloyd M. "Special Education for the Mildly Retarded: Is Much of It Justifiable?" *Exceptional Children* 35, no. 1 (September 1968): 5–22.

Dunn, Timothy A. "Teaching the Meaning of Work: Vocational Education in British Columbia, 1900–1929." In Jones, Sheehan, and Stamp, *Shaping the Schools*, 236–56.

Dyck, Erika. *Facing Eugenics: Reproduction, Sterilization, and the Politics of Choice*. Toronto: University of Toronto Press, 2013.

Edwards, R.A.R. "Sound and Fury; or, Much Ado about Nothing? Cochlear Implants in Historical Perspective." *Journal of American History* 92, no. 3 (December 2005): 892–920.

- *Words Made Flesh: Nineteenth-Century Deaf Education and the Growth of Deaf Culture*. New York: New York University Press, 2012.

Ellis, Jason. "'All Methods – And Wedded to None': The Deaf Education Methods Debate and Progressive Educational Reform in Toronto, Canada, 1922–1945." *Paedagogica Historica* 50, no. 3 (2014): 371–89.

– "Brains Unlimited: Giftedness and Gifted Education Canada before *Sputnik* (1957)." *Canadian Journal of Education/Revue canadienne de l'éducation* 40, no. 2 (2017): 1–26.

– "Early Educational Exclusion: 'Idiotic' and 'Imbecilic' Children, Their Families, and the Toronto Public School System, 1914–50." *Canadian Historical Review* 98, no. 3 (September 2017): 483–504.

– "'Inequalities of Children in Original Endowment': How Intelligence Testing Transformed Early Special Education in a North American City School System." *History of Education Quarterly* 53, no. 4 (November 2013): 401–29.

Ellis, Jason, and Paul Axelrod. "Continuity and Change: Special Education Policy Development in Toronto Public Schools, 1945–Present." *Teachers College Record* 118, no. 2 (February 2016). http://www.tcrecord.org/Content.asp?ContentId=18228.

Fallace, Thomas D. *Race and the Origins of Progressive Education, 1880–1929.* New York: Teachers College Press, 2015.

Fass, Paula S. "The IQ: A Cultural Historical Framework." *American Journal of Education* 88, no. 4 (1980): 431–58.

Ferri, Beth A., and David J. Connor. "In the Shadow of Brown: Special Education and Overrepresentation of Students of Color." *Remedial and Special Education* 26, no. 2 (March/April 2005): 93–100.

Fiamengo, Janice. "Rediscovering Our Foremothers Again: Racial Ideas of Canada's Early Feminists, 1885–1914." In Mona Gleason and Adele Perry, eds., *Rethinking Canada: The Promise of Women's History*, 5th ed., 144–62. Don Mills, ON: Oxford University Press, 2006.

Frager, Ruth. *Sweatshop Strife: Class, Ethnicity, and Gender in the Jewish Labour Movement of Toronto, 1900–1939.* Toronto: University of Toronto Press, 1992.

Franklin, Barry M. *From "Backwardness" to "At-Risk": Childhood Learning Difficulties and the Contradictions of School Reform.* Albany: SUNY Press, 1994.

– "Progressivism and Curriculum Differentiation: Special Classes in the Atlanta Public Schools." *History of Education Quarterly* 29, no. 4 (winter 1989): 571–93.

Friedland, Judith. *Restoring the Spirit: The Beginnings of Occupational Therapy in Canada, 1890–1930.* Montreal: McGill-Queen's University Press, 2011.

Gaffield, Chad. *Language, Schooling, and Cultural Conflict: The Origins of the French-Language Controversy in Ontario.* Montreal: McGill-Queen's University Press, 1987.

Gaffield, Chad, Lynne Marks, and Susan Laskin. "Student Populations and Graduate Careers: Queen's University, 1895–1900." In Paul Axelrod and John G. Reid, eds., *Youth, University and Canadian Society: Essays in the Social History of Higher Education*, 3–25. Montreal: McGill-Queen's University Press, 1989.

Galer, Dustin. "A Friend in Need or a Business Indeed? Disabled Bodies and Fraternalism in Victorian Ontario." *Labour/Le Travail* 66 (fall 2010): 9–36.

Gelman, Susan. "'The "Feminization" of the High Schools'? Women Secondary School Teachers in Toronto: 1871–1930." *Historical Studies in Education/Revue d'histoire de l'éducation* 2, no. 1 (1990): 119–48.

Gershman, Janis. *The Evaluation of Special Education Programs: Past Attempts and Present Directions*. Report no. 134. Toronto: TBE Research Department, 1975.

Gidney, Catherine. *Tending the Student Body: Youth, Health, and the Modern University*. Toronto: University of Toronto Press, 2015.

Gidney, R.D., and W.P.J. Millar. "How to Teach English to Immigrant Children: Canadian Pedagogical Theory and Practice, 1910–1960." *Historical Studies in Education/Revue d'histoire de l'éducation* 26, no. 2 (fall 2014): 98–115.

– "Medical Students at the University of Toronto, 1910–40: A Profile." *Canadian Bulletin of Medical History/Bulletin canadien d'histoire de la médecine* 13 (1996): 29–52.

– *How Schools Worked: Public Education in English Canada, 1900–1940*. Montreal: McGill-Queen's University Press, 2012.

– *Inventing Secondary Education: The Rise of the High School in Nineteenth-Century Ontario*. Montreal: McGill-Queen's University Press, 1990.

Gleason, Mona. "Disciplining the Student Body: Schooling and the Construction of Canadian Children's Bodies, 1930–1960." *History of Education Quarterly* 41, no. 2 (summer 2001): 189–215.

– "'Lost Voices, Lost Bodies?' Doctors and the Embodiment of Children and Youth in English Canada from 1900 to the 1940s." In Mona Gleason, Tamara Myers, Leslie Paris, and Veronica Strong-Boag, eds., *Lost Kids: Vulnerable Children and Youth in Twentieth-Century Canada and the United States*, 136–54. Vancouver: University of British Columbia Press, 2010.

– *Normalizing the Ideal: Psychology, Schooling, and the Family in Postwar Canada*. Toronto: University of Toronto Press, 1999.

– "Size Matters: Medical Experts, Educators, and the Provision of Health Services to Children in Early to Mid-Twentieth Century English Canada." In Cynthia Comacchio, Janet Golden, and George Weisz, eds., *Healing the World's Children: Interdisciplinary Perspectives on Child Health in the Twentieth Century*, 176–202. Montreal: McGill-Queen's University Press, 2008.

– *Small Matters: Canadian Children in Sickness and Health, 1900–1940*. Montreal: McGill-Queen's University Press, 2013.

Goodman, Joyce. "Pedagogy and Sex: Mary Dendy (1855–1933), Feeble-Minded Girls and the Sandlebridge Schools, 1902–33." *History of Education* 34, no. 2 (2005): 171–87.

Gould, Stephen J. *The Mismeasure of Man*. New York: W.W. Norton, 1981.

Graham, John R. "The Haven, 1878–1930: A Toronto Charity's Transition from a Religious to a Professional Social Work Ethos." In John Coates et al., eds., *Spirituality and Social Work: Selected Canadian Readings*, 47–64. Toronto: Canadian Scholars Press, 2007.

Grant, Julia. *The Boy Problem: Educating Boys in Urban America, 1870–1970*. Baltimore: Johns Hopkins University Press, 2014.

Hackett, Gerald T. "The History of Public Education for Mentally Retarded Children in the Province of Ontario 1867–1964." EdD diss., University of Toronto, 1969.

Hanley-Maxwell, Cheryl, and Lana Collet-Klingenberg. "Chapter 4: Biographies of Key Contributors in the Field." In Hanley-Maxwell and Collet-Klingenberg, eds., *Education*, The Sage Reference Series on Disability Key Issues and Future Directions, 145–201. Thousand Oaks, CA: Sage, 2011.

Hardy, E.A., and Honora M. Cochrane. *Centennial Story: The Board of Education for the City of Toronto 1850–1950*. Toronto: Thomas Nelson, 1950.

Harney, Robert F. "Ethnicity and Neighbourhoods." In Harney, *Gathering Place*, 1–24.

– ed. *Gathering Place: Peoples and Neighbourhoods of Toronto, 1834–1945*. Toronto: Multicultural History Society of Ontario, 1985.

Harney, Robert F., and Harold Troper. *Immigrants: A Portrait of the Urban Experience, 1890–1930*. Toronto: Van Nostrand-Reinhold, 1975.

Harris, Richard. *Unplanned Suburbs: Toronto's American Tragedy, 1900 to 1950*. Baltimore: Johns Hopkins University Press, 1996.

Heap, Ruby. "'Salvaging War's Waste': The University of Toronto and the 'Physical Reconstruction' of Disabled Soldiers during the First World War." In Edgar-André Montigny and Lori Chambers, eds., *Ontario since Confederation: A Reader*, 214–34. Toronto: University of Toronto Press, 2000.

Heron, Craig. "The High School and the Household Economy in Working-Class Hamilton, 1890–1940." *Historical Studies in Education/Revue d'histoire de l'éducation* 7, no. 2 (1995): 217–59.

Hogan, David John. *Class and Reform: School and Society in Chicago, 1880–1930*. Philadelphia: University of Pennsylvania Press, 1985.

Hogeveen, Bryan. "'The Evils with which We Are Called to Grapple': Elite Reformers, Eugenicists, Environmental Psychologists, and the Construction of Toronto's Working-Class Boy Problem, 1860–1930." *Labour/Le Travail* 55 (spring 2005): 37–68.

Homel, Gene. "James Simpson and the Origins of Canadian Social Democracy." PhD diss., University of Toronto, 1978.

Hooper, Nadine A. "Toronto: A Study in Urban Geography." MA thesis, University of Toronto, 1941.

Houston, Susan E. "Victorian Origins of Juvenile Delinquency: A Canadian Experience." In Michael B. Katz and Paul H. Mattingly, eds., *Education and Social Change: Themes from Ontario's Past*, 83–109. New York: New York University Press, 1975.

Hutchison, Iain. "Oralism: A Sign of the Times? The Contest for Deaf Communication in Education Provision in Late Nineteenth-Century Scotland." *European Review of History* 14, no. 4 (2007): 481–501.

Iacovetta, Franca, and Wendy Mitchinson. "Introduction: Social History and Case Files Research." In Iacovetta and Mitchinson, eds., *On the Case: Explorations in Social History*, 3–24. Toronto: University of Toronto Press, 1998.

Iozzo, Alessandra. "'Silent Citizens': Citizenship Education, Disability and d/Deafness at the Ontario Institution of the Deaf, 1870–1914." PhD dissertation, University of Ottawa, 2015.

Jackson, Mark. *The Borderland of Imbecility: Medicine, Society and the Fabrication of the Feeble Mind in Late Victorian and Edwardian England*. Manchester: Manchester University Press, 2000.

James, Mary E. "Edith Groves School to Continue." *Globe and Mail*, 17 March 1951, 14.

Johnston, Charles M. *E.C. Drury: Agrarian Idealist*. Toronto: University of Toronto Press, 1986.

Jones, David C., Nancy M. Sheehan, and Robert M. Stamp, eds. *Shaping the Schools of the Canadian West*. Calgary: Detselig, 1979.

Jones, Kathleen. *Taming the Troublesome Child: American Families, Child Guidance, and the Limits of Psychiatric Authority*. Cambridge, MA: Harvard University Press, 1999.

Jordan, Anne, Christine Glenn, and Donna McGhie-Richmond. "The Supporting Effective Teaching (SET) Project: The Relationship of Inclusive Teaching Practices to Teachers' Beliefs about Disability and Ability, and about Their Roles as Teachers." *Teaching and Teacher Education* 26, no. 2 (February 2010): 259–66.

Katz, Michael B. "Occupational Classification in History." *Journal of Interdisciplinary History* 3, no. 1 (summer 1972): 63–88.

Kevles, Daniel J. *In the Name of Eugenics: Genetics and the Uses of Human Heredity*. Berkeley: University of California Press, 1985.

Klee, Marcus Aurelius. "Between the Scylla and Charybdis of Anarchy and Despotism: The State, Capital, and the Working Class in the Great Depression, Toronto, 1929–1940." PhD diss., Queen's University, 1998.

Kliebard, Herbert. *The Struggle for the American Curriculum 1893–1958*. New York: Routledge, 1987.

Kline, Wendy. *Building a Better Race: Gender, Sexuality, and Eugenics from the Turn of the Century to the Baby Boom*. Berkeley: University of California Press, 2001.

Kode, Kimberly. *Elizabeth Farrell and the History of Special Education*. Edited by Kristin E. Howard. Arlington, VA: Council for Exceptional Children, 2002.

Koester, C. Elizabeth. "An Evil Hitherto Unchecked: Eugenics and the 1917 Ontario Royal Commission on the Care and Control of the Mentally Defective and Feeble-Minded." *Canadian Bulletin of Medical History/Bulletin canadien d'histoire de la médecine* 33, no. 1 (spring 2016): 59–81.

Koven, Seth. "Remembering and Dismemberment: Crippled Children, Wounded Soldiers, and the Great War in Great Britain." *American Historical Review* 99, no. 4 (October 1994): 1,167–202.

Kudlick, Catherine L. "Disability History: Why We Need Another 'Other.'" *American Historical Review* 108, no. 3 (June 2003): 763–93.

Ladd-Taylor, Molly. *Mother-Work: Women, Child Welfare, and the State, 1890–1930*. Urbana: University of Illinois Press, 1994.

Lane, Harlan. *The Mask of Benevolence: Disabling the Deaf Community*. New ed. San Diego: Dawn Sign Press, 1999.

Langfeld, Herbert S. "Walter Fenno Dearborn: 1878–1955." *American Journal of Psychology* 68, no. 4 (December 1955): 679–81.

Lazerson, Marvin. "The Origins of Special Education." In Jay G. Chambers and William T. Hartman, eds., *Special Education Policies: Their History, Implementation, and Finance*, 15–46. Philadelphia: Temple University Press, 1983.

– *Origins of the Urban School: Public Education in Massachusetts, 1870–1915*. Cambridge, MA: Harvard University Press, 1971.

Lazerson, Marvin, and Timothy Dunn. "Schools and the Work Crisis: Vocationalism in Canadian Education." In Hugh A. Stevenson and J. Donald Wilson, eds., *Precepts, Policy and Process: Perspectives on Contemporary Canadian Education*, 285–303. London, ON: Alexander, Blake Associates, 1980.

Lazerson, Marvin, and Norton W. Grubb. "Introduction." In *American Education and Vocationalism: A Documentary History*, 1–56. New York: Teachers College Press, 1974.

Lee, Ronald. "The Gypsies in Canada: An Ethnological Study [Part 1]." *Journal of the Gypsy Lore Society* (third series) 46, no. 1–2 (January–April 1967): 38–51.

– "The Gypsies in Canada: An Ethnological Study [Part 2]." *Journal of the Gypsy Lore Society* (third series) 47, no. 1–2 (January–April 1968): 12–28.

Lemon, James T. *Toronto since 1918: An Illustrated History*. Toronto: James Lorimer and National Museums of Canada, 1985.

Levi, Charles Morden. *Comings and Goings: University Students in Canadian Society, 1854–1973*. Montreal: McGill-Queen's University Press, 2003.

Levine-Rasky, Cynthia. *Writing the Roma: Histories, Policies, and Communities in Canada*. Halifax: Fernwood Publishing, 2016.

Lombardo Paul A., ed. *A Century of Eugenics in America: From the Indiana Experiment to the Human Genome Era*. Bloomington: Indiana University Press, 2008.

Longmore, Paul K., and David Golberger. "The League of the Physically Handicapped and the Great Depression: A Case Study in the New Disability History." *Journal of American History* 87, no. 3 (December 2000): 888–922.

Longmore, Paul K., and Lauri Umansky. "Introduction: Disability History: From the Margins to the Mainstream." In Longmore and Umansky, *The New Disability History*, 1–29.

Longmore, Paul K., and Lauri Umansky, eds. *The New Disability History: American Perspectives*. New York: New York University Press, 2001.

Lorinc, John, Michael McClelland, Ellen Scheinberg, and Tatum Taylor, eds. *The Ward: The Life and Loss of Toronto's First Immigrant Neighbourhood*. Toronto: Coach House, 2015.

Lupart, Judy, and Charles Webber. "Canadian Schools in Transition: Moving from Dual Education Systems to Inclusive Schools." *Exceptionality Education International* 22, no. 2 (2012): 8–37.

McConnachie, Kathleen. "Methodology in the Study of Women in History: A Case Study of Helen MacMurchy, M.D." *Ontario History* 75, no. 1 (1983): 61–70.

MacDougall, Heather. *Activists and Advocates: Toronto's Health Department, 1883–1983*. Toronto: Dundurn Press, 1990.

McLaren, Angus. *Our Own Master Race: Eugenics in Canada, 1885–1945*. Toronto: Oxford University Press, 1990.

MacLeod, Malcolm. "Parade Street Parade: The Student Body at Memorial University College, 1925–49." In Paul Axelrod and John G. Reid, eds., *Youth, University and Canadian Society: Essays in the Social History of Higher Education*, 51–71. Montreal: McGill-Queen's University Press, 1989.

Malacrida, Claudia. *A Special Hell: Institutional Life in Alberta's Eugenic Years*. Toronto: University of Toronto Press, 2015.

Mann, Lester. *On the Trail of Process: A Historical Perspective on Cognitive Processes and Their Training*. New York: Grune & Stratton, 1979.

Marks, Lynne. "Kale Meydelach or Shulamith Girls: Cultural Change and Continuity among Jewish Parents and Daughters – A Case Study of Toronto's Harbord Collegiate Institute in the 1920s." *Canadian Woman Studies/Les cahiers de la femme* 7, no. 3 (1986): 85–9.

– "New Opportunities within the Separate Sphere." MA major research paper, York University, 1984.

Maynard, Steven. "'Horrible Temptations': Sex, Men, and Working-Class Male Youth in Urban Ontario, 1890–1935." *Canadian Historical Review* 78, no. 2 (June 1997): 191–235.

Mercer, Jane R. *Labelling the Mentally Retarded: Clinical and Social System Perspectives on Mental Retardation*. Berkeley: University of California Press, 1973.

Millar, W.P.J.. "'We Wanted Our Children Should Have It Better': Jewish Medical Students at the University of Toronto, 1910–51." *Journal of the Canadian Historical Association* 11, no. 1 (2000): 109–24.

Millar, Wyn, Ruby Heap, and Bob Gidney. "Degrees of Difference: The Students in Three Professional Schools at the University of Toronto, 1910 to the 1950s." In Ruby Heap, Wyn Millar, and Elizabeth Smyth, eds., *Learning to Practise: Professional Education in Historical and Contemporary Perspective*, 155–87. Ottawa: University of Ottawa Press, 2005.

Myers, Tamara. *Caught: Montreal's Modern Girls and the Law, 1869–1945*. Toronto: University of Toronto Press, 2006.

Nelson, Adam R. "Equity and Special Education: Some Historical Lessons from Boston." In Kenneth K. Wong and Robert Rothman, eds., *Clio at the Table: Using History to Inform and Improve Education Policy*, 157–79. New York: Peter Lang, 2009.

Nicolas, Serge, Bernard Andrieu, Jean-Claude Croizet, Raysid B. Sanitioso, and Jeremy Trevelyan Burman. "Sick? Or Slow? On the Origins of Intelligence as a Psychological Object." *Intelligence* 41 (2013): 699–711.

Nielsen, Kim. E. *A Disability History of the United States*. Boston: Beacon Press, 2012.

Norden, Martin F. *The Cinema of Isolation: A History of Physical Disability in the Movies*. New Brunswick, NJ: Rutgers University Press, 1994.

Oakes, Jeannie. *Keeping Track: How Schools Structure Inequality*. 2nd ed. New Haven, CT: Yale University Press, 2005.

Olneck, Michael R. "American Public Schooling and European Immigrants." In William J. Reese and John L. Rury, eds., *Rethinking the History of American Education*, 103–41. New York: Palgrave Macmillan, 2008.

Olneck, Michael R., and Marvin Lazerson. "The School Achievement of Immigrant Children, 1900–1930." *History of Education Quarterly* 14, no. 4 (winter 1974): 453–82.

Osgood, Robert L. *For "Children Who Vary from the Normal Type": Special Education in Boston, 1838–1930.* Washington: Gallaudet University Press, 2000.

– *The History of Inclusion in the United States.* Washington: Gallaudet University Press, 2005.

– *The History of Special Education: A Struggle for Equality in American Public Schools.* Westport, CT: Praeger, 2008.

Palmer, Bryan D. "Emperor Katz's New Clothes; Or with the Wizard in Oz." Review of Michael B. Katz, Michael J. Doucet, and Mark J. Stern, *The Social Organization of Early Industrial Capitalism* (Cambridge, MA: Harvard University Press, 1982). *Labour/Le Travail* 13 (spring 1984): 190–9.

Palmer, Bryan D., and Gaetan Heroux. "'Cracking the Stone': The Long History of Capitalist Crisis and Toronto's Dispossessed, 1830–1930." *Labour/Le Travail* 69 (spring 2012): 9–62.

Paul, Diane B. *Controlling Human Heredity: 1865 to the Present.* Atlantic Highlands, NJ: Humanities Press, 1995.

Pearce, Joanna L. "Not for Alms but Help: Fund-Raising and Free Education for the Blind." *Journal of the Canadian Historical Association* 23, no. 1 (2012): 131–55.

Pennacchio, Luigi G. "The Defence of Identity: Ida Siegel and the Jews of Toronto versus the Assimilation Attempts of the Public School and Its Allies, 1900–1920." *Canadian Jewish Historical Society Journal* 9, no. 1 (spring 1985): 41–60.

– "Toronto's Public Schools and the Assimilation of Foreign Students, 1900–1920." *Journal of Educational Thought* 20 (1986): 37–48.

Perlmann, Joel. *Ethnic Differences: Schooling and Social Structure among the Irish, Italians, Jews, and Blacks in an American City, 1880–1935.* Cambridge, MA: Cambridge University Press, 1988.

Philpott, David, and Christina Fiedorowicz. "The Supreme Court of Canada Ruling on Learning Disabilities." Learning Disabilities Association of Canada, 2012. http://www.ldac-acta.ca/downloads/pdf/advocacy/Education%20Implications%20-%20Moore%20Decision.pdf.

Pierson, Ruth Roach. *"They're Still Women after All": The Second World War and Canadian Womanhood.* Toronto: McClelland and Stewart, 1986.

Pitt, David. *E.J. Pratt: The Truant Years 1882–1928.* Toronto: University of Toronto Press, 1984.

"Pioneer Teacher of Deaf and Dumb." *Globe and Mail,* 4 September 1945, 4.

Piva, Michael J. *The Condition of the Working Class in Toronto, 1900–1921.*
Ottawa: University of Ottawa Press, 1979.

Pletsch, Vera C. *Not Wanted in the Classroom: Parent Associations and the Education of Trainable Retarded Children in Ontario: 1947–1969.* London, ON: Althouse Press, 1997.

Pols, Hans. "Between the Laboratory and Life: Child Development Research in Toronto, 1919–1956." *History of Psychology* 5, no. 2 (2002): 135–62.

– "Divergences in American Psychiatry during the Depression: Somatic Psychiatry, Community Mental Hygiene, and Social Reconstruction." *Journal of the History of the Behavioral Sciences* 37, no. 4 (fall 2001): 369–88.

Raftery, Judith R. "Missing the Mark: Intelligence Testing in Los Angeles Public Schools, 1922–1932." *History of Education Quarterly* 28, no. 1 (1988): 73–93.

Read, Jane. "Fit for What? Special Education in London, 1890–1914." *History of Education* 33, no. 3 (May 2004): 283–98.

Reaume, Geoffrey. "Disability History in Canada: Present Work in the Field and Future Prospects." *Canadian Journal of Disability Studies* 1, no. 1 (2012): 35–81.

– *Lyndhurst: Canada's First Rehabilitation Centre for People with Spinal Cord Injuries, 1945–1998.* Montreal: McGill-Queen's University Press, 2007.

– *Remembrance of Patients Past: Patient Life at the Toronto Hospital for the Insane, 1870–1940.* Don Mills, ON: Oxford University Press, 2000.

Reese, William J. "After Bread, Education: Nutrition and Urban School Children, 1890–1920." *Teachers College Record* 81, no. 4 (1980): 496–525.

– *Power and the Promise of School Reform: Grassroots Movements during the Progressive Era.* Boston: Routledge and Kegan Paul, 1986.

Reynolds, Roy, and Donald J. Netherty. *An Annotated Guide to the Manuscripts in the Historical Collection of the TBE,* Educational Records series, OISE, no. 13. Toronto: TBE, 1977.

Richardson, Theresa. *The Century of the Child: The Mental Hygiene Movement and Social Policy in the United States and Canada.* Albany: SUNY Press, 1989.

Riendeau, Roger E. "Servicing of the Modern City 1900–1930." In Victor L. Russell, ed., *Forging a Consensus: Historical Essays on Toronto,* 157–70. Toronto: University of Toronto Press, 1984.

Roberts, Wayne. "'Rocking the Cradle for the World': The New Woman and Maternal Feminism, Toronto 1877–1914." In Linda Kealey, ed., *A Not Unreasonable Claim: Women and Reform in Canada 1880s–1920s,* 15–45. Toronto: Women's Educational Press, 1979.

Robinson, Helen Caister. *Decades of Caring: The Big Sister Story.* Toronto: Dundurn Press, 1979.

Rooke, Patricia T., and R.L. Schnell. *Discarding the Asylum: From Child Rescue to the Welfare State in English Canada (1800–1950)*. Lanham, MD: University Press of America, 1983.

Rousmaniere, Kate. *City Teachers: Teaching and School Reform in Historical Perspective*. New York: Teachers College Press, 1997.

– "Those Who Can't, Teach: The Disabling History of American Educators." *History of Education Quarterly* 53, no. 1 (February 2013): 90–103.

Ruis, A.R. "'The Penny Lunch has Spread Faster than the Measles': Children's Health and the Debate over School Lunches in New York City, 1908–1930." *History of Education Quarterly* 55, no. 2 (May 2015): 190–217.

Rutherford, Paul. "Introduction." In Rutherford, ed., *Saving the Canadian City: The First Phase 1880–1920*, ix–xxiii. Toronto: University of Toronto Press, 1974.

– "Tomorrow's Metropolis: The Urban Reform Movement in Canada, 1880–1920." In Gilbert A. Stelter and Alan F.J. Artibise, eds., *The Canadian City: Essays in Urban and Social History*, 435–55. Montreal: McGill-Queen's University Press, 1984.

Rutty, Christopher. "The Middle-Class Plague: Epidemic Polio and the Canadian State, 1936–37." *Canadian Bulletin of Medical History/Bulletin canadien d'histoire de la médecine* 13 (1996): 277–314.

Ryan, Ann Marie. "From Child Study to Efficiency: District Administrators and the Use of Testing in the Chicago Public Schools, 1899 to 1928." *Paedagogica Historica* 47, no. 3 (2011): 341–54.

Ryan, Ann Marie, and Alan Stoskopf. "Public and Catholic School Responses to IQ Testing in the Early Twentieth Century." *Teachers College Record* 110, no. 4 (2008): 894–922.

Salo, Matt T. "Gypsies/Rom." In Paul Robert Magocsi, ed., *Encyclopedia of Canada's Peoples*, 642–8. Toronto: Published for the Multicultural History Society of Ontario by the University of Toronto Press, 1999.

Samson, Amy. "Eugenics in the Community: Gendered Professions and Eugenic Sterilization in Alberta, 1928–72." *Canadian Bulletin of Medical History* 31, no. 1 (2014): 143–63.

Sarason, Seymour B., and John Doris. *Educational Handicap, Public Policy, and Social History: A Broadened Perspective on Mental Retardation*. New York: The Free Press, 1979.

Schoen, Joanna. *Choice & Coercion: Birth Control, Sterilization, and Abortion in Public Health and Welfare*. Chapel Hill: University of North Carolina Press, 2005.

Scruggs, Thomas E., and Margo A. Mastropieri. "Teacher Perceptions of Mainstreaming/Inclusion, 1958–1995: A Research Synthesis." *Exceptional Children* 63, no. 1 (October 1996): 59–74.

Shammai, Shmuel. "The Jews and the Public Education System: The Students' Strike over the 'Flag Fight' in Toronto after the First World War." *Canadian Jewish Historical Society Journal* 10, no. 1 (fall 1988): 46–53.

Sheehan, Nancy M., J. Donald Wilson, and David C. Jones. *Schools in the West: Essays in Canadian Educational History*. Calgary: Detselig, 1986.

Stern, Alexandra Minna. *Eugenic Nation: Faults and Frontiers of Better Breeding in America*. 2nd ed. Berkeley: University of California Press, 2016.

Sullivan, Ellen B., Roy M. Dorcus, Bennet M. Allen, and Louis K. Koontz. "Grace Maxwell Fernald: 1879–1950." *Psychological Review* 57, no. 6 (November 1950): 319–21.

Simmons, Harvey G. *From Asylum to Welfare*. Toronto: National Institute on Mental Retardation, 1982.

Skiba, Russell J., Ada B. Simmons, Shana Ritter, et al. "Achieving Equity in Special Education: History, Status, and Current Challenges." *Exceptional Children* 74, no. 3 (2008): 264–88.

Smith, Nila Banton. *American Reading Instruction*. Newark: International Reading Association, 1965.

Spagnuolo, Natalie. "Defining Dependency, Constructing Curability: The Deportation of 'Feebleminded' Patients from the Toronto Asylum, 1920–1925." *Histoire sociale/Social History* 49, no. 98 (May 2016): 125–53.

Speisman, Stephen A. *The Jews of Toronto: A History to 1937*. Toronto: McClelland and Stewart, 1979.

Stamp, Robert M. "The Response to Urban Growth: The Bureaucratization of Public Education in Calgary, 1884–1914." In Jones, Sheehan, and Stamp, *Shaping the Schools*, 109–23.

– *The Schools of Ontario, 1876–1976*. Toronto: University of Toronto Press, 1982.

Stanley, Timothy J. *Contesting White Supremacy: School Segregation, Anti-Racism, and the Making of Chinese Canadians*. Vancouver: University of British Columbia Press, 2011.

Stephen, Jennifer. "The 'Incorrigible,' the 'Bad,' and the 'Immoral': Toronto's 'Factory Girls' and the Work of the Toronto Psychiatric Clinic." In Louis A. Knaffa and Susan W.S. Binnie, eds., *Law Society and the State: Essays in Modern Legal History*, 405–39. Toronto: University of Toronto Press, 1995.

– *Pick One Intelligent Girl: Employability, Domesticity, and the Gendering of Canada's Welfare State, 1939–1947*. Toronto: University of Toronto Press, 2007.

– "Unemployment and the New Industrial Citizenship: A Review of the Ontario Unemployment Commission, 1916." In Robert Adamoski, Dorothy E. Chunn, and Robert Menzies, eds., *Contesting Canadian Citizenship: Historical Readings*, 155–77. Peterborough, ON: Broadview Press, 2002.

Stiker, Henri-Jacques. *A History of Disability*. Translated by William Sayers. Ann Arbor: University of Michigan Press, 1999.

Strange, Carolyn. *Toronto's Girl Problem: The Perils and Pleasures of the City, 1880–1930*. Toronto: University of Toronto Press, 1995.

Strange, Carolyn, and Jennifer A. Stephen. "Eugenics in Canada: A Checkered History, 1850s–1990s." In Alison Bashford and Phillipa Levine, eds., *The Oxford Handbook of the History of Eugenics*, 523–38. Oxford: Oxford University Press, 2010.

Strong-Boag, Veronica. "Canada's Women Doctors: Feminism Constrained." In Linda Kealey, ed., *A Not Unreasonable Claim: Women and Reform in Canada 1880s–1920s*, 109–29. Toronto: Women's Educational Press, 1979.

– "'Children of Adversity': Disabilities and Child Welfare in Canada from the Nineteenth to the Twenty-First Century." *Journal of Family History* 32, no. 4 (October 2007): 413–32.

– "'Forgotten People of All the Forgotten': Children with Disabilities in English Canada from the Nineteenth Century to the New Millennium." In Mona Gleason, Tamara Myers, Leslie Paris, and Veronica Strong-Boag, eds., *Lost Kids: Vulnerable Children in Twentieth-Century Canada and the United States*, 33–50. Vancouver: University of British Columbia Press, 2010.

– *Fostering Nation? Canada Confronts Its History of Childhood Disadvantage*. Waterloo, ON: Wilfrid Laurier University Press, 2011.

– *The New Day Recalled: Lives of Girls and Women in English Canada, 1919–1939*. Markham, ON: Penguin, 1988.

– *The Parliament of Women: The National Council of Women of Canada 1893–1929*. Ottawa: National Museums of Canada, 1976.

– "Taking Stock of the Suffragists: Personal Reflections on Feminist Appraisals." *Journal of the Canadian Historical Association* 21, no. 2 (2010): 76–89.

– "'Wages for Housework': Mothers' Allowances and the Beginnings of Social Security in Canada." *Journal of Canadian Studies* 14, no. 1 (1979): 24–34.

Struthers, James. *The Limits of Affluence: Welfare in Ontario*. Toronto: University of Toronto Press, 1994.

Sutherland, Gillian. *Ability, Merit and Measurement: Mental Testing and English Education 1880–1940*. Oxford: Clarendon Press, 1984.

Sutherland, Neil. *Children in English-Canadian Society: Framing the Twentieth-Century Consensus*. Toronto: University of Toronto Press, 1976.

– "When You Listen to the Winds of Childhood, How Much Can You Believe?" *Curriculum Inquiry* 22, no. 3 (autumn 1992): 235–56.

Thomas, Robert McG., Jr. "Samuel A. Kirk, 92, Pioneer of Special Education Field." *New York Times*, 28 July 1996. http://www.nytimes.com/1996/07/28/us/samuel-a-kirk-92-pioneer-of-special-education-field.html.

Thomson, Gerald E. "'Not an Attempt to Coddle Children': Dr Charles Hegler
   Gundry and the Mental Hygiene Division of the Vancouver School Board,
   1939–1969." *Historical Studies in Education/Revue d'histoire de l'éducation* 14,
   no. 2 (fall 2002): 247–78.
– "'Remove from Our Midst These Unfortunates': A Historical Inquiry into
   the Influence of Eugenics, Educational Efficiency as Well as Mental Hygiene
   upon the Vancouver School System and Its Special Classes, 1910–1969."
   PhD diss., University of British Columbia, 1999.
Tomlinson, Sally. *A Sociology of Special Education*. London: Routledge, 1982.
Treiman, Donald. *Occupational Prestige in Comparative Perspective*. New York:
   Academic Press, 1977.
Trent, James W., Jr. *Inventing the Feeble Mind: A History of Mental Retardation
   in the United States*. Berkeley: University of California Press, 1994.
Trethewey, Lynn. "Producing the Over-Aged Child in South Australian
   Primary Schools." *Historical Studies in Education/Revue d'histoire de
   l'éducation* 10, no. 1–2 (1998): 159–79.
Tropea, Joseph L. "Bureaucratic Order and Special Children: Urban Schools,
   1890s–1940s." *History of Education Quarterly* 27, no. 1 (1987): 29–53.
– "Bureaucratic Order and Special Children: Urban Schools, 1950s–1960s."
   History of Education Quarterly 27, no. 3 (1987): 339–61.
Tulchinsky, Gerald. *Branching Out: The Transformation of the Canadian Jewish
   Community*. Toronto: Stoddart, 1998.
– *Taking Root: The Origins of the Canadian Jewish Community*. Toronto: Lester,
   1982.
Tyack, David B. *The One Best System: A History of American Urban Education*.
   Cambridge, MA: Harvard University Press, 1974.
Tyack, David B., and Elisabeth Hansot. *Learning Together: A History of Co-
   education in American Public Schools*. New York: Russell Sage, 1990.
Tyack, David B., Robert Lowe, and Elisabeth Hansot. *Public Schools in Hard
   Times: The Great Depression and Recent Years*. Cambridge, MA: Harvard
   University Press, 1984.
Tyler, Fred T. "David H. Russell, Past-President, APA Division 15 1906–1965."
   Educational Psychologist 2, no. 2 (April 1965): 1.
"'U' Professor, P. Sandiford, Dies, Aged 59." *Globe and Mail*, 13 October 1941, 4.
Uditsky, Bruce. "From Integration to Inclusion: The Canadian Experience." In
   Roger Slee, ed., *Is There a Desk with My Name on It? The Politics of Integration*,
   79–92. London: Falmer, 1993.
Valverde, Mariana. *The Age of Light, Soap, and Water: Moral Reform in English
   Canada, 1885–1925*. Toronto: McClelland and Stewart, 1991.

Vance, Bruce, ed. *The Schools and the Polio Epidemic*. Education in TBE Public Schools, a Series of Historical Sketches, 2. TBE Sesquicentennial Museum and Archives, 1994.

Vipond, Robert C. *Making a Global City: How One Toronto School Embraced Diversity*. Toronto: University of Toronto Press, 2017.

von Heyking, Amy. *Creating Citizens: History and Identity in Alberta's Schools, 1905–1980*. Calgary: University of Calgary Press, 2006.

– "Ties that Bind? American Influences on Canadian Education." *Education Canada* 44, no. 4 (fall 2004): 30–4.

Weaver, John C. "The Modern City Realized: Toronto Civic Affairs, 1880–1915." In Alan F.J. Artibise and Gilbert A. Stelter, eds., *The Usable Urban Past: Planning and Politics in the Modern Canadian City*, 39–72. Montreal: McGill-Queen's University Press, 1979.

– "'Tomorrow's Metropolis' Revisited: A Critical Assessment of Urban Reform in Canada, 1890–1920." In Gilbert A. Stelter and Alan F.J. Artibise, eds., *The Canadian City: Essays in Urban and Social History*, 393–418. Montreal: McGill-Queen's University Press, 1984.

Wilson, Daniel J. "Psychological Trauma and Its Treatment in the Polio Epidemics." *Bulletin of the History of Medicine* 82, no. 4 (winter 2008): 848–77.

Wilson, J. Donald. "'The Picture of Social Randomness': Making Sense of Ethnic History and Educational History." In David C. Jones, Nancy M. Sheehan, Robert M. Stamp, and Neil G. MacDonald, eds., *Monographs in Education V: Approaches to Educational History*. Winnipeg: University of Manitoba, 1981.

– "Some Observations on Recent Trends in Canadian Educational History." In J. Donald Wilson, ed., *An Imperfect Past: Education and Society in Canadian History*, 7–29. Vancouver: Centre for the Study of Curriculum and Instruction, University of British Columbia, 1984.

Winfield, Ann Gibson. *Eugenics and Education in America: Institutionalized Racism and the Implications of History, Ideology, and Memory*. New York: Peter Lang, 2007.

Winzer, Margret A. *From Integration to Inclusion: A History of Special Education in the 20th Century*. Washington: Gallaudet University Press, 2009.

– *The History of Special Education: From Isolation to Integration*. Washington: Gallaudet University Press, 1993.

Wright, David. *Downs: The History of a Disability*. Oxford: Oxford University Press, 2011.

Wright, E.N. *Student's Background and Its Relationship to Class and Programme in School, the Every Student Survey*. Toronto: TBE Research Department, 1970.

Yoshida, Karen K., Fady Shanouda, and Jason Ellis. "An Education and Negotiation of Differences: The 'Schooling' Experiences of English-Speaking Canadian Children Growing up with Polio during the 1940s and 1950s." *Disability and Society* 29, no. 3 (2014): 345–58.

Zenderland, Leila. *Measuring Minds: Henry Herbert Goddard and the Origins of American Intelligence Testing*. Cambridge: Cambridge University Press, 1998.

Index

intelligence quotient; intelligence tests; intelligence testers
intelligence quotient, and classification of feebleminded, 55; effects on auxiliary education, 7, 58–9, 79–80; tests of (*see* intelligence tests); use in vocational guidance, 114–16; theory of, 53–9. *See also* Goddard, H.H; mental age; Stern, William; Terman, Lewis
intelligence testers, 53–9, 66, 83, 94, 163, 171. *See also* Brigham, Carl; Goddard, H.H.; intelligence; intelligence quotient; intelligence tests; Sandiford, Peter; Terman, Lewis; Yerkes, Robert
intelligence tests, 53–9, 203; administered to Toronto children, 59–73, 166–70, 191–4; auxiliary education placements and, 66–71, 153–4, 166–70, 191–4; bias in, 56, 171; Canadian Intelligence Examination, 264n65; children's reactions to (intelligence testing moment), 71–4; and diagnosis of feebleminded, 54–5, 64; National Intelligence Test, 58, 67; opponents and critics, 54, 58, 157, 159, 162–3, 262n31; school reorganization and, 57–65; Stanford-Binet (test), 57, 60, 67–8, 70–2; streaming and, 57. 57; *See also* intelligence; intelligence quotient; intelligence testers; mental age; special-subject disability; tests, diagnostic
International Council for Exceptional Children, 196–7, 201
International Council of Women, 20. *See also* Local Council of Women

(of Toronto); National Council of Women
Iowa State Psychopathic Hospital, 155, 157
IPRC (Identification, Placement, and Review Committee), 210
IQ. *See* intelligence quotient
Italians, in auxiliary classes, 76–7, 171; in junior vocational schools, 105–6; in opportunity classes, 171; in Toronto, 12

J., Alexandra, 169
Jackson, Mark, 249n63
Jacobs, Rabbi, 48
Jarvis Collegiate Institute, 92, 131
Jarvis Junior Vocational School, 92, 95–8, 103–4, 108–11, 114–15, 120–2, 137, 148–9, 180, 186, 194, 200; Home and School Association of, 118–19, 124
Jesse Ketchum Public School, sight-saving classes at, 146
Jews, in auxiliary classes, opportunity classes, 76–7, 170–1; deaf, 144; ethnic origin inferred from pupil records, 227; in foreign classes, 38; in forest schools, 34, 36; ideas about and education, 39, 76–7, 266n94; immigrants, decisions about education, 105–7, 116, 124, 276–7nn87–9; in junior vocational schools, 105–7, 116, 124; in Toronto, 12, 218–19, 314n44
Johnstone, E.R., 25
Jones, Kathleen, 71, 186–7
Judge Baker Guidance Clinic (Boston), 292n16. *See also* child guidance, clinics

teasing. *See* disability, children's
views of other children's. *See also*
adjustment
technical high schools, curriculum
in, 92–3. *See also* Central Technical
School
Terman, Lewis, 7, 52, 54–60, 64,
72–3, 77, 93–4, 161, 203–5. *See also*
intelligence; intelligence quotient;
intelligence testers; intelligence
tests
tests, diagnostic, 161, 177–8. *See also*
intelligence tests
Toronto, Board of Control, 12, 40, 49;
industrial development of, 11–12;
Toronto City Model School, 14;
"Toronto the Good," 11
Toronto Board of Education, 11,
14–15, 20–1, 48–9, 125, 138; at-
tendance department, 120. *See also*
individual trustees' names; Toronto
District School Board
Toronto Collegiate Institute, 16
Toronto Committee on Mental
Hygiene, 131
Toronto Daily Star, 42, 44, 48, 140–1
Toronto District School Board, 209,
215, 242n20. *See also* Toronto
Board of Education
Toronto General Hospital, 42, 60,
217; occupational therapy depart-
ment, 135; psychiatric clinic, 60
Toronto Transit Commission.
See Toronto Transportation
Committee
Toronto Transportation Committee,
131, 133
tracking. *See* streaming
Trades and Labour Congress, 89,
147

Trefann Court, 207–8
Tropea, Joseph L., 78
truants, 22. *See also* attendance laws;
Toronto Board of Education,
attendance department
tuberculosis, 7, 30–2; of the bone, 130
Tyack, David, 4, 28, 109

Understanding the Child, 190, 193
unemployed, 6, 19, 87, 90, 115, 124,
208, 224–5
ungraded classes, 22–4
United Farmers of Ontario, 50, 88
University of California, Los
Angeles. *See* California State
Normal School at Los Angeles
University of Chicago, 95, 158
University of Heidelberg, 156
University of Manchester, 56
University of Toronto, 16, 78, 90, 132;
Institute of Child Study, 186, 200

V., Ella, 193
V., Fred, 73, 83
V., Henry, 169–70
Vancouver, auxiliary education in,
51
Victoria Park Forest School, 30–1,
36, 203
Victoria Street Public School, 37–9
Vineland Training School (New
Jersey), 24–6, 43, 54
Vipond, Robert, 146
visiting teachers. *See* extramural
teaching for children with
disabilities or illnesses
visual impairment, partial. *See* sight-
saving classes
Vocational and Technical Education
Act (Canada), 89